Understanding Alternative Dispute Resolution

Carolina Academic Press Understanding Series

Understanding Alternative Dispute Resolution

Kristen M. Blankley

Associate Professor of Law
University of Nebraska

Maureen A. Weston

Professor of Law
Pepperdine University School of Law

Carolina Academic Press
Durham, North Carolina

Library of Congress Cataloging-in-Publication Data

Names: Blankley, Kristen M., author. | Weston, Maureen A., author.
Title: Understanding alternative dispute resolution / Kristen M. Blankley,
    Maureen A. Weston.
Description: Durham, North Carolina : Carolina Academic Press, [2017] |
    Series: Understanding series | Includes bibliographical references and
    index.
Identifiers: LCCN 2017009373 | ISBN 9780769862507 (alk. paper)
Subjects: LCSH: Dispute resolution (Law) | Mediation. | Compromise (Law) |
    Arbitration (International law)
Classification: LCC K2390 .B53 2017 | DDC 347/.09--dc23
LC record available at https://lccn.loc.gov/2017009373

eISBN 978-0-32718-327-3

Carolina Academic Press, LLC
700 Kent Street
Durham, North Carolina 27701
Telephone (919) 489-7486
Fax (919) 493-5668
www.cap-press.com

Contents

Acknowledgments

Kristen Blankley would like to thank Dezi Medina, Mary Rose Richter, Karlus Cozart, and Jenna Woitaszewski for their research and editing assistance. This book is dedicated to my husband, Mike Douglass, Jr.

Maureen Weston would like to thank Ryan Storms for his helpful research assistance, her good friend and inspiring co-author Kristen Blankley, and Brian, Cedric, Lily, and Rosie for their support and love.

Understanding Alternative Dispute Resolution

Chapter 1

Introduction to Alternative Dispute Resolution

§ 1.01 Introduction

Understand yourself. Understand your client. Understand your case. Understand your dispute resolution processes and options.

This book on *Understanding Alternative Dispute Resolution* aims to assist lawyers, law students, neutrals, and parties in conflict in effectively addressing, managing, and resolving legal disputes and transactions. This process requires not only an understanding of legally relevant facts and theories, but also of the importance of communication and relationships with clients, involved parties, neutrals, and ourselves. The ability of lawyers to understand both how we work and operate—personally, emotionally, and professionally—and to understand these aspects with our clients is critical to our effectiveness.

Too often, clients and lawyers instinctively seek redress from a court, even when courts are ill-equipped to deal with the disputes at hand. If lawyers and clients are equipped to resolve disputes in the most appropriate way for each circumstance, clients will likely discover better and longer-lasting solutions to their problems. A few examples may be helpful in illustrating this point.

Breach of Contract—Consider a contract between two businesses where the Seller is to provide to Buyer a raw material to construct a finished product. The Seller's raw material is not of a high enough quantity for the finished product, and the Buyer rejects the shipment. The Buyer, however, is under a strict deadline and must produce the finished product to meet retail obligations. Even in a case of a clear breach of contract, litigation over the matter could take years, and Buyer needs to produce the product now. How can alternatives to court help resolve this matter?

Family Law—Mom files a no-fault divorce against Dad. In Mom and Dad's jurisdiction, a statute creates a presumption that Mom and Dad will each have 50 percent parenting time and that the children will spend seven days with Mom followed by seven days with Dad, and so on. Dad, however, is an airline pilot who travels significantly and has an unpredictable schedule. The court process would impose an inflexible schedule that does not meet either parent's needs and both will need to communicate with each other into the future. How can alternatives to court help resolve this matter?

Employment Dispute—Female Employee works for Factory, and she begins to receive unwanted attention from male employees. Female Employee would like to keep her job, but she feels uncomfortable at work and would like the unwanted attention to stop. The Factory values the work of Female Employee and would like to resolve the issue before the situation gets out of hand and before Factory receives any bad publicity. How can alternatives to court help resolve this matter?

3

§ 1.02 Why Alternative Dispute Resolution?

Alternative Dispute Resolution is a comparatively young area of legal scholarship and practice. The area of the law, however, is of paramount importance in today's legal landscape. With fewer than one percent of civil cases reaching trial, most disputes are resolved pursuant to some type of alternative dispute resolution mechanism, such as negotiation, mediation, arbitration, collaborative law, or other type of dispute resolution procedure.

Every lawyer's career will involve some aspect of dispute resolution. All lawyers need to understand client interviewing and counseling, as well as negotiation, whether or not those lawyers have a litigation-based practice. Today's lawyers need to advise their clients on preventing, managing, and resolving disputes—whether those lawyers counsel their clients at the contract drafting stage or well after a dispute arises.

Most clients are not interested in litigation, for one reason or another. Litigation, in and of itself, is almost never a client goal. At best, litigation is a means to an end. Instead, clients are interested in receiving the proper widgets to make their business work, in creating a parenting plan for children that meets their best interests, or in ensuring that the workplace is free from sexual harassment. When lawyers understand what clients really want, they will begin to see that they can help their clients achieve these goals in any number of different ways, with litigation as one option among many.

Courts too have largely endorsed alternative dispute resolution. Recent trends in arbitration law have nearly guaranteed enforcement of pre-dispute agreements to arbitrate. Many courts have court-connected mediation programs that attempt to settle cases short of trial. In addition, many laws (such as those involving divorce) mandate the use of mediation before a court will hear a contested case. Negotiation and client counseling are integral to the processes and forms of dispute resolution themselves.

Given these trends, today's law schools teach alternative dispute resolution in some fashion or another. Most schools teach a "survey" course covering topics such as negotiation, mediation, and arbitration. Many schools teach stand-alone courses in client interviewing and counseling, negotiation, mediation, and arbitration. In addition, schools are beginning to teach more specialized courses in areas like collaborative law and advocacy in mediation. Many law schools have clinical offerings in alternative dispute resolution, such as mediation clinics, where students act as mediators. Even in traditional civil clinical classes, many student lawyers must prepare their clients to attend negotiation, mediation, or arbitration sessions.

§ 1.03 The Spectrum of Dispute Resolution Processes

Disputes or conflict generally may be handled, or not, in a variety of ways. Among the spectrum of approaches one may employ to address a dispute may be:

(1) *Avoidance:* simply deny, ignore, or avoid that conflict. While sometimes the conflict may "go away," in general, doing nothing results in the problem

persisting or becoming worse, especially if the parties involved have a continuing relationship.

(2) *Negotiation:* involves the direct engagement by the parties or their representatives in a discussion and exchange of their respective positions and interests to reach an agreement on how to resolve a dispute.

(3) *Mediation:* is a form of facilitated negotiation and a non-binding, consensual process in which a neutral third party assists the disputing parties in their efforts to negotiate a settlement or resolution.

(4) *Arbitration:* typically is premised upon the parties' private agreement to have their case heard, and decided by, a third-party arbitrator or panel to result in a final and binding decision.

(5) *Litigation:* involves a public justice system in which parties, usually through attorneys, directly present their legal claims and defenses for resolution before a judge or jury. Many public agencies also have adjudicative processes to resolve a certain type of dispute, such as immigration or social security issues.

(6) *Other Methods:* in addition to the foregoing basic methods of dispute resolution, a number of hybrid private processes may be available, such as *Ombudsmanship*, involving a neutral hired by a company to facilitate internal disputes; *Med-Arb*, when parties agree that arbitration will result in the event a mediation settlement is not reached; *Mini-Trial*, a private, voluntary, and less formal trial procedure in which disputants present their respective cases before a selected neutral advisor; and *Summary Jury Trial*, involving a truncated trial presentation before a judge and mock jury, which renders an advisory verdict and may be questioned by the court or attorneys to provide a preview of how a jury may evaluate a dispute.

(7) *Dispute Resolution through Power:* although not discussed here, conflicts may be resolved through power, such as war, authoritative decision, or democratic processes, such as elections. In some instances, resolving disputes through power is justified; more likely, the disputes may be resolved more efficiently through more collaborative means.

§ 1.04 Selecting the Appropriate Dispute Resolution Process

Although litigation is also a form of dispute resolution, this book focuses on private processes parties may employ, typically outside the public justice system. These processes are generally called *Alternative Dispute Resolution ("ADR")*, but they may also be effective in dispute prevention and management. The term *Appropriate Dispute Resolution* is also apt, in that the unique circumstances for each case and client should be considered.

Selecting the most appropriate dispute resolution process should involve an assessment of factors as they relate to the needs of the respective parties, such as:

- **Public or Private Process**—Are the parties interested in a process that is public, such as a court, or would they prefer to resolve their matter privately between the parties? In some instances, bringing issues to light is a goal of the process, while at other times the parties may benefit from resolving their dispute outside of the public light.

- **Need for Precedent**—Is this the type of dispute that involves a significant issue of public policy and a need to establish a uniform policy, public record, or judicial oversight? Or is this the type of case involving primarily private parties where setting a precedent may not have much value?

- **Cost**—Cost is a motivator in resolving all manners of disputes. Hiring a lawyer is expensive, and taking a case all the way to trial may cost anywhere from $20,000 to more than $10 million in legal fees alone. Both individual and business clients seek to reduce legal fees and costs, and lawyers should be aware of the pressure to keep legal fees low.

- **Party Control and Participation**—Does the client want to have a role in the process? Some clients want to be involved in the process, while others would like the lawyer to handle everything. Some clients have a better ability to be involved than others, due to the emotional content of the dispute or their ability to communicate effectively.

- **Confidentiality**—Are the clients interested in keeping the proceedings or any resulting agreements confidential? If so, a court proceeding may not be ideal because the court process and any resulting verdicts are public records. Parties interested in confidentiality for any reason (embarrassment, publicity reasons, sensitive information) may need to find an alternative way of resolving the dispute.

- **Process Informality or Formality**—Court proceedings are extraordinarily complex and unrepresented parties have difficulty navigating the rules, accessing the system and mounting a successful case. Other processes, such as negotiation and mediation, are less structured and allow for more client participation.

- **Binding or Non-binding**—*Adjudicatory processes*, such as litigation and arbitration, will result in a binding outcome for the parties. In contrast, *consensual processes*, such as mediation or negotiation, require the parties agreement to resolve the disputes. Adjudicative processes ensure the resolution of a dispute, while consensual processes place the decision to resolve a dispute or not squarely in the hands of the parties.

- **Timing**—The court process often takes years to resolve civil disputes, but clients may want resolution to a dispute more immediately. The business that needs the widgets today to meet manufacturing deadlines may choose a different type of dispute resolution process compared to a dispute that does not have pressing interests.

- **Relationship**—In many situations, preserving or maintaining a relationship may be important to the clients. Cases involving families, such as divorce or probate cases, obviously have a relationship component. Many other cases also involve important relationships, such as business partners, employers/employees, or neighbors, that parties may want to preserve.

- **Third-Party Expertise**—Cases that have complicated factual or legal issues may require the involvement of specialized experts. The range of types of experts is vast; examples include financial, technology, medical, vocational, and mental health experts. Expert witnesses are common in litigation, but they also have a role in arbitration, collaborative law, and other processes.

- **Multiple Parties**—Although many people assume that disputes involve two parties, many situations actually involve many different parties (and non-parties behind the scenes). For instance, insurance adjusters may be involved in disputes, whether or not they are named as parties. Will contests may involve dozens of potential heirs or beneficiaries. Some processes may be better equipped than others to handle large groups of stakeholders.

These are only a few of the process-based interests that may be at issue in any given case. By reading this text, we hope to leave you with the realization that dispute resolution is not a "one size fits all" process. Conflict and conflict prevention and resolution can be e extraordinarily complex, largely because of the legal, psychological, economic, and other individualized factors in any given conflict. Over the last few decades, the use of ADR methods has grown rapidly and touches the practices of nearly all lawyers in our state, country, and internationally. ADR has transformed the nature of lawyers' practice and roles as client counselor, advocate, and neutral.

Our goal is to help you understand the nature, advantages, and disadvantages of the various ADR processes so that, as lawyers or other professionals, you can assist clients and other individuals and institutions select—and participate in—the most effective and appropriate method for preventing, managing, and resolving disputes. A hallmark feature of ADR is that the parties consent to the process and thus have more control to agree to the formality or flexibility of the process.

§ 1.05 How This Book Is Organized

The following chapters focus on these processes, beginning with the important foundational process of Client Interviewing and Counseling. Working with clients and understanding client situations and needs is the bedrock of any attorney/client relationship. Only through effective client counseling will a lawyer be able to serve clients in an effective and meaningful way.

The following chapters focus on the variety of processes commonly known as "Alternative Dispute Resolution." This book is organized by discussing the processes from the most conciliatory to the most adjudicative. Thus, the chapters proceed in the order of Negotiation, Mediation, Collaborative Law, and Arbitration. The materials for Mediation and Arbitration are so robust that we have divided them into two chapters each—one chapter to cover the process, and a second chapter to cover the legal issues arising from using those processes. In addition, we provide a chapter on Mediation Advocacy, which focuses on the lawyer's unique role in the mediation process. The final chapter, "Other Processes," covers additional processes that involve hybrid or tiered approaches or variations of ADR methods tailored to a specific type of problem or setting.

Ethical considerations are highlighted throughout this book. A lawyer's ethical practice is not only a duty, but also a best practice. This text discusses the ethical issues arising from every process and notes how lawyers and neutrals can work within these guidelines to help their clients achieve the best possible results.

ADR processes continue to evolve and grow in popularity. In today's practice, a lawyer can rarely be effective without understanding these skills and these processes. Our goal is to introduce you to the multitudes of available processes for resolving disputes and provide a solid framework for dealing with these issues in practice.

Chapter 2

Interviewing and Counseling

§ 2.01 Introduction

The process of effectively interviewing and counseling a client is a fundamental skill for lawyers and the foundation for any dispute resolution process. In fact, interviewing and counseling a client is a dispute resolution process in itself. Why might that be?

The interviewing and counseling process is an ongoing communication process between the lawyer and client that involves a trusted flow of information by the client to assist the lawyer in making an informed analysis of a client's case and in helping the client make informed choices among possible courses of action.[1] An effective interviewing and counseling process can help a lawyer and client understand the nature and underlying basis of the dispute, as well as help the client make an informed decision whether to pursue, or even drop, a claim in a legal context or to pursue other non-legal remedies.

Interviewing is the first step and process in which the lawyer begins to understand the client, the client's goals, expectations, and perspective on the situation.[2] The interviewing portion involves the attorney gathering information from a prospective client and the facts surrounding the client's problem. From the lawyer's perspective, the purpose of the client interview is to understand the nature and factual basis for the client's presenting case, to establish (and assess) rapport and trust with the client, to evaluate the strengths and weaknesses of the dispute, and to determine whether to accept the client and the case.[3] The client interview lays the foundation for every interaction that follows and is essential to building a trusting attorney-client relationship.

In counseling the client, the attorney attempts to identify options for resolution, both those based in the law and those based on other problem-solving approaches, and to help the client choose a course of action that will best satisfy the client's needs and objectives.[4] The counseling process is ongoing and involves the attorney assisting the client in making decisions to adopt the most appropriate course of action. Although related, the essential aspects of interviewing and counseling involve distinct stages, skills, and processes.

---

1. *See* Clark D. Cunningham, *What Do Clients Want from Their Lawyers*, 2013 J. Disp. Resol. 143, 156 (2013).

2. Leonard L. Riskin et al., Dispute Resolution and Lawyers 83 (3d ed. 2005).

3. Linda F. Smith, *Was it Good For You Too? Conversation Analysis of Two Interviews*, 96 Ky. L.J. 579, 609 (2008).

4. G. Nicholas Herman & Jean M. Cary, A Practical Approach to Client Interviewing, Counseling, and Decision-Making 4 (2009) (identifying five goals for the attorney to reach during the whole of the attorney-client relationship).

§ 2.02 Lawyer-Client Relationship Models

Establishing an effective attorney-client relationship is fundamental to a successful representation.[5] Each interaction between attorney and client shapes the overall functioning of their relationship and affects important characteristics of it, such as how the lawyer and client will work with each other and the extent of involvement in decisions regarding the representation.

Rules of professional conduct address various ethical aspects of the attorney-client relationship. Model Rule 1.2 concerns the allocation of decision-making authority between attorney and client. Under this Rule, lawyers are to abide by a client's decision regarding the objectives and overall goals of the representation, including whether to settle a matter. Although lawyers must confer with the client, lawyers have decisional authority as to the means used in the representation. Clients may, and generally do, defer to a lawyer's specialized skill and knowledge regarding the means used in the representation. In some instances, the "goals" versus "means" test is difficult to apply. In those instances, the best practice is for the attorney and client to consider which "means" or process steps will help best achieve the client's goals and make those decisions together.

Within this ethical boundary of decision-making authority, the attorney-client relationship may involve various degrees of control and participation. The respective roles of the attorney and the client in this relationship have been characterized in two basic models: the traditional or lawyer-centered model, and a more participatory, client-centered approach.[6] Each model has its advantages and disadvantages and may be appropriate depending on the specific situation or stage in the representation.[7] Neither approach is "good" or "bad" in the abstract, but different client needs may dictate the appropriate model to use in individual circumstances.

[A] Lawyer-Centered/Traditional Model

The traditional or "lawyer-centered" model is the more stereotypical view of an attorney-client relationship in which the attorney controls major aspects of the representation. This largely paternalistic model assumes that the lawyer "knows best," gives limited involvement to the client in the decision-making process, and focuses primarily on legal remedies. A lawyer adopting the traditional approach might ask the client to narrate the events leading to the matter presented, and the lawyer's questions focus on a legal theory and remedy fitting the case. The lawyer's counsel may involve a monologue on a recommended course of action.

The traditional model may be appropriate in certain situations with clients, such as where the lawyer has significant expertise, the representation involves a continuing relationship with a client, or the client wants the lawyer to take control and handle the legal representation and does not want to actively participate in the details of the

---

5. Cunningham, *supra* note 1 at 146 (a survey of professional negligence claims revealed that "failure to listen to the client, failure to ask appropriate questions, and failure to explain relevant aspects of the matter" were the top three causes of complaint).

6. Riskin, *supra* note 2 at 84; Herman & Cary, *supra* note 5 at 5–6.

7. *See* Robert F. Cochran et al., The Counselor-at-Law 2-6 (1999) (listing disadvantages to the client-centered and traditional models); Riskin, *supra* note 2 at 88–89 (describing a situation where the traditional model might be best).

representation.[8] Under these circumstances, the traditional model may be effective, provided the client is fully informed and the lawyer understands the client's objectives, values, and interests. A risk of this approach, however, is that the lawyer may influence the client's decision and recommend a narrow course of action such as focusing on a "rational" e.g., legal or economic, remedy, as opposed to what may be right for that particular client's situation, feelings, relational, or long-term needs.

More often, however, the traditional approach is not conducive to a productive attorney-client relationship. The limited involvement by the client risks the client not "owning" the problem or the outcome and later blaming the lawyer. Another concern with this traditional model regards the lawyer's role as a "hired gun" or in an authoritarian role and not necessarily optimal for meaningful interaction between lawyers and clients.[9] This model thus rarely produces satisfactory, optimal, or cost-effective outcomes. Both the lawyer and the client can become aggravated and disenfranchised by an aggressive approach. Where the lawyer, instead, adopts a client-centered approach and seeks to understand a client's true needs and objectives, conflict can become an opportunity for resolution, satisfaction, and even transformation.

[B] The Client-Centered/Participatory Model

A client-centered/participatory model involves shared power between the lawyer and client in which the lawyer educates and involves the client in the process.[10] This approach values the dual concepts that client interests in seeking legal counsel can involve both legal and non-legal aspects and that clients are in the best position to bring about the most effective resolutions to their own particular situations. Studies report that clients who actively participated in the representation tended to achieve better results than those whose participation was passive.[11] In a client-centered interview, the lawyer encourages the client to do most of the talking, explores legal and non-legal considerations, and involves the client in exploring possible solutions most acceptable for the client. This approach promotes collaborative problem-solving and helps guides the client to an informed decision.

The client-centered approach may also reduce attorney costs. When a client is more involved, the client may be able to perform some tasks that might otherwise fall on the lawyer. For instance, in a litigated case involving discovery requests, an involved client may be able to provide preliminary answers or responsive documents to the lawyer. The lawyer then can refine the answers and prepare the documents for exchange. Clients who assist in these preliminary tasks have a greater understanding of the cost, work, and complexity of the matter. This dynamic can apply to any type of representation, from drafting a patent, to preparing documents for a business transaction, to participating in a negotiation, mediation, or complex adjudication.

---

8. Herman & Cary, *supra* note 1 at 7. Riskin, *supra* note 2 at 89 (suggesting four factors: "(a) The solutions . . . require knowledge or expertise within the lawyer's exclusive control; (b) The lawyer fully understands the needs and values of the client; (c) The lawyer can be neutral; and (d) The client is unwilling or unable to make a decision.").

9. *See* Cunningham, *supra* note 1 at 156.

10. *See* David A. Binder et al., Lawyers as Counselors 3 (3d ed. 2012).

11. Riskin, *supra* note 2 at 88–89.

[C] Models Along the Spectrum

The traditional and the client-centered models represent two points along a spectrum of the dynamic in an attorney-client working relationship. The primary distinction between the two models lies in the level of client involvement and control in the representation. The approach adopted by the attorney will dictate much of what happens throughout the representation. The attorney should consider the approach that best fits the particular client's needs and objectives. In the course of a representation, an attorney may utilize multiple approaches depending on the client and requirements and stage of the particular case.[12]

Most attorney-client relationships fall within the spectrum, rather than on the edges of the two models. A lawyer may adopt one approach with one client and a different approach with a different client, depending on the client's needs and abilities. A single lawyer may have an individual client who feels strongly about participating in the case and a different client who is emotionally traumatized by the underlying events and not capable of active involvement. Even sophisticated business clients may be cost-sensitive and willing to take on some of the legwork, while another client may be too busy and want the lawyer to handle the representation.

The attorney-client relationship is the foundation upon which a lawyer's ethical and fiduciary duties are based. Effective communication skills are essential to a successful attorney-client relationship and to assist clients in understanding the legal process.[13] In fact, "[t]he most effective legal counselors are those who are instilled with respect for the client, cognizant of building rapport, aware of the psychological dynamics of the lawyer-client relationship, and equipped with technical communication skills that enable them to gather information without sacrificing rapport."[14] These communication skills in the context of a lawyer-client interviewing and counseling process are explored next in the context of the client interview.

Part I: The Client Interview

§ 2.03 Overview

Legal practice occurs at the nexus of facts, law, and procedure. Legal problems arise in the morass of daily life, in personal and business interactions, and in commerce. The backstory of any particular claim may be simply one variation on a common theme, or it may involve new and novel characters in unprecedented situations. A client dispute

---

12. *See* Riskin, *supra* note 2 at 88–89; Cochran, *supra* note 7 at 9 ("[The template provided in this book] must be adapted to the individual lawyer and refined according to circumstances.").

13. Cunningham, *supra* note 1 at 146 (noting that a survey of professional negligence claims revealed that "failure to listen to the client, failure to ask appropriate questions, and failure to explain relevant aspects of the matter" were the top three causes of complaint).

14. Cochran, *supra* note at 7. Stefan Krieger & Richard K. Neumann, Essential Lawyering Skills: Interviewing, Counseling, Negotiation, and Persuasive Fact Analysis (4th ed. 2011) (listing the purposes of the client interview as being to form an attorney-client relationship; to learn the client's goals; to learn as much as the client knows about the facts; and to reduce the client's anxiety without being unrealistic).

may involve a single issue or multiple issues; the dispute may, and often does, involve non-legal concerns that the client may value more than legal vindication; and there may be key facts that the client deems unimportant but are highly relevant from a legal perspective. Clients can range from individuals of any socioeconomic segment of society to the small business or multinational corporation. Lawyers need to consider all of these possibilities. The interview is not only a search for legally significant facts, but also an opportunity to better understand the overarching factual and legal context, underlying motivations, and possible courses of relief most appropriate for the client.

§ 2.04 Why Meet with a Lawyer?

Consider why a prospective client seeks to meet with a lawyer. Individuals and organizations may seek a lawyer's help for many reasons, at many different points in a dispute or in life. Some may want advice, options, solutions, vindication, or policy precedent. The resort to seek legal counsel is likely the result of failed negotiations and attempts at conciliation, thus the entire process may be fraught with anxiety. Others, particularly in the business world, may see the involvement of attorneys as a necessary and routine— whether or not desirable—aspect of their professional work. Still others seek the advice of counsel for planning purposes, such as estate planning or protecting vulnerable persons such as minors or those with disabilities.

A prospective client meeting with the lawyer will want to tell his or her story. This process provides an opportunity for the client's needs to be heard and for the client to be educated about the legal process, clarification of roles, and financial implications of their case. It is important that the client understands the strengths and weaknesses of their case in terms of legal, financial, practical, logistical, and emotional considerations. The client often wants to know "Do I have a case?" "Can I win?" or "How do I accomplish that?" The lawyer's role is to assist the client in assessing these questions and to understand viable options. To engage in this process, a lawyer needs to develop rapport with the client and gather sufficient information and facts about their matter to understand the client's legal case, as well as their needs, interests, and expectations.

§ 2.05 Purposes and Goals

The first interview and meeting between the attorney and client provides an important opportunity to establish a successful attorney-client relationship. The purpose of a client interview is not only to learn whether the client has a strong legal case or issue, but also to help a client consider the best approach for them to obtain optimal resolution of their dispute and situation. The client interview allows the lawyer to gather information about the matter presented and is an opportunity to get to know the client. This interview involves a unique situation where the attorney and client both acquaint themselves, while also evaluating each other, to determine whether or not they would be able to work together. The initial conversations are a two-way street: the client is deciding whether to hire this particular lawyer (and perhaps whether to retain counsel at all), while the lawyer is deciding whether to accept or refer this particular client. The decision of whether to accept representation of a particular client is as important as the client's decision of whether to select a lawyer. An uncooperative or untrustworthy client could seriously impair a lawyer's ability to effectively represent the client and potentially risk a malpractice lawsuit. Although these serious ethical issues are generally only background considerations for a canonical understanding of the attorney-client interview, they are nevertheless important considerations to take into account. An effective interview will reveal these considerations.

The client interview provides the forum for the client to tell their story and express their views of the disputed events in a confidential setting. The lawyer should create a comfortable working atmosphere that encourages a client's willingness to talk candidly with the lawyer. Clients seeking legal representation are often experiencing major life event—such as a divorce, accident, injury, change in employment, or a business concern. Making the clients comfortable by meeting in a comfortable room or offering them something to drink can go a long way in establishing a productive professional relationship. Rapport is built through preparation, listening, and showing attention and empathy to the client.

§ 2.06 Preparing for the Client Interview

Before the initial client meeting, preliminary tasks to complete include: conducting a conflicts check; determining referral sources; clarifying the consultation fee; scheduling the in-person appointment; and informing the client of what to bring and expect in the first meeting.[15]

[A] Conflicts of Interest Check

Prior to arranging the client interview, a lawyer should gather basic information about the client, potential parties/participants, key witnesses, and the nature of the dispute. The attorney should perform a conflicts of interest assessment to determine whether representation of this prospective client would pose a potential or actual conflict of interest. An Internet search of the client and potential parties may also provide useful background information. A lawyer is ethically prohibited from representing a client if the representation involves a conflict of interest with another client of the lawyer or lawyer's firm. A conflict exists if "(1) the representation of one client will be directly adverse to another client; or (2) there is a significant risk that the representation of one or more clients will be materially limited by the lawyer's responsibilities to another client, a former client or a third person or by a personal interest of the lawyer."[16] These rules seek to ensure client loyalty and the lawyer's independent, professional judgment. Absent informed consent by an affected client, the lawyer should not pursue discussion regarding the disputed claim with the prospective client.

---

15. James Feldman, *The First Contact is Crucial—Have Your Ducks in a Row*, FAMILY ADVOCATE (Am. Bar Ass'n 1990).

16. Am. Bar Ass'n, Center for Professional Responsibility, MODEL RULES OF PROF'L CONDUCT r. 1.7(a) [hereinafter "MODEL RULES" or "MODEL RULES OF PROF'L CONDUCT"]. *See also* MODEL RULES 1.9 (former clients) and 1.8–1.13 (conflicts generally).

For example, if the lawyer learns that the prospective client's dispute involves one of the lawyer's current clients (even on a totally different matter), a conflict of interest exists, and the lawyer must decline that representation. Conflict may also arise because of a lawyer's work at a different law firm or other type of prior employer, complicated client business structures, or a professional or personal relationship.

Although new lawyers might assume that they would want to take any client who walks through the door, they should remember that a "lawyer is not a bus." In other words, a lawyer need not accept every client seeking representation. Although "[a] lawyer's representation of a client does not constitute endorsement of the client's political, economic, social or moral views or activities,"[17] many legitimate reasons exist to decline taking on a new client, including inability to pay, low chance of obtaining the client's goal, personal conflict with the client (i.e., refusing to represent a member of an organized crime group), and certainly when the representation involves a client's ongoing or illegal activity or would require the lawyer to violate professional conduct rules.

[B] Advance Communication with Prospective Client

In advance of the meeting, a lawyer should prepare the client about what to expect in the interview. The lawyer may ask that the client bring documentation, correspondence, and information potentially relevant to their case. Depending on the type of representation, the relevant information may include contracts, employment documents, wills, or insurance information. The lawyer should also explain whether the consultation will require a fee, as well as the likely duration and format of the initial interview. Providing this information helps to manage client expectations and to avoid misunderstandings early in the representation.

[C] Referral Source

Asking how the client came to find your services is helpful to assist in learning about business sources, as well as to ascertain whether the client has consulted or retained other lawyers. A client who has hired multiple attorneys on the same matter could be an indication concerning the merits of the case or identify a potential problem if the client seems highly litigious.

§ 2.07 Conducting the Client Interview: Stages of the Client-Centered Interview Process

The client interviewing and counseling process involves several stages, which start before and conclude after the actual client meeting. The goals of the first interview with the client are both factual and relational. The lawyer needs to gather sufficient information to be able to provide an initial assessment on the relative merits of the case and to advise the client of potential legal options, as well as anticipated legal fees and expenses.

---

17. Model Rules of Prof'l Conduct r. 2.1(b).

In order to understand the client's situation, goals, and expectations, the lawyer must establish a level of rapport with the client to reduce the client's anxiety and to foster client candor and trust essential for effective representation.

[A] Opening and Rapport Building

In meeting with the prospective client, the lawyer should explain the purposes of the client interview process. Clients are likely anxious to meet with the lawyer and reluctant to discuss their concerns, particularly negative aspects of their case or matter. The lawyer should assure the client of confidentiality and explain that attorney-client privilege protects the communications provided no one unnecessary to the discussion is present.[18] An in-person interview with the client facilitates establishing rapport with the client and the attorney's ability to assess the prospective representation.

The lawyer should engage with the client and use the initial interview as an opportunity to begin developing rapport and relationship with their client. To effectively engender trust and begin to understand the client's goals, the initial interview should proceed more as a conversation, not an interrogation or checklist of questions required to draft legal documentation. While it is possible to gain important information in a swift manner through the use of intensive questioning, a lawyer-dominated interview may inhibit important communication and the potential for a collaborative working relationship. Important nonverbal cues are often missed when the lawyer's focus is on gathering specific information rather than attending to the prospective client. As part of this conversational style, the lawyer should make eye contact with the client, engage in active-listening skills, and be mindful of his or her own body language.

[B] Client Story and Problem Description

The opening stage of the interview is particularly important to understanding the client, the client's concerns, interests, motivation, and goals. In the opening stage of an interview, clients should be invited to explain their situation or "story" in their own words, with minimal interruption by the lawyer.[19] Start simply with broad, open-ended questions, such as "What brings you here today?" and "What happened?" Open-ended questions allow the client to provide a narrative in describing their situation in their own words, which can be therapeutic to the client's need to express their concerns as well as reveal their intentions.

During this phase, lawyers should primarily listen and seek to put the client at ease as they describe their situation. Encourage the client to provide as much information as possible in a narrative fashion with additional open-ended questions, such as "Please

---

18. Attorney-client confidential communications made for the purpose of legal representation are privileged under state or federal laws. Such privilege may be waived by the unnecessary presence of a third party or other revelation of the communications. A lawyer is obligated not to reveal communications related to the representation of a client or a prospective client. *See* MODEL RULES OF PROF'L CONDUCT r. 1.6 and 1.18.

19. Smith, *supra* note 3 at 580 (recommending that clients be permitted to describe the situation in their own words and to give a narrative or timeline, that the attorney listen, avoid interrupting the client, engage in "active listening" and otherwise show empathy.").

tell me more . . ." or, "Are there other concerns . . . ?"[20] Taking notes along with verbal recognition ("yes" — "okay") and nonverbal cues (head nodding) signals to the client that you are providing your full attention to understanding their situation.

Lawyers should pay particular attention to the client's opening words, as crucial information about the client and their case is often revealed very early in the interviewing process.[21] A client may demonstrate emotion and reveal underlying motivations for seeking legal consultation. Important insights about the client may be revealed at this point.[22]

Many times, *how* clients tell their story is as important as the story they tell. Lawyers not only advocate for clients' legal rights, they are also the "tellers" of their clients' stories. Often these stories involve personal or painful incidents in a client's life. Sociologist Erving Goffman's theory of "facework" suggests that when people interact, they present their positive image "face" to society.[23] A sensitive or emotional interaction presents a "face-threatening" situation to one's self-image or social standing. A perceived power imbalance in the attorney-client relationship may hinder communication when a client perceives judgment to their reputation or credibility. How a client talks about issues may reveal areas of heightened interest or emotion, which are not apparent from the bare facts, but are legally and practically significant.

The interviewing lawyer should aspire "[t]o hear, begin to understand, and acknowledge the clients' particular concerns or problems and their context from the clients' point of view."[24] Encouraging clients to tell their stories helps the lawyer understand more about the client, why they are consulting a lawyer, and the relationship of their "legal" issues to other events in the client's world.

[C] Information Gathering

Once the client has provided a narrative timeline of the situation, the lawyer may proceed to inquire more specifically about the facts of the case. Even here, the lawyer must be aware of the client's reactions, as emotionally significant information is not confined to the opening narration. This phase of the interview generally permits the lawyer to seek facts in a more direct manner without unduly limiting the client's expression.

Information gathering is facilitated through the techniques of effective questioning, active listening, demonstrating empathy and non-judgment, and attention to nonverbal cues.

---

20. Gay Gellhorn, *Law and Language: An Empirically-Based Model for the Opening Moments of Client Interviews*, 4 CLINICAL L. REV. 321, 348 (1998).

21. Gellhorn, *supra* note 20 at 347 (finding that "[c]lients reveal critical self-information in their opening words . . . ").

22. Gellhorn, *supra* note 20 at 350 (advising that lawyers be attentive, do not interrupt, and use linguistic strategies that encourage complete responses and client full expression in opening moments of the client interview).

23. Erving Goffman, *On Face Work: An Analysis of Ritual Elements in Social Interaction*, 18 PSYCHIATRY 213 (1955).

24. Gellhorn, *supra* note 20 at 350.

[1] Questions

The client's narrative should also include an explanation of the chronological timeline.[25] Asking the five "Ws" (what, where, when, who, and why) questions is helpful when gathering information relevant to the client's general situation. When beginning a new line of questioning, engage in open-ended questions to permit the client to relay his or her story with the personal bias barriers that might unintentionally present themselves within the question. Even simple questions such as "Can you tell me more about that?" show a deeper reflection on the part of the speaker.[26]

A progression from open, broad questions proceeding to more narrow and focused inquiries allows for both flexibility and specificity. A "T" or inverted funnel sequence of questioning, starting with open-ended, then proceeding to more specific and close-ended questions, and even the use of silence will help to elicit important information. Be mindful of the timing, purpose, and context in which the questions are asked. The type of question and degree of sensitive information sought should depend on the personal dynamics and development stage of the interview.

Lawyers may not only ask questions chronologically, but also ask questions topically. In many situations, the timeline of events is particularly important. If a client seeks legal help based on a car accident, the exact timing of where cars were positioned at various times may be very important. On the other hand, if the client is seeking estate planning, the lawyer will more likely ask the client questions topically, focusing on heirs, assets, debts, and other relevant issues.

[2] Exploring Client Goals, Interests, Resources and Options

A thorough interview involves not only gathering a comprehensive understanding of the client's stated problem, but also identifying the client's needs, interests, and goals for the representation. A client's motivation for seeking legal relief may not always be obvious or readily forthcoming. A client may take a certain "position" regarding an issue, but exploring the underlying reasons for such a position can unveil a rich source of information that may be helpful to creative options. The seemingly simple question of "Why?" is powerful in this respect. A needs and interests inquiry should explore the client's hierarchy of substantive, procedural, and intangible psychological needs with respect to the disputed situation. For example, a client may have felt disrespected and seeks recognition or relief beyond money. A need for validation or security may be more important than legal issues or relief sought. Understanding client feelings and emotions can reveal true client motivations in pursuing legal recourse.

---

25. Binder, *supra* note 10, at 167, 64–77 (advising the interviewer to follow the timeline or narrative with "Tunnel" questioning by beginning with "open" questions and proceeding to more narrow and closed questioning); Krieger, *supra* note 3 at 98 (interviewers to "take up each topic separately" and "on each topic, start with broad questions . . . and gradually work your way toward narrow ones.").

26. John Barkai, *Teaching Negotiation and ADR: The Savvy Samurai Meets the Devil*, 75 Neb. L. Rev. 704 (1996) (commenting that "[e]ven though the questions are quite simple ("Tell me more about that"), the responder often gives very serious consideration to his or her answers. Though simple, these questions are thought provoking.").

[3] Listening Actively and with Empathy

Listening involves not only attentiveness to the message being communicated, but also intentional feedback communicated to the speaker. Active listening is the verbal return of the speaker's main ideas or feelings. The active listener restates the essential content and feelings associated with speaker's statement. This helps ensure that the speaker was heard correctly and provides the opportunity to correct and clarify any misunderstandings.

Various verbal and nonverbal cues apprise the speaker—in this case, the client—that the message is heard and understood. Classic active listening involves the speaker restating introductory phrases, but it is also achieved through various techniques such as restating, reflecting, and summarizing. Asking more detailed and probing questions helps to clarify and focus the inquiry. Active listening can be used to avoid prematurely answering questions. It can also provide an opportunity to demonstrate empathy and nonjudgment in acknowledging emotion and the client's feelings, emotions, or descriptions. The topic of active listening is also covered in Chapter 4, The Mediation Process.[27]

[4] Body Language and Emotional Awareness

A focus on words alone can lose important messages communicated by nonverbal behavior. Understanding the client's narrative involves more than learning the "dry facts" of the client's situation. Nonverbal communications can convey silent messages that more accurately reflect the client's beliefs than mere words. Messages can be conveyed nonverbally, by way of body posture, movement, or distance, eye contact, and vocal pitch, pace, and repeated speech. As much as 93 percent of communication is expressed through body language and the tempo, tone, and pitch of a person's voice. Attentiveness to nonverbal communication will give the lawyer a more complete picture of the situation facing the client.

To assess the quality of information provided, counsel must also consider emotional aspects of the client's situation. Emotional intelligence includes knowing one's emotions through self-awareness and emotional self-control and recognizing emotions in others through empathy and relationships. Demonstrating empathy, nonjudgment, and understanding with the client can help elucidate important client needs, interests, and underlying concerns. These factors are often intangible but essential needs relating to security, status, respect, and fairness. Understanding why a person is emotional, taking a position, or demanding relief can help to frame the issues to be negotiated and to empower cooperation between the attorney and client.[28]

[5] Reality Testing

Attorneys should recognize certain barriers common during client interviews. Clients may withhold information that might cast them in a negative light, that they think will

---

27. *See infra* Chapter 4.

28. Cochran, *supra* note 7 at 39 (noting Professor Howard Gardner's theory of multiple intelligences and describing "interpersonal [or emotional] intelligence," as "[t]he ability to understand other people, what motivates them, how they work, how to work cooperatively with them.").

hurt their case, or that is traumatic to discuss. Lawyers should demonstrate empathetic listening by recognizing what the client is saying and refraining from judgment, and re-assure the client that the lawyer can best help the client if they are prepared to respond to potentially critical or adverse information.

Exploring potential weaknesses of the case with the client is important when assessing the viability of pursuing the client's legal claim and to manage client expectations. The client should be encouraged to consider the situation from the viewpoint of the opposing party. Assuring that the "reality testing" questions are intended to assess the strength of the client's case and not to pass judgment, the lawyer should pose a series of probing questions, such as: What are the strengths and weakness of your case? How is the opposing party like to respond? Are there prior incidents suggesting a similar pattern? Has the client talked to other lawyers? What would happen if you did not get the desired outcome or resolution? These questions may also prompt the client to correct or clarify their perceptions of the dispute and to consider aspects of the dispute they previously ignored.

[D] Preliminary Assessment

After the client has provided the attorney with the relevant facts and context, a lawyer may want to provide a preliminary overview of the law generally applicable to the case, reality test projections of the case, and estimate the time frame, expenses, and various elements that go along with the process to prepare the client's expectations.

Whether to provide a preliminary assessment is appropriate at this stage is a matter of discretion. Where the case is simple and/or the attorney is familiar with the particular legal issues involved, an assessment may be a valuable tool in shaping the course of the representation. However, in many cases, a preliminary assessment would be little more than an educated guess and as likely to wrongly influence expectations as to assist informed decision-making.

§ 2.08 Concluding the Interview and Plan of Action

In concluding the initial interview, the lawyer should summarize main points of understanding and clarify client goals and expectations. Client interviews should conclude with communication about next steps for both the attorney and the client. A client should be informed about whether the attorney will further evaluate the case, the timing, and costs.

[A] Client Communications

Prospective clients should be informed as to the status of their case and relationship with the lawyer and firm. Failing to communicate this information may be malpractice, or at minimum, will result in a dissatisfied client.[29] The client should also be advised that a statute of limitations may require filing an action by a certain date.

If the lawyer knows at the conclusion of the initial interview that he or she will not enter into an attorney/client relationship, the attorney may want to provide the client with a referral list of other attorneys. For example, if the client consults a business lawyer but really needs an intellectual property lawyer, the business lawyer may want to refer the client to the appropriate type of lawyer. If the client cannot afford a lawyer's services, that lawyer may want to refer the client to a more affordable lawyer or to low-cost or free legal services available in the community. If the client is in a situation that is time-sensitive, the lawyer should decide promptly whether to take the case or to refer the client to another attorney. If the lawyer does not accept or anticipate accepting representation, a letter confirming non-engagement should be sent to the prospective client.

If additional meetings are expected, the attorney should provide the client with a list of instructions to complete before their next meeting. These might include providing copies or originals of key documents, financial records/summaries, signing and returning the engagement letter, and advising the client not to communicate with various parties.

[B] Attorney Post-Interview Actions and Assessment

After the interview, an attorney should prepare an internal office memorandum; confirm ability to accept the representation, draft a letter outlining the terms of engagement and representation (or non-engagement, as appropriate); decide on staffing; and thank the referral source if applicable.

File Memoranda. Following the client interview, the interviewing lawyer should draft a memoranda summarizing the information gained from the interview, indicating both subjective impressions as well as objective facts. This record preserves the lawyer's understanding of information and should include questions for additional research.

Aside from a conflict of interest, other conditions may limit an attorney from accepting the representation. The case could be outside of the attorney's expertise, beyond the statute of limitations, possibly jeopardize the ability to competently handle existing clients (i.e., the lawyer may be "too busy" already), or there could be disagreement on the proper fee arrangement.[30] Also consider whether this client is someone you can work with and, just as important, is this someone you can help? It is not easy to "fire" a client after entering an appearance on their behalf. Personal incompatibilities can derail the representation, even if the lawyer is entirely competent to address legal issues in the case.

---

29. *See* Togstad v. Veseley, 291 N.W.2d 686, 694 (Minn. 1980) (recognizing an attorney-client relationship was established by virtue of legal advice given in an initial interview with a prospective client and affirming lawyer's malpractice liability to the prospective client for failing to inform as to the risk of statute of limitations and for not following up with client post interview).

30. Lonny H. Dolin, *The Fine Art of Turning Clients Away*, Vol. 20 GP SOLO No. 5 (Am. Bar Ass'n, 2003) ("[t]he case may not be in my area of expertise, the case may be beyond the applicable statute of limitations, I may be unable to take the case on a contingent fee basis as requested, or I may be so busy at the moment that it would jeopardize my ability to competently handle my existing clients' matters if I currently took on the case.").

Engagement Letter. If representation is agreed upon, an engagement letter should define the scope of the representation, identifying the matters covered by the engagement, the respective roles and obligations of the lawyer and client, responsibility for fees and expenses, termination provisions; and dispute resolution provisions.[31] Many law firms have standard engagement letters, and new lawyers in solo or small practice should develop engagement letters for their own firms.

Part II: Counseling the Client

Getting to know a client is a prerequisite to the larger goal of helping the client toward a satisfactory result. The counseling process involves understanding the client's problem, interests, and motivations; and then exploring options that are best suited to meet the client's goal. Not all client problems are legal, and even a client with a viable legal case may be seeking an outcome other than a strictly legal remedy. In a counseling session, the lawyer will work with the client to identify alternatives, priorities, creative options, and a course of action.

§ 2.09 Lawyer's Role as Counselor

A lawyer's role in counseling clients extends to more than an analysis of the legal viability of a particular claim or defense. While mere fact-gathering may prepare an attorney to win a legal claim, it is entirely possible that the attorney's narrow focus will preclude other options and considerations that would have better served the client's interests.

In counseling a client, a lawyer provides an informed understanding of the client's rights and obligations and explains practical implications. A lawyer's counseling role may refer not only to the law, but also to other considerations such as moral, economic, social, and political factors that may be relevant to the client's situation.

The Model Rules of Professional Conduct emphasize the lawyer's ethical duties not only as an Advocate, but also as an Advisor or Counselor. Rule 1.2 provides that:

> In representing a client, a lawyer shall exercise independent professional judgment and render candid advice. In rendering advice, *a lawyer may refer not only to law but to other considerations such as moral, economic, social, psychological, and political factors* that may be relevant to the client's situation. (Emphasis added).

Although the clients make the ultimate decision on questions such as setting disputes, the clients look to the lawyer to provide sound counsel and are influenced by the lawyer's advice. Thus, lawyers have the extraordinary responsibility to ensure that clients make informed decisions. The lawyer, as a problem-solver and counselor, can help clients consider the best approach to their problem by advising them on the law as well as

---

31. Steven P. Jones & Melissa Beard Glover, *The Attack on Traditional Billing Practices*, 20 U. Ark. Little Rock L. Rev. 293 (1998) (describing various fee arrangements and presenting a sample engagement letter).

the myriad of other practical, emotional, financial, and social consequences of certain options.

Examples of nonlegal counseling are plentiful. In a divorce case, a lawyer may counsel a spouse on how protracted litigation may have an effect on children or deplete marital assets. If a current employee wants to file a lawsuit against the employer, the lawyer could counsel the employee on how that litigation might change the working environment or affect professional references and reputation. If a business intends to breach a contract with a government entity, the lawyer should discuss the reputational and political harm that may arise from the breach. Very few "legal" problems involve solely legal issues. The lawyer's role as counselor makes clear that lawyers have a duty to consider how the legal matter may have an effect on other aspects of the client's life.

§ 2.10 The Counseling Process

After the client has provided the attorney with the relevant facts and context, the lawyer provides an initial case assessment and presentation of process options. The counseling process is aptly called a "process." Conferring with and counseling the client is an element that integrates itself in every stage, from the initial case evaluation to the conclusion of the representation. The counseling process involves a discussion of legal and nonlegal considerations. In relation to the legal consequences, clients need to understand the realistic merits and weaknesses of their case as it integrates the specific facts to precedent and legal doctrine. Regarding nonlegal considerations, clients need to understand the time, financial, emotional, and overall demanding effects a particular approach can have on them and others. The process works most productively when the client regards the lawyer as a trusted advisor.

[A] Establishing Trust and Clarifying Client Goals, Priorities and Interests

The counseling session involves meeting with the client and reestablishing rapport and trust to make the client feel comfortable and open to the attorney's objective analysis. The lawyer-counselor should review and clarify the facts and the client's goals, interests, and priorities developed from the initial interview session. The lawyer should also ask the client whether anything has changed or whether the client has any additional thoughts on the matter since their last discussion. The lawyer may then report on any new developments or factual information learned as a result of the lawyer's independent investigation and analysis. Again, the techniques for active listening and empathetic understanding should be used throughout the representation.

[B] Preparatory Statement

Like the preparatory statement in an initial interview, the lawyer in the counseling session gives the client a preview of what to expect, both in terms and content, and clarifies the role expectations for both attorney and client. Explaining the purpose of the counseling session and its structure helps reduce client anxiety about the process. The preparatory statement should convey the attorney's role as an objective advisor in the counseling process, and the client's role as ultimate decision-maker for the representation. The lawyer should ensure that the client understands the process and provide the client with the opportunity to discuss any questions. The main task is to identify the matter requiring a decision and to further explore the client's objectives and assess options and consequences.

[C] Case Assessment

Counseling the client includes a lawyer's assessment of the applicable law, relative case strengths and weaknesses, reality testing projections, an estimated time frame, and a range of options that may meet the client's objectives.

In explaining the legal aspects of the client's case, the lawyer should communicate in a manner so that the client understands the strengths as well as the weaknesses of the case, and the possibility of counterclaims and associated expenses. The legal process can be a time-intensive, emotionally draining, and financially consuming endeavor. The lawyer should discuss the legal as well as the potential emotional, reputational, political, and financial implications of various courses of action. The lawyer should also give time to the client to raise questions or clarify points confusing to the client.

§ 2.11 Generating and Identifying Options

Based on the case analysis and provided information, the attorney should work with client to understand various legal and nonlegal options. The discussion can begin with a simple, "Now let's turn to what choices you have in meeting your needs, interests, and goals. As I see it, you can do X, or you can do Y, and we can explore other options as well." Invite the client to select which option to explore first to assess priority preferences, and conduct a similar analysis of each option. The range of options should be developed consistent with client interests, resources, and needs for fair process and relationships.[32]

The process of identifying alternatives should revolve around the client's interests and ultimate goals. If the client has not been forthcoming or the attorney has failed to uncover key concerns, determining the best course of action is more difficult. Effective initial discussions facilitate the lawyer's understanding of the client's situation and ability to counsel on an appropriate course of action.

---

32. Krieger & Neumann, *supra* note 14 at 29 ("To generate the largest number of possible solutions, you must be willing to look below the surface of the facts and law for deeper possibilities and meaning. Solution-generation depends on an uninhibited flow of association, during which judgment is suspended and ideas that later evaluation might show to be sound arrive mixed together with ideas that eventually turn out to be wrong or even silly . . . The key is to avoid premature judgment, to defer evaluation until after you have created an array of alternatives.").

§ 2.12 Assessing and Weighing Consequences

For each option identified, the legal and non-legal consequences should be considered. The legal assessment includes discussion of case strengths and weaknesses, timing, and procedural details. Nonlegal considerations include the range of financial, social, personal/emotional, reputational, and ethical and moral implications upon the client and other affected parties. The lawyer should work with the client to methodically consider the advantages and disadvantages of each option and likely consequences. A written chart laying out the advantages and disadvantages of every option, grouped in categories such as economic, social, psychological, and ethical/moral may be helpful to weigh the consequences of alternative courses of action and to identify client priorities in reaching a decision. A sample chart setting forth these considerations appears at the end of this chapter.

In addition to substantive decisions, the attorney and client should discuss what processes may be used to achieve the client's goals. While some clients have a particular process firmly in mind, many others are undecided regarding a desired course of action. Even clients who foresee litigation as the only option can benefit from a discussion of non-litigation options, such as negotiation or mediation.

§ 2.13 Informed Decision-Making

A client-centered and participatory decision-making process involves helping the client make an informed decision and identify steps to accomplish their objectives. Empowering the client to be the focal point of the decision-making process can be beneficial in identifying the problems and underlying interests, formulating solutions, and making decisions based on client values. The lawyer should ensure that the client understands the lawyer's advice and gives adequate time to answering client questions before proceeding.

The process of identifying client objectives, interests, alternatives, and weighing consequences assists the client in making an informed decision. The lawyer and client have established an understanding of the determined course of action, time parameters, and next steps. The rapport and relationship developed through the representation is affirmed through an intentional client-focused counseling process.

§ 2.14 Ethical Considerations

The decision whether to accept representation of a client matter involves considering moral and ethical issues that can arise during the representation. A survey conducted by the American Bar Association reported that 56 percent of lawyers have been asked by their clients to do something that the client knew was unethical.[33] This statistic indicates an alarming tendency for clients to hope, if not expect, that their attorneys will disregard

---

33. Terry Carter, *Ethics by the Numbers*, 83 A.B.A.J. 97, 97 (1997).

ethical rules on their behalf. This societal belief is furthered by many stereotypical images of the aggressive, ambulance-chasing lawyer willing to do whatever it takes to secure a win. What these portrayals fail to acknowledge, however, is that the legal profession holds itself to high ethical standards and rules of professional conduct. A lawyer must know how to handle unethical requests and how to counsel clients on moral and ethical issues that arise during the course of the representation, as well as to know when to withdraw and to decline representation. These skills ensure that the lawyer is adequately prepared for the variety of unique ethical issues that any client will present.

[A] Vetting Clients for Moral Compatibility

To avoid ethical or client management dilemmas, lawyers should get to know their clients at the outset of the representation.[34] Rapport building is helpful, but additional vetting of potential clients can ensure the attorney is compatible with the client and the representation from a legal, ethical, and moral perspective. Although representing a client does not constitute an endorsement, a lawyer may consider whether the client's representation is consistent with the lawyer's own values in deciding whether to represent a client. Once an attorney agrees to represent a client, termination of representation may require court approval.

[B] Moral Counseling

A lawyer *may* withdraw from the representation because of moral incompatibility,[35] but the lawyer should first attempt to guide and persuade the client to make a morally acceptable decision. Legal counseling may involve advising clients on non-legal considerations, ranging from the practical, political, financial, emotional, business, reputational, as well as moral questions that a client's actions and decisions may have on others. Although moral counseling is distinctive in that the focus turns away from legal issues, in practice it is no different from legal counseling. Client-centered counseling on nonlegal aspects may be done by discussing client values, goals, needs, and interests, and then analyzing the choices in light of those factors to determine the most appropriate steps for the given situation.

[C] Ethical Limits on Lawyer Advocacy

Lawyer professional conduct rules provide guidance on authorizing or requiring a lawyer to withdraw from representing a client who is acting illegally.[36] For example, lawyers

---

34. *See* Paul J. Zwier, Ethics in Litigation 16–17 (1995) (encouraging lawyers to get to know their clients as well as possible in the initial interview); W. Bradley Wendel, *Institutional and Individual Justification in Legal Ethics: The Problem of Client Selection*, 34 Hofstra L. Rev. 987, 993–95 (2006).

35. Model Rule 1.16(b)(4) (allowing an attorney to withdraw from the representation if the course of action chosen by the client is "repugnant" or "fundamental[ly] disagree[able]" to the attorney).

36. Model Rule 1.16(a)(1) (requiring a lawyer to withdraw from the representation when its continuation would violate the law); Model Rules of Prof'l Conduct r. 1.16(b)(2)-(3) (allowing a lawyer to withdraw if the client commits a crime or uses the lawyer's services to do so).

are prohibited from helping a witness commit perjury, engaging in fraud or illegal conduct, or otherwise abusing legal process.[37] A lawyer may be permitted to give an opinion on the legality or likely consequences of certain conduct, but a lawyer may not assist a client in fraudulent or criminal conduct.[38] In the event the lawyer would not objectively be able to represent that client due to incompatibly, moral repugnancy, or illegality, withdrawal is appropriate and possibly mandated.

§ 2.15 Duty to Advise Clients of ADR Options?

The ABA's Ethics 2000 Commission recommended that an attorney has a duty to advise clients of ADR options. The reasons advanced to impose such a duty were that knowledge of ADR options is needed for informed client decision-making. "Informed consent" is defined as agreement "after the lawyer has communicated adequate information and explanation about the material risks of and reasonably available alternatives to the proposed course of conduct."[39]

The ability to conduct an effective legal client interview and counseling session is a foundational skill required of all lawyers. The following chapters explain the various other ADR processes that should be presented to the client.

---

37. MODEL RULE 3.4(b).
38. MODEL RULE 1.2(d) ("A lawyer shall not counsel a client to engage, or assist a client, in conduct that the lawyer knows is criminal or fraudulent, but a lawyer may discuss the legal consequences of any proposed course of conduct with a client and may counsel or assist a client to make a good faith effort to determine the validity, scope, meaning or application of the law.); Rule 1.2(e) ("When a lawyer knows that a client expects assistance not permitted by the rules of professional conduct or other law, the lawyer shall consult with the client regarding the relevant limitations on the lawyer's conduct.").
39. MODEL RULE 1.0.

Client Interview & Counseling Checklist

Matter: _____   Attorney(s): _____

Client: _____   Date: _____

Problem Description: _____

---

1. Working Atmosphere: Establish effective relationship with prospective client.

2. Problem Description: Learn how client views the situation.

3. Client's Goals: Learn client's initial goals and expectations.

4. Problem Analysis: Analyze the client's situation or problem.

5. Moral/Ethical Issues: Recognize and deal with potential ethical issues.

6. Alternative Courses of Action: Develop options.

7. Client's Informed Choice: Assist client in understanding and making informed choices among possible courses of action. For each option, consider likely consequences (legal, economic, social/political, personal/emotional, and moral) in light of the client's goals and interests.

8. Effective Conclusion: Effectively conclude the interview.

9. Post-Interview Reflections.

10. Other Comments, Strategy, Research, Follow-Up.

Chapter 3

Negotiation

§ 3.01 Introduction

Negotiation is a communication and interpersonal decision-making process that people engage in to reach agreements in varied factual contexts, whether a personal, professional, or business transaction, or to resolve conflict. The scope of a negotiation can range from a one-on-one interaction to the highly complex, multi-party, multi-issue, and high-dollar-amount transactions. People negotiate not only for a material or financial outcome, but also may seek particular conduct, information, enhanced reputation, improved relationships, governance structures, and even political, personal, or community transformation. Whether the subject is money, property, convenience, liability, policy, parenting time, or peace, people choose to negotiate because they believe that they can improve upon what they are seeking by attempting to reach an agreement with another.

Often, people are unaware that they are "negotiating," they negotiate out of instinct, or believe that good negotiators are just "born that way."[1] However, negotiation is a strategic communication process that can be learned as a structured bargaining process and has dimensions based in psychology that are important and accessible to learn, understand, and strategically employ.

Negotiation is one of the most frequent and important activities of lawyers and of executives, leaders, and managers in business or politics. The word *negotiation* comes from the Latin "to carry on business." Certainly, negotiation is integral to the operation of commerce and any public or private governance structure. Lawyers negotiate in an effort to achieve optimal results for client concerns, as well as to help them avoid the delay, expense, stress, and uncertainty of litigation.

Negotiation advocacy calls upon a range of skills, including a trusted attorney-client relationship, thorough preparation, an understanding of the legal, social, and ethical parameters of representation, and the patience and ability to engage effectively with the client and involved parties throughout the negotiation process.

This chapter: (1) provides an overview of the negotiation process; (2) presents a roadmap for negotiation preparation; (3) discusses two basic, yet varied, approaches to negotiation; (4) identifies techniques, skills, and tactics that are used in the negotiation process; and (5) highlights certain heuristics and other psychological aspects that influence a negotiation.

---

1. Leigh L. Thompson, The Mind and Heart of the Negotiator 8 (5th ed. 2012).

§ 3.02 The Negotiation Process

A negotiation can vary based upon the complexity of the issues and parties involved. However, the basic process involves a predictable flow. Negotiation is a process, even a "dance." In some contexts, a negotiation exchange may be customary or expected, and a party who does not engage in the process may have a suboptimal outcome. For example, a buyer paying the asking price for a home or car may have paid more than the seller was willing to accept. Likewise, a defendant who pays a plaintiff's initial demand may have overpaid. The same situation also applies when a deal is made on the first counter-offer. While an agreement was reached, the asking party may later experience the "winner's curse" in wondering whether he perhaps did not set the initial offer price high enough while "buyer's remorse" may beset the buyer paying sticker price. As a corollary, the right offer proposed at the wrong time may be the wrong offer if the other side is not yet ready to engage in a deal and has not felt heard. The negotiation process provides parties with an opportunity to discuss, exchange information, persuade, and explore whether an agreement may be achieved. Planning, understanding of negotiation strategies and techniques, and patience are necessary to achieve optimal results.

A typical negotiation involves four basic stages. In the *opening* stage, parties present their perspectives of the situation, state their positions and ostensible demands, and display basic orientations as a competitive or collaborative bargainer. This stage generally involves an opening statement and presentation of factual and legal arguments (positioning). But unlike an opening argument in a legal trial, parties in a negotiation have the opportunity to frame the discussion to indicate their expectations, hope, and willingness to engage in a productive conversation about how to come to an agreement in a negotiation. The parties can set an agenda of the topics or issues to be discussed. As will be described more fully below, strategies and tactics used in this and other stages can be extreme, equitable, or integrative, depending upon the strategy and style employed.

The second stage involves *information gathering and exchange.* Here, the parties have the opportunity to communicate, share and express their perspectives, clarify issues, engage in fact-finding, and ask questions to understand the various interests, motivations, and goals. This communication process of articulating and understanding interests, goals, and alternatives can facilitate and reveal opportunities for mutual gain and resolution.

With greater understanding of perspectives and information, the parties emerge from positioning and can enter the third stage *bargaining* process. Here, the parties present offers, counteroffers, concessions, and proposals for alternatives. A variety of techniques and tactics may be used in this bargaining process. Depending upon whether the parties approach the negotiation as a distributive and integrative situation, and whether competitive or problem-solving techniques are used, the bargaining stage can appear quite different. A typically distributive bargaining may involve an exchange of positions, demands, and counteroffers resulting in a compromise outcome, whereas an integrative problem-solving negotiation can focus on exploring options that satisfy important interests and can provide a mutually beneficial outcome.

Each party's goal in the bargaining process is to achieve the best deal considering their own objectives and thus to determine areas of agreement as well as impasse. As deadlines approach, the parties enter the final stage of a negotiation. In the *closing* stage, parties take steps to summarize and finalize agreement or, if unable to agree, they may acknowledge deadlock but clarify areas of agreement and disagreement, and perhaps even commit to a future meeting. Even if a deal is not reached, negotiation can be a worthwhile process in itself when it increases the parties' understanding and ends in an informed decision to make the deal or walk away.

Inexperienced attorneys often misperceive at which stage of the negotiation process the case is in and perhaps settle or give up too soon. A variety of psychological principles and heuristics are at work in the very human endeavor of negotiation. An understanding of these tendencies, principles, and arguable traps that affect decision-making provide fascinating insight to the study and practice of negotiation.

§ 3.03 Negotiation Preparation

The client interviewing and counseling process, as discussed in Chapter 2, addresses the importance of understanding the client's legal problem as well as the client's goals, interests, resources, and options. This analysis provides a valuable foundation for negotiation preparation.

The importance of preparation for negotiation cannot be overemphasized. According to the "80-20" rule, 80 percent of the negotiator's effort should go to preparation, and 20 percent should be the actual work in the negotiation.[2] Yet flexibility in the negotiation process is also important. "Overprepare, then go with the flow" is an apt guiding principle. A well-prepared negotiator has sufficiently conducted advance assessments of the client, the counterpart, and the situation. Accordingly, the negotiator can work confidently in the negotiation to create value and opportunities for resolution.

Preparation for a negotiation encompasses an assessment of three components: (1) self; (2) the other party; and (3) the situation.[3] In this section, the self-assessment refers to the assessment of the client (in a represented case) or the negotiator (if the party does not need or have an attorney). Based upon this analysis, the negotiator can determine which strategy is most appropriate for the client and for the situation. Consider the negotiation chart provided at the end of this chapter as a rubric for negotiation preparation.

[A] Self-Assessment

Self-assessment certainly requires examining the factual and legal aspects of a client's matter. Identifying the issues to be discussed and items to negotiate helps to set the agenda for the negotiation. But critical self-preparation begins with clarifying the client's objectives, rationale, ideal outcome, realistic alternatives, resources, and risk propensity. First, what is the client's goal, aspiration, or target point? Prepare to articulate the client's objectives and reasoning for engaging in the negotiation. Second, what outcomes are consistent with those objectives? Third, what are the client's viable alternatives to a negotiated agreement? The negotiated deal should be better than other alternatives. Determining one's Best Alternative to a Negotiated Agreement (BATNA)

---

2. Thompson, *supra* note 1 at 13.
3. *Id.*

provides valuable information, power, and guidance in negotiation. Knowing and improving upon alternatives helps clarify one's bargaining leverage and walkaway point. Next, evaluate, quantify, and prioritize the alternatives to determine the reservation point or "bottom line" in the negotiation. The reservation point is essentially the BATNA quantified. Analyzing client objectives, ideal outcome, BATNA, and reservation point provides the framework for negotiation planning and for identifying a credible bargaining zone. With this, one may avoid premature concessions, setting an offer too low (winner's curse), or becoming unnecessarily positional and rejecting offers simply because of the source and not the merits (reactive devaluation).

Self-assessment also involves identifying a client's genuine needs, interests, and motivation in the negotiation, as well as possibilities for resolution of conflict. Interests are distinct from issues. Issues are the "what" or the discrete topics for discussion and matters to be negotiated. Interests are the "why" or underlying reason for the stated position or goal. Interests are often intangible, but very real and important in negotiation. Interests operate on three levels. Consider a "triangle of satisfaction" representing basic human needs or interests. This includes recognition of a person's: (1) substantive needs, in terms of the content, money, time, goods, tangible, and measurable product that is necessary for client survival or security; (2) procedural needs for fairness in the process, participation, and "buy-in" of how decisions are made; and (3) personal/psychological needs for respect, relationship, and security.[4] Identifying these aspects helps explain the client's motivation for the requested relief and expands possibilities for presenting proposals that meet these requirements.

Understanding client interests helps promote creative options and assess various offers. Alternatives or other deal packages may be presented in a manner that satisfies the substantive, psychological, and procedural interests equivalent to, or even better than, the stated demand. In this analysis, also consider the parties' risk propensity—is their aversion to loss (risk-averse) greater than value of gain (risk-seeking)? Frame your proposal accordingly. Prepare for the emotional aspects of negotiation and for dealing with difficult negotiations and negotiators. It may be tempting to walk away from the bargaining table where positions seem entrenched and emotions are heated. The opportunity to reach a deal may then be lost. Identify in advance the reservation point, circumstances, and manner in which it is appropriate to walk away. Otherwise prepare to be patient and prepared to negotiate.

Self-assessment is an ongoing process but important to undertake intentionally at the outset to clarify objectives, rationale, alternatives, and bargaining approach. In represented cases, the attorney/client counseling process should be used to uncover the needs, interests, and objectives of the client.

[B] Assessing the Other Side

Negotiation preparation involves a similar analysis of the counterpart. A critical first step is to clarify who is the counterpart. Does this party have decision-making authority? Is there a "hidden table" of principals, constituents, or other stakeholders? Who has authority to negotiate a deal? Consider the counterpart's likely agenda, stated position, goals,

---

4. Christopher W. Moore, The Mediation Process 231–33 (2d ed. 1996).

interests, and BATNA. Can a proposal be presented that would especially appeal to the counterpart's interests that might also align with your client's interests and agenda?

The ability to assess the interests of the counterpart will be easier in some situations than others. When the parties have a long relationship with one another—such as business partners, neighbors, or spouses—the client may be able to predict what the other side would like to obtain in a negotiation. When the parties do not know each other well—such as in negotiations with a new business counterpart or while resolving a dispute between strangers—the parties should consult available research and resources. Effective negotiators consider both monetary and non-monetary interests of the other side.

[C] Situation Assessment

Assessing the situation involves considering the substantive and relationship context of the negotiation. Does the negotiation involve a proposed transaction or dispute settlement? Is the negotiation a one-shot transaction or anticipated repetitive or long-term relationship? Deal-making negotiations are generally focused on the future, often have a positive tone, and involve creating new relationships between the parties—such as forming a business partnership, buying a house, determining a salary, or entering into a long-term purchase contract. In these negotiations, the "buyer" may have several alternatives (i.e., BATNA), such as multiple houses to purchase or multiple employment offers to consider. Depending upon the market, of course, the seller may also have significant alternatives.

Lawsuit or dispute-settling negotiations may involve actual or perceived wrongs, violations, and injuries. At least initially, these negotiations tend to focus on the past (what happened and who was at fault), involve a monetary demand, and have a more adversarial and emotional tone (contested liability and damages). Although an obvious BATNA in dispute negotiations is the threat (and risk) of going to court, dispute resolution in negotiation is also a deal-making opportunity. For instance, in a lawsuit alleging a product defect, the attorney may be able to turn the negotiation from one involving a payment of money for past wrongs into a negotiation regarding new product safety and a future business deal between the parties.

Situation assessment helps to clarify the focus and goal of the negotiation and to avoid becoming diverted or bogged down in the negotiation or come to an agreement of all listed agenda issues only to find that one issue was left out. Questions to answer during this stage include: What are the actual problems to be solved and the decisions to be made? What opportunities can be created? What are the issues to be negotiated? Does this negotiation involve a one-shot or long-term relationship? Does this negotiation involve scarce resources, ideologies, or both? Is this negotiation an opportunity for partnership, business development, or dispute resolution? What are the time constraints, costs, or other needs for precedent, power, or validation?[5] Preparation for these contingencies increases the likelihood for success in the negotiation.

---

5. *See* Thompson, *supra* note 1 at 31.

§ 3.04 Negotiation Approaches and Techniques

Negotiation is a mixed-motive decision-making process. Parties want to get the best outcome or deal possible, but need an agreement with the counterpart in order to achieve those objectives. A negotiator thus needs to cooperate with the counterpart, while also competing to maximize for the desired resources. Negotiation literature describes two primary approaches to negotiation: distributive bargaining and integrative bargaining. Almost all negotiations involve some elements of both. Consider how, and when, each approach may be most appropriate for the negotiation at issue.

§ 3.05 Distributive Bargaining and Claiming Value

[A] Defined

Distributive bargaining is a negotiation strategy that views negotiation as involving a limited resource (fixed pie). It is a process by which parties "distribute" the substance over which they are bargaining. Distributive bargaining is a competitive strategy and seeks to claim value by obtaining the largest possible share of resources available for distribution.[6] Distributive bargaining is perceived as a zero-sum exchange in that a gain for one negotiator requires less for the other. Distributive bargaining generally occurs in situations involving a limited and fixed resource, such as a specific amount of money, or a one-shot relationship.

Distributive bargaining generally focuses on positions and assumes that the parties' interests conflict. It proceeds in a series of concessions and exchanges in order to reach an agreement or "compromise." Distributive bargaining can occur in a variety of contexts, typically involving money, the treasured family heirloom, or parenting time. Parties may assume that "one for you is one fewer for me," such that every night the kids stay at Mom's house is time that Dad will never have with the kids at his house. This assumption tends to limit the options parties consider in discussing a resolution to a dispute or claim. A drawback in utilizing this approach is that it can miss opportunities to generate mutually beneficial value-creating options or to foster reputational or future relationships with the other party. But suppose that the resources are truly limited and distributive bargaining is necessary. The remainder of this section discusses how to engage in this type of negotiation.

[B] Stages in a Distributive Negotiation

Distributive bargaining generally proceeds in a series of reciprocated compromises through continuously diminishing moves. This pattern involves: (1) competitive initial offers and statements of client positions; (2) gradual relinquishment of those positions through concessions and exchanges; (3) establishing a bargaining zone of possible

---

6. Carrie Menkel-Meadow, *Toward Another View of Legal Negotiation: The Structure of Problem Solving*, 31 UCLA L. Rev. 754, 765, 783 (1984).

agreement; and (4) employing various techniques to reach agreement. A deal is likely reached (if a deal can be reached at all) near the midpoint between the first two reasonable offers.

[1] Initial Positioning

A distributive bargainer attempts to maximize his or her individual position while minimizing that of the "opponent." The distributive bargainer tends to engage in positional bargaining, open with a firm high demand, and make small, infrequent concessions. An aggressive initial offer may act as a psychological "anchor" to influence the bargaining range; however, an extreme offer may be perceived as an insult or so unreasonable that the other party will avoid negotiation. Usually, the distributive bargainer will make an opening offer that is significantly better than what he is ultimately willing to accept (i.e., well above that person's "bottom line"), while hoping to make few small concessions in an attempt to retain as much surplus value as he possibly can. An aggressive counteroffer likewise may represent a counter-anchor, rather than true bargaining position. These initial offers may seem as though a deal is not possible and that the negotiation is in a negative bargaining zone.

The astute negotiator will recognize when the situation is seemingly distributive and know the varied tactics that may be employed. But other constructive techniques may be used to generate momentum and divert impasse. Techniques to address positional offers include asking questions, requesting clarification of how they arrived at that offer, ignoring the offer, and presenting your own offer. Although an aggressive first offer may seem to establish a psychological anchor, the best defense is to be highly informed about the true evaluations of what is being offered. In a distributive bargaining process, the parties seek to claim as much of the bargaining zone as possible but are at the negotiationn table and thus open to some form of compromise.

[2] Concessions and Exchanges

In a distributive negotiation, initial opening positions are generally just that. Parties expect an exchange of offers and some movement toward compromise. Getting to that next round may require saving face from firmly stating the opening offer to demonstrating willingness to compromise. Techniques to relinquish one's initial position include citing to new information learned in the negotiation, suggesting an exchange in various categories, or simply to counter-offer in the spirit of negotiating in good faith.

[a] Recognizing and Overcoming Tactics

A typical distributive negotiation can involve a variety of tactics used to implement a value-claiming strategy. Where the goal is to gain the upper hand, a party may seek to establish control and begin with a seemingly firm, aggressive offer or position. An adversarial bargainer might seek to elicit information or concessions from the other side, while revealing little and making few commitments.

Parties may use any number of other techniques or tactics to persuade or pressure the other to make concessions. Competitive tactics include the use of arguments, threats, ridicule, humor, silence, patience, guilt, and voice reflection. Threats in the context of negotiation could be pursuing litigation or publicity of the dispute. The difficulty in implementing this tactic is that it could escalate the conflict and lead to the mutual exchange of threats. Similarly, the gentle use of ridicule or humor in the negotiation could have the effect of challenging the negotiation counterpart's offer, without a direct confrontation. For example, implying that an offer is comical, and couldn't possibly be serious, has the effect of rejecting the offer but providing a way for the other party to save face by stating that it was not a serious offer. The use of silence or guilt as negotiation tactics draw on the strength of social discomfort. People tend to be uncomfortable with silence and strive to fill that silence with more words than necessary. Thus, a negotiator who is patient or silent before responding to an offer could cause the presenter to question whether the offer was too much, add words of clarification, or even bid against oneself. Voice inflection is another tactic that can be used to give emphasis to certain points. If a negotiator has been speaking in one voice inflection throughout the negotiation, changing inflection during the delivery of an offer or a rejection of an offer could provide greater emphasis to what was said.

If used correctly, a well-employed and timed tactic could motivate the other party to focus on agreement. However, tactics used to pressure the other side can also backfire where received as insulting or offensive. On the other hand, a party may extend an incentive to elicit a positive response. A party who engages in competitive tactics may encounter a "tit for tat" exchange, meaning that the counterpart may, and perhaps should, lest they risk exploitation, match the competitive move and make similarly sized concessions in response to one another and result in limited progress or movement. "Tit-for-tat" also applies to information exchanges. Likewise, where a party is cooperative, the other party may be more willing to provide other information in exchange.[7]

Although there are numerous tactics in negotiation, the main goal in negotiation is identifying underlying interests and working with the negotiation counterpart in crafting a deal that satisfies both parties. Attempts to employ tactics are likely to be easily noticed by skilled negotiators and run the risk of damaging the deal, the relationship, and the reputation.

[3] Establishing the Bargaining Range

Parties to a negotiation typically seek as much as they can. They have a target point of where they would like to reach a deal, but they will also identify a reservation point or bottom line at which they would not make a deal. The BATNA is the quantification of the reservation point that focuses on alternatives to the negotiation. The bargaining zone is the range between the buyer's high and the seller's low. A negative zone occurs where there is no overlap. The overlap otherwise represents a zone of possible agreement.

For example, a seller willing to accept $7,000 for a certain result may state an opening demand of $10,000. While the buyer may be willing to pay up to $8,500 but will first offer $5,000. The parties may make various concessions during the course of the negotiation process and settle on $8,500, thus gaining a surplus value of $1,500. Note there is a $1,500 overlap between what the seller is willing to accept and what the buyer is willing to pay. This bargaining zone is the range of possible agreements that would be acceptable

---

7. Robert Axelrod's "Tit-for-Tat" Theory is based on concepts of altruism and retaliation. This strategy maintains that a negotiator start cooperatively, be willing to retaliate if provoked by the other side, but also to forgive and respond in kind where the other party acts cooperatively. The strategy helps prevent exploitation and promotes reciprocal cooperation. *See* Thompson, *supra* note 1 at 291–93.

by both parties, also referred to as the Zone of Possible Agreement ("ZOPA"). When there is an overlap between the parties' ZOPAs, an agreement is theoretically possible.

A Zone of Possible Agreement is more likely found in deal-making negotiations than in dispute-resolving negotiations. When a buyer and seller negotiate over the price of a home, a bargaining range of a few thousand dollars is not uncommon. On the other hand, when parties attempt to settle a litigation matter, the parties often have no ZOPA and instead are working toward closing that gap to create a ZOPA of one number.

[4] Allocating Surplus Value

Once the parties to the negotiation have defined the bargaining zone, they must decide how to distribute the surplus value. Regardless of the bargaining power held by either party, a final agreement that both parties perceive as fair will help ensure that they follow through with the agreement.[8] If one party with inferior bargaining power reluctantly agrees to a solution that strongly favors the other party, the reluctant party may end up delaying performance of the negotiated agreement, or even refusing performance altogether.

Given that the ultimate goal of a negotiation is to ensure that the parties perform in accordance with the final agreement, the question then arises: what methods of allocating surplus value are generally perceived as fair?

Bridging the gap is facilitated by focusing on objective criteria, considering opportunities for continued relationships, and analyzing prospects for meeting both sides' key interests and priorities. The tactic of *splitting the difference* between the last two offers may seem to present a fair resolution.[9] For example, if the bargaining zone for the sale of a car is $10,000–$20,000, splitting the difference would mean agreeing on a price of $15,000. However, the fairness of simply "splitting the difference" is illusory. It is not legally justified nor does it meet party objectives.

If we return to the concept of the triangle of satisfaction, the parties may think "splitting the difference" is "fair" from a psychological standpoint, even if no other reason justifies using this tactic. Parties are also more likely to perceive the agreement as fair if both parties have made concessions to arrive at a final agreement. Continuing with the car sale example, the buyer might be more willing to pay a higher total price if the seller agrees to smaller, less frequent payments. In the end, however the parties choose to allocate surplus value, performance of the agreement is more likely if both parties perceive that a fair procedure was used to determine the final outcome. Although it should go without saying, negotiation culture teaches that bargainers do *not* reveal the true limits of their bargaining range post-negotiation. Such disculosures only hurt feelings and damage relationships between negotiators.

---

8. Charles B. Craver, *The Negotiation Process*, 27 Am. J. Trial Advoc. 271, 324–25 (2003).
9. Russell B. Korobkin, *A Positive Theory of Legal Negotiation*, 88 Geo. L.J. 1789, 1823 (2000).

§ 3.06 Integrative Bargaining

Distributive bargaining itself may not result in an agreement or a satisfying deal for either party. The classic example of two sisters fighting over an orange appears to illustrate the limitations of distributive bargaining over a fixed resource. Both sisters want the orange. The parent settles the dispute by cutting the orange in half as a compromise, so that both children receive an equal "fair share."[10] The children are still furiously crying? Why?

Asking "why" is a critical diagnostic question that can bridge an impasse in distributive bargaining and reveal interests that may align so that each party, or sister, can achieve their objectives in a single negotiation. Had the parent asked the fighting sisters why they wanted the orange, it would have been revealed that one wanted pulp to make juice, while the other wanted the rind for baking.[11] Here, therefore, an even split compromise resulted in the loss of 100 percent of the value of what each wanted, although each party's interests could have been 100 percent satisfied given the different interests in the fixed resource.

A focus on what outcome is a seemingly *fair compromise* can fail to achieve satisfactory value for either, when maximum value is possible for both sides. Integrative bargaining provides a process for joint resolution by moving to a problem-solving mode in which, instead of focusing on differences, parties attempt to work together for integrative interests. Discussing the underlying reasons why parties are in dispute can reveal opportunities for integrative agreements so that each can achieve their objectives.

[A] Defined

An integrative or problem-solving approach seeks to obtain the best possible outcome for both parties. As opposed to the zero-sum perspective of distributive bargaining, integrative bargaining seeks to satisfy each party's primary interests and thereby negotiate an agreement that produces a "win-win" result.[12] Thus, if distributive bargaining is seen as distributing a fixed pie, integrative bargaining can be seen as an attempt to expand the pie available for distribution.

Integrative bargaining can be used in nearly every type of dispute or transaction if the parties are willing to approach negotiation in a collaborative manner. Unlike distributive bargaining, integrative bargaining can utilize nonmonetary options to meet party interests. Multidimensional and multi-issue negotiations may be particularly well-suited for integrative bargaining because of the range of opportunities for varied priorities, deal packages, and options.

[B] Shifting to Integrative Bargaining

In GETTING TO YES, Roger Fisher and William Ury proposed a four-step framework for an integrative problem-solving negotiation approach: (1) separate the people from

---

10. *Id.*

11. Dan Kirk, *Mental Contrasting Promotes Integrative Bargaining*, 22 IJCMA, Vol. 4, 324 (2011), available at http://www.psych.nyu.edu/gollwitzer/Mental_contrasting(2).pdf

12. Craver, *supra* note 8 at 300.

the problem; (2) focus on interests, not positions; (3) invent options that have potential for mutual gain; and (4) use objective criteria to evaluate potential solutions.[13] This approach allows the parties to "[r]each a gradual consensus on a joint decision efficiently without all the transactional costs of digging into positions only to have to dig [oneself] out of them"[14] and allows for a value-creating, rather than claiming, outcome.

[1] The People Factor

The first step of separating the people from the problem does not mean that people are not necessarily *the* problem. Negotiations often involve conflict, high emotions, and hurt feelings. The people problem factor can be addressed through perception, communication, and empathy. Consider how the counterpart perceives the situation and acknowledge the other's point of view without expressing judgment, even though you may not agree with the position. Avoid blame. Don't react. Understand both sides' need to vent or to express emotions and the need to be heard. Listen. Empathy helps to foster rapport, trust, and a working relationship so the parties can jointly proceed to attack the problem (and not each other).[15]

"Separating the people from the problem" seeks to turn negotiating opponents into teammates tackling the same problem. To foster this mindset, a negotiator may use a visual aid or whiteboard to list issues for joint discussion or even physically sit side-by-side to signal that the parties are not opponents. Primarily, the problem-solving approach is accomplished through effective communication skills and understanding the parties' respective needs, interests, and priorities.

[2] Focus on Interests

Integrative bargaining is also known as interest-based bargaining because of the focus on the parties' respective interests, as opposed to positions. Recall that *Preparing for Negotiation* discussed the importance of identifying and assessing client and party interests. Again, these interests are more than the underlying reason for the stated demand and include not only substantive needs, but also needs for process fairness, and social/emotional needs for security, reputation, dignity, vindication, and more.[16] By explicitly discussing party interests, the parties can better understand the conflict and move to discuss responsive solutions.

A party in a negotiation may be "interested" in more than monetary compensation. Inquiring into the underlying concerns of the party may reveal a multitude of alternative solutions, such as providing an apology, confidentiality, recognition, or transparency, or instituting a system to prevent a similar problem.

Identifying interests also helps frame the issues to be discussed and the "how" interests can be satisfied. Listing the issues in a proposed negotiation agenda can reveal a mix of alternatives that can be unbundled, prioritized, or traded in order to craft satisfactory outcomes. Rather than negotiating one issue or item of value, each party receives more overall value by trading, or "logrolling," different items of value that satisfy their

---

13. Roger Fisher & William Ury, Getting to YES: Negotiating Agreement without Giving In 12 (2d ed. 2011).

14. *Id.* at 14–15.

15. *Id.* at 40.

16. Moore, *supra* note 4 at 233. *See also* Riian Williams, *Toward a New Theory of Mediation,* available at http://www.asiapacificmediationforum.org/resources/2003/williams.pdf.

respective needs and interests.[17] As Professor Carrie Menkel-Meadow states, "because not all individuals value the same things in the same way, the exploitation of differential or complementary needs will produce a wider variety of solutions which more closely meet the parties' needs."[18] Working with interests requires a certain amount of vulnerability. When parties are honest about their interests, they often agree to take less money in exchange for non-monetary options. The parties thus need a certain level of trust to engage in this type of bargaining.

[3] Creating Options and Value

Understanding each other's positions, underlying needs, interests, and motivations allows the parties to explore creative problem-solving strategies and to identify potential mutually satisfactory outcomes.[19] This principle involves the concept of thinking creatively or "outside the box" in order to achieve a result that solves a mutually shared problem. Many problems cannot be solved on the two-dimensional plane of a financial give-and-take tug-of-war. A client's emotions and hidden interests may lie below the surface of the dispute. Focusing on traditional distributive notions could not only lead to lengthy and costly litigation, but also decreased client satisfaction.

The option-generation phase goes beyond the initial issues on the table.[20] Through beneficial trades, the parties stand to enlarge the scope of the possibilities and come to an agreement that better satisfies mutual interests. For example, parties in a negotiation who understand their respective interests can move to consider and brainstorm various solutions which provide value for both. Techniques such as brainstorming allows parties working together to develop ideas, improve upon ideas, and inspire creative solutions from a new perspective. Questions to consider are: What are the substantive, emotional, and procedural interests of each party? What possible solutions can address those needs? Therefore, in sharing the "why" of what is desired, it is possible to create value by getting more from each other without putting either in a zero-sum position. Communicating interests and exploring options increases the likelihood of achieving a Pareto-optimal outcome.[21]

[4] Evaluating Solutions with Objective Criteria

The GETTING TO YES approach also urges parties to present and evaluate proposals by using *objective criteria*.[22] Using objective criteria, such as market price and expert opinion, is more likely to be seen as fair by both parties and to lead to a final negotiated agreement

---

17. Craver, *supra* note 8 at 279.

18. Menkel-Meadow, *supra* note 6 at 795.

19. H. ROBERT MNOOKIN, BEYOND WINNING: NEGOTIATION TO CREATE VALUE IN DEALS AND DISPUTES (2000).

20. *Id.*

21. "According to the criterion of Pareto-superiority, a reallocation of resources [e.g., in a give-and-take negotiation between two or more persons] is preferred if some persons are made better off and no person is worse off . . . changes that will make some people better off without making anybody worse off are undoubtedly quite rare . . . . All points [as on a tradeoff curve] for which there is no move which will make someone better off and no one else worse off are defined as 'Pareto-optimal.'" PETER S. MENNELL & RICHARD B. STEWART, ENVIRONMENTAL LAW AND POLICY 47–48 (1994).

22. Fisher & Ury, *supra* note 13 at 17–18.

if both parties but into the value of the outside opinion. For example, if negotiating the price for the sale of a car, the parties may wish to use the current market price as an objective method for measuring the fairness of a price. Using this same example, other objective criteria might include bringing in an expert on cars to help determine value. The party paying for the car would more likely view a final price term determined by a neutral, detached expert as a fair price than a price term determined by the seller.

In addition to its intrinsic "fairness," the technique of using objective criteria helps the parties agree on a smaller matter, which may prompt them ultimately to agree on a bigger matter. For instance, if the parties are working on a long-term supply contract for wheat and cannot determine price on their own, they may be able to agree on a reputable pricing index to determine the price over time.

§ 3.07 Negotiation Styles and Techniques

Negotiators may adopt a particular negotiation style, such as a "hard" or competitive, a "soft" or cooperative/accommodating, or a collaborative, principled, or problem-solving approach.[23] Competitive bargainers may be more distributive and employ tactics involving extreme opening offers, small concessions, manipulative techniques to strengthen their position. They may not be concerned with facilitating long-term relationships with their counterparts. A competitive strategy may obtain better value claiming results, but risk greater distrust, impasse, and deteriorating relationships. A cooperative bargainer may initiate concessions to develop trust and to create a moral obligation on the other side to reciprocate. A risk is vulnerability to exploitation by a competitive negotiator. Collaborative bargainers typically use an integrative approach and seek to achieve the maximum value that they can, while working with their counterpart to satisfy their interests in the deal.

A negotiator likely needs to employ a varied negotiation style depending on the circumstances and stage of the negotiation. In a hybrid approach, a negotiator may adopt both the cooperative style but also be prepared to meet a competitive counterpart in order to avoid exploitation. In the "Prisoner Dilemma" scenarios, Roger Axelrod introduced the "tit-for-tat" strategy, which is based upon concepts of altruism and retaliation.[24] Beginning a negotiation cooperatively increases the likelihood that the other party will also cooperate. If the other party instead is competitive, a competitive countermove may be necessary to get their attention. Techniques may include identifying the tactic, informing the counterpart that aggressive methods will not be productive, or simply not acknowledge the tactic at all and not respond until the party convenes a more cooperative, integrative approach. Realizing that the tactics will not be effective and could potentially derail the entire deal should motivate them to back off such techniques and pursue an integrative mutual-gain approach throughout the rest of the negotiation.

---

23. *See* Andrea K. Schneider, *Teaching a New Negotiation Skills Paradigm*, 39 WASH. U. J. L. & POL'Y 13 (2012).

24. *See supra* note 7.

§ 3.08 Psychological Influences in Negotiation

Negotiation involves more than the parties' positions, interests, facts, and legal theories. A variety of research has been conducted on the psychological aspects of negotiation. This chapter has discussed a number of these concepts, such as the fixed-pie perception and tit-for-tat strategy.[25] Other influences and heuristics, unconscious behavior, implicit bias, body language, language, culture, gender, and emotion, for example, can have a significant impact in a negotiation. Many of these psychological influences are identified and captured in a negotiation parlance. A few examples of these terms are described below and include concepts such as: (1) anchoring; (2) the endowment effect; (3) loss aversion; (4) satisficing; (5) confirmation bias; (5) reactive devaluation; and (6) time and the evaluation on money.[26]

[A] Anchoring

Anchoring is the psychological effect of focusing first on the offer and having that focus influence the evaluation throughout the entire negotiation. The greatest defense to an anchor is to be well-informed about the topic being anchored. For example, if you are attempting to buy a lamp at a flea market, and the Seller drops a high anchor of $15, the well-informed knowledge that similar lamps in this area are typically sold for $10 mitigates the psychological effects of the anchor.[27]

[B] Endowment Effect

The endowment effect involves the tendency to overvalue or place an unjustifiable evaluation on something one owns or has proposed in a demand. In the negotiation context, viewing a product as one's own gives it more worth than if the same item belonged to someone else. For example, assume that a person must sell his or her deceased mother's house as part of a probate case. The child may have an inflated sense of how much the property is worth because of the memories and good times that occurred in the family home over the years. In a negotiation to resolve a lawsuit, both parties are usually overconfident in determining the value of the case or how a jury would resolve the issue. This effect can serve as a potentially dysfunctional anchor.

---

25. Karsten K.W. Dreu et al., *Unfixing the Fixed Pie: A Motivated Information-Processing Approach to Integrative Negotiation*, 79 J. PERSONALITY & SOC. PSYCH. 975–87 (2000) (positing that that negotiators often believe that their views and the other party's views are completely opposite and when a fixed pie perception is not revised during a negotiation, then it is unlikely integrative bargaining can occur, accountability reduces this perception during face-to-face negotiation and produces a more integrative agreement).

26. Weingart Kwon, *Unilateral Concessions from the Other Party: Concessions Behavior, Attributions, and Negotiation Judgments*, 89 J. APPLIED PSYCH. 263–78 (2004).

27. Mussweiler Galinsky, *First Offers as Anchors: The Role of Perspective-Taking and Negotiator Focus,* 18 J. PERSONALITY & SOC. PSYCH. 657–69 (2001).

[C] Loss Aversion

This psychological effect involves the tendency to avoid loss. In the negotiation context, if we hear an offer phrased in a way that highlights a potential loss, it will carry greater weight than if we heard the equivalent offer in terms of what we might stand to gain. For example, the statement "your client stands to lose $100 per day if a settlement is not reached" carries greater weight than "your client will not get the benefit of $100 per day profit if a settlement is not reached." People generally take greater risks when they stand to lose and fewer risks if they stand to gain. Framing an offer as a gain or a loss can be used strategically in a negotiation.

[D] Satisficing

Some negotiators fall short of their aspiration and reservation points because of the human tendency to satisfice. Satisficing is settling for something less than one could otherwise have. The opposite of satisficing is optimizing. In any negotiation, it is important to optimize one's strategy. One should set high aspirations and attempt to achieve as much as possible.[28]

[E] Consistency Principle

The "consistency principle" stands for the idea that a negotiator seeks to act consistently with prior commitments made or to act in accordance with the negotiator's strongly held beliefs or reputation.[29] Negotiators with a reputation as being tough bargainers will likely continue to use tactics to live up to that reputation. If a negotiator can fashion an agreement that comports with the counterpart's reputation or strongly held (and often public) beliefs, then the offeree will have a difficult time rejecting the offer.

[F] Body Language

Conflict in relationships arises less from *what* a person says than *how* he or she says it. According to research, our communication involves 55 percent body language, followed by tone inflection and sound making up 38 percent, and seven percent from the content itself.[30] In taking account of the 93 percent of what is being communicated, special consideration should be placed on: attraction, similarity, kinesics, proxemics, haptics, and

---

28. Thompson, *supra* note 1 at 7.
29. Chris M. Curris, *Mediating Off the Grid*, 59 J. Disp. Resol. J. 9 (2004) (asserting that the drive to satisfy basic human psychological needs underlies human conflict and that conflict is largely predictable, not random; inter-dependence and cooperation contribute more to success than competition); Michael R. Carrell, Matthew Shank & Jose Luis Barbero, *Fairness Norms in Negotiation: A Study of American and European Perspectives*, 64 Disp. Resol. J. 54 (2009) (consistency and fairness principle); Robert J. Condlini, *Legal Bargaining Theory's New"Prospecting" Agenda: It May Be Social Science, But Is It News?*, 10 Pepp. Disp. Resol. L.J. 215 (2010). Attraction is defined as the positive temperament to respond to another in an agreeable way. Studies show that people view attractive people in a more positive light.
30. *See generally* Albert Mehrabian, Silent Messages (1971).

vocalics.[31] A good negotiator is fully present and paying attention to what is said, how it is said, and what is not said. Negotiations that take place online or over the telephone can miss valuable information that can be gained by observing body language.

A glossary of select negotiation terms includes the following:[32]

Frame: One's individualized way of perceiving and defining a situation, based on one's past experiences and knowledge; a subjective mechanism through which one evaluates and makes sense out of situations; a perspective or point of view one uses in gathering information and solving problems. The parties' frames change as a negotiation evolves.

Halo effect: Assigning a variety of attributes (positive or negative) to an individual based on the knowledge of one attribute. A form of perceptual distortion.

Haptics involves using physical contact in order to establish a greater level of affiliation, comfort, or intimacy. An example of what this could look like in a negotiation is seen in the first initial firm handshake with solid eye contact. Further physical contact should be tailored to the situation, and conducted within the parameters of gender and cultural sensitivities and from a place of warmth and connection with your counterparts.

Kinesics involves the use of head, facial, eye, and other body movements that give off a variety of often-subliminal messages. Body language can be an effective tool to communicating effectively. Similarly, it is possible for negotiators to unintentionally give away too much information through the use of kinesic body language. For example, when your negotiation counterpart states their offer, unintentionally responding in a positive way might lead that counterpart to think that the offer is acceptable, and push for more. Just as important as knowing your client and knowing the subject matter of the negotiation, a prudent negotiator must also know themselves and the messages they are communicating to their counterpart.

Projection: Ascribing to another the characteristics or feelings that one possesses oneself. A form of perceptual distortion.

Proxemics involves a negotiator being aware of the space and distance between themselves and their negotiation counterparts. For example, being spatially too close to a person could potentially make the other person feel that their personal space is violated, and triggers an uncomfortable response. Conversely, too much distance from their counterpart may create suspicion (compromising the trust needed for proper building of rapport). Throughout the negotiation it is important to take into account the culture of your negotiation counterpart, and what spatial distance is socially acceptable given the situation and the relationship developed between the parties.

Reactive devaluation: Tendency to devalue the other party's concessions simply because the other party has made them. A form of cognitive bias.

---

31. Pamela Peters, *Gaining Compliance through Non-Verbal Communication*, 7 Pepp. Disp. Resol. L.J. 87 (2007) (noting that the similarity effect recognizes that the receiver identifies similarities between himself or herself and the message, it reinforces their own self-concept. People have a tendency to view themselves as better than average, typically correct, and rarely at fault. When a negotiation counterpart sees a piece of themselves in their counterpart's appearance, views, or ideas, they are more likely to accept those statements as more credible).

32. *See* Thompson, *supra* note 1.

Recency effect: Tendency for the last item presented to be the best remembered when items are uninteresting, unfamiliar, or not very important.

Reframing: Influencing the other party to share a new frame, thereby shaping his decision-making process in evaluating alternatives and outcomes.

Selective perception: Singling out certain information that supports or reinforces a prior belief and filtering out information that does not confirm that belief. A form of perceptual distortion.

Settlement point: The point at which both parties believe that the outcome is the best they could achieve and that it is worth accepting and supporting.

Shadow negotiation: Subtle, complex interaction (e.g., power moves, process moves, appreciative moves) lurking beneath formal negotiation itself, where issues of power imbalance, conversational tone, and influence over process are settled.

Signaling: Conveying information to the other party through one's pattern of concessions.

Snow job: Overwhelming the other party with so much information that he or she can no longer distinguish what is important. A hardball tactic.

Tit-for-tat strategy: Cooperation on the first move, and thereafter doing whatever the opponent has done on the previous move, i.e., either cooperating or competing.

Uncertainty avoidance: Hofstede's dimension of culture describing the extent to which a society programs its members to feel uncomfortable in ambiguous, unpredictable, or risky situations (high uncertainty avoidance), or comfortable with a lack of structure, stability, and predictability (low uncertainty avoidance).

Unilateral strategy: One chosen without active involvement of the other party. Often called a "take it or leave it" proposal.

Winner's curse: Tendency of negotiators to feel discomfort following a resolution that came too quickly and easily, akin to "buyer's remorse."

Vocalics involves using tone, pitch, vocal expressiveness, fluency, and rate of speech in order to present your client's position, interest, or offer in the most beneficial light possible.

§ 3.09 Negotiation Ethics

Negotiation generally involves a series of back-and-forth statements, positions, offers, competitive tactics, and puffery in the sense that the parties ultimately agree to less or something different from the initial demands or requests. A lawyer's duty is to advocate and protect client interests, and rules of professional conduct apply to this advocacy even in a negotiation. Professional conduct rules prohibit lawyers from making false statements, misrepresentations, deceptive statements, or exerting undue influence. Under Model Rule 4.1, a lawyer may not knowingly "(a) make a *false statement of material fact* or law to a third person; or (b) *fail to disclose* a material fact to a third person when disclosure is necessary to avoid assisting in a criminal or fraudulent act by a client . . ." However, a lawyer may reveal confidential communications to prevent or rectify a fraud under the Model Rules 1.6(b)(2)(3).

When a lawyer is engaged in negotiations on behalf of a client, a distinction is made between acceptably puffing and improper misstatements of material facts. Puffery or statements regarding a party's negotiation goals or willingness to compromise made in a negotiation is acceptable, whereas statements that materially misrepresent facts in a negotiation constitute fraud, dishonesty, or deceit. Active concealment of material facts also constitutes a breach. A lawyer may not engage in "dishonesty, fraud, deceit or misrepresentation."[33] Ethical conduct rules also restrict an attorney from engaging in negotiating tactics that are abusive or not made in good faith; threaten inappropriate legal action, arbitrary deadlines; or are used solely to gain an unfair advantage or take unfair advantage of a superior bargaining position; or that do not accurately reflect the client's wishes or previous oral agreements.

---

33. Model Rules of Prof'l Conduct r. 8.3.

§ 3.10 Negotiation Plan Template

Introductions — Parties/Counsel	Negotiation Counterparty
Party 1: _____ *Lawyer:* _____ *Client:* _____	*Party 2:* _____ *Lawyer:* _____ *Client:* _____
Factual Context — Opening/Initial Perspective	**Counterparty's Opening/Initial Position**
Appreciation for both parties' willingness to meet *Storytelling* — Explain client's perspective on the situation; initial position and rationale *Case Theme* *Hopeful Tone:* High Hopes (relationship, goals); bump in the road (concerns/current issue or dispute); high hopes (for meaningful outcome) _____ _____	_____ _____ _____ _____ _____ _____
Goals — What You Want to Accomplish	**Their Likely Goals**
_____ _____	_____ _____
Needs & Interests *** *Why? Consider substantive, process, and emotional/psychological.*	**Interests of Counterparty?**
_____ _____	_____ _____
Relationship Significance of continuing relationship?	
Issues/Topics/Agenda	**Issues/Topics/Agenda**
What issues would an agreement need to address? Possible elements of a framework agreement with key terms left blank to be negotiated. 1. _____ 2. _____ 3. _____	[Get agreement on topics/agenda/other] 1. _____ 2. _____ 3. _____
Initial Positions/Rationale	**Counterpoint**
My BATNA/Alternatives/Reservation Point	**Their BATNA**
If no agreement is reached, backup plan?	
Private Offer Strategy —	**Counterparty's Likely Strategy**
Aspiration/Target Point: _____ _____ Reservation Point/BATNA: _____ Other: _____	

Information Gathering/Questions	Their Questions
What would you like to learn? Strategies for doing so? *Q's?* 1. _____ 2. _____ 3. _____ Info to Disclose v. Keep Confidential _____ _____ _____	*Questions you expect they will ask you?* 1. _____ 2. _____ 3. _____ Info they likely want to keep confidential? _____ _____
Options & Offers/Packages	**Counteroffers**
Brainstorm possible ways to meet each side's interests for each key issue/topic that needs to be resolved; 1st Offer (Anchor) _____ 2nd _____ 3rd _____	_____ _____ _____
Objective Criteria/Legitimacy	
Identify objective standards or principles that might suggest fair ways to resolve conflicting interests with respect to each key issue/topic area to be resolved: • _____ • _____ • _____	_____ _____ _____
Commitments & Deal Points	
(Shared info/mutual understanding, options explored, joint recommendation, tentative agreement, firm deal)? If not seeking final agreement in this meeting, what sequence of meetings with what goals makes sense?	_____ _____ _____
Concluding the Session	
• Summarize points of agreement • Clarify outstanding issues • Plan for future course of action	
Process Reminder	
• Active listening; Clarify; Reframe • Cues to partner; Teamwork & Balance • When to call for a break • What to do if you get stuck	• Body Language • Summarize • Be careful not to interrupt • Show appreciation
Protect Client's Interests!	
Teamwork — Balance	
Notes:	

Chapter 4

The Mediation Process

§ 4.01 Overview

Mediation can be broadly defined as a dispute resolution process in which a third party assists two or more parties in negotiating a resolution to a dispute. Unlike arbitration, the neutral party does not have any decision-making authority. The authority to resolve a dispute lies squarely with the parties. Unlike traditional negotiation, mediation involves a third party to help the parties resolve the conflict.

Mediation is a notoriously difficult concept to encapsulate. If mediation only involves a third party who helps others resolve their disputes, then many everyday scenarios will fall into this category. For instance, family members often help other family members resolve conflict over things such as holiday plans, acceptable parenting styles, or housing choices for an elderly parent. Resident assistants in college dormitories resolve conflict between roommates or among multiple residents. Friends sometimes help other friends solve problems within their circle. One can easily imagine any number of informal situations involving this broad definition of mediation.

This chapter focuses on the more formalized and professionalized system of mediation that has developed in the United States, beginning primarily during the Civil Rights movement in the 1960s. At that time, interested community members used facilitative processes in order to solve disputes within neighborhoods and workplaces. Over the last five or more decades, mediation has evolved into a system that usually involves a neutral third party to resolve a legal dispute. Mediation can be used in almost every type of dispute, and it is commonly used in civil and family cases.

This chapter focuses on the mediation process, beginning with an overview of the history of mediation in the United States, followed by a discussion of the benefits and drawbacks of the mediation process. It then covers how cases get into mediation and traces the mediation process from intake to post-mediation. It concludes with discussions of mediator techniques and mediator styles. Chapter 5 considers legal issues arising from mediation.

§ 4.02 The History of Mediation

While mediation, broadly defined, has likely existed since the dawn of time, the process that we know today as "mediation" has many different roots. Early European settlers to the United States, such as the Puritans and Quakers, used alternative processes such as mediation to resolve differences between group members. These mediation processes were largely used within the group, as opposed to governmental action imposed upon the group.

In the late nineteenth century and into the twentieth century, the Congress began passing statutes that authorized the use of mediation for labor cases. The Erdman Act of 1898[1] authorized mediation and arbitration of labor cases in the railroad industry. In 1913, Congress created the U.S. Department of Labor. Part of the duties of the Secretary of Labor was to "act as mediator and to appoint commissioners of conciliation in labor disputes."[2] Mediating disputes was (and continues to be) a better alternative than going on strike. Utilizing the mediation process has the potential to resolve labor disputes earlier and with better outcomes than either going to court or going on strike.

In the 1960s, social activists used the mediation process to help resolve community disputes resolving around racial unrest. Many of these disputes involved equality in education and housing. Mediators in many major metropolitan areas sought to open a dialogue among community leaders, government employees, and business entities to resolve community tensions. Mediation was used to promote dialogue and peace, as well as to avoid the negative consequences of rioting that was already occurring in some major metropolitan areas.

§ 4.03 Benefits and Drawbacks of the Mediation Process

Given the rise of mediation to resolve litigated cases in today's legal system, understanding the benefits and drawbacks of the mediation process is a useful exercise for lawyers, clients, and mediators. This section details some of the primary reasons mediation can be an excellent process for parties in conflict, as well as some of the drawbacks to using the process. Not surprisingly, many of the benefits of mediation may also be considered drawbacks. Some of the qualities that make mediation beneficial for some cases also serve as reasons mediation may not be appropriate in a different situation.

[A] Benefits of the Mediation Process

Mediation is an informal, consensual, flexible, and confidential process. These four characteristics are often considered the hallmarks of the mediation process.[3] As discussed in the next section, these characteristics are also sometimes detriments to the process, depending on the situation.

Mediation is generally an informal process. Mediation allows parties to communicate with one another and work toward resolving their differences.[4] Unlike the court process, mediators can hear, and parties can discuss, any information that might be helpful to the successful resolution of the dispute because mediators are not bound to follow the formalities of rules of evidence or procedure.[5] The informality makes mediation

---

1. Erdman Act of 1898, June 1, 1898, Ch. 370, 30 Stat. 424.
2. 37 Stat. 738 (1913), 29 U.S.C. § 51 (1913).
3. Rodney A. Max, *Mediation Comes of Age in Alabama*, 59 Ala. Law. 239, 243 (1998).
4. John L. Estes, *Advocacy in Mediation*, 23 Advocate (Texas) 41, 48.
5. Richard P. Sher, *Mediation*, 41 St. Louis B. J. 10, 15 (1994–1995).

accessible to unsophisticated parties and allows them to have their own "voice" in the decision-making process.[6]

The mediation process is generally considered consensual or voluntary.[7] The parties decide whether they will participate, how long they will participate, whether they will settle their case, and what the terms of any settlement may be.[8] The consensual nature of the process puts an incredible amount of power (sometimes described as party autonomy) in the hands of the parties, as opposed to a third-party decision-maker. Compared to adjudicatory processes (such as litigation and arbitration), mediation is the parties' process, and how a mediation progresses largely depends on how the parties would like to see the mediation proceed.

These qualities of informality and voluntariness lead into the next benefit of mediation—flexibility. Mediation's flexibility extends to both the process and the outcomes. With respect to the process, no two mediations are exactly alike. The mediators' skills and the parties' needs can take mediation into any number of different directions.[9] The parties may stay in the same room, or the mediator may travel from room to room in order to negotiate a deal. The mediation may involve intense expressions of emotion, or it may be conducted in a more "businesslike" manner. The mediation may resolve all, some, or none of the issues facing the parties. The negotiated outcomes available in mediation are also extraordinarily flexible. Courts have limited remedies available to the parties—namely monetary, injunctive, and declaratory relief. In mediation, the parties are free to settle for any mutually agreeable settlement (provided that the settlement is not illegal).[10] Mediators can help parties negotiate an unlimited variety of settlement options, including options such as reinstatement, an apology, a business deal, a referral or recommendation, housing options, and any other types of remedies appropriate for the situation.

In addition to the benefits of informality, voluntariness, and flexibility, mediation is also confidential. Mediation is almost always confidential by law, court rule, or agreement, and mediation confidentiality is discussed in more detail below.[11] The mediation process is protected space for participants to have full and frank discussions without worry that what is said may be used against a party at a later date.[12] Confidentiality protects parties and allows them to discuss information that may be detrimental to their legal case in order to come to a settlement. The protections of confidentiality may pave the way for things such as apologies or other types of information that would not usually be shared between the parties in the course of a litigated case.[13]

Other benefits surround the mediation process. Courts support mediation because settled cases help control congested court dockets.[14] More information on court-connected mediation is detailed below.[15] Mediation is intended to be a process that is efficient in

---

6. *Id.*

7. *See infra* Section 4.04.

8. David Matz, *The Mediation Movement*, 28 Boston Bar J. 7, 10 (1984).

9. *Id.*

10. Steve Brutsche, *Mediation Cross-Examined*, 53 Tex. B.J. 580, 584 (1990).

11. *See infra* Section 4.08.

12. Kristen Blankley, *How to Make Mediation Safer in Cases of High Conflict*, 24 Alternative Resol. 11, 13 (2014).

13. Deborah L. Levi, *The Role of Apology in Mediation*, 72 N.Y.U. L. Rev. 1165, 1167 (1997).

14. Kathy L. Shuart et al., *Settling Cases in Detroit: An Examination of Wayne County's Mediation Program*, 8 Just. Sys. J. 307, 324 (1983).

15. *See infra* Section 4.09.

time and cost.[16] The time and preparation for mediation is significantly less than the preparation needed for trial.[17] If a case is mediated and settled early, the parties can save a significant amount of time.[18] Whether mediation will benefit a particular case is a discussion that attorneys and clients (or just clients) should discuss on a case-by-case basis. Although mediation has significant benefits for individual cases, the process is not the answer in all situations.

[B] Drawbacks to the Mediation Process

The qualities mentioned in the subsection above—notably informality, voluntariness, flexibility, and confidentiality—can also serve as drawbacks to the process. Depending on the case and the situation, the benefits of mediation may also be detrimental to individual cases or society as a whole.

The informality of mediation may serve as a negative characteristic of the process. Parties and lawyers may not take the process seriously, especially compared to court proceedings. While the informality theoretically makes the process more accessible to more people, laypeople who do not understand the mediation process may be frustrated by the lack of rules and expected procedures.[19] In addition, some parties and attorneys may not appreciate a mediator discussing otherwise non-relevant information, issues, and evidence, even if that information may otherwise help a case settle.

Because mediation is a voluntary process, the parties are free to not participate or not continue at any time. Adjudicative processes, such as court and arbitration, guarantee a result at the end (even if such decisions could be appealed).[20] Non-adjudicative processes, such as mediation and negotiation, may not result in a settlement.[21] Mediation parties, and their counsel, may consider mediation to be a waste of time if the parties do not reach settlement. Such feelings of discontent may be exacerbated if one of the parties entered the mediation unprepared or otherwise not ready to have serious discussions about settlement. When this type of behavior occurs, one party may accuse the other of not mediating "in good faith."[22] These types of distracting behaviors exist precisely because mediators do not have any authority to make decisions, and one party has the ability to waste another party's time and money.

The flexibility of mediation is sometimes not welcomed by the parties. Given the great variance in mediation styles and techniques (which can vary across mediators or even the same mediator in different circumstances), parties may not know what to expect or how to prepare for the session. The flexibility of outcomes may also cause concern for parties. While non-monetary options may be preferable for one party, not all mediation participants are willing to give (or receive) non-monetary options. Some parties want to deal solely in money, and some attorneys pressure their clients to either give or take

---

16. Gerald F. Phillips & Vanessa A. Ignacio, *Entertainment Industry Recognizing Benefits of Mediation*, 17 Ent. & Sports Law. 29, 32 (2000).

17. Harold Jr. Baer, *Mediation—Now Is the Time*, 21 Litigation 5, 65 (1995).

18. *Id.*

19. Stephanie A. Beauregard, *Court-Connected Juvenile Victim-Offender Mediation: An Appealing Alternative for Ohio's Juvenile Delinquents*, 13 Ohio St. J. Disp. Resol. 1005, 1020 (1998).

20. Robert D. Lang, *ADR: A Smart Solution for Crowded Court Dockets*, 86 N.Y. St. B.J. 23, 30 (2014).

21. *Id.*

22. *See infra* Section 4.04 regarding good faith requirements.

solely monetary offers.[23] Parties who chose mediation for its potential for flexibility may be disappointed when the other party is not willing to engage in the same type of flexibility.

While many choose mediation to take advantage of the confidentiality and legal privileges afforded, confidentiality has potential drawbacks. Critics of mediation and other forms of alternative dispute resolution may view the confidentiality mediation affords as allowing for a private system of justice, outside of the view of the courts, the papers, and the public in general.[24] Cases resolved outside of the public justice system do not add to the common law system of precedent, and taking too many cases out of the public justice system has the potential to stunt the growth of the common law.[25] Confidentiality may also shield the public from knowing about important wrongs. Critics argue that some types of wrongs should be known publicly, especially in situations involving product liability, environmental damage, civil rights, or other cases of importance to the public at large.[26]

Finally, the cost and efficiency benefits of mediation are not always realized. When mediation is unsuccessful, the parties may incur more time and expenses by having participated in an extra step before resorting to an adjudicative process.[27] Parties usually have to pay for the cost of the mediator,[28] which may be an added expense if the parties do not settle.

Despite these drawbacks, mediation is a beneficial process in most cases. The benefits usually outweigh the negatives, and more and more cases are resolved through mediation. The next section details how cases enter into the mediation process.

§ 4.04 Getting into Mediation

Mediation is generally considered to be a voluntary process.[29] Traditionally, "voluntary" meant that the parties agreed to go to mediation after a dispute arose.[30] Many cases still go to mediation in this fashion, through a post-dispute agreement to mediate. Increasingly, courts, court rules, and statutes require individual cases or entire categories of cases to go to mediation before a court will hear the case. In addition, many contracts include a requirement that the parties will mediate any later-arising dispute between the parties, and this type of requirement is known as a pre-dispute mediation agreement.

---

23. Beth Deere, *Federal Court Mediation,* 43 Ark. Law. 22, 23 (2008).

24. Martin H. Malin & Robert F. Ladenson, *Privatizing Justice: A Jurisprudential Perspective on Labor and Employment Arbitration from the Steelworkers Trilogy to Gilmer,* 44 Hastings L.J. 1187, 1240 (1993).

25. Robert A. Baruch Bush & Joseph P. Folger, *Mediation and Social Justice: Risks and Opportunities,* 27 Ohio St. J. Disp. Resol. 1, 5 (2012).

26. Stephanie Brenowitz, *Deadly Secrecy: The Erosion of Public Information under Private Justice,* 19 Ohio St. J. Disp. Resol. 679, 708 (2004).

27. Stephen B. Goldberg, *The Mediation of Grievances Under a Collective Bargaining Contract: An Alternative to Arbitration,* 77 Nw. U. L. Rev. 270, 287 (1982).

28. In some instances, a mediator may work *pro bono.* In some jurisdictions, courts have full-time mediators on staff, and those mediators do not charge an hourly fee for using their services.

29. Martha Weinstein, *Mediation: Fulfilling the Promise of Democracy,* 74 Fla. B.J. 35, 37.

30. Jill I. Gross, *Securities Mediation: Dispute Resolution for the Individual Investor,* 21 Ohio St. J. Disp. Resol. 329, 376 (2006).

Voluntariness is considered a hallmark of mediation.[31] Early in mediation's history, "voluntary" meant that the parties agreed to participate in the mediation process. If one or more parties did not agree to mediate, then no mediation would occur. Mediation is also considered to be voluntary because the parties decide whether or not to settle their dispute, and on what terms. Mediation is often court ordered, which appears to be contrary to the fundamental concept of voluntariness.[32]

Court-connected and other forms of "mandatory" mediation occur in a number of different situations. Often, courts will order specific cases to mediation based on a local court rule authorizing the procedure.[33] In the federal courts, every district and appellate court has a local rule governing mediation, in accordance with the federal Dispute Resolution Act of 1988.[34] Many jurisdictions have programs such as "settlement day" or "settlement week," during which many civil cases are referred to mediators for free or a reduced fee.[35] Court-ordered mediation, discussed in more detail below, alleviates overburdened court dockets and allows the parties to find solutions that courts otherwise could not order.

In other circumstances, legislation or court rule may require certain types of disputes to be mediated prior to receiving a judicial resolution to the case. Many states require mediation of cases involving parenting time for children of divorcing or separating parents before a court will hear contested custody cases.[36] Given the necessity of parents continuing to work together following the divorce or separation, legislatures have favored mediation in these cases to promote the relationships between the parents, reduce parental conflict, and open lines of communication going into the future.[37] Some jurisdictions have mandated mediation in cases involving residential foreclosures.[38] Mediation in these cases may foster creative solutions for homeowners that courts cannot provide— such as loan modifications or "cash for keys" resolutions.[39] In some cases, statutes or court rules may require mediation for a specific type of case, such as fence disputes between neighbors.[40]

In other situations, the contractual arrangement between parties at the beginning of a relationship may require mediation as a method of dispute resolution. For example, employment agreements may involve a mediation clause that would require mediation of all disputes relating to the employment contract.[41] In unionized workplaces, mediation

---

31. *Court-Ordered Mediation*, 62 Disp. Resol. J. 5 (2007).

32. Peter N. Thompson, *Good Faith Mediation in the Federal Courts*, 26 Ohio St. J. Disp. Resol. 363, 365 (2011).

33. Rebecca Wetzel, *New Local Rule 21.2 (E) Mediation*, 67 Clev. B.J. 5, 7 (1996).

34. The Alternative Dispute Resolution Act of 1988 directed federal district courts to develop local rules to implement ADR processes for civil actions. 28 U.S.C. §651(b) (2006).

35. The Ohio State Bar Association's description of Settlement Week is at http://www.ohiobar .org/pub/lycu/index.asp?articleid=98.

36. *See, e.g.,* Ariz. Rev. Stat. Ann. 25-381.18 (West 1991); Fla. Stat. Ann. 984.04 (West Supp. 1999); Minn. Stat. Ann. 518.619 (1990); Wash. Rev. Code Ann. 26.09.015 (West 1990).

37. *See, e.g.,* Ariz. Rev. Stat. Ann. 25-381.01 (West 1991); Fla. Stat. Ann. 984.01 (West Supp. 1999).

38. *See, e.g.,* Nev. Rev. Stat. Ann. § 107.086 (West); Md. Code Ann., Real Prop. § 7-105.1 (West); Ohio Rev. Code Ann. § 2323.06 (West).

39. Richard P. Sher, *Mediation*, 41 St. Louis B. J. 10, 15 (1994–1995).

40. *See, e.g.,* Neb. Rev. Stat. Ann. § 34-112.02 (West).

41. *See, e.g., Gilmer v. Interstate/Johnson Lane Corp.*, 500 U.S. 20 (1991) (holding a broker was "bound to arbitrate his claim under the Age Discrimination in Employment Act because he had . . . agreed to arbitrate all claims arising out of his employment").

is sometimes a required step in the dispute resolution process for employee grievances.[42] Consumer contracts may also permit or require mediation, usually as a step prior to arbitration.

"Voluntariness" in these mandated or contractually required situations is generally limited to voluntary participation within the mediation process. Unlike arbitrators, mediators do not have any decision-making authority over the disputants, and the parties will ultimately decide whether or not they settle their dispute and on what terms. Mediation is considered voluntary because the parties retain these decisions regarding participation at the table and ultimate settlement.

Although the vast majority of parties comply with mandated mediation, few consequences exist for failing to mediate or failing to take full advantage of the mediation process. In some situations, courts may refuse to proceed on a case until the case is mediated in accordance with the law or court order.[43] If a party appears at mediation either unprepared or unwilling to mediate, the opposing party may seek sanctions for failure to mediate "in good faith."[44] Given the confidentiality protections over the process, such sanctions for failure to mediate "in good faith" are notoriously difficult to prove.[45]

§ 4.05 The Mediation Process

The mediation process is both an art and a science, and no two mediations are the same. Mediation's informality allows for great flexibility in the process itself and in the techniques that the mediator may employ. Mediators generally consider the process to flow through a series of "steps" or "shifts" as the mediation progresses. Programs that train new mediators include a varying number of steps, usually between three and 15 steps.[46] Although packaged in different ways, many of these training modules have significant similarities and can be synthesized to give an overview of the process.

This Section considers mediation to be a four-phase process. The first phase, *intake and preparation*, occurs before the parties arrive at the table. The next phase, *information gathering*, generally consists of the first half of the mediation. During this phase, the mediator and parties make opening remarks, and the mediator works with the parties to exchange and expand information. Once the parties have sufficient information, the mediation usually shifts into a *problem-solving* phase, during which settlement ideas are generated and critiqued, and the parties decide whether or not they will settle the case. After the parties settle or reach impasse, the mediator will move into the fourth phase, or *closure* of the session. The closure phase may also include post-mediation issues, such as agreement writing or other follow-up.

---

42. Sarah Rudolph Cole, *Let the Grand Experiment Begin: Pyett Authorizes Arbitration of Unionized Employees' Statutory Discrimination Claims*, 14 Lewis & Clark L. Rev. 861 (2010).

43. Jonathan C. Myers, *Is There an Obligation to Mediate in Good Faith?*, 21 J. Bankr. L. & Prac. 2 Art. 6 (2012).

44. *Nadeau v. Nadeau*, 2008 ME 147, 957 A.2d 108 (Me. 2008).

45. Myers, supra note 44.

46. *See e.g.*, Jennifer E. Beer & Caroline C. Packard, The Mediator's Handbook (2013); Prudence B. Kestner & Larry Ray, The Conflict Resolution Training Program (2002); Christopher W. Moore, The Mediation Process: Practical Strategies for Resolving Conflict (2d ed. 1996).

The mediation process, however, should not be considered linear. Although mediation is regularly presented in a linear fashion, the process is fluid and the mediator may take these steps out of order. For instance, additional questions may arise during the problem-solving phase that would require the parties to step back into the information-gathering phase. In other instances, parties may begin a mediation with a settlement proposal, and the parties may begin by working on problem solving instead of information gathering. In essence, no one "right" way to mediate exists. This Section gives an overview of what to expect in a typical mediation session.

[A] Intake and Preparation

Intake and preparation for mediation are crucial parts of the mediation process that often get overlooked. The mediation process actually begins well before the parties sit at the table with the mediator. Careful intake and preparation help ensure that the process will be successful when the parties arrive for their session. For the purposes of this section, "intake" refers to the process of having all of the parties agree to mediate with a particular mediator. "Preparation," then, refers to the stage occurring after the parties agree to mediate with a particular mediator but before the parties arrive for mediation.

[1] Intake

Intake is the specific process of deciding to mediate with a particular mediator—and it is separate from the question of whether the parties should mediate at all. Intake usually begins with one party calling a mediator or a mediation office. The initiating party, or "party one," contacts the mediator either because party one voluntarily agrees to mediate or because the parties are required to mediate pursuant to court order or other law.[47]

Mediators must carefully consider a number of issues during the intake process. First, mediators should consider how much information they collect from each party at the beginning of the process. Second, mediators should decide who should approach "party two" and any other parties that should attend the mediation process.

[a] Information Collection

With regard to the first question, what is the appropriate amount of information to collect during intake? Mediators must balance the amount of information that they need to prepare for the mediation but not gather too much information such that they might develop biases or pre-conceived notions about the case.

Mediators should collect certain types of information at intake in order to satisfy mediation ethics standards. For instance, mediators should collect the full names and addresses of all of the parties and their attorneys, if any. Once the mediators collect this information, they should run a conflicts check to determine whether the mediator has any professional, personal, or other types of relationships with any of the parties or attorneys involved.[48] If mediators discover conflicts, they must disclose them. Disclosure obligations and other ethical requirements are discussed in Chapter 5. For instance, a

---

47. *See supra* § 4.04.
48. Laura E. Weidner, *Model Standards of Conduct for Mediators*, 21 Ohio St. J. Disp. Resol. 547, 567 (2006).

mediator would want to discover early in the process that the mediator had previously represented one of the parties as an attorney.

Mediators should also collect information regarding the nature of the dispute to be mediated. This information is critical for mediators to determine if they have the competency to mediate the dispute. Although mediators are often considered process experts, some familiarity with the subject matter in dispute might be required for mediators to have the requisite level of competency to mediate the dispute.[49] Family law mediators may not feel comfortable mediating a patent dispute, and intellectual property mediators might not feel competent to mediate a divorce. In some jurisdictions, mediators must meet training and other requirements in order to mediate certain types of cases.[50] In many states, mediators who mediate family disputes involving children must have training in family dynamics, domestic violence, and other issues relating to parenting plans.[51] Having a basic understanding of the type of dispute to be mediated will help mediators determine if they meet competency requirements and comfort levels with the type of dispute.

Although some basic information collection is essential to intake, mediators should be careful to not solicit too much information such that they might form biases before the mediation sessions commence.[52] Generally, the intake process occurs in a series of ex parte conversations (i.e., with only one party at a time). Savvy counsel and parties might try to take advantage of these one-on-one conversations and try to "win over" the mediator before all of the parties are at the table.[53] Careful mediators should keep these types of discussions to a minimum and collect only information relevant to ethical and logistical issues.

[b] Approaching "Party Two"

Once "party one" approaches the mediator with a request to mediate, how should mediators convince "party two" to mediate? A variety of options are available to mediators, each with pros and cons. This section considers the most common methods of engaging "party two" and bringing that party to the table.

One approach is for the mediator to approach "party two." The mediator can approach "party two" with the information gathered from "party one." The mediator can approach "party two" by telephone, mail, electronic communication, or other means. Commonly, a mediator will reach out to the other party by telephone.[54] When the mediator is on the telephone with the party, the mediator will likely discuss the fact that "party one" requested the mediation, intake information relating to "party two," and give an explanation of the mediation process. Although the telephone is the most direct way to get a response out of "party two," the mediator should be careful not to "sell" the mediation process too hard or appear biased in favor of "party one," who already wants

---

49. Weidner, *supra* note 54, at 558 (citing Model Standards Standard IV(A) (2005)).

50. *See, e.g.,* Neb. Rev. St. §43-2938; N.H. Rev. Stat. Ann. §328-C:5; Ind. R. Alternative Disp. Resol. 2.5; La. Ch. C. Art. 439.

51. Utah Code Ann. §30-3-39 (West); S.D. Codified Laws §25-4-58.1.

52. Kimberlee K. Kovach, Mediation in a Nutshell 133 (2003).

53. *See infra* Chapter 6.01 (introducing mediation advocacy as a different type of skill set for lawyers to master).

54. John A. Fiske & Michael L. Leshin, *Mediation and other Dispute Resolution Alternatives*, MDLPM MA-CLE 3-1 (2014).

to mediate the case with the mediator.[55] Other methods of communication, however, may not require an immediate response, and it may become difficult to convince "party two" to engage in mediation solely through mail or even electronic mail communications.

If a mediator has an administrative assistant, the assistant could take the initiative to contact "party two." Because of the buffer between the assistant and the mediator, the mediator would be less likely to be swayed by and develop bias due to anything said by any of the parties to the assistant. "Party two" may not think that the administrative assistant has the same type of profit motivation that the party may think the mediator has. Not all mediators, however, have an administrative assistant. Many new mediation operations consist of solo practices on budgets that may not include assistants. On the other hand, many community mediation centers may have the capacity to have staff conduct all of the intake activities, so the mediators can handle the cases after all parties have committed to the process.

Another option would be for the mediator to convince "party one" to contact "party two" and convince "party two" to mediate. In some ways, this situation is ideal. If "party one" and "party two" can agree on their own to mediate, they have already agreed on one thing—i.e., the mediation process.[56] If the parties can agree to mediate with a particular mediator, they may be more likely to work cooperatively in the mediation. Having "party one" approach "party two" reduces the risk of the appearance of bias, particularly the appearance that the mediator is biased in favor of "party one" due to "party one's" decision to mediate. Having "party one" reach out may also limit the amount of information the mediator may learn prior to the beginning of the sessions. The biggest drawback to this approach is that not all parties will be cooperative and agree to mediate, even if required by statute or court order. Mediators may be able to discuss with "party one" who should approach "party two" and make these decisions on a case-by-case basis.

[2] Mediator Preparation

Once the parties have agreed to mediate with a particular mediator (or mediation organization, such as a community mediation center), the stage of mediation preparation begins. Preparation encompasses both the preparation by the mediator to handle an individual case, as well as preparing the facilities for the participants.

Careful mediators take a wide variety of steps to prepare for a mediation. Often, mediators who work on civil cases will ask the parties or their counsel to prepare written mediation submission statements.[57] Those submissions usually cover topics such as the background of the case, an overview of the legal issues, a discussion of the settlement efforts to date, and other information pertinent to the mediation.[58] Mediators will review these statements and documents the parties attached to them (such as pleadings, contracts, or other exhibits) prior to the mediation. Mediators may gather this type of information in pre-mediation conference calls, as well.

---

55. *Id.*

56. Tom Mulligan, *An Overview of the Mediation Process*, 71 Clev. B.J. 8, 9 (2000).

57. *Id.*

58. Chapter 6 covers the mediation submission statements from an advocate's perspective.

In addition to preparing for the specific case, many mediators will engage in some type of meditation or centering activities prior to mediating.[59] Impartiality is crucial for mediators and being in the right frame of mind can help mediators be (and appear to be) free from bias. Centering activities, such as deep breathing, meditation, or visualization, can also help mediators set aside other concerns and be fully present for the mediation session.[60]

Mediators must also prepare the facilities that will be used. Sometimes mediators use space belonging to one of the parties. In some instances, these mediators work from home or without a home office. Mediators may be able to save a significant amount of money by utilizing the offices of the parties, but sometimes parties feel uncomfortable mediating at the office of the other party. Often, mediating at a neutral location will make the parties the most comfortable, and they will consider the mediator to be more neutral.[61] Some mediators choose to mediate in a courthouse. Mediators who have concern about the presence of weapons or a party's propensity for violence may prefer mediating in a courthouse so the parties must go through a security checkpoint.[62] Court security officers may also be able to help step into a situation if the parties become violent. Additional safety concerns are addressed in Chapter 5.

Most mediations occur in some type of conference room, usually in a neutral location. Many mediators give consideration to the size and shape of the table that will be used for the mediation. Research demonstrates that certain types of seating arrangements are more likely to stimulate conversation compared to other arrangements.[63] Mediators who use visual aids, such as flip charts or whiteboards, must consider how to arrange participants so that the charts or whiteboards are accessible and easily read by everyone in the room. Mediators should be acquainted with basic hospitality features of the facility, such as the availability of snacks and beverages, the location of the restrooms, and places the parties can go during a break or a private meeting with the mediator. Some mediations require multiple rooms so that each party can have a separate room while the mediator travels from room to room while dealing with the different parties. In cases involving co-mediators, the two mediators should plan together on how they plan on conducting the mediation together.

Although an office setting is the most typical type of arrangement for mediations, some mediators prefer secluded and picturesque locations. For instance, Jim Malamed, the founder of Mediate.com, owns a yurt in the country, and he asks his divorcing clients to meet him at the yurt for their mediation.[64] He reports significant success because the parties must drive through beautiful scenery on their way to the yurt, and the yurt itself is deliberately decorated to encourage peacefulness and tranquility. This example illustrates the great flexibility that mediators have in preparing the surroundings to foster settlement.

---

59. Leonard L. Riskin, *The Contemplative Lawyer: On the Potential Contributions of Mindfulness Meditation to Law Students, Lawyers, and Their Clients*, 7 Harv. Negot. L. Rev. 1, 40 (2002).

60. *Id.* at 45.

61. William L. Thomas, *Mediation: The Future is Now — The Whys and Hows of this Method of Resolving Disagreement*, 71 Iowa Law. 3, 2 (2011).

62. *See* Jason Lazarus, *Note, Vision Impossible? Imaging Devices — The New Police Technology and the Fourth Amendment*, 48 Fla. L. Rev. 299, 318 n.137 (1996).

63. Douglas N. Frenkel & James H. Stark, The Practice of Mediation 105 (2008).

64. *See, e.g.*, http://www.internetmediator.com/

[B] Information Gathering

The next phase of the mediation process centers around information gathering. One of the most common barriers to settlement is parties not having sufficient information to make a decision.[65] Mediation is an opportunity for parties to share information needed in an informal manner. Mediators can also diagnose what information one party may need to make a decision and try to obtain that information. Mediators, too, use these information-gathering stages in order to gain more information for them to move the process forward.

As noted above, these stages are not rigid. Although the information-gathering portion of a mediation typically happens in the first half of the process, mediators often find themselves seeking more information later in the process when the parties are working on solving the problem before them. This section, while presented in a linear manner, simplifies the explanation of how the process works. How any mediation is conducted in practice will depend on the mediator, the circumstances of the case, the settlement history of the parties, and other relevant factors.

[1] Mediator Opening Remarks

Almost every mediation begins with some type of opening remarks by the mediator. The term for these opening remarks varies. In some training manuals, this opening is referred to as an "introduction."[66] Others call this part of the mediation an "opening statement."[67] Other, additional terms can also be found to label this portion of the mediation.[68] This chapter will call all of these variations the opening remarks. This portion of the mediation has both informational and psychological purposes.

The opening remarks convey important information to the parties. The mediator will introduce himself or herself, ensure that everyone is present (including necessary third parties, such as insurance adjusters), determine how each participant would prefer to be addressed, and likely make some type of small talk with all of the participants.

The mediator will usually describe the mediation process to be used in the session, the role of the mediator, the style of mediation that will be utilized, and perhaps how the mediator's role is different from the role of an attorney or judge.[69] Many mediators will describe whether the mediation will take place with all the parties together (i.e., a joint mediation session) or in separate rooms (i.e., a caucus-style mediation).[70] The mediator may let everyone know how long the session will last and determine whether any time constraints (such as travel plans) exist for the mediation session.

---

65. Jean R. Sternlight, *Lawyers' Representation of Clients in Mediation: Using Economics and Psychology to Structure Advocacy in a Nonadversarial Setting*, 14 Ohio St. J. Disp. Resol. 269, 299 (1999).

66. John W. Cooley, Mediation Advocacy 15 (NITA 1996).

67. *See supra* note 3, at 243.

68. Dwight Golann, Mediating Legal Disputes: Effective Strategies for Lawyers and Mediators 62 (1996) (opening session); Pamela L. Reeves, *Working it Out: Mediation Advice for Employment Law Disputes*, 39 Tenn. B.J. 34, 37 (2003) (opening remarks).

69. Judy Cohen, *How Preliminary Conferences Lay Groundwork for a Productive Process,* 30 Alternatives to High Cost Litig. 169, 179–80 (2012).

70. These types of techniques are discussed in Section 4.06[E].

The mediator will likely also discuss the fact that the session is confidential, privileged, or both.[71] Usually, a mediator will state that the session is confidential and something along the lines of "what is said in this room stays in this room." Some mediators may explain exceptions to confidentiality. The explanation of exceptions may be most common in family law cases where mediators are mandatory reporters if allegations of child abuse are made during the session.[72] A mediator may also state professional credentials, some of which may be required under state law or court rule.[73]

A mediator may also want the parties to feel comfortable in their surroundings. Some mediators assure the parties that they may break for any reason, including hospitality breaks or checking in with important advisors not present at the session.[74] The mediator may offer the parties pen, paper, a beverage, snack, or other types of items, so the participants feel comfortable at the session. Some mediators like to establish "ground rules" or "codes of conduct" for the session (such as acting with common courtesy or allowing one person to speak at a time),[75] and other mediators ask the parties what guidelines they would like to follow for the session.[76]

The opening remarks by the mediator serve an important informational purpose. Many participants are not sure what to expect from the process, and this information should give the parties a sense of what to expect during the session. In addition, the mediator's opening remarks serve an important psychological purpose. The mediator intends to instill trust and participant "buy in" from the beginning of the session.[77] If the parties trust the mediator, they will be more likely to participate fully and be satisfied with the session.[78] The mediator will also try to establish authority and control of the session, demonstrating competence.

The length of these opening remarks depends on the mediators. Some mediators will cover these types of issues in pre-mediation communications, so the parties are already familiar with what to expect when they enter the mediation session.[79] Other mediators will handle all of these introductory issues in three to five minutes and quickly turn the session over to the parties. Other mediators take a much longer time to establish these

---

71. Confidentiality and privilege issues are discussed infra in Chapter 5.2.

72. National Conference of Commissioners on Uniform State Laws, Uniform Mediation Act §§ 1 to 17 (2003). *See also* Kan. Stat. Ann. [j0] 38-2223(a)(1)(D) (2006); LA Chil Code 610; Va. Code Ann. [j0] 63.2-1509(a)(10) (2002); Wis. Stat. [j0] 48.981 (2005).

73. The Model Rules of Professional Conduct require that lawyers disclose to mediation clients their legal training if the mediation clients are not represented by counsel. Model Rules of Prof'l Conduct r. 2.4. In addition, the Model Rules require the mediator to state that the mediator may not give any legal advice other than recommending that the parties seek independent legal counsel. *Id.*

74. When clients attend mediation without their attorneys, breaks can be helpful for calling attorneys with questions about settlement options or other concerns. Sometimes, trusted advisors, such as spouses, friends, parents, or others may need to be consulted during a mediation session for a client to feel comfortable about a settlement option.

75. Peter N. Thompson, *Enforcing Rights Generated in Court-Connected Mediation-Tension Between the Aspirations of a Private Facilitative Process and the Reality of Public Adversarial Justice*, 19 Ohio St. J. Disp. Resol. 509, 568 (2004).

76. *Id.*

77. Thomas W. Cavanagh Jr., *The Mediation Process in the General Equity Division*, 287 N.J. Law. 69, 70 (2014).

78. *Id.*

79. Paul E. Mason, *What's Brewing in the International Commercial Mediation Process: Differences from Domestic Mediation and Other Things Parties, Counsel and Mediators Should Know*, 66 Disp. Resol. J. 64, 66 (2011).

introductory issues and use the first hour or more before proceeding to the issues presented by the parties.

Each mediator's opening remarks are different, and some mediators do not present the same opening remarks for each mediation. This section is intended to give an idea of what might occur during this opening phase of the mediation, but every mediator develops his or her own style in how to open the session.

[2] Opening Remarks by the Parties

After the mediator opens the session, the session is usually turned over to the parties to give their own opening remarks, sometimes called the parties' "opening statements."[80] The purpose of the parties' opening remarks is to allow them some uninterrupted time in order to state, in their own words, why they are in mediation.[81]

The purpose of these opening remarks is, again, both informational and psychological. This portion of the mediation is informational because the each party has the opportunity to educate the mediator and the other side of the reasons for the mediation.[82] The parties can present any information they think would be helpful to reaching a settlement. The length of time each party uses for these opening remarks varies. Pro se parties in small claims mediation may speak for few minutes each. In complicated cases, attorneys and clients may script opening statements complete with PowerPoint displays, evidentiary presentations, and narratives from the clients. Additional consideration to crafting opening remarks from the advocate's perspective is discussed in Chapter 6, Advocacy in Mediation.[83]

Many mediators prefer that these opening presentations to be made in joint session, with all of the parties together.[84] When all parties can be together for the opening statements, then everyone has access to all of the same information. Other mediators prefer that the parties present their opening remarks solely to the mediator, in caucus.[85] Mediators who worry that the opening presentations will be inflammatory or otherwise detrimental to the settlement process may find that this phase is best conducted in a private audience with the mediator so that the parties have the chance to make their presentation without jeopardizing the atmosphere for settlement.[86] Some mediators choose to skip this step.[87] Those mediators will often try to get a good overview of the case through pre-mediation conference calls and submission statements so that they already have a good sense of what the mediation is about. The mediators who skip this portion fear that the opening remarks will polarize the parties, entrench parties in their positions, or offend the other parties at the table.[88]

---

80. Bobby Marzine Harges, *The ABCs of Effective ADR Ten Practical Tips for Representing Clients in Mediations*, 43 LA. B.J. 142, 144 (1995).

81. *Id.*

82. *Id.*

83. *See infra* Chapter 6 regarding the advocate's role in mediation.

84. *See supra* note 88.

85. Melanie A. Vaughn, *Mediation Tips*, 36 MD. B.J. 46, 50 (2003).

86. *Id.*

87. Larry R. Rute, *The Evolution of Commercial Mediation in the Midwest: Best Practices, Confidentiality and Good Faith*, 79 J. KAN. B. Ass'N. 24, 26 (2010).

88. *Id.*

The parties' opening remarks may help psychologically and give the parties a "voice" in the session.[89] This portion of the mediation allows the parties to participate personally or through their lawyers to discuss openly the reasons they are in mediation. Because of the informality and flexibility of the process, the parties are free to use their opening narrative to discuss "irrelevant" or non-legal reasons that are important to the parties. Often, the legal dispute that has brought parties to mediation was the "straw that broke the camel's back" and discovery and discussion of underlying problems is imperative to a successful mediation. Allowing the parties to begin this process during the opening remarks may help the parties feel heard and may create greater party satisfaction in the process.[90]

[3] Information Sharing and Expanding

The vast majority of the first "half"[91] of mediation involves a process of sharing and expanding information for both the mediator and the parties. Parties need a certain amount of information before they can accept a settlement offer. Parties must be able to assess whether a proposed offer is fair, reasonable, or otherwise acceptable. The information-sharing portion is crucial for preparing for the later problem-solving stage.

Mediators use a wide variety of techniques in order to expand the available information. The techniques of questioning, actively listening, summarizing, reframing, dealing with emotions, and other tools are discussed later in this chapter.[92] The types of information gathered and exchanged during this time may include information on: the factual background of the case, the value of the case, emotional content felt by the parties, information relating to legal arguments and theories, information regarding damages suffered or reparations sought, settlement history to date, and anything else that might help uncover the story between the parties or move the parties closer to settlement.

Given the timing of the information sharing phase, the mediators and parties may have questions about the parties' opening statements. If the parties do not give lengthy or detailed opening statements, the mediator will likely have many questions about the case and what the parties would like to achieve during the session. If the parties give highly detailed opening statements, the mediator and other party may still want to clarify information discussed or determine the basis for certain information disclosed. Questions may also arise not by what is said, but by what has been *omitted* by the opening statements. If an opening statement omits a discussion of an element of a legal claim, such as causation or damages, the mediator or opposing party can seek clarity on those issues.

How the information gathering occurs largely depends on whether the parties are together in joint session or are in separate caucus rooms. In joint session, mediators will often ask parties questions and may have the parties reflect on the new information that has just been received. For example, if one party offers an apology in joint session, the mediator may turn to the other party and ask how that party feels, having heard the apology. In joint session, the parties also have the opportunity to ask each other's questions directly. Lawyers in mediation have the unique opportunity to speak directly to

---

89. *Id.*

90. *Id.*

91. Most mediation sessions involve the two major portions of information gathering and problem solving. These two phases are the two "halves" of the mediation session. Although described as "halves," the time for each half will vary greatly from mediation to mediation.

92. *See infra* Section 4.06.

the opposing client and ask questions to that client.[93] During this phase of the mediation, the mediators will commonly seek areas of agreement, engage in active listening, and try to improve the communication between the parties. When the parties are together in joint session, the information expansion is most transparent because all of the parties are hearing all of the same information at the same time. Of course, parties may interpret what has been said in open session differently,[94] but they have at least all had access to the same information.

Information gathering and expansion still occurs in caucus, but it occurs in a different manner. The mediator will ask each party questions, but the information will only be shared with the mediator, and not necessarily with the other party. When mediators use a caucus style, many of them will have the ground rule that whatever is said in caucus is confidential from the other party, unless the party gives consent to share the information with the other side.[95] A ground rule like this one will encourage parties to share freely with the mediator and the neutral; however, often that information is not exchanged with the other party. The mediator, then, learns a considerable amount of information about the dispute but is placed in the precarious position of being the only one who has knowledge of the proverbial "whole story."[96] Mediators sometimes can convince a party to share information if they are able to show them that disclosure would be beneficial or essential to settlement. Attorneys and clients can also use the shuttle diplomacy style of mediation to ask questions of the mediator and request that the mediator find out the answer to those questions.

How long the information gathering and expanding portion of a mediation takes depends on each mediation. One common rule is that this portion of the mediation goes on until the parties begin to repeat information and no new information is disclosed.[97] By the close of this phase, the mediator and the parties should all have a good idea of the nature of the dispute that brings them to mediation and the issues to be mediated. Sometimes, parties will suggest solutions or otherwise try to engage in problem/dispute solving early in the mediation session. If the mediator determines that no additional information is needed, then the mediator may simply shift to problem-solving. Often, however, these early solutions are premature, and the mediator will put them aside and return to them in the problem-solving portion of the mediation.

[C] Problem Solving

After information gathering is complete, the mediation moves to the problem-solving stage. At this point, the mediator and the parties stop talking about the factual and legal background of the case and start moving toward trying to settle the problem. During this phase, parties will generate and test options, brainstorm new ideas, create settlement proposals, and ultimately determine whether they will settle.

---

93. Model Rule of Professional Conduct 4.2 generally prohibits attorneys from contacting represented clients without consent of the attorney.

94. *See generally*, Edward E. Jones et al., *Attribution: Perceiving the Causes of Behavior*, General Learning Press (1972).

95. Carrie Menkel-Meadow, *Ethics and Professionalism in Non-Adversarial Lawyering*, 27 Fla. St. U. L. Rev. 153, 181 (1999).

96. Kent B. Scott & Cody W. Wilson, *Questions Clients Have About Whether (and How) to Mediate and How Counsel Should Answer Them*, 63 Disp. Resol. J. 26, 34 (2008).

97. Gary A. Goodpaster, Guide to Negotiation and Mediation 209 (1997).

The problem-solving phase can be considered the second "half" of the mediation. Again, the term "half" is used conceptually and not literally. Some mediations move very quickly into the problem-solving "half," while others spend a significantly longer portion of time in the information gathering "half." This section details some of the highlights of the problem-solving portion of the mediation.

[1] Setting the Table for the Rest of the Mediation

At this shift from information gathering to problem solving, the mediator plays a key role in creating an environment where parties can express and share ideas and work toward solutions for solvable[98] problems (referred to here as "mediatable issues"). In order to do this, the mediator must first determine (on his or her own or with the help of the parties) which issues are ripe for mediation. Second, the mediator or the parties must determine in which order to discuss the mediatable issues.

[a] Determining the Mediatable Issues

Not all things that the parties may wish to discuss are items that can be mediated. The mediator must determine what are the major items that the parties can resolve, which are sometimes called "issues." The term "issues," as used here, is separate from the underlying "interests." Interests, discussed above,[99] are the parties' underlying motives and needs. Interests are not mediatable. The issues, on the other hand, are items that can be discussed and solved, if the parties choose to solve them.

In order for an issue to be mediatable, that issue must be capable of multiple possible outcomes.[100] Some items that parties would like to discuss are not capable of any outcomes. Historic facts, parties' feelings, and parties' interests are just some examples of issues that are not capable of having any mediated outcome. Consider a dispute regarding the freshness of a shipment of apples between an apple grower and a store owner. The parties may disagree vehemently regarding the day that they were harvested from the orchard. One party claims that they were harvested the day before shipment, but the other party strongly suspects that the party is lying because the apples arrived bruised and soft. No amount of mediation will help the parties agree on the date that the apples were picked. Furthermore, determining the precise date of harvest is generally immaterial to whether or not the parties can resolve the dispute and move on with their businesses.

The feelings and interests of the apple harvester and the store owner are also not mediatable issues. No matter how frustrated, hurt, angry, or disappointed the store owner feels, the parties cannot resolve to make the store owner feel less of any of those emotions. The emotions simply "are." Good mediators know how to deal with strong emotions in a mediation room, but they are not items that can themselves be mediated. The apple harvester may have underlying interests of getting paid and maintaining a good reputation, but those interests, too, cannot be mediated. When mediators work with parties to develop solutions, they will often keep the interests in mind and ensure that the solutions satisfy the parties' interests.[101] The interests, however, are not subject to compromise or solution.

---

98. As discussed in Section 4.05[C][1][a], not all issues that the parties may wish to discuss can be mediated.

99. See Chapter 3, Negotiation.

100. Douglas N. Frenkel & James H. Stark, The Practice of Mediation: A Video-Integrated Text 228 (2d ed. 2012).

101. See Section 4.05[C][2].

When mediators discover items that are important, but not mediatable, they can set these items as "discussion items" as opposed to "mediatable issues." Discussion items are simply that—items that can be discussed, but not items that require any action. Sometimes items must be discussed, such as factual issues or feelings, before the parties can feel comfortable moving on to solving the problem. Having these discussions would move the mediation back into the "information gathering" portion of dispute resolution, but often these discussions are crucial to ultimate resolution.

The mediator can determine the issues to be solved or can ask for assistance from the parties in so doing.[102] Common issues in cases involving parenting time include: the regular schedule for the children, the holiday schedule, legal and physical custody, child support, insurance, education, and the like. Common issues in landlord/tenant disputes include: past due rent, damaged property, repairs requested, and whether the parties will continue their rental relationship. Common issues in contract cases include damages for breach of contract and whether the parties will continue their business relationship. Although some issues become predictable for mediators who regularly mediate a specific type of case (consider, for example, a patent mediator who has a significant amount of experience mediating licensing agreements), most cases will have unique issues that need to be addressed. Mediators will often discuss with the parties the identification of the issues and then ensure that they have not missed anything. At that point, parties may discuss issues that the mediator did not mention.

[b] Setting the Agenda

Setting the agenda is a crucial step in the mediation process, even though this phase often only takes a few minutes. Having a logical and sound agenda makes nearly every meeting progress smoothly, and a mediation is no different. Mediators, however, cannot set an agenda until they have identified the mediatable issues. Once the issues have been identified and settled, then the mediator or the parties can set the agenda.

Some mediators decide the agenda for themselves, while other mediators will have the parties decide the agenda. Pros and cons exist for both approaches. When the mediator decides, the mediator can make the decision quickly and efficiently, drawing on past experience to determine the best way to proceed. When the parties decide, they may become empowered to resolve the dispute in the way that is best for them. Not all parties may be able to agree on how to set the agenda, and this method can become cumbersome if the mediator is required to mediate the creation of the agenda. Optimally, the mediator works with the parties to develop the agenda and to ensure issues important to the parties will be discussed.

Mediators who set their own agenda can do so in a variety of ways. Some mediators prefer to start with something easy, reasoning that the parties will build momentum and the problem-solving portion will get off to a good start.[103] Some family mediators like to start by asking the parents where the children will spend Mother's Day and Father's Day because they can expect easy agreement on these issues. Other mediators like to work on the most difficult issue first.[104] Those mediators sense that the parties are at

---

102. Mark E. Appel, *Selecting Cases for Mediation*, 17 Colo. Law. 2007, 2010 (1988).

103. Lancelot L. Esteibar, *To Kill A ~~Mockingbird~~ Mediator?: Assessing the Need for Third-Party Neutrals in Federal Bankruptcy Courts' Home Foreclosure Avoidance Programs*, 13 Cardozo J. Conflict Resol. 527, 554 (2012).

104. Arnold H. Gold, *Make Parting Less Painful*, 39 Trial 44, 45 (2003).

mediation in order to solve the hard issues, so starting with the hardest issue makes sense. Mediators who start with the hardest issues might also be trying to gauge whether the parties really want to settle or if they are just going through the motions. In some mediations, some issues are dependent on other issues. In those cases, starting with the independent issues and moving to the dependent issues might be an excellent way to structure the agenda.[105] Consider a case of employment discrimination where a potential issue is reemployment. Tackling the reemployment issue first may be desirable because the settlement options surrounding reemployment may look substantially different from the settlement options surrounding a severance package. In some mediations, emergency issues may need to be addressed first.[106] For example, if parents are having a difficult time mediating a large number of issues in August, one logical place to start is to have the parents agree on which school the children should attend before the school year starts.

Another consideration is whether the mediator should set the whole agenda at once or simply take the agenda issue by issue as they are resolved.[107] When mediators set an entire agenda at once, the parties know what to expect for the rest of the mediation, and they can mentally plan for the rest of the session. Mediations, however, are fluid and rarely go as planned, so the mediator may take issues outside of the agenda order, especially when one issue naturally flows into another issue. Parties may lose confidence in the mediator if the agenda is not followed. Other mediators will only set one issue at a time and then pick another issue to work on after that first issue is complete.[108] This type of scheduling allows for significant flexibility, but the parties do not have a clear roadmap of how the rest of the mediation will proceed.

Some mediators go back to the agenda as a way to break impasse on a difficult issue.[109] Consider a situation in which the parties agree to start with the hardest issue first. After working on this issue for a while, the parties get frustrated and are ready to declare an impasse. Astute mediators may simply choose a different agenda item and try to make some headway on a different issue. In some cases, the parties will come to agreement on the other issues, and that leads to agreement on the issue previously considered insurmountable. In other instances, the parties may be able to reach a partial agreement. Of course, some mediations will end in complete impasse.

After mediators identify the issues to be mediated and determine the agenda, the real work begins — helping the parties propose and analyze solutions. These issues are addressed in the next section.

[2] Decision Making

The bulk of the problem-solving portion of the mediation occurs in the decision-making stage. This phase actually encompasses a number of different aspects. First, it includes helping the parties engage in the creation of options. Next, this phase involves assessing the options that have been proposed. Finally, this phase includes

---

105. Christopher Moore, *The Mediation Process: Practical Strategies for Resolving Conflict* (3d ed. 2004).

106. *Id.*

107. *Id.*

108. *Id.*

109. Additional information on impasse breaking is found in Section 4.05[C][3].

drafting any resulting agreements or (at a minimum) the major terms for a memorandum of understanding.

[a] Generating Settlement Ideas

In some mediations, parties and their attorneys will come to the mediation with their own settlement ideas and concession strategies. When the parties have come with their own options, the mediator can work with these options and see whether the other party will agree to them.

If the parties do not come to the mediation having already considered settlement options, the mediator must help the parties generate those options at the mediation session. Any number of techniques can be used to generate these options.

One common method is brainstorming. The purpose of brainstorming is for the parties to generate as many ideas as possible and to refrain from evaluating any of those ideas until the parties exhaust their options.[110] For the brainstorming technique to be successful, the mediator must set certain ground rules—namely that the generation of ideas be separated from evaluation of those ideas.[111] The parties should be encouraged to suggest any and all options aloud and in front of the other party, including wild and crazy options. Suggestions may be combined or modified to create additional ideas. The mediator should also instruct the parties that no one takes any ownership of ideas generated, and that parties could suggest options even if they would not later agree to them. The separation of creation and evaluation of options is crucial for brainstorming to be successful. The act of evaluating items often stifles creativity, makes parties defensive, and otherwise disrupts the flow of option generation. As the parties generate options, the mediator should capture those options on paper or a whiteboard so that they can be referred to later.

Some mediators use variations of brainstorming in order to create potential settlement options. Parties could sit and think quietly about potential settlement options and write those options down on a paper, on note cards, or on sticky notes. The mediator could collect the potential options and then read them all aloud. This technique works particularly well in mediations involving three or more parties because the authors of individual options remain anonymous.

Other mediators forego the creation of many options and simply start to work on assessing options that the parties suggest as they are suggested. If the parties suggested an option early in the mediation, this would be an appropriate time to revisit that option and address the potential solution.

Mediators usually let the parties generate their options, rather than suggest options themselves. The principle of party autonomy suggests that the parties know their problem best and therefore know best how to resolve it. The parties are intimately aware of their businesses, communities, families, and others that might be affected by any decision made by the parties. They will best know what is feasible and the best way to resolve their dispute.

---

110. Kay Elkins-Elliott & Frank W. Elliott, *Settlement Advocacy*, 11 Tex. Wesleyan L. Rev. 7, 15 (2004).
    111. *Id.*

In some instances, mediators may need to suggest options.[112] The parties may not be very successful at creating their own options and may seek help from the mediator. Some risk surrounds mediator suggestions. Mediators are not as familiar with the parties' situation and therefore mediator options may not be workable or best for the parties. Mediator options may also carry some weight as a "preferred option," and the parties may give these types of options undue weight.[113] Some benefits exist for giving mediator options. Mediators who regularly work in a specific area of the law may be familiar with typical settlement options. Mediators may also see options that the parties may have overlooked. Some mediators, if they were to suggest options, prefer to suggest multiple options so as to not provide a single "mediator option."

The purpose of this phase of the mediation is to move toward resolution by creating potential options for settlement. Only after the options are brought to light can the parties begin the process of narrowing and refining options for potential agreement.

[b] Choosing the Right Option

After the options have been generated, the parties must begin the often difficult work of choosing the right option for them and coming to an agreement. This portion of the mediation may be highly contentious, rife with emotion, or smooth, depending on the parties. How this phase of the mediation proceeds will likely depend on whether the mediator helps generate many options or simply works with one option at a time.

Mediators who engage the parties in brainstorming will likely have a rich list of potential options. The number of options will differ depending on the parties, but the parties may be considering from among a handful of options to more than a few dozen potential solutions. Mediators have a variety of techniques that they can use in order to narrow the list of options to those that are potential solutions.[114] One option is for mediators to suggest that they remove from the list any option that is unrealistic, unworkable, dangerous, harmful, or unacceptable to a party. When the unacceptable options are removed, the mediator can focus on the options that are most likely to result in resolution. Another option would be for the mediator to ask which options are most likely to lead to resolution and then start with those options.

Once the mediators have identified workable options, they can test the options using a technique commonly called "reality testing."[115] This technique involves asking pointed questions regarding the feasibility of the options suggested, and it is described in more detail below.[116] The purpose of reality testing is to ensure that the solutions are workable, so the parties can make a lasting agreement. Mediators may also consider if the options satisfy the parties' underlying interests, meet stated needs, and are sustainable. For example, if a proposed settlement is complicated, the mediator might ask the parties questions about their dedication to a complicated plan and whether simpler ideas might better serve the parties. If the parties express dedication to the more complicated plan, then the mediator should defer to the parties' wishes.

---

112. Lenden Webb, *Brainstorming Meets Online Dispute Resolution*, 15 AM. REV. INT'L ARB. 337, 381 (2004).

113. Jamie Henikoff & Michael Moffitt, *Remodeling the Model Standards of Conduct for Mediators*, 2 HARV. NEGOT. L. REV. 87, 110 (1997).

114. Lela P. Love & Kimberlee K. Kovach, *ADR: An Eclectic Array of Processes, Rather Than One Eclectic Process*, 2000 J. DISP. RESOL. 295, 304 (2000).

115. *Id.*

116. *See* § 4.06[D].

In caucus-based mediations, the mediators usually shuffle offers and counter-offers between the mediation rooms.[117] During those individual sessions, mediators may ask the parties questions about their BATNA, other alternatives, "bottom line," concession strategy, and any number of other considerations. In mediations primarily revolving around the payment of money, the mediator will often try to shrink and ultimately close the numeric gap until the parties reach a final dollar amount. Mediators can also try to work with additional, non-monetary options, such as letters of recommendation, apologies, or employment or business opportunities, to name a few. Ultimately, this portion of the mediation is all about choosing a suitable option and making sure that the option the parties choose is feasible.

[c] Agreement Drafting

If the parties come to an agreement, the next portion of the mediation involves drafting the contract or ensuring that someone else, usually a lawyer, will draft the contract after the session. How the drafting occurs is a style preference for most mediators.

Some mediators prefer to draft the agreement in the room and have the parties sign it before they leave the session.[118] In some situations, like small claims court, the agreement may be drafted by hand and then signed by the parties. In other situations, the mediator will bring or have access to a computer and printer in order to type an agreement on the spot. Numerous advantages exist for drawing up an agreement in the moment at the session.[119] If an agreement is drafted then and there, the parties will leave the session knowing that they have agreed to something. The parties can jointly work on the language of the agreement, rather than allowing one party to fill in its own "boilerplate" later. Having an agreement in writing might give the parties a good sense of closure and certainty going forward. Drafting the agreement "on site" is not without some downsides, however.[120] First, wordsmithing a contract can be a laborious and time-consuming process. Laboring over specific language could create unnecessary tension and may destroy any agreements reached. Depending on the length and circumstances in the session, parties may later try to rescind the agreement on the basis of undue pressure or similar challenges.

Other mediators will ask the parties if they would like to draft the agreement after the session and take care of ensuring that the resulting agreement is fully executed. If the parties are represented, one of the attorneys may offer to draft the agreement after the session is over. Whether an attorney should offer to draft a mediated agreement is discussed in more detail in Chapter 6.[121] Attorneys who draft an agreement after the session have the opportunity to use their own standard terms, or boilerplate, into the settlement agreement.[122] The parties may be able to think more deeply and have time to reflect on an agreement drafted after the session because they will be less hurried and

---

117. Richard M. Calkins, Esq., *Mediation: A Revolutionary Process That Is Replacing the American Judicial System*, 13 Cardozo J. Conflict Resol. 1, 47 (2011).

118. *Id.*

119. David Plimpton, *Mediation of Disputes: The Role of the Lawyer and How Best to Serve the Client's Interest*, 8 Me. B.J. 38, 46 (1993).

120. Michael S. Wilk & Rik H. Zafar, *Mediation of A Bankruptcy Case*, 22 Am. Bankr. Inst. J. 12, 58 (2003).

121. *See infra* Chapter 6.

122. *See generally*, R. W. Thorpe & Jennifer Boyens, *Mediation Settlement Agreements: Legal, Ethical, and Practical Issues*, 16 Alternatives To High Cost Litig. 93 (1998).

pressured.[123] On the other hand, parties may back out of the agreement if nothing is signed at the session.[124] The element of time may actually work against agreement if one or more parties have cold feet.

For mediators who allow the parties to draft the agreement after the session, those mediators will often draft a "Memorandum of Agreement" to memorialize the understandings of the parties.[125] The purpose of such memorandum is to set forth the major points of agreement while allowing for the details to be filled in at a later date. In many jurisdictions, however, a memorandum of agreement is not a contract and does not hold up in a court of law if one party seeks enforcement of the agreement.[126] Although a memorandum of agreement may not be legally binding, it will aid the parties in drafting the contract when they undertake it at a later date. Another option is that the mediator can draft the agreement for the parties after the mediation session. When the mediator drafts the agreement, the parties will be required to pay the mediator for the time spent drafting, but if one party drafts the agreement, only that party will pay his or her lawyer to draft the agreement.

[3] Impasse Breaking

Although not technically a "phase," parties often head toward impasse and mediators can use a variety of techniques in order to put the mediation back on track. Certainly, not every mediation can or will result in a settlement, but most mediators will not simply throw in the towel if the mediator senses that progress can still be made. Mediators can terminate a session if one or more parties are completely unwilling to proceed, but sometimes these impasse-breaking techniques will keep the parties working toward settlement.

Impasse occurs when the parties are no longer making progress.[127] Impasse is actually quite common within a mediation session, and impasses may occur multiple times throughout the course of a mediation. Impasse, standing alone, is not failure. Another way to think about impasse is that the parties have become "stuck" in the mediation. Often, impasse occurs when the parties claim to have reached their respective "bottom lines" or when parties cannot agree on the resolution of a certain issue. Breaking impasse, then, requires the mediator to find a way around the sticking point and help the parties back into moving forward with progress.

Often, the key to breaking impasse is by changing something in the mediation. When the parties appear to be at impasse, the mediator could call a break and give people some time to think, call a trusted friend or advisor, or simply have a cigarette break. If impasse is reached near a meal time, the mediator could call a break for lunch or dinner. The parties could have a meal together,[128] or the parties could dine separately. Rather

---

123. *Id.*

124. Wilk & Zafa, *supra* note 132.

125. Thorpe & Boyens, *supra* note 135.

126. *See, e.g.,* Golding v. Floyd, 261 Va. 190, 539 S.E.2d 735 (2001); Cabarrus Cty. v. Systel Bus. Equip. Co., 171 N.C. App. 423, 614 S.E.2d 596 (2005); U.S. S.E.C. v. Halek, 537 Fed. Appx. 576 (5th Cir. 2013).

127. Peter Guyon Earle, *The Impasse Doctrine*, 64 Chi.-Kent L. Rev. 407, 409 (1988).

128. Breaking bread eventually led to an agreement after the NFL's 2011 labor dispute between owners and players. Mark Grabowski, *Both Sides Win: Why Using Mediation Would Improve Pro Sports*, 5 Harv. J. Sports & Ent. L. 189, 209 (2014).

than taking a break, the mediator could also call a caucus (if the parties were previously in joint session) in order to ask them each separately about the reasons for the impasse.

Sometimes, when parties reach impasse on one subject, the mediator may change the subject and see if headway can be made in a different area.[129] Consider a family mediation involving issues of parenting time, property division, and child support. If the parties are stuck on the issue of property division, the mediator might want to try to discuss issues relating to the children and parenting time. If the parties make headway on the parenting time issue, they may be ready to discuss and reach settlement on the property division issue. Similar to changing the subject, the mediator might try to combine issues or break issues apart in order to find agreement. In the family law context, if the parties cannot agree on the issue of child support standing alone, the mediator may try to have a discussion about child support *and* parenting time together to see if the mediator can package an agreement regarding when the children reside with which parent and the financial repercussions of both of those issues combined. In other contexts, breaking issues into smaller components can help generate party agreement. Again, in the family context, if the parents disagree on who will make important decisions for the children (i.e., the global issue of "legal custody"), a mediator may be able to talk about specific types of decisions and determine whether one parent or the other should make those decisions. In some families, one parent may want to be in charge of the decisions regarding education or religion, while the other parent might be most interested in making decisions on health care or choice of daycare. By breaking the issues down into more manageable and concrete issues, the mediator may be able to generate agreement.

In disputes involving money, mediators also have a wide variety of "gap bridging" measures when the impasse involves one party asking for more money than the other party is willing to pay. The parties may claim that they have reached their respective "bottom lines," but mediators can use varying techniques to move away from these claimed "bottom lines" and reach agreement on an amount in the middle.[130] One way to try to bridge the gap is to simply see if the parties are willing to split the difference and meet in the numerical middle of the last offers.[131] Another option would be to ask the parties to make significant, simultaneous moves to see if settlement discussions could be continued—a technique sometimes called "bracketing."[132] For instance, if the parties are stuck at the plaintiff demanding $250,000 and the defendant willing to pay $200,000, a mediator might try to get a simultaneous move that the plaintiff would accept $230,000 if the defendant also agreed to pay $220,000. If both parties agree, then the parties will have closed the gap $40,000 and can continue negotiating the last $10,000 gap. In another version of bracketing, the mediator may have the parties agree that the parties can give 'blind bids' and if those bids are within the agreed range, the mediation will continue. Again, assume that the plaintiff is at $250,000 and the defendant is at $200,000. The parties agree that they will submit blind proposals to the mediator (i.e., not exchanged with the other party), and they agree that if the proposals are within $10,000 of each other, they will continue negotiating. If the plaintiff submits a blind proposal of $230,000 and the defendant submits a blind proposal of $220,000, then the mediator

---

129. *See supra* 4.05[C][1].

130. Kristen M. Blankley, *10 Things I Wish The Mediator Asked Me. . . . None of Which Are "What Is Your Bottom Line?* Nebraska Mediation Association's Mediator Minute 1 (2012).

131. James J. Alfini, *Trashing, Bashing and Hashing it Out: Is This the End of "Good Mediation?* 19 FLA. ST. U. L. REV. 47, 66–75 (1991).

132. Joan Stearns Johnsen, *Understanding Impasse: How to Prevent, Avoid and Break Deadlock,* 20 PIABA B.J. 373, 381 (2013).

would reveal the proposals and the parties would continue negotiating. If, on the other hand, the plaintiff submitted a blind bid of $235,000 and the defendant submitted a blind bid of $220,000, the mediator would keep both bids secret and the mediation would end in impasse. Creative mediators likely have other methods for moving parties toward resolution in cases revolving around money.

[D] Closure and Post-Mediation

The final phase of the mediation session is closure. Closure is an important step, whether or not the session ends in an agreement. The session must be closed if there is agreement or impasse. Mediators should close the session in a way that is respectful of the parties. The formality of closure can help the parties feel as if the process is legitimate. How the session is closed might vary depending on the progress made or not made during the session.

If the parties reach agreement, the mediator should congratulate the parties and review the terms of the agreement.[133] The mediator should review with the parties any next steps, if applicable, such as the process for getting parties final documents (if they are not drafted and distributed at the session) and ensuring compliance with any upcoming deadlines.[134] If the mediator is tasked with drafting the agreement after the session, the mediator should remind the parties how and when the mediator will deliver the draft for signature.

If the parties do not reach agreement, the mediator should still compliment the parties, thank them for coming to mediation, and review the progress they made during the session.[135] In the overwhelming majority of mediations, progress does take place, and the parties and their attorneys can build on that progress after the session. In most mediations, the parties learn new information that can inform their ability to settle the case at a later date, or the parties can agree to provide additional, necessary information after the session. If necessary, the mediator can schedule a later session with the parties or simply remind the parties that the mediator may be available to assist the parties at a later date.

Whether or not settlement is reached, the mediator may have logistical items to discuss with the parties at this point. Some mediators like to have parties fill out surveys regarding the mediation process as a method of self-assessment and self-improvement.[136] Mediators may need to collect payment for the session or review with the parties how the fees for the session will be billed. In cases involving co-mediation, the co-mediators can debrief with each other after the mediation to discuss how the session evolved and how the co-mediators can grow in their skills.

This overview of the mediation process highlights how mediations can occur, but parties and advocates may experience the mediation process in a different order or focused on different objectives than those mentioned here.

---

133. Ann Begler, *Mediation Sessions: Philosophy and Structure*, 3 Lawyers J. 4 (2001).

134. Susan T. Mackenzie, *Mediator's Perspective on Effective Mediation Advocacy, A*, 12 Prac. Litig. 17, 34 (2001).

135. Jerry M. Slusky, *Mediating the Commercial Lease Dispute*, 24 Prac. Real Est. Law. 9, 18 (2008).

136. John Lande, Lawyering with Planned Early Negotiation: How You Can Get Good Results for Clients and Make Money 143 (ABA Publishing, 2015).

§ 4.06 Mediation Techniques

While the previous section highlighted the typical mediation process, this section considers the specific techniques that mediators use during the process. Because mediation is a fluid process, mediators will choose among the tools in the "toolbox." Some mediations will call for a great number of different tools and techniques, while other mediations may not. Because mediators have different philosophical ideas about the proper role of the mediator, some mediators use certain techniques that fit within their mediator philosophy but not others. The discussion of mediator styles, sometimes described as "mediator orientations" is detailed in the next section.[137]

The techniques listed below are among the most common performed by mediators. Mediation is an innovative and flexible practice, so techniques that are not described here may be used in individual cases or developed over time. The purpose of this section is to be exemplary of tools often employed in mediation.

[A] Questions

Questions are the stock-in-trade of every mediator. During the course of a mediation, the mediator will likely ask more questions than make declarative statements. Questions serve many functions and are extraordinarily useful during mediation. This section covers the many different types of questions that mediators use, the "T-funneling" technique, and some of the dangers that questions may pose.

One common way to characterize questions is to divide them between "closed-ended" questions and "open-ended" questions. Closed-ended questions are those that elicit a "yes" or "no" answer.[138] Open-ended questions allow the speaker to give a narrative, a list, or other type of free flow of information.[139] Consider a case involving sexual harassment in the workplace, and the mediator wants to learn more about the working environment. If the mediator asks the plaintiff, "Did you feel like your employer discriminated against you?" the mediator will likely receive a "yes" or a "no" answer. While this answer yields some important information, the mediator may discover even more useful information from an open-ended question, such as, "What about the working environment made you feel like the victim of discrimination?" This open-ended question will more likely yield a narrative of the different reasons why the plaintiff initiated the legal action.

Closed-ended questions and open-ended questions each serve an important role in mediation. Open-ended questions, in the abstract, are not necessarily "better" than closed-ended questions, or vice versa. Instead, they each serve a different purpose. The skilled mediator understands how these questions are used and chooses the question to ask based on the type of information the mediator hopes to gain.

Open-ended questions are a good tool for gathering a large amount of information. Open-ended questions generally start with words like "who," "what," "where," "when,"

---

137. *See infra* Section 4.07.
138. Thomas D. Lyon, *Interviewing Children*, 10 ANN. REV. L. & SOC. SCI. 73, 78 (2014).
139. *Id.* at 79.

"why," and "how."[140] In addition to these questions, imperative statements, such as "Tell me more about . . ." or "Describe in more detail . . . ." can also serve the same purpose of gathering a large amount of information.[141] Open-ended questions are efficient, and they allow the parties to frame the dispute in the narrative of their choice. These types of questions are also non-threatening; and psychologically, open-ended questions give parties the chance to be heard in their own words and their own voice.[142] Open-ended questions also serve the underlying goal of party empowerment by putting the power of the narrative in the hands of the parties.

Open-ended questions can be used to gather many kinds of information. These questions can be used to learn factual information, allow parties to express emotional content, discover underlying interests, and generate options and solutions, among numerous other purposes. Allowing free narrative can help inform not only the mediator, but also the other party at the table.[143] The parties may not have had an opportunity to truly listen to one another before the mediation, and these questions may open the lines of communication.

Closed-ended questions also serve an important function in the mediation process. These questions can efficiently elicit short responses in order to cover a significant amount of information in a short amount of time.[144] Closed-ended questions can solidify information, especially if a party's answers are wavering or otherwise unclear. Yes/No questions can also be used to confirm or summarize information. For example, a mediator could summarize what the mediator believes a party may have said, followed by, "Did I summarize that correctly?" or "Do I have that right?" If the party says "yes," the party will hopefully feel heard by the mediator, and if the party says "no," the mediator can go back and clarify where he or she went wrong.

Law-trained mediators may have a tendency to ask more closed-ended questions than other mediators. Lawyers are generally trained the art of asking specific, closed-ended questions during the course of deposition and trial practice.[145] Mediators, unlike advocates, should not fear the open-ended question because the information received usually does not hurt the mediation process in the same way an ill-advised question may hurt a client's adversarial position.

One common questioning technique is called "T-Funneling." The T-Funneling technique starts with a broad, open-ended question that is intended to elicit a number of topics.[146] For example, the mediator could ask the plaintiff, "What are the sources of the damages that you are asking for here?" The plaintiff then responds with a list of types of damages, such as medical bills, lost past wages, lost future wages, and pain and suffering. The mediator continues to ask questions like "what other damages have you suffered?" until the plaintiff agrees that the list is exhaustive. Once the list of topics is

---

140. Nancy Neal Yeend, *Are Mediation Settlement Rates Linked to Advocate Competency?*, 11 Nev. Law. 16, 17 (2003).

141. *Id.*

142. Alexander S. Polsky, *10 Tips to Make Mediation Work*, 51 Orange County Law. 30, 31 (2009).

143. Justin S. Teff, *Human Memory Is Far More Fallible and Malleable Than Most Recognize*, 76 N.Y. St. B.J. 38, 41 (2004).

144. *See generally*, Scott Jensen, *Questions that Count*, 6 CPA Prac. Mgmt. F. 5, 8 (2010).

145. Lisa Blue et al., *Effective 30-Minute Voir Dire in a Criminal Case: The Good, the Bad, and the Ugly*, 73 Tex. B.J. 534, 536 (2010).

146. David Binder et al., Lawyers as Counselors: A Client-Centered Approach 167–73 (2004).

created, the mediator will start with one topic and begin to ask open-ended questions about that topic.[147] The mediator might ask, "What medical expenses have you incurred?" The mediator will then ask follow-up questions in that topic. When the mediator thinks that the topic is exhausted, the mediator will summarize and use a closed-ended question to determine if the summary is correct.[148] If the summary is correct, the mediator will ask whether there is any anything the party would like to add.[149] If not, then the mediator moves to the next topic and starts the process again. T-Funneling is a comprehensive technique that utilizes both open- and closed-ended questions to exhaustively cover a topic. In a mediation, this technique might be time-consuming, and the mediator should be careful to ensure that all of the parties to the mediation are incorporated into the conversation.

Although questions are considered a "low-risk" type of technique, some dangers exist in asking questions. Some parties do not like to give long answers, and they might be uncomfortable answering open-ended questions. Close-ended questions, especially if made in succession to one party, might make a party feel defensive or as if that party is being cross-examined. Poorly worded questions may indicate a bias (real or perceived) in favor of a party. In rare cases, questions might also signal to the parties that the mediator is uninformed or not properly prepared, thus causing the parties to lose trust in the mediation process.

Despite the downsides, questions are a key technique for mediators. They elicit a large amount of information. Because information development and exchange is such a large part of the mediation process, asking and answering questions will occur throughout the entire session. Usually, parties are willing and happy to answer the questions, giving the parties a true voice in the mediation process. As discussed above, questions play a key role throughout the process. Questions begin the process of the parties' opening remarks (i.e., "What brings you to mediation today?") and is crucial during the information-gathering phase. Questions regarding the issues, interests, and agenda items ensure clarity and buy-in from the parties during the middle portions of the mediation. When the parties engage in problem-solving, the mediator will ask questions to generate, test, and finalize options for the parties. The mediation process only concludes when the mediator questions the parties about their willingness to settle or to conclude the session. In all, questions are omnipresent in mediation.

[B] Active Listening

Active listening is a broad term for a number of different techniques intended to demonstrate to the parties that the mediator is interested, paying attention, and truly listening to the parties. The techniques under this umbrella generally include a "feedback loop" in order to check back in with the parties in order to ensure that the mediator understands what the parties are saying and how the parties are feeling.[150] Good active listening can help parties feel heard and understood, and these techniques can foster buy-in and comfort in the process. Common active listening techniques include positive body language,

---

147. *Id.*
148. *Id.*
149. *Id.*
150. Robert E. Lee Wright, *Mediator Listening Skills for All Attorneys*, 89 MICH. B.J. 32, 33 (2010).

allowing silent times in the mediation, clarifying, summarizing, rephrasing, and acknowledging feelings. These techniques are discussed in turn.

Careful mediators are aware of their body language and the messages that body language sends to the parties. Open body language, such as arms uncrossed, signals that the mediator is open to listening.[151] Head nodding (while sometimes mistaken for agreement) is generally understood to be acknowledgment of hearing what the speaker is saying.[152] Eye contact with the parties also shows that a mediator is paying attention to the parties.[153] Mediators who take notes during the session balance notetaking with making meaningful eye contact and nonverbal communication with the parties.

The mediator's physical location may also be used as a nonverbal signal. Some mediators like to physically push away from the table if the parties are communicating well with each other. The mediator in that situation is physically removing him- or herself from the table as a signal that the parties can continue to communicate on their own. When the parties are not communicating well, the mediator may take an opposite tactic and physically move between the parties or act as a buffer. Good non-verbal communication by a mediator is often unnoticed by the parties. The converse, however, is not always true. If the mediator does not maintain good non-verbal communication with the participants, the parties may consider the mediator to be bored, uninterested, or worse.

Another technique of active listening is to allow for silence, when appropriate. Many people are uncomfortable with silence and try to fill in the silence with talking. When mediators become comfortable with silence in the room, the parties or their advocates will often fill that silence with additional information. Silence following the answer to a question may lead to additional information if the mediator is not too quick to jump in and reply.

When mediators do not understand something said by a party, they can ask simple clarifying questions. These types of clarifying questions demonstrate that the mediator is interested, paying attention, and wants to be clear as to the information being conveyed. Clarifying questions, such as "What did you mean by . . . ?" are a simple way to avoid assumptions and ensure a common understanding for everyone at the table. These types of questions may be particularly appropriate when parties use jargon, terms of art, acronyms, or when the mediator simply could not understand the words spoken. When the parties are in joint session, clarifying questions may ensure that all of the parties are on the same page because they will all hear the clarifying answers. Sometimes mediators will ask clarifying questions for the sake of the other party, even when the mediator already knows the answer to the question.[154] If a mediator senses that another person in the room is not following what the speaker is saying, the mediator can seek to clarify for others. Little risk attends clarifying questions, other than the risk of appearing as if the mediator is not paying attention, is uninformed, or ill prepared.

Summarizing what a party has said is another active listening technique. Summaries can occur at any number of points during the mediation. Often, the first time that

---

151. Sheldon E. Friedman, *The Basics of Effective Mediation*, 38 COLO. LAW. 73, 76 (2009).

152. Alan Krause, *Striking Accord: Composing a High Quality and Meaningful Mediation*, 33 U. LA VERNE L. REV. 147, 158 (2011).

153. *Id.* at 157.

154. Gregory D. Hoffmann, *Applying Principles of Leadership Communication to Improve Mediation Outcomes*, 64 DISP. RESOL. J. 24, 28 (2009).

mediators summarize is following both parties' opening remarks. Some mediators will summarize each party's statement separately, while others like to combine the statements into a "third story" on which both parties can agree.[155] Mediators often summarize after a party gives a long narrative answer to a question that was asked. Some mediators will give a summary of "where we are" in the mediation, especially as the mediation moves from one phase to the next. For instance, the mediator might summarize the factual history after the information-gathering phase before moving into problem solving. As another example, a mediator may summarize the terms of an agreement that the parties appear to have reached to ensure that the mediator and parties are all on the same page. As with asking clarifying questions, summarizing is generally a low-risk technique. If the mediator incorrectly summarizes, the parties may correct the mediator. A mediator runs a slight risk of appearing incompetent for an incorrect summary, but most mediators can brush off an incorrect summary or apologize for not understanding correctly.

Finally, mediators can label the underlying feelings of the parties as a technique to identify and validate emotions. Acknowledging the underlying feelings may signal to the parties that the mediator is listening and cares about how the dispute is making them feel. In some cases, the parties may be at impasse because of unacknowledged feelings, and validating the feelings may help the parties move toward resolution.[156] Mediators can acknowledge feelings with phrases such as "I hear that this situation has made you frustrated and angry," or "It sounds like you felt despair when you suddenly lost your job." Often, the parties will respond with an affirmation that the mediator was correct, and some parties are exceptionally grateful for having someone understand the emotional content of the dispute.[157] As with the other types of active listening, the mediator takes some risk of misidentifying the feelings. In addition, some parties may shy away from a discussion of feelings.

In many mediations, parties may use words or phrases that are not helpful to the settlement process. Parties may use heated or inflammatory language, insult each other, or engage in other types of harmful communication. Some mediators will simply ignore these types of comments. Other mediators will use the technique of rephrasing. When a mediator rephrases, that mediator will reflect back the idea of the parties, but use less inflammatory language.[158] For example, if one party calls the other a "stubborn jerk," the mediator could rephrase and say, "I hear you saying that you think that your neighbor is set in his ways." The mediator could use this type of technique in order to set an example of the type of respectful language that the parties should be using in the session.[159] But the rephrase still tries to capture the feeling that the speaking party feels, albeit in more subdued language. Rephrasing has the benefit of keeping the conversation civil and "coming to the defense" of the insulted party. On the other hand, the party whose words are rephrased may feel insulted that the mediator has "watered down" the content that the speaking party expressed.[160]

---

155. *Id.*

156. *Id.*

157. Russell M. Ware, *"I'm Too Mad to Settle!" Working with Angry Plaintiffs in A Mediation*, 81 Wis. Law. 16, 18 (2008).

158. John M. Livingood, *Reframing and Its Uses*, 57 Disp. Resol. J. 42, 47 (2003).

159. *Id.* at 42.

160. *Id.*

These active listening techniques utilize varying levels of mediator intrusiveness, and they are presented here in order of least intrusive to most intrusive. Mindfulness of body language and utilizing silence require the mediator to do very little and leave the mediation in the hands of the parties. Clarifying and summarizing involve the mediator interjecting into the process, but not in an intrusive manner. Identifying feelings and rephrasing, although still subtle, require the mediator to draw conclusions and put words in the mouths of the parties. All of these techniques have value, but the astute mediator will be careful to only use them as he or she feels comfortable.

Ultimately, these active listening techniques serve to aid understanding. Many mediators live out the saying: "Seek first to understand, and then to speak."[161] Mediators seek understanding both for themselves, as well as for the other participants. The purpose of the mediator is to aid communication, rather than to give advice or otherwise insert him- or herself into the conflict.

[C] Issue and Interest Identification

During the course of the mediation, mediators should be listening to determine the mediatable issues and the underlying interests of the parties. What constitutes a "mediatable issue" is described above.[162] During the course of the information-gathering phase, the mediator should be trying to determine what issues need to be addressed and ultimately solved. Those issues will then be put into an agenda and discussed in a logical manner.[163]

Mediators should also be mindful of interests, or the underlying motivations of the parties. Interests are described in greater detail in Chapter 3, Negotiation.[164] Through the use of active listening, mediators should be able to identify the interests the parties bring to the mediation. Some mediators will explicitly identify the issues for verification by the parties.[165] Other mediators will simply keep these interests in mind. Understanding the interests involved is particularly helpful in the problem-solving portion of the mediation. Mediators who have considered the interests can ask the parties whether certain options will meet the parties' needs. In addition, the mediators can help the parties generate options that specifically meet the underlying needs.

[D] Brainstorming

Brainstorming is a technique that allows the parties to generate a large number of potential options in a judgment-free environment. This technique is described above in the section on the problem-solving phase of the mediation.[166] In order to create the judgment-free environment, the mediator must take care to protect the space so the parties can participate in a meaningful way.

---

161. STEPHEN R. COVEY, 7 HABITS OF HIGHLY EFFECTIVE PEOPLE (1st Fireside ed. 1990). *See also* Peace Prayer of St. Francis at http://www.shrinesf.org/franciscan-prayer.html.

162. *Supra* 4.05[C][1].

163. *Supra* 4.05[C][2].

164. *See* Section 3.06 for a more thorough discussion about negotiation based on interests.

165. *See* Slusky, *supra* note 148, at 11.

166. *See supra* Section 4.05[C].

The brainstorming technique centers on separating out the creation of ideas from the evaluation of ideas. Mediators are usually explicit and set ground rules for this exercise. The most important rule is that the parties will first generate as many ideas as possible and then evaluate them after all of the options have been put on the table. Often, parties brainstorm by simply shouting out possibilities while the mediator records those options on a piece of paper or a whiteboard.[167] The mediator usually encourages any and all options, including crazy options, impossible options, unworkable options, unacceptable options, and wild options. Allowing for great creativity in brainstorming may lead to options that are workable and desirable. Wild and crazy ideas may ultimately yield practical and useful ideas.

The brainstorming session need not be done with the parties together or aloud. The mediator can set up the same ground rules and gather a wide variety of options from parties in different rooms. If the parties feel uncomfortable suggesting options aloud, the mediator could offer the parties note cards or pieces of paper so that the parties can think and write down options. Those options can then be shared with all parties with or without attribution.

Of course, not all parties enjoy brainstorming. Some people do not consider themselves creative. Others have difficulty refraining from evaluation while the parties are supposed to be generating options. People may be hesitant to suggest options to which they would never agree out of a worry that they will be misinterpreted as endorsing their own ideas. Whether brainstorming is appropriate depends on the parties to the dispute and their comfort level. Mediators who want to employ this technique can always describe it to the parties and see if they are willing to try it.

[E] Reality Testing

The reality-testing technique was first described above in Section 4.05[C][2], on making decisions in mediation.[168] Reality testing occurs when a mediator asks serious questions about the parties' proposed solution to ensure that it is workable and desirable. Reality-testing questions are often close-ended questions, with the mediator seeking confirmation that the parties are ready, willing, and able to accept the terms presented.

Reality-testing questions can be used to determine whether a solution is reasonable, feasible, meets party interests, and is capable of being completed.[169] Consider the following example. A former employer sues a former employee for failure to return the company phone. At the mediation, the mediator learns that the phone has been destroyed and that the employee attempted to replace the phone with a refurbished phone that the employer found to be unacceptable. At the conclusion of the mediation, the parties have a tentative agreement that the former employee will identify four or five potential replacement phones. Then the employee will email the potential choices to the former employer. The employer will then choose one, and the employee will purchase the phone. When the phone arrives, the employee agrees to give it to the former employer.

A mediator would likely have a lot of different reality-testing questions for this potential agreement. The mediator may ask whether the parties, who appear to have a strained

---

167. David E. Spencer & Michael Brogan, Mediation Law and Practice 65 (2007).
168. *See supra* Section 4.05[C][2][b].
169. Kovach, *supra* note 126.

relationship, are willing to work with each other through all of these steps in order to put the situation behind them. The mediator might ask questions about the time limits on each of these steps and the financial constraints under which the parties are operating. The mediator will also need to ask questions about what will happen if any of these steps fails. How will the parties deal with unexpected circumstances over the course of the agreement?

The purpose of reality testing is to create lasting and workable agreements. Mediators hope that parties actually adhere to agreements reached during the mediation session. Although mediators generally do not engage in follow-up to ensure that the parties follow the terms of the agreement, the reality-testing technique helps the parties think through the consequences of potential agreements before any agreement is drafted and signed.

[F] Breaking and Caucusing

Breaks and caucuses are two different techniques that can be helpful, especially if the mediation is not progressing well. When the mediator calls a break, all parties, including the mediator, take some time off, and the mediator is not working with any party. In contrast, a caucus is a private meeting between the mediator and a subset of the participants. Usually, a caucus involves a meeting between the mediator and one side, but mediators can also caucus with just clients, just lawyers, all of the plaintiffs or defendants in a multi-party case, or only certain parties and their attorneys.

Breaks can serve many important purposes in mediation. Sometimes breaks are called for hospitality reasons, such as bathroom, smoking, or meal breaks. Parties to a mediation should be comfortable, and breaking can give the parties a certain amount of relief from the session.[170] Breaks can be helpful if the tensions in mediation run high. Some mediators will call a break if the exchange between the parties becomes heated or potentially dangerous.[171] The break, then, serves as a "cooling off" period. Sometimes parties need a break in order to confer on how to proceed. They can use mediation breaks to make telephone calls to lawyers, family members, or other trusted advisors. Mediators, too, can use breaks in order to assess the mediation session and regroup as necessary.

Sometimes, a mediator may call a break to have the parties go home for the night and reconvene at a later date.[172] Breaking the mediation into multiple sessions may give the parties time to do necessary research, talk with loved ones or attorneys, think more deeply about the situation, or formulate new options. Depending on the availability of the mediator, parties, and attorneys, the next session could be scheduled the next day or within the next few weeks or even months.

A mediator may call a caucus session for many of the same reasons that a mediator would call a break. The difference, however, is that the mediator will meet privately with each of the parties before returning to joint session, if they return to joint session at all. During a caucus, parties feel more free to tell the mediator potentially adverse information because the party will not be making admissions in front of the other party. The mediator, too, may feel more free to empathize with the parties without appearing biased.

---

170. Michael Schofield, *Practice & Professionalism Tips from A Mediator, Arbitrator and Appraiser*, 25 TRIAL ADVOC. Q. 6, 9 (2006).

171. Safety issues in mediation are discussed in Section 5.04[C].

172. *See supra* note 187.

Caucusing can be particularly helpful when parties are showing signs that they are getting uncomfortable in joint session. Verbal cues such as "I don't really want to talk about that," or nonverbal cues of discomfort may cause a mediator to break the parties apart and talk to them separately. The mediator can then use the caucus as a safe space for the parties to talk about the uncomfortable information. The mediator and the party can jointly decide whether to disclose this information to the other side or keep the information private.

Caucusing can also be helpful when the parties are negotiating. Some parties do not like to negotiate in front of the other party, so a mediator can use caucusing to facilitate shuttle diplomacy between them. Mediators can often ask harder questions of the parties in a caucus, whether they are reality testing or trying to help a party realistically assess the settlement value of a case. Because the other side is not present, the mediator does not appear biased when speaking with one party, and the party can freely respond to tough questions when the other party is not in the room.

Despite its benefits, significant drawbacks may exist to using the caucus structure. At a purely practical level, caucusing in mediation extends the time of the mediation considerably. The mediator generally only works with one party at a time, and working with the parties individually greatly lengthens the time that the mediation takes.[173] In addition, because the mediator works with the parties one at a time, the party who is not meeting with the mediator may have a significant amount of down time during the course of the session.[174] If attorneys are at the mediation, attorneys and clients can discuss the mediation on their own while the mediator is working with the other party. Otherwise, a party may need to bring a book, magazine, or other work in order to pass the time and not enter into "crazy think."[175] Some mediators avoid caucusing because caucusing creates an informational asymmetry.[176] Unlike joint session, when all parties hear what the other party is sharing, the caucus style of mediation involves the mediator knowing all of the information and then the mediator distilling or summarizing the information (that is allowed to be shared) to the other party.

[G] Evaluating and Giving Opinions

Although the evaluative style of mediation is discussed in more detail below,[177] mediators who do not self-identify as "evaluative" may still use evaluative techniques. A mediator "evaluates" when the mediator gives an evaluation or an opinion on something in the mediation — usually the merits of a case.[178]

Evaluative mediators must have expertise — usually legal expertise — in order to give informed opinions. Most mediators who give evaluations are attorneys or former judges who have a lot of experience trying cases in the same area of law in which they

---

173. Richard M. Calkins, Esq., *Mediation: A Revolutionary Process That Is Replacing the American Judicial System*, 13 Cardozo J. Conflict Resol. 1, 47 (2011).

174. Larry C. Hunter, *Mediation — Behind Closed Doors*, 49 Advocate 24, 25 (2006).

175. Tom Arnold, *Twenty-Two Client Preparation Pointers for Mediation*, 8 Prac. Litig. 35, 40 (1997).

176. *See* Robert A. Creo, *Mediation 2004: The Art and the Artist*, 108 Penn St. L. Rev. 1017, 1061 (2004).

177. See infra Section 4.7[B].

178. *See generally,* Jeffrey W. Stempel, *The Inevitability of the Eclectic: Liberating ADR from Ideology*, 2000 J. Disp. Resol. 247, 248 (2000).

mediate. The parties can trust the evaluations because of the background of the mediator.

Mediators may be asked to give opinions on any number of aspects of the case. Mediators may evaluate the settlement value of a case, the likelihood of victory of a particular cause of action, the credibility of a party as a witness, the likelihood of evidence or an expert witness being admitted as evidence, the chance of success on appeal, and the collectability of a judgment, among numerous other questions that may arising during the course of a litigated case.

Some parties need mediator evaluations in order to fill informational gaps. Often, parties to a legal dispute cannot resolve their case because the plaintiff's and defendant's sides have highly varying ideas of what the case is "worth." A plaintiff and defendant, knowing the exact same information (which never actually happens) may still have widely divergent views of the value of the case. Even with the same information, the plaintiff may view the case as a $200,000 case, and the defendant may view the case as worth only the $50,000 it would cost the lawyers to defend it. If asked in caucus, the plaintiff might view her chance of success at trial to be 75 percent. When the mediator asks the defendant the same question, the defendant may assess his chance of winning at 50 percent. A mediator, after hearing all of this information, could make an independent assessment of the situation and recommend a settlement option to the parties.

One specific type of evaluation is the practice of making a "mediator's proposal." The mediator's proposal almost always occurs at the end of a mediation that appears to be heading toward impasse.[179] A mediator's proposal is a suggestion by the mediator, usually in writing, of a single settlement value that the mediator believes the parties may both accept in order to settle the case. Sometimes a mediator will make a mediator's proposal after the parties have asked the mediator to do so. In other instances, the mediator will offer the possibility of making a proposal and obtain the parties' consent prior to making the recommendation.[180] The mediator's proposal is essentially a recommendation made to both parties based on the mediator's judgment after hearing everything the parties have presented up to that point in time. Mediators may use a variety of criteria in making the proposal, including the value of the case and the likelihood that the parties would settle on a certain solution. The parties are under no obligation to accept the mediator's proposal, and if one or more parties reject the proposal, the mediation ends in impasse.

Some mediators are known by advertisement or reputation as those willing to give opinions. Other mediators will only give opinions if asked. Few mediators will give legal evaluations to pro se parties out of fear that the pro se party will mistake the evaluation for legal advice.[181] Mediators should tell counsel in advance if the mediator plans on giving an evaluation so they can adjust their advocacy styles accordingly. As discussed in Chapter 6, advocates will present their cases differently if the parties

---

179. Stephen A. Hochman, *A Mediator's Proposal—Whether, When, and How It Should Be Used*, MEDIATE (Feb. 2012) at http://www.mediate.com/mobile/article.cfm?id=8503 (discussing pros and cons).

180. *Id.*

181. *See* MODEL RULES OF PROF'L CONDUCT r. 2.4(b) ("A lawyer serving as a third-party neutral shall inform unrepresented parties that the lawyer is not representing them. When the lawyer knows or reasonably should know that a party does not understand the lawyer's role in the matter, the lawyer shall explain the difference between the lawyer's role as a third-party neutral and a lawyer's role as one who represents a client.").

expect an evaluation.[182] Giving an evaluation is a mediator technique that is significantly more intrusive than the others described in this section. An evaluation will likely favor one party or the other, and the non-favored party may view the mediator as biased.

[H] Co-Mediation

Mediating with a co-mediator brings a number of advantages to the process, but also adds some complications. Co-mediation is not necessarily a technique, but a form of mediation that has some distinct pros and cons. Co-mediation usually involves a mediator pair that practice facilitative mediation. Because co-mediation is not particularly cost-effective, it is a model used most often in community mediation centers, as opposed to private mediation practice.

Co-mediation pairs can bring a lot of complementary skills to the table. Male/female co-mediators may be helpful in cases in which one party is a man and one party is a woman, such as in a divorce or sexual harassment case.[183] Mediators of different backgrounds or races might be able to relate to one party or another or bring an understanding of relevant cultural issues.[184] Mediators with different professional backgrounds may also be helpful. Pairing attorney mediators with mediators who are trained in counseling, psychology, or accounting may provide the parties with two valuable skill sets that could be helpful in resolving disputes.[185]

When two people mediate, the mediators have a chance to plan for the session, divide responsibilities, and help each other during the mediation. Although both mediators are in the same room, the two mediators may hear different things, pick up on different nonverbal cues, or understand the parties differently.[186] Two mediators can also model constructive communication for the parties to witness. With two mediators, less stress exists for tasks such as note taking and using visual aids, because one mediator can be attending to the parties while the other mediator is taking notes or writing on a flip chart or whiteboard. During the mediation, the mediators can check in with each other to discuss how the mediation is going and what next steps should be taken, if any. Co-mediators also have the opportunity to debrief following a mediation in order to learn from mistakes and grow from the mediation experience. For these reasons, co-mediation is also a good model for training new mediators because they are paired with more experienced mediators.[187]

Co-mediation is not without some drawbacks. If the co-mediators have competing styles or clash due to lack of preparation, the presentation by the mediators might be sloppy, fail to model constructive communication, or be disruptive to the process.[188]

---

182. *See infra* Chapter 6. When a lawyer participates in an evaluative mediation, the lawyer's goal will be to do everything possible to gain a positive evaluation. The lawyer can afford to be more open and forthcoming with the mediator if the lawyer knows that disclosing potentially harmful information will not be used to the disadvantage of the client.

183. Lee A. Rosengard, *Learning from Law Firms: Using Co-Mediation to Train New Mediators*, 59 Disp. Resol. J. 16, 18 (2004).

184. *Id.*

185. *Id.*

186. *Id.*

187. *Id.*

188. *See generally*, Joe Epstein & Susan Epstein, *Co-Mediation*, 35 Colo. Law. 21, 22 (2006).

Two mediators have the potential to be more expensive than one mediator, and coordinating with an extra person may make scheduling more difficult.[189] Co-mediation takes work because the co-mediators need to be attentive to the parties and the co-mediator, and everyone needs to be on the same page for the parties to make progress.

Although the co-mediation model is not standard among private mediators, community mediation centers have had significant success using this model.[190] The process offers benefits for the individual mediators, the parties, and the mediation system—and it is a viable alternative for mediation centers or collaborations among mediators.

§ 4.07 Mediation Styles

As mediation emerged within the dispute resolution community, significant theoretical research and analysis was conducted to better explain the various styles and types of mediation. One of the first influential individuals who described the differences in mediation styles was Leonard Riskin. Through Riskin's own research, assessment, and analysis of mediation, he introduced what he described as the "grid" system.[191] The Riskin grid uses two intersecting continuums to describe four types of mediator orientations.[192] These four mediator orientations are: evaluative narrow, evaluative broad, facilitative narrow, and facilitative broad, in each of their respective quadrants.[193] Evaluative mediators, who tend to focus on the strengths and weaknesses of a legal case, fall at one end of the continuum, as opposed to facilitative mediators, who help the parties communicate by facilitating a discussion without providing their own opinions of the case.[194] The other axis on the grid describes the breadth with which issues are discussed in a mediation, ranging from very narrow issues to extremely broad ones.[195] The narrow-to-broad spectrum describes how mediators define the problems that will be discussed. Some mediators focus on very narrow issues and only the stated topic, whereas other mediators will encourage the parties to delve further into their issues and interests surrounding the original issue that required mediation. For example, a family mediator adopting a narrow approach may only focus on the topic of developing a parenting plan and creating a schedule for the children during a mediation, while a mediator with a broad style encourages the parties to explore issues such as communication, the involvement of significant others, and the emotions the parties may hold toward each other. The four quadrants of the grid represent a mediator's overall "orientation," which helps mediators understand their own approaches and gives attorneys and clients

---

189. *Id.*

190. *Id.*

191. Leonard L. Riskin, *Mediator Orientations, Strategies and Techniques*, 12 ALTERNATIVES TO HIGH COST LITIGATION, 111 (1994); Leonard L. Riskin, *Understanding Mediators' Orientations Strategies, and Techniques: A Grid for the Perplexed*, 1 HARV. NEGOT. L. REV. 7 (1996).

192. Leonard L. Riskin, *Understanding Mediators' Orientations, Strategies, and Techniques: A Grid for the Perplexed*, 1 HARV. NEGOT. L. REV. 7 (1996).

193. *Id.* at 25.

194. Riskin, *supra* note 2, at 24.

195. *Id.*

the opportunity to choose mediators in the quadrant of the grid that they believe would best serve their needs.[196]

Although these original four categories helped present the idea of different mediator styles, Riskin acknowledged, after some misunderstandings by users and criticisms from colleagues, that the grid categories of mediator styles did not sufficiently represent the flexibility and varied approaches mediators employ in practice. Some mediators may be strictly facilitative or evaluative; however, other mediators may act in both a facilitative and evaluative way, depending on what is needed in a particular mediation.[197] In a single mediation, a mediator may be facilitative on one topic and evaluative on another.[198] Another issue with the grid dealt with describing evaluative mediators. An evaluative mediator may only tell clients which points of their argument are weak while another evaluative mediator may give an opinion on the exact amount of money they think someone's case is worth.[199] Riskin also garnered criticism for using the term *evaluative*. Instead, he realized "directive" may be a better term for describing how the mediator acts in mediation.[200] On the other grid's axis, the terms *broad* and *narrow* were also criticized. A broad discussion in mediation may also include a discussion of narrow topics.[201] While this spectrum did not receive as much criticism and was often ignored, it required some changes as well. The original Riskin grid was too simple, and did not allow for the many changes that occur throughout a mediation session.[202] This wide range of mediator types and styles was not captured on the original grid.

In order to address these issues and enhance the original grid beyond the four distinct quadrants, Riskin introduced a new grid.[203] Riskin proposed two types of changes to his original grid. The first was to replace the terms "facilitative" and "evaluative" with new terms: "elicitive" and "directive."[204] He felt these new terms better represented the wide range of mediator behaviors and represented a continuum that more closely represents the impact a mediator can have on the parties and their autonomy.[205] While Riskin embraced these changes to his old grid, he was not satisfied with the outcome.[206] Instead of only making these changes to the original, he created an all-new grid system to incorporate the many dynamics involved in mediation.[207]

Riskin's new system included a series of grids, which focus not only on the mediator but also on the parties.[208] The first change Riskin included was to divide mediation decision-making into three categories: substantive, procedural, and meta-procedural.[209] These categories allow for characterizations based on various styles such as which substantive issues will be addressed during the mediation and which procedural methods

---

196. Leonard L. Riskin, *Decisionmaking in Mediation: The New Old Grid and the New Grid System*, Notre Dame L. Rev. 79:1 (2003).
197. *Id.*
198. *Id.*
199. *Id.*
200. Riskin, *supra* note 6, at 20.
201. Riskin, *supra* note 6, at 23.
202. Riskin, *supra* note 6, at 29.
203. *Id.*
204. Riskin, *supra* note 6, at 30.
205. *Id.*
206. Riskin, *supra* note 6, at 33.
207. Riskin, *supra* note 6, at 34.
208. *Id.*
209. *Id.*

will be used to go about discussing them.[210] Riskin's new grids categorize the mediation as a process undertaken by a group, which involves the mediators and clients equally.[211] Viewing the mediation as a journey puts more control in the hands of the parties and allows the mediators to make decisions about which topics to discuss and when throughout the mediation.[212]

Despite the criticisms to the first Riskin grid, the mediation community and users of mediation services often identify according to a predominant style. The most common styles are facilitative, evaluative, and transformative. Other styles, such as narrative mediation, are continuing to emerge. These dominant mediation styles are discussed below in more detail.

[A] Facilitative Mediation

Facilitative mediation was the first style of mediation to emerge in the dispute resolution community. Many still refer to facilitative mediation as "classic mediation." The main focus of this type of mediation is on the parties and their interests. The philosophy underlying facilitative mediation is that a mediator is a "process expert" and understands how to promote discussion and communication between the parties.[213] Facilitative mediators avoid offering their own suggestions and opinions, relying on the parties to generate ideas and come up with options that will work with their situations.[214] Facilitative mediators use techniques and strategies that "allow the parties to communicate with and understand one another."[215] For example, facilitative mediators will allow the parties to direct the course of the mediation, asking the parties which topics they would like to discuss first. Facilitative mediators also encourage the parties to generate their own ideas and ask questions to help the parties realize whether their suggestions will work in the real world.

During a facilitative mediation, the parties are encouraged to voice their concerns and address any issues they have regarding the conflict at hand. Facilitative mediation often begins with both parties discussing issues in a joint session, but private sessions may be used as needed. The main idea behind a facilitative mediation process is that the parties know their situation best so they are in the best position to create solutions that will work for them.[216] The mediator's role is not to give insights or opinions as to what the outcome of the mediation should be, but to help the parties generate their own ideas and solutions. One benefit to the parties playing an active role in option generation and decision making is based on the theory that holding the parties accountable will encourage them to implement and stick to the plan they created.[217] Having ownership and a hand in the solution process encourages the parties to stick to their agreement.

Because the parties are encouraged to be highly involved in the process, facilitative mediators are focused on guiding the discussion of the parties rather than contributing

---

210. *Id.*

211. Riskin, *supra* note 6, at 51.

212. *Id.*

213. Albert Fiadjoe, Alternative Dispute Resolution: A Developing World Perspective 62 (2004).

214. John Lande, *Toward More Sophisticated Mediation Theory*, 2000 J. Disp. Resol. 322 (2000).

215. Riskin, *supra* note 2.

216. *Id.*

217. *Id.*

their own thoughts and opinions about the ideas and possible solutions. The role of facilitative mediators is to help the parties navigate the mediation process by facilitating the communication between the parties and provide them with a neutral environment in which to do so. Facilitative mediators encourage parties to communicate in a healthy and productive way by modeling appropriate communication and asking the right questions.[218] A facilitative mediator can assist the parties in identifying and recognizing the interests when the parties become too focused on expressing their immediate thoughts and concerns regarding the issues, often based on emotional responses and reactions to stress. Facilitative mediators use tools such as active listening, summarizing, asking open-ended questions, reality-testing ideas, and ensuring commitment to a potential settlement. These types of techniques emphasize party involvement and autonomy.

[B] Evaluative Mediation

In contrast to the interest-based approach in a facilitative model, evaluative mediation is a more direct and outcome-oriented approach. Evaluative mediation was developed and modeled after court settlement conferences, where judges would listen to the facts and issues and make a decision about each case.[219] An evaluative mediation style tends to have a more adversarial feel, which is especially true if attorneys are involved. The adversarial feel can also be the result of the role of the mediator, who brings experience to the table and may offer insights regarding the value of a case. Evaluative mediators often provide feedback, give assessments, and provide their own opinions about the strengths and weaknesses of each case.[220]

While facilitative mediations are often conducted in joint sessions with all parties in the same room, evaluative mediations are generally conducted in separate rooms, with the mediator "shuttling" back and forth between the parties.[221] This approach is more akin to a negotiation, with the mediator acting as both the messenger and evaluator of the case. The mediator may help each party to consider their respective legal positions and arguments and to assess how their case would likely play out in the courtroom. Parties may defer to the mediator and weigh their options to determine what would be most beneficial to them. Parties may decide to come to an agreement in mediation or take their case to court based on the opinions an evaluative mediator may provide. The focus in evaluative mediation is less on the parties discovering the interests behind the issues and more about the outcome of the case.

The role of an evaluative mediator is to assist the parties in valuing and discussing the possible outcomes. Without providing direct opinions or rulings on each case, an evaluative mediator may provide opinions about the strengths and weakness of each argument. Evaluative mediators help the parties make decisions by explaining to the parties what a judge or jury is likely to do.[222] Evaluative mediators are not as focused on the interests of the parties, but rather on the rights of the parties and what the most likely outcome would be if the dispute were settled in court.[223] Evaluative mediators not only

---

218. *Id.*
219. Zena Zumeta, *Styles of Mediation: Facilitative, Evaluative, and Transformative Mediation*, http://www.mediate.com/articles/zumeta.cfm.
220. Id.
221. *Id.*
222. *Id.*
223. *Id.*

point out strengths and weaknesses of a case, but often assume that the parties want them to provide guidance as to the best grounds for settlement.[224]

Evaluative mediators give opinions based on their own experience and qualifications. Many evaluative mediators are lawyers who have experience in the courtroom or are retired judges who can give an educated opinion about the possible outcome of a case based on their own experience. However, not all evaluative mediators are lawyers. For example, in construction disputes, parties may want mediators who understand the administrative aspects, practical outcomes, and dynamics involved within the construction field. A former contractor, architect, engineer, or builder with mediation experience and training may be sought out for construction disputes because of their experience and understanding of the business. Parties in a medical dispute may want a former nurse, doctor, or hospital administrator mediating the case because they have firsthand knowledge about different medical issues and the various dynamics involved in hospital administration. A parent in a special education dispute that involves their child with special needs may want a mediator who has teaching experience or has worked with children with disabilities to mediate their case. Because parties are looking for an informed opinion, mediators with specialized experience or expertise may conduct evaluative mediations. These mediators may evaluate not only the strengths and weaknesses of the legal case but also help guide the parties to appropriate settlement solutions.[225] Evaluative mediators often ask pointed legal questions about the merits of the legal case. Evaluative mediators may also provide advice, offer a "mediator's proposal," or give opinions about what a jury or judge might decide if the case continues to court.

[C] Transformative Mediation

Transformative mediation is the third and a more recently developed type of mediation. While evaluative mediation moved the focus of a session toward the outcome and away from the parties' interests, transformative mediation puts the attention back on the parties. Transformative mediation is focused almost exclusively on the parties and the conversation between them. The mediation occurs with all parties in the same room, with the mediator facilitating the discussion between them.

Transformative mediation allows the parties to structure both the process and outcome of the mediation.[226] A mediator in a transformative mediation takes a back seat to the parties. While the mediator's job is to help facilitate the process, the parties provide primary input as to the speed and direction of the mediation. While still important for the parties to try to determine a solution to their conflict, developing a written agreement by the end of mediation is not of the greatest importance. There is less perceived pressure to come to an agreement in transformative mediation. The transformative process is driven by two primary goals: empowerment and recognition.[227]

The first important aspect of transformative mediation is empowerment. This goal is all about giving the parties the power and control to voice their concerns and make

---

224. Riskin, *supra* note 2, at 24.
225. Riskin, *supra* note 2, at 24.
226. *Id.*
227. R. Baruch Bush & J. Folger, J., The Promise of Mediation, Responding to Conflict Through Empowerment and Recognition (1994).

their own decisions. A successful transformative mediator empowers the parties by encouraging them to clarify goals, options, and resources. The second goal of transformative mediation is recognition. The mediators encourage the parties to listen to each other and recognize what is said. Transformative mediators do not use caucuses because they believe all parties must be in the room together to allow recognition to occur. Transformative mediations encourage recognition and empowerment to arrive at solutions.

[D] Narrative Mediation

Narrative mediation is another relatively new type of mediation, which is based on the theory that both parties will come to the mediation with their own version of the story.[228] Narrative mediation was influenced by Narrative Family Therapy, which developed in the mid-1980s from the work of Michael White and David Epston.[229] The theory developed by White and Epston in narrative family therapy is based on the postmodern tradition's theory that "one's point of view is never completely objective."[230]

To better understand narrative mediations, it is important to understand the underlying use of storytelling, which can be very subjective, based on the language used to give the story meaning and the interpretation of the "facts" involved.[231] Stories are developed in two ways: through content and telling.[232] The actual set of events is the content of the story, while the way the story is delivered is its telling. Narratives change and develop over time, as participants in the dispute and later mediation elaborate and modify portions of their own and each other's stories.[233] This usually creates the role of a victim and the other the antagonist within the story.[234] In order to dispel these categorizations, narrative mediation gives the parties the opportunity to recognize that there is more than one way to interpret a series of events.[235]

Language is a crucial aspect of narrative mediation. Stories are told through language, which can transform or distort a story. The focus of narrative mediation is on the communication and relationship between the parties and is focused on the broad interests of the parties instead of narrow positions.[236] The focus of narrative mediation is not on the substantive issues that appear on the surface. Instead, the primary goal is to work on the relationship between the conflicting parties in order for them to develop ways of dealing with conflict in the future.[237] As John Winslade and Gerald Monk developed narrative mediation, they concentrated on the mediator's role to shape the parties'

---

228. Toran Hansen, *The Narrative Approach to Mediation*, September 2003, http://www.mediate.com/articles/hansent.cfm.

229. *See* Cheryl White, *Where Did It All Begin? Reflecting on the Collaborative Work of Michael White and David Epston*, CONTEXT, October 2009.

230. JOHN WINSLADE & GERALD MONK, NARRATIVE MEDIATION (2001).

231. Toran Hansen, *The Narrative Approach to Mediation*, September 2003, http://www.mediate.com/articles/hansent.cfm.

232. *See* Sara Cobb, *A Narrative Perspective on Mediation: Toward the Materialization of the Storytelling Metaphor*, in NEW DIRECTIONS IN MEDIATION: COMMUNICATION RESEARCH AND PERSPECTIVES (Joseph P. Folger & Tricia S. Jones eds., 1994).

233. *Id.*

234. *Id.*

235. Toran Hansen, *The Narrative Approach to Mediation*, September 2003, http://www.mediate.com/articles/hansent.cfm.

236. *Id.*

237. *Id.*

perspectives on the dispute by focusing on the meaning of the stories rather than the facts.[238] The three stages involved in narrative mediation include engaging the parties, deconstructing the story, and constructing an alternate story. These stages are used throughout the mediation and mediators may find themselves jumping back and forth throughout these stages to best help the parties come to resolution.[239] While there are three stages described, they are not distinct stages and mediators guide the parties in and out of these stages throughout the mediation.[240]

As with all types of mediation, narrative mediation is not without its disadvantages. For instance, the role of the mediator in narrative mediation is to help the parties deconstruct their old stories and create a whole new story between them.[241] While a mediator's job is to remain neutral, it is important to recognize that no one can be completely objective and the mediator may inject some of his or her own opinions and views into the new version of the story. In addition to the mediator's role, the relationship between the parties may matter in the success of the mediation. Narrative mediation tends to work best when the parties have an ongoing relationship.[242] A possible disadvantage is that narrative mediation may not work well in mediations where the parties do not have an ongoing relationship. Parties without that relationship prior to the mediation may want to focus more on the actual problem than on describing and rewriting the story.

[E] Other Types of Mediation

As mediation develops over time, other types of mediation may also emerge. For example, Maryland has another type of mediation called "inclusive mediation."[243] This mediation style helps the parties meet their own needs by always using two mediators in a co-mediator model.[244] The mediator's role is to focus on the emotions expressed by the parties and then appropriately reflect these expressions back to the parties using language that best captures the intensity of the emotion.[245] It is a defined process involving various stages, including identifying topics to resolve, clarifying what is important, and generating options based on the parties' goals.[246]

Another form of dispute resolution that has developed, but differs from mediation itself, is facilitation. Facilitation is a dispute resolution process specifically used with large and multi-party groups.[247] In their article *Preventing Conflict through Facilitation*, Janice Fleischer and Zena Zumeta define facilitation as "the use of a third party neutral to help multi-party work groups accomplish the content of their work by providing process leadership and process expertise."[248] They describe facilitation as a process with a

---

238. JOHN WINSLADE & GERALD MONK, NARRATIVE MEDIATION (2001).

239. *Id.*

240. *Id.*

241. *Id.*

242. Jon Linden, *Mediation Styles: The Purists vs. the Toolkit*, www.mediate.com/articles /linden4.cfm

243. Mediation Approaches, last updated April 2014, http://www.peoples-law.org/mediation -approaches.

244. *Id.*

245. *Id.*

246. *Id.*

247. Janice M. Fleischer & Zena D. Zumeta, *Preventing Conflict through Facilitation*, December 1999 http://www.mediate.com/articles/zenandflei.cfm.

248. *Id.*

beginning, middle, and an end. The beginning might include pre-meeting agendas, surveys, and protocols. This is also where the facilitator meets with parties involved to determine what is being asked of the mediator and for the mediator to think about how to approach the particular facilitation. The middle would include meeting guidelines for participants, using sills to keep the meeting moving, and keeping the group memory.[249] The mediator's role is to encourage participation by all involved. Group memory is also an important aspect of this part of the facilitation, which involves keeping notes of what is discussed.[250] Writing down thoughts and ideas is helpful during the meeting to provide a visual for all to show recognition of what is said and it is helpful to write up the report after the meeting is over. It is also important during the actual meeting to invite everyone to speak and to calm the group and reduce tension. A debrief is then involved to summarize what was discussed and to allow members to reflect on their feelings about what occurred or what the result was.[251] The end of the facilitation involves preparing a meeting report and follow-up duties, although sometimes an official report is not necessary if the facilitated meeting resulted in a written document, which may serve as the report.

[F] The "Toolbox" Approach

Each of these models of mediation involves different ways of conducting the process and leaves a great deal of discretion to the mediator. Mediators address the parties and direct the mediations differently, both during the mediation process and while attempting to arrive at a solution or settle upon an agreement. While an evaluative mediator may offer advice about what is likely to happen in front of a judge, a facilitative or transformative mediator may encourage the parties to generate ideas and solutions of their own. In a facilitative or transformative mediation, the role of the mediator is to empower the parties to make their own decisions and the mediator's role is to facilitate that process. An evaluative mediator plays a more active role, giving the parties advice about the possible outcomes of their situation if their case would continue to court. Different situations call for different styles of mediation.

The training of various mediators also falls on a continuum. Regulations and requirements for mediation training differ not only in style, but in location and in the types of individuals who are trained. Facilitative mediation is the most widely taught approach for training new mediators, while transformative mediation is the newest and most recent approach used in training. Evaluative mediation is more likely to involve training of individuals who are former judges or those within the legal field with enough experience to provide educated opinions about the strengths and weaknesses of a case.

Mediations not only differ in the style and training, but each individual mediator brings his or her own unique approach to mediation. Facilitative, evaluative, and transformative mediators all may differ in how they conduct mediation. Even mediators who took the same type of training may use different approaches to resolving conflict. These differences may make mediation difficult to strictly regulate, but the various approaches allow for unique styles to be used in different situations. Though there are some defined "styles" of mediation, at the root of any mediation is the requirement that

---

249. *Id.*
250. *Id.*
251. *Id.*

a mediator remain impartial, neutral, and unbiased.[252] Although each style of mediation appears to differ from each other, all mediators must follow a standard of ethics. Mediators are held to a high standard of conduct and have to remain neutral in a mediation in order to provide the best possible service to the parties, whether in a facilitative, evaluative, transformative, or narrative approach.

Successful mediators use many techniques or "tools" within a single mediation. Mediators may employ a variety of tools, depending on the needs of the parties and the issues in the mediations. Even mediators who identify with a certain mediation style often use tools from a number of different approaches. For instance, a facilitative mediator may need to ask more pointed questions that an evaluative mediator might typically ask if a mediation requires it. Or an evaluative mediator may use techniques from a facilitative style to allow parties to open up and address specific interests in order to move the mediation forward.

The various styles of mediation differ in significant ways but are not completely separate and distinct styles. Instead these styles fall within a continuum.[253] In terms of the mediator's role, transformative mediation appears to fall on one end of the spectrum, with the least involvement from the mediator. Evaluative mediation falls on the opposite end of the spectrum, with the most intervention and involvement from the mediator. Facilitative mediation falls somewhere in the middle. While these are each described as different styles of mediation, the styles do overlap because they all have the same goal: resolving conflict.

---

252. MODEL STANDARDS OF CONDUCT FOR MEDIATORS (2005).

253. Samuel J. Imperati, *Mediator Practice Models: The Intersection of Ethics and Stylistic Practices in Mediation*, 706 WILLAMETTE L. REV. 33:3 (1997).

Chapter 5

Legal Issues in Mediation

§ 5.01 Overview

The mediation process is typically private and occurs outside of the court system. Mediation has some regulatory oversight, and legal implications may result from an unsuccessful mediation. Mediation is largely unregulated; however, mediation ethics and potential malpractice exposure influence mediator behavior and attempt to improve the process. When mediation is unsuccessful, mediation parties may want to use the information learned during the process to their benefit in subsequent litigation. To preserve the mediation process, many jurisdictions have comprehensive confidentiality or privilege legislation or court rules to protect the communications made in mediation.

This chapter considers the most prevalent legal issues surrounding mediation. These legal issues include confidentiality and privilege, issues surrounding court-connected mediation, mediation ethics, and mediator malpractice.

§ 5.02 Confidentiality and Privilege

Confidentiality and privilege are two terms that have distinct meanings but are often erroneously used synonymously. This confusion lies in the fact that both terms represent concepts that intend to keep information private. As discussed in more detail below, confidentiality and privilege rules apply in different realms, and the disclosure of information in one realm may not affect the legal protections for mediation communications in another realm.

Broadly speaking, a confidentiality obligation prohibits a person from disclosing certain information (in this case, "mediation communications") to third parties. The protections of confidentiality are quite broad because they cover nearly all third parties. Privilege, on the other hand, applies significantly more narrowly, and this concept protects information from being introduced as evidence in court, legislative hearings, administrative hearings, or other types of tribunals. Compared to other privileges (such as attorney/client or patient/physician), the confidentiality and privilege aspects are separate legal duties that are not necessarily co-extensive or even co-existent.

The legal rules governing confidentiality and privilege are governed primarily by state law, although some case law exists regarding a federal mediation privilege.[1] In 2001, the Uniform Law Commissioners adopted the Uniform Mediation Act (UMA), which has

---

1. Olam v. Congress Mort. Co., 68 F. Supp. 2d 1110 (N.D. Cal. 1999).

since been adopted in 12 jurisdictions.[2] This section will highlight the UMA and certain influential state acts, to serve as a guide to confidentiality and privilege laws throughout the United States.[3]

This section begins with a discussion of the policy justifications, as well as the drawbacks, for protecting mediation communications. It then details the legal and contractual bases for confidentiality, followed by a discussion of evidentiary privileges.

[A] Policy Justifications

Protection for mediation communications is extraordinarily important, and many parties choose mediation precisely because of these protections. The primary reason for protecting mediation communications is to encourage full and frank discussion in the mediation process.[4] Mediators often ask difficult questions and broach sensitive topics, and the promise of confidentiality and privilege give comfort to the parties to answer honestly as they work toward settlement.[5] Some parties and their advocates may be hesitant to have these discussions outside of the mediation process (i.e., in traditional negotiations) concerned that statements made during the mediation might be later used against them in litigation or another forum. Mediators routinely remind the parties of these protections as early as the opening remarks,[6] if not prior to the mediation during the preparation that mediators may do with the parties.[7]

Settlement rarely occurs without the parties making some type of concessions. Confidentiality and privilege allow parties to discuss potential concessions and, in fact, make concessions without fear that those concessions will be discussed outside of the session. Confidentiality also protects statements, such as apologies, that parties may not be willing to make if the possibility exists that the admissions and apologies could be used outside of the session.

Confidentiality and privilege also protect the mediator. Privilege, in particular, protects the mediator from being called as a witness in court. To preserve the integrity of the process and their neutrality, mediators do not want to be called as witnesses to discuss who said what during a mediation. When a mediator is called to testify, the mediator's words may be used to aid one party at the expense of another party, even if the mediator simply restates true statements uttered at the session. The mediator will likely appear biased (even if the mediator is not, in fact, biased) in favor of one party or another given the adversarial nature of the trial process. Thus, the promise of confidentiality and privilege assures mediators that they will not be hauled into court in every unsuccessful (and some successful) mediations. Some legislatures have passed these types of protections, in part, to encourage people to volunteer and work with community mediation centers that provide low-cost mediation services to the public at large.[8]

---

2. Uniform Law Commission, *Legislative Fact Sheet*, available at http://www.uniformlaws.org /LegislativeFactSheet.aspx?title=Mediation%20Act

3. Sarah R. Cole et al., Mediation: Law, Policy & Practice Ch. 8 (2016).

4. Uniform Mediation Act, Prefatory Note (2003).

5. *Id.*

6. *See supra* 4.05[B][1].

7. *See supra* 4.05[A].

8. *See, e.g.*, Neb. Rev. Stat. § 25-2914 (2015) (applying only to community mediation centers).

Confidentiality and privilege allow mediators to spend their time providing mediation services and not being involved in post-mediation legal actions and defending subpoenas.

Of course, comprehensive protection for mediation communications has some downsides. Statements that are made *only* in mediation may not be later used to prove or defend a case or claim. In other words, the protection of mediation statements may result in a loss of evidence. Those statements may have been helpful, and a party may not be able to have the other party make those statements again—especially if the statement regarded responsibility for certain events or promises to pay or accept certain amounts of money. Confidentiality protections may also cover up misuse of the mediation process. Claims of one party mediating in "bad faith" (by failure to prepare, harassment of other parties, or other improper deeds) are notoriously difficult to prove if the mediation communications are protected.[9] These protections may even encourage parties to enter mediation with ill intentions, such as using mediation as a form of inexpensive discovery or a stalling technique, because no real recourse exists for these harmful actions.

Confidentiality in mediation may protect more powerful parties at the expense of less powerful parties, especially for "repeat players," such as businesses and employers. Asymmetrical access to information already exists because business entities generally have more case information than individual consumers and employees, and the confidentiality of mediation will preserve the informational imbalances in individual cases as well as across similar cases. Cases resolved in mediation are resolved outside of the public eye, and thus important information for society may never come to light.[10]

The use of the term "mediation communication" is used quite deliberately in this chapter. For the most part, the laws regarding confidentiality and privilege apply only to what is *said* during the mediation process.[11] Observations of objective facts may not be protected—such as whether a plaintiff who alleges certain injuries arrives at mediation without the assistance of a neck brace, crutches, or the like. The presence or absence of certain parties or their representatives is also not covered as a "communication." If the defendant's insurance agent is notably absent, this type of fact is likely not protected. Underlying facts in a given situation are also not covered by most privilege and confidentiality statutes. If parties admit new factual information in an unsuccessful mediation, the parties can further explore that information in formal discovery after the mediation has concluded.[12]

Despite the drawbacks, the benefits of confidentiality outweigh the downsides, and mediation's popularity has grown, in part, because of the promise of the protections of statements made in mediation. The technical details of confidentiality and privilege are detailed next.

---

9. *See, e.g.,* Maureen A. Weston, *Checks on Participant Conduct in Compulsory ADR: Reconciling the Tension in the Need for Good-Faith Participation, Autonomy, and Confidentially,* 76 Ind. L. J. 591 (2001).

10. *See supra* Section 4.03.

11. *See, e.g.,* Uniform Mediation Act § 2(2).

12. *See, e.g.,* Uniform Mediation Act § 4(c).

[B] Confidentiality

A statement is confidential if that statement cannot be repeated outside of the forum in which it was made. Under this definition, statements made in mediation cannot be repeated in a courtroom or in a hair salon, or anything in between. Generally, confidentiality applies to everyone in attendance at a mediation, including the parties, their attorneys, the mediator, and any third parties. Confidentiality obligations may be found in the parties' private agreements to mediate or from state law or court rule.

[1] Confidentiality by Contract

As discussed above, one way for parties to begin the mediation process is to have an agreement to mediate.[13] For parties who have an agreement to mediate in writing, a confidentiality requirement is generally written into the contract, among other terms, as an express confidentiality requirement. Other parties will enter into a specific confidentiality agreement with the other party to the mediation. Leading ADR service provider JAMS makes available on its website a sample confidentiality agreement for parties who are looking for a sample form governing this area.[14]

In addition to contracts for confidentiality between the parties, many mediators ask the parties to execute agreements to mediate that explicitly include confidentiality agreements. James Malamed, founder of Mediate.com, makes available a sample mediation agreement for parties and mediators, and he suggests using the following language regarding confidentiality:

> 4. Absolute Confidentiality
> It is understood between the parties and the mediator that the mediation will be strictly confidential. Mediation discussions, written and oral communications, any draft resolutions, and any unsigned mediated agreements shall not be admissible in any court proceeding. Only a mediated agreement, signed by the parties may be so admissible. The parties further agree to not call the mediator to testify concerning the mediation or to provide any materials from the mediation in any court proceeding between the parties. The mediation is considered by the parties and the mediator as settlement negotiations. The parties understand the mediator has an ethical responsibility to break confidentiality if s/he suspects another person may be in danger of harm.[15]

The primary difference between confidentiality agreements between the parties and those among the parties and the mediator is the express inclusion of the mediator.

Some parties submit their dispute to a provider organization and use one of the organization's mediators. When the parties submit their dispute to that organization or include an organization's rules into their agreement to mediate, the parties and the mediator will be bound by the provider organization's own rules regarding confidentiality. For example, contracts submitted to the American Arbitration Association (AAA) for mediation or that incorporate the AAA's mediation rules into their contract will be obligated to follow AAA's confidentiality rule. AAA has an extensive rule regarding confidentiality, which provides:

---

13. *See supra* Section 4.03.
14. See http://www.jamsadr.com/mediation-forms/.
15. http://www.mediate.com/articles/melamed6.cfm.

M-10. Confidentiality

Subject to applicable law or the parties' agreement, confidential information disclosed to a mediator by the parties or by other participants (witnesses) in the course of the mediation shall not be divulged by the mediator. The mediator shall maintain the confidentiality of all information obtained in the mediation, and all records, reports, or other documents received by a mediator while serving in that capacity shall be confidential.

The mediator shall not be compelled to divulge such records or to testify in regard to the mediation in any adversary proceeding or judicial forum.

The parties shall maintain the confidentiality of the mediation and shall not rely on, or introduce as evidence in any arbitral, judicial, or other proceeding the following, unless agreed to by the parties or required by applicable law:

(i)   Views expressed or suggestions made by a party or other participant with respect to a possible settlement of the dispute;

(ii) Admissions made by a party or other participant in the course of the mediation proceedings;

(iii) Proposals made or views expressed by the mediator; or

(iv) The fact that a party had or had not indicated willingness to accept a proposal for settlement made by the mediator.[16]

This particular rule by the AAA sets forth both the mediator's and the parties' confidentiality obligations. Other provider organizations have similar mediation confidentiality rules.[17]

[2] Confidentiality by Statute or Court Rule

In some jurisdictions, state law or court rule may also provide for confidentiality of mediation communications. The applicability of these laws is necessarily specific to individual jurisdictions. Some states have blanket rules regarding confidentiality of mediation communications.[18] For example, in California, state law provides: "All communications, negotiations, or settlement discussions by and between participants in the course of a mediation or a mediation consultation shall remain confidential."[19] In Oregon, "Mediation communications are confidential and may not be disclosed to any other person."[20] In other states, statutes and court rules may apply to specific types of mediations, such as family mediations.[21] Some state law specifically applies to state-created mediation

---

16. The American Arbitration Association (AAA) Commercial Mediation Procedures can be found at www.adr.org. https://www.adr.org/aaa/faces/rules/searchrules/rulesdetail?_afrWindowId =o65qldcf2_278&_afrLoop=727978351118618&doc=ADRSTG_004130&_afrWindowMode=0& _adf.ctrl-state=o65qldcf2_281.

17. *See, e.g.,* JAMS, Comprehensive Arbitration Rules, Rule 26 (confidentiality and privacy).

18. *See, e.g.,* Florida Rules for Certified & Court-Appointed Mediators, Rule 10.360 (2014) (Confidentiality).

19. Cal. Evid. Code 1115–1128.

20. Or. Rev. Stat. § 36.220.

21. *See, e.g.,* N.D. S. Ct. Rules, R. 8.1 (e)(5) (2016) (Confidentiality) ("The program requires the highest ethical standards, including confidentiality. Mediators may not discuss or reveal the details of any mediation proceeding or any information provided by a party in a mediation proceeding to any judge, magistrate, or third party.").

centers and provides for confidentiality of proceedings that take place at the approved center.[22]

In court-connected mediation, the local court rules may also provide for mediation confidentiality. Some jurisdictions, such as the Southern District of New York, have comprehensive rules on confidentiality, among other mediation rules. That jurisdiction requires:

(d) Confidentiality

(1) The parties will be asked to sign an agreement of confidentiality at the beginning of the first mediation session to the following effect:

> (A) Unless the parties otherwise agree, all written and oral communications made by the parties and the mediator in connection with or during any mediation session are confidential and may not be disclosed or used for any purpose unrelated to the mediation.

> (B) The mediator shall not be called by any party as a witness in any court proceeding related to the subject matter of the mediation unless related to the alleged misconduct of the mediator.

(2) Mediators will maintain the confidentiality of all information provided to, or discussed with, them. The Clerk of Court and the ADR Administrator are responsible for program administration, evaluation, and liaison between the mediators and the Court and will maintain strict confidentiality.

(3) No papers generated by the mediation process will be included in Court files, nor shall the Judge or Magistrate Judge assigned to the case have access to them. Information about what transpires during mediation sessions will not at any time be made known to the Court, except to the extent required to resolve issues of noncompliance with the mediation procedures. However, communications made in connection with or during a mediation may be disclosed if all parties and, if appropriate as determined by the mediator, the mediator so agree. Nothing in this section shall be construed to prohibit parties from entering into written agreements resolving some or all of the case or entering and filing with the Court procedural or factual stipulations based on suggestions or agreements made in connection with a mediation.[23]

In the state of Illinois, the Supreme Court required each court jurisdiction to establish mediation rules, which needed to address, among other things, confidentiality.[24] These are simply illustrative of court rules that exist throughout the United States.

Some statutes will have exceptions to confidentiality. Common exceptions include threat of harm to self or others, allegations of child or elder abuse, and plans to commit a crime. Exceptions also exist in situations involving claims of malpractice against a mediator or attorney based on mediation conduct.

Interestingly, the UMA does not address confidentiality at all. The UMA simply provides that mediation communications are confidential to the extent authorized by law

---

22. Neb. Rev. Stat. §§ 25-2901 et seq. (2016); Rev. Code Wash. Ch. 7-75 (2016) (Dispute Resolution Centers).
23. S.D.N.Y. Local Rule 83.8(d).
24. Ill. Sup. Ct. Rules R 99.

or agreement by the parties.[25] Under the UMA, a breach of confidentiality does not affect the privilege that the statements are afforded.[26] A more in-depth discussion of privileges and waiver follows.

[C] Privilege

A privilege is the legal mechanism under which information is protected from being presented in a tribunal (such as a court, arbitration, legislative, or administrative hearing) or from being subject to the mechanisms of discovery. Privilege only applies to disclosures in these contexts and not to disclosure generally. In other words, the rules of privilege will apply during a court proceeding but not at the hair salon.

[1] Federal Rule of Evidence 408

Evidence regarding offers of compromises and negotiations have been inadmissible in federal court since at least 1978.[27] The rule, originally drafted to cover communications made during negotiations, has been applied to the mediation context as well.[28]

The current version of Rule 408 reads:

(a) Prohibited Uses. Evidence of the following is not admissible — on behalf of any party — either to prove or disprove the validity or amount of a disputed claim or to impeach by a prior inconsistent statement or a contradiction:

(1) furnishing, promising, or offering — or accepting, promising to accept, or offering to accept — a valuable consideration in compromising or attempting to compromise the claim; and

(2) conduct or a statement made during compromise negotiations about the claim — except when offered in a criminal case and when the negotiations related to a claim by a public office in the exercise of its regulatory, investigative, or enforcement authority.

(b) Exceptions. The court may admit this evidence for another purpose, such as proving a witness's bias or prejudice, negating a contention of undue delay, or proving an effort to obstruct a criminal investigation or prosecution.[29]

Rule 408 protects offers to compromise in order to encourage and incentivize parties to settle their cases outside of the court system.[30] The purpose of the rule is to prohibit one party from putting into evidence the fact that the other party offered to settle the case as proof of an admission of guilt or a determination of the value of a case. For instance, if a defendant insurance company agrees to settle an automobile accident case for $50,000, the plaintiff cannot use that settlement offer to either prove the liability of the defendant or the value of the lawsuit.

---

25. Uniform Mediation Act § 8.
26. Uniform Mediation Act § 5.
27. Fed. R. Evid. 408 (1978).
28. *See, e.g.,* State v. Tracy, 991 A.2d 821, 829 (Me. 2010) (applying state version of Rule 408 to mediation communications); Acquilla v. Davies, 198 P.3d 730 (Haw. Ct. App. 2009) (applying Rule 408 to mediation communications in a failed mediation).
29. Fed. R. Evid. 408.
30. Committee Notes to FRE 408.

This rule, however, provides only limited evidentiary protection and not particularly well suited for the mediation process. Rule 408 only protects the offers of compromise and not all of the other mediation communications. Further, the protected statements are only protected for the limited purpose of establishing liability and value. Rule 408 only protects statements from the trial process, and this rule does not protect communications during the discovery process. Under Rule 408(b), the evidence is still admissible for any other purpose, including as evidence of knowledge, bias, delay, bad faith, or any other purpose. Given these limitations, states have generally opted to enact legislation providing for specific and generally broader confidentialy for mediation communications.

[2] Uniform Mediation Act

The Uniform Mediation Act (UMA) is a comprehensive statute providing privilege (but not necessarily confidentiality) to mediation communications. The UMA drafters acknowledged the many benefits of protecting mediation communications.[31] The drafters, however, also recognized the limits to confidentiality and some of the competing policies that require disclosure in certain situations.

The UMA begins with definitions of mediation and mediation communication. Mediation is broadly defined as "a process in which a mediator facilitates communication and negotiation between parties to assist them in reaching a voluntary agreement regarding their dispute."[32] This definition does not limit *mediation* to a particular style or use of any particular techniques. A "mediation communication," then, is a "statement, whether oral or in a record or verbal or nonverbal, that occurs during a mediation or is made for the purpose of considering, conducting, participating in, initiating, continuing, or reconvening a mediation or retaining a mediator."[33] This definition is also broad, including communications made before, during, or after the mediation process, yet still connected with the mediation.[34] The term *mediation communication* does not include actions[35] or turn otherwise admissible evidence into inadmissible evidence simply because the parties discussed it at the mediation.[36]

Under the UMA, the parties, mediator, and any non-party participants (lawyers, support persons, experts, etc.) each hold a mediation privilege.[37] As privilege-holders, each participant has the ability to "refuse to disclose" mediation communications during *both* the discovery process and before a tribunal.[38] In other words, any mediation participant has the independent right to refuse to disclose mediation communications. In addition, the privilege holders can also prevent others from disclosing mediation communications. Parties hold the broadest privilege and can prevent any person from disclosing

---

31. UMA Preamble.
32. UMA § 2(1) (definition of mediation).
33. UMA § 2(2) (definition of mediation communication).
34. Whether pre-mediation communications are protected depends on state law. In 2015, the Oregon Supreme Court ruled that pre-mediation communications are not covered by the mediation privilege. Alfieri v. Solomon, 365 P.3d 99 (2015).
35. UMA § 2(2).
36. UMA § 4(c).
37. UMA § 4.
38. UMA § 4(b).

any mediation communication.[39] Mediators and third parties can prevent other people from disclosing statements that a particular person made.[40]

The UMA does not protect all mediation communications. Exceptions to the privilege generally exist for: agreements reached in mediation, mediations subject to sunshine laws, threats of bodily harm, statements commissioning crimes, statements sought to prove or disprove mediator or attorney malpractice, or statements regarding child or elder abuse.[41] In some circumstances, an exception to privilege will apply in criminal cases and cases in which the parties seek to rescind a mediated agreement.[42] The UMA also prohibits mediators from making reports to courts and other decision-makers.[43] Mediators may disclose whether a mediation occurred, who attended, and whether the parties settled.[44] Mediators may also disclose reports of abuse to the appropriate agency, such as the state's Department of Health and Human Services.[45]

Unlike other privileges,[46] the mediation privilege is independent of confidentiality and a breach of confidentiality does not serve as a waiver of the privilege. The privilege can be waived if all parties agree (and the mediator/third-party agrees for their statements).[47] In other words, a mediation communication is still privileged, even if the mediation participants discuss what happened at the mediation with friends, loved ones, or even strangers. The drafters specifically wanted this type of flexibility to allow mediation parties to consult with others when making these types of important decisions.

[3] Other State Laws

Many states, too, have laws that operate as evidentiary privileges. Some of these laws are labeled as "confidentiality" protections, but in actuality they operate as privileges because they keep mediation communications from being disclosed in courts or before other adjudicative bodies.

Some jurisdictions have very comprehensive privilege statutes. In Florida, "A mediation party has a privilege to refuse to testify and to prevent any other person from testifying in a subsequent proceeding regarding mediation communications."[48] The mediation communications are protected from the compulsory process and during discovery.[49] The California Evidence Code also provides a robust privilege for mediation communications.[50]

Because of the variety of laws governing confidentiality and privilege on a state-by-state and court district-by-court district basis, this chapter could not possibly detail them all. The most comprehensive resource is the treatise *Mediation: Law, Policy, and Practice*, a publication that contains state-by-state information on mediation statutes,

---

39. UMA § 4(b)(1).
40. UMA § 4(b)(2)-(3).
41. UMA § 6(a).
42. UMA § 6(b).
43. UMA § 7.
44. UMA § 7(b)(1).
45. UMA § 7(b)(3).
46. The attorney/client privilege, for example, is waived if the communications are not also confidential.
47. UMA § 5(a).
48. Fla. Stat. § 44.405(2).
49. Fla. Stat. § 44.403(5).
50. Cal. Evid. Code § 1115–1128.

including confidentiality and privilege.[51] Mediators and lawyers practicing within a given jurisdiction should take time to research the laws governing that jurisdiction. This type of preparation will help manage expectations as well as influence the type of information the parties may be willing to disclose in mediation.

§ 5.03 Court-Connected Mediation

Given the benefits of mediation, such as earlier resolution of cases, creative settlements, and party satisfaction, courts often mandate that parties use mediation. Court-connected mediation has a secondary benefit for court systems, i.e., docket control. Cases settled through mediation do not need final resolution by a judge or jury, and mediation programs have the potential to save judicial resources. Court-connected mediation programs are currently a part of every federal district and appellate court across the United States, and most state courts have mediation programs at the trial or appellate levels.

[A] The Rise of Court-Connected Mediation

The modern, facilitative mediation process traces its roots to the 1960s and 1970s, as described in more detail in Chapter 4.[52] Ironically, mediation's roots lie with general dissatisfaction with the court system because the parties lacked control over the process and judicial remedies could not truly remedy the problems between disputants.[53] Attorneys and judges, however, became proponents of the mediation process and advocated to institute mediation within the traditional legal system. Courts experimented with mandatory mediation in small claims and family cases, often with significant success. Based on these programs, courts began mandating mediation in a wide variety of civil cases.[54]

Courts have significant power to order mediation. The Federal Alternative Dispute Resolution Act of 1998 required each federal district court (including bankruptcy courts) to implement an alternative dispute resolution program.[55] Most, if not all, of these programs rely heavily on the use of mediation. Many of these programs allow the courts to mandate that the parties attend mediation, even if the parties otherwise would not consent. In the absence of a specific court rule or statute, case law suggests that courts have the inherent power to mandate that parties attend mediation.[56]

Court-connected mediation has significant benefits for parties, judges, and mediators. Most civil cases settle, and mediation is a natural forum for cases to settle earlier (with potentially fewer costs) than in the traditional system. In this regard, parties

---

51. Cole et al., *supra* note 3.

52. *See supra* Section 4.01.

53. *See* Nancy A. Welsh, *The Thinning Vision of Self-Determination in Court-Connected Mediation: The Inevitable Price of Institutionalization?*, 6 HARV. NEGOT. L.J. 1, 16–17 (2001) (describing the early mediation movement).

54. *Id.* at 23–24.

55. 28 U.S.C. § 651 (1998).

56. In re Atlantic Pipe Corp., 304 F.3d 135 (2002) (holding that the inherent power of the courts would allow a court to mandate that otherwise non-consenting parties participate in mediation).

benefit from earlier resolution of disputes and potentially creative options. In jurisdictions with heavy case dockets or with too few judges, cases settled through mediation can ease the burdens on the judiciary. When mediation is mandatory, more cases are mediated, giving mediators more work. In other words, the market for mediation services is stronger when the court systems mandate that parties participate.

[B] Criticisms of Court-Connected Mediation

Court-connected mediation is not without its criticisms. In many jurisdictions, court-connected mediation involves a mediator who uses an evaluative style, thus resembling a judicial settlement conference.[57] Due to market forces, attorneys representing clients hire evaluative mediators in order to give a legal evaluation of the case for the purpose of determining a monetary settlement value. Parties may feel as if they lack control over the process, thus diminishing the opportunity for self-determination.[58]

Another concern is whether court-connected mediation is voluntary if parties are required to mediate? Parties may have any number of reasons for not wanting to participate in the process, ranging from a good-faith belief in the success of their case at trial, to simply being are too upset with the other party to want to consider compromise or working together. The counter-argument is that the parties need not settle their cases, so voluntariness means coming to a voluntary resolution. This answer, however, may not be satisfying to parties who do not want to be at mediation.

A final criticism is the question of who is responsible for paying for court-connected mediation. Some courts have resources to hire a full-time mediator who can mediate cases within a given jurisdiction at no cost to the parties. Some programs, such as small-claims court mediations and "settlement week" programs,[59] may also provide free mediation services. In other jurisdictions, mediators may offer free mediation services for a limited number of hours—such as the first two or four hours of a mediation—and then charge the participants for any time exceeding the number of free hours. These programs, however, likely constitute the minority of cases in court-connected mediation. Instead, most court-connected cases require the parties to pay private mediators to mediate their cases, potentially imposing a financial burden on parties, especially when the mediation is unsuccessful.

§ 5.04 Mediation Regulation and Ethics

Mediation is primarily an unregulated profession, and most regulation that does exist consists of self-regulation. Despite the regulatory void, the mediation profession relies on ethical practice and codes of conduct so that individual parties and the public can buy into and trust the mediation process. Because mediators are third-party neutrals, ethical conduct is a cornerstone of mediation's legitimacy.

---

57. Welsh, *supra* note 53, at 25–27.

58. *Id.* at 31–33.

59. A "settlement week" is a program where a significant number of civil cases are scheduled for mediation in a given calendar week. The mediators come from the private sector, and they agree to volunteer their time for that mediation.

This section covers mediation regulation and ethics. The ethical obligations generally stem from mediation regulation, but there do exist a number of aspirational standards even when a mediator is not otherwise bound by them. This section also covers related issues, such as mediator safety, and power and control.

[A] Mediation Regulation

A discussion of mediator ethics should begin with a discussion of mediation regulation. Mediation is largely an unregulated industry. As discussed above, today's mediation is rooted, in part, in a grassroots effort of community mediators from all walks of life with a peacemaking mission.[60] Mediators come to the profession with a wide variety of backgrounds and mediate in a wide variety of ways. As noted in Chapter 4, mediators use a wide variety of tools and techniques.[61] In other words, mediation is a far cry from a "one size fits all" type of profession.

Two primary problems arise in the issue of mediator regulation. The first problem is in the definition of mediation. The second problem lies in how mediators should be credentialed and regulated. As to the first question, the great diversity of the field offers challenges as to who should or should not be regulated. The definition of mediation is not universal, and regulation turns on being able to define the profession. Many people informally mediate all the time, and most mediation policymakers would not want to cover the friend who helps two other friends resolve disputes or the parent who "mediates" disagreements among the children.

The second problem of mediator regulation lies in the question of what criteria mediators must meet in order to be credentialed. Little agreement within the profession exists on the proper credentialing criteria. Certainly, a number of options for credentialing exist, such as required training, supervised mediations, years of experience, written examinations, and other means to ensure mediator competency.[62] In 2004, a Task Force on Mediator Certification recommended that the Association of Conflict Resolution (ACR) establish a Mediator Certification Program involving a portfolio of years and training, a written examination, periodic re-certification, a process for de-certification, and the ability to waive some of the certification requirements.[63] Ultimately, the members of this Task Force could not agree on the proper model for a single program. Instead, in 2011, the ACR adopted the Model Standards for Mediator Certification Standards,[64] which sets forth some guiding principles to other organizations that credential mediators. Standard 1 states that the program will assess mediators' abilities to: "attend to procedural justice," "support self-determination, collaboration, and/or exchange among the parties," "manage content and issues," and "appropriately deal with personal, emotional and relational issues."[65] Standard 2 requires that performance evaluation be part of the

---

60. *See supra* Section 4.02.

61. *See supra* Section 4.06.

62. *See* Ignazio J. Ruvolo, *Appellate Mediation — "Settling" the Last Frontier of ADR*, 42 SAN DIEGO L. REV. 177, 222 (2005).

63. ACR Mediation Certification Task Force: Report and Recommendations, *at* http://www.mediate.com/articles/acrcert1.cfm.

64. Association of Conflict Resolution, Model Standards for Mediator Certification Programs (2011), available at http://www.imis100us2.com/acr/ACR/Resources/ACR_Stand/ACR/Resources/Standards_of_Practice.aspx?hkey=5f21719d-8d65-4ced-8931-2a31d6b676a9.

65. Model Standards for Mediator Certification Programs, Standard 1.

assessment.[66] In most other respects, these standards allow for great flexibility in determining the actual standards that the certifying bodies may use to certify mediators within a given program or jurisdiction. In other words, this long effort did not yield any concrete advice for programs on this important issue.

Part of the frustration within the field regarding certification efforts lies in the fact that little empirical research exists regarding the qualities of a good mediator.[67] Studies to date show that the best indicator of mediator quality is mediation experience.[68] Herein lies one of the most difficult problems—the best indicator of quality is experience. How does the profession determine whether *new* mediators can provide competent services?

Ultimately, mediator regulation is largely a question for individual programs and associations. Private mediators working without affiliation with a court, program, or association continue to be largely unregulated. Organizations that do have credentialing decide on their own criteria, including training and mediation experience, and any other subject-matter experience. The American Arbitration Association, for example, requires that its mediators have at least 10 years of "senior-level experience in business, industry, or a profession," in addition to training and previous mediation experience.[69] To be a "Certified Transformative Mediator," a mediation applicant must meet training requirements, participate in an interview, submit a video of the candidate's mediation, and engage in periodic re-evaluations.[70] Some court-connected mediation programs have requirements to mediate those cases. Florida rules certify mediators based on a point system, where different types of mediators must accumulate a different number of points, and the points are awarded based on training, education, mentorship, and experience.[71]

Programs of mediation certification have certain benefits and drawbacks for the program, the individual mediators, and the system of mediation as a whole. The benefits to certification systems include improved mediator quality, increased public trust in mediation, marketable credentials for mediators, and oversight protections.[72] On the other hand, these types of systems require a significant amount of cost for the oversight (staffing time and expense), struggles of determining the proper credentialing requirements, as well as the need to create a system of periodic re-certification and de-certification for non-complying mediators.[73] Given the hurdles involved in certification, most certification programs exist in the areas of private membership organizations (such as the AAA) and court-connected mediation programs.

---

66. Model Standards for Mediator Certification Programs, Standard 2.

67. ACR Standard 1 is based in part on the available research regarding the making of a good mediator and a desirable process from the parties' view. *See* Nancy A. Welsh, *Disputants' Decision Control on Court-Connected Mediation: A Hollow Promise without Procedural Justice*, 2002 J. Disp. Resol. 179 (2002).

68. Roselle Wissler, *Mediation and Adjudication in Small Claims Court: The Effects of Process and Case Characteristics*, 29 L. & Society Rev. 323, 341, 343 (1995).

69. American Arbitration Association, AAA Panel of Mediators Qualifications Criteria, available at https://www.adr.org/aaa/ShowPDF?doc=ADRSTG_003877.

70. Institute for the Study of Conflict Transformation, Description of the Summative Assessment Process, available at http://www.transformativemediation.org/wp-content/uploads/2012/11/Description-of-the-Summative-Assessment-Process2011.pdf.

71. How to Become a Florida Supreme Court Certified Mediator, available at http://www.flcourts.org/core/fileparse.php/534/urlt/HowtoBecomeaMediatorDecember2015.pdf.

72. Sarah Rudolph Cole, *Mediator Certification Has the Time Come?*, 11 No. 3 Disp. Resol. 7 (Spring 2015) (describing the benefits of mediator certification).

73. Donald T. Weckstein, *Mediator Certification: Why and How*, 30 U.S.F. L. Rev. 757, 788 (1996) (discussing continuing mediator certification).

[B] Mediator Standards of Conduct

Mediators who are affiliated with an organization, panel, or list, are often required to adhere to certain ethical standards. Failure to meet those standards could result in a disciplinary procedure or removal from the credentialing organization entirely. Private mediators are not necessarily subject to any particular set of ethical standards, but ethical standards certainly serve as a best practice for mediators. Although private mediators, by definition, cannot be excluded from membership in a particular organization because of an ethics violation, private mediators may still be liable to individual parties in a mediator malpractice action based on a breach of a common ethical standard.[74]

The ethical standards may vary slightly based on the individual organization, but most ethical standards share many commonalities. In 2005, the American Arbitration Association, the American Bar Association, and the Association for Conflict Resolution each adopted the Model Standards of Conduct for Mediators ("Model Standards"). This document has been cited by courts as a national standard for mediation conduct.[75] Individual mediators affiliated with various organizations and court-connected lists may be required to adhere to some different or additional standards. The remainder of this section highlights the most prominent provisions of the Model Standards.

[1] Party Autonomy or Self-Determination

Standard I of the Model Standards concerns the guiding principle of party autonomy or self-determination.[76] Self-determination is defined as "the act of coming to a voluntary, uncoerced decision in which each party makes free and informed choices as to process and outcome."[77] The principle of party autonomy encompasses both substance and process. Self-determination as to the outcome of the dispute means that the parties make their own decisions and make the determination whether or not to settle in mediation. The mediator does not pressure any party to settle. The mediator should also be mindful of self-determination as to the process. Mediators are generally considered to be mediation process experts, but that expertise must sometimes yield to the needs of the parties. Some examples of party autonomy with respect to process may include: whether to mediate together or in separate rooms, when to take breaks, whether certain subjects are off-limits for discussion, whether confidential information will be shared with the other party, and any number of other items. Mediators may not believe that a party's choices are wise, but the mediator should respect the party's wishes.

Party autonomy also means that the goals of the parties outweigh the goals of the participants. A mediator should not let extraneous factors, such as settlement rates (personal or within an organization), organizational pressures, ego, increased fees, or the like interfere with the process and the self-determination of the parties.[78]

[2] Bias

The ethics governing bias and neutrality flow from the parties' overarching goals of party autonomy and self-determination. Mediation is the process, and the neutrality of

---

74. A more detailed discussion of mediator malpractice can be found infra Section 5.06.
75. *See, e.g.,* CEATS, Inc. v. Continental Airlines, 755 F.3d 1356 (Fed. Cir. 2014).
76. Model Standards of Conduct for Mediators, Standard I.
77. Model Standard of Conduct for Mediators, Standard I(A).
78. Model Standard of Conduct for Mediators, Standard I(B).

the mediator ensures that the parties can make an informed decision to settle that is not influenced by the personal feelings of the mediator. Bias is generally defined as "freedom from favoritism, bias or prejudice."[79] Mediator bias is generally a nuanced subject. Although the parties retain the ability to decide whether they will settle, bias may manifest itself in subtle ways. A biased mediator will likely not outwardly act on the bias. Instead, the mediator may ask harder questions of one party than another because of a bias, or a mediator may recommend that one party accept a settlement that they may not want to accept. The source of bias may stem from the characteristics of a party (such as race, gender, beliefs, or values) or from the party's behavior at the mediation (cooperative or non-cooperative).[80] Mediators who believe that they cannot conduct the mediation in an impartial manner should withdraw from the mediation.[81]

Mediators should also refrain from the appearance of bias, in addition to actual bias. Mediators must be constantly aware of their biases as they arise in the moment. If a mediator determines that he or she is feeling biased, the mediator must try to set that bias aside and continue the mediation without being biased or showing bias. If the mediator determines that the bias is too overwhelming, then the mediator needs to withdraw so that the parties can have a fair process.

[3] Conflicts of Interest

Conflicts of interest are similar to bias, but they are a very specific type of bias. Bias, generally, is a favoritism in favor of or against a particular party. A conflict of interest is a bias that arises either because the mediator has a relationship with one of the parties or attorneys involved or because the mediator has a personal stake in the outcome of the mediation.[82]

Prior to the commencement of the mediation, the mediator should collect sufficient information to determine whether a conflict exists. As discussed regarding the intake process in Chapter 4,[83] gathering information regarding the type of dispute and the participants involved satisfies the mediator's obligation to make a "reasonable inquiry" to determine if a conflict exists.[84] Mediators should assess whether they have a financial, personal, business, or other relationship with any of the participants or if the mediator has some type of stake in the outcome. For instance, if the mediator owns stock in the company of one of the parties, then that would be a financial conflict of interest because the value of the stock may change based on the outcome of the mediation. A mediator should also be aware of personal relationships with the parties or attorneys, such as serving on a board of directors with a particular party or knowing a participant from church attendance.

Once the mediator discovers the conflict of interest, the mediator must disclose it to the parties.[85] After the disclosure, the parties can determine whether or not the mediator can still serve. If the parties agree, the mediator can serve, but if one party wants a different mediator, the mediator must withdraw.[86] The requirement to disclose conflicts of

---

79. Model Standards of Conduct for Mediators, Standard II(A).
80. Model Standards of Conduct for Mediators, Standard II(B)(1).
81. Model Standards of Conduct for Mediators, Standard II(C).
82. Model Standards of Conduct for Mediators, Standard III(A).
83. *See supra* Section 4.05[A].
84. Model Standards of Conduct for Mediators, Standard III(B).
85. Model Standards of Conduct for Mediators, Standard III(C).
86. *Id.*

interest is a continuing duty, meaning that the mediator must disclose even if the conflict arises well into the mediation.[87]

[4] Competency

The Model Standards require that a mediator "has the necessary competence to satisfy the reasonable expectations of the parties."[88] Competency spans across multiple grounds. First, the mediator must be competent in the skills of being a mediator. This competency may be achieved through training or experience. Second, the mediator may need competency in the subject matter of the dispute. Family law mediators may need extra training in issues such as family dynamics and domestic violence, in addition to knowledge of family law. Mediators who work in the areas of securities disputes might want to have a background in that area of law. Third, mediators should also consider cultural competency and other special areas of competency. A mediation involving members of a minority population (race, religion, disability, education, etc.) may require additional types of competency in order to better understand the disputants and the bargaining culture.

As with conflicts of interest, competency is something that mediators should be able to determine during the intake process. Simple questions, such as "what is the nature of this dispute?" should elicit the type of information needed to determine whether the mediator is competent. At its core, competency is an ethical standard that protects the parties and ensures a quality experience for them.

[5] Confidentiality

The rules of confidentiality are discussed above.[89] Confidentiality is not only a legal obligation, but also an ethical matter.[90] Parties expect that mediation will be a confidential process. In particular, parties expect that the mediator will maintain confidentiality. Mediation communications are generally confidential outside of the mediation process, but some communications may be confidential even *within* the process. When meeting with the parties in a caucus, the general expectation is that the communications that occur during the caucus will be confidential from any other parties in the process.[91] Of course, mediators can obtain permission to disclose communications learned in caucus to other parties.

[6] Ethics Governing the Business of Mediation

Ethical standards also govern the business side of mediation. As with lawyer advertising,[92] mediator advertising must be truthful.[93] The duty of truthfulness governs communications regarding the mediator's "qualifications, experience, services and fees."[94] Along the same lines, the mediator may not make any statements that promise certain

---

87. Model Standards of Conduct for Mediators, Standard III(D).
88. Model Standards of Conduct for Mediators, Standard IV(A).
89. *See supra* Section 5.02.
90. Model Standards of Conduct for Mediators, Standard V.
91. Model Standards of Conduct for Mediators, Standard V(B).
92. Model Rules of Professional Conduct, R. 7.1.
93. Model Standards of Conduct for Mediators, Standard VII (A).
94. *Id.*

outcomes, such as promises that the parties will settle in mediation.[95] A mediator may only claim to be certified by an organization or a part of a program if the governing body actually bestows such status upon the mediator.[96] When advertising, the mediator may only refer to specific clients or use client testimonials with the permission of the clients.[97]

With respect to mediation fees, the mediator should charge reasonable fees, explained to the client in writing, which are based on the mediator's experience, the complexity of the case, and prevailing fees in the local marketplace.[98] In order to protect the mediator's neutrality, fees cannot be contingent on the result of a settlement or the amount of the settlement.[99] In many instances, the mediator will accept an unequal division of fees between the parties, but the mediator must still be able to conduct the mediation in an impartial manner.[100] For instance, in consumer and employment cases, the business entity may shoulder all of the mediation fees. Despite this fact, the mediator must remain impartial and not favor the party paying the mediation fees.

[C] Ensuring Participant Safety

The mediation process involves the possible resolution of people in conflict. Given the conflict, mediation is a potentially volatile situation. Safety for the participants and the mediator is an ethical obligation that often goes undiscussed. And yet safety is an important concern. Safety issues arise in a wide variety of situations, from threats uttered in extreme emotion to displaying a weapon, and other types of violent actions. Safety issues may also arise in a more subtle context, particularly in family disputes, when parties know how to push each other's buttons. A variety of techniques exist to help mediators ensure safety for the participants and the mediator.[101]

Before the mediation begins, a mediator should be familiar with the physical surroundings, such as knowing the exits and entrances of the building, the location of fire alarms and telephones, and the security of the parking lot. If a dangerous situation arises, the mediator can help victim parties stay safe or escape to safety. Mediators can use the intake procedure to assess the conflict level and plan for the session. Mediators can also research case information, looking for past violent activity or protection orders in appropriate cases.[102]

During the mediation, the mediator can arrange the room so that potential victims sit closest to the door. The mediator can remove dangerous objects from the room, such as scissors, if necessary. If the parties cannot be in the same room together, the mediator can use caucus sessions to ensure participant safety. In some cases, it may be necessary to meet with parties on different days or online so that they are not even in the building at the same time. If the mediator suspects that there are safety issues, the mediator may want to mediate during business hours in a location with other people

---

95. *Id.*
96. Model Standards of Conduct for Mediators, Standard VII(A)(2).
97. Model Standards of Conduct for Mediators, Standard VII(C).
98. Model Standards of Conduct for Mediators, Standard VIII(A).
99. Model Standards of Conduct for Mediators, Standard VIII(B).
100. Model Standards of Conduct for Mediators, Standard VIII(B)(2).
101. *See* Kristen M. Blankley, *How to Make Mediation Safer in Cases of High Conflict*, available at http://www.mediate.com/mobile/article.cfm?id=11344&type=.
102. *Id.*

present. Further, a co-mediator may be helpful to assert additional authority in the room.[103]

When the mediation is over, the mediator should take care that the parties can safely exit the building. Staggering the parties' exit times may help prevent altercations in the parking lot. Making sure that the parties do not leave on the same elevator car is also a good practice. In extreme cases, having a police escort may be necessary to make sure that everyone leaves safely.[104]

Mediators should be mindful of safety throughout the process. The participants have a right and an expectation to a safe process. Mindfulness to the complex dynamic of conflict and everyone's safety is important to the future of the practice.

[D] Power and Control in Mediation

Issues of power and control in the mediation process must also be considered. Power is a complex dynamic, and power in dispute resolution may shape the outcome of the process. Generally speaking, power is the ability to influence another or convince another to make a certain decision. Many sources of power exist in mediation, including financial resources, personal charisma, having a good legal case, having the benefit of time on one party's side, being on the side of the status quo, and structural power in a culture or organization, among many other sources of power in bargaining.

There are many sources of legitimate or structural power. In workplace disputes, supervisors generally have more power than employees. In disputes within families, parents have more power over minor children. In a lawsuit, a party with an objectively better legal argument will likely have more power than the person with a weaker legal argument.

Other types of power give mediators pause. Should power that comes from great personal resources, affiliation with people in powerful places (in government, business, or the community), or personal characteristics, such as beauty, confidence, or charm, be allowed to affect a mediation? Mediators have different views on whether their job is to "balance the power" of the parties in the room.[105] Some mediators may try to help a party in a weaker position of power through techniques as benign as giving equal time and attention to both parties, to more questionable techniques such as giving legal, financial, or other types of advice to one party.

The issue of power in mediation, at its core, is an ethical question. The guiding principle of self-determination or party autonomy assumes that each party is capable of making choices regarding the mediation process and the ultimate resolution of the dispute. In extreme cases, the power differential may be so great that the person of lesser bargaining power may not be able to make these choices out of his or her own free will, but only out of capitulation to the power. The power dynamics associated with

---

103. *Id.*

104. *Id.*

105. *See, e.g.*, Susan Nauss Exon, *How Can a Mediator Be Both Impartial and Fair? Ethical Standards of Conduct Create Chaos for Mediators*, 2006 J. Disp. Resol. 387 (2006) (describing how mediators may balance power, but that other ethical standards may be infringed); Penelope E. Bryan, *Killing Us Softly: Divorce Mediation and the Politics of Power*, 40 Buff. L. Rev. 441 (1992) (arguing against balancing the power in mediation because the mediator may not know what causes the power imbalance);

domestic violence is an example of an area where power issues turn into control issues, and domestic violence is addressed in more detail below.[106] Power and control issues in mediation, however, are not limited to cases involving families, and mediators should be cognizant of the power dynamics between the parties.

§ 5.05 Challenges to Mediated Agreements

If parties settle a case in mediation, the resulting agreement is a contract. Parties are sometimes dissatisfied with their agreement the next day or after talking to a friend or lawyer. Because mediated agreements are treated as contracts, ordinary contract law would apply to a legal challenge to a mediated agreement. Challenges to mediated agreements are rare, and winning such a challenge is difficult. The most common ground for challenge to a mediated agreement is based on duress—usually aimed at the mediator. A party may claim that the mediator put undue pressure on a party to settle, and that the party did not sign the contract out of self-determination. As with other contracts, oral agreements are subject to the statute of frauds.

Mediation confidentiality and privilege may make a claim against the mediated agreement difficult to prove. Under the Uniform Mediation Act, a written mediated agreement signed by the parties is not privileged,[107] so the terms of a written contract can be presented to a court. But other evidence may be difficult to present to challenge the agreement because of general confidentiality and privilege statutes or rules. Although the Uniform Mediation Act has an exception to privilege in these types of cases, the exception is not absolute, and the court must conduct a balancing test, following a hearing *in camera*, to determine if the need for the evidence "substantially outweighs" the interest in confidentiality.[108] Parties in jurisdictions that do not have a similar exception for post-mediation challenges to agreements may have a difficult time proving the duress if information from the mediation session cannot come into court.

§ 5.06 Mediator Malpractice

Parties in a mediation proceeding may feel injured and seek redress against a particularly bad mediator. As an empirical matter, few lawsuits have been filed against mediators, and little precedent exists in the area of mediator malpractice. The most common complaints about mediators involve ethical violations—such as mediator bias, pressure on one or more parties to settle, or breach of mediation confidentiality. In some instances, parties are upset with the mediator when they agree to something they later regret. In other instances, the parties may not have settled the case at mediation, but they still seek some type of recompense from the mediator.

---

106. *See* Section 4.10[G].
107. Uniform Mediation Act §6(a)(1).
108. Uniform Mediation Act §6(b)(2).

Pursuing a lawsuit against a mediator can be an uphill battle. In some jurisdictions, mediators are protected by common law or statutory immunity.[109] Even in a jurisdiction where mediators might be subject to liability, establishing the standard of care may be difficult given the varying practices of mediation.[110] The standard of care for a facilitative mediator may be different from that of an evaluative mediator or a transformative mediator. As noted above, not all mediators are regulated, and ethical standards may vary.[111] The standards are often broad, encompassing a wide variety of behavior. Even if a party could prove that the mediator fell below a standard of care, determining damages—beyond the costs of mediation—would be difficult. Finally, as with challenging a mediated agreement, confidentiality and privilege laws may prevent a party from presenting critical evidence to the court. The Uniform Mediation Act excludes mediation communications that are used to pursue or defend a claim of professional malpractice from protection,[112] but the UMA is not the law in every state.

Although difficult, mediator malpractice claims are not impossible. Further, parties may be able to report mediator misconduct to ethics boards or service providers. If the mediators are licensed or credentialed through a government or private agency, the entity may have a procedure for imposing sanctions on the mediator. Market forces may also help keep bad mediators from performing services if people stop using the mediator.

§ 5.07 Special Issues for Family Mediators

Family mediators may wncounter certain challenges not present in other types of mediation because of the complicated dynamics in families. Perhaps the most common challenge for family mediators is to recognize and report domestic violence, child abuse, or other types of dangerous conditions within the home. Family mediators must also be aware of family dynamics, property and financial issues, as well as child development issues. This section highlights some of the issues facing family mediators on a regular basis.

"Family mediation" generally refers to cases dealing with divorce or child custody issues. Mediation typically occurs in three different types of cases. Most people equate family mediation with divorce, and many divorcing couples use mediation to help peaceably resolve their differences. Parents often mediate child custody issues in paternity cases, or cases involving parents who never married (and therefore, do not need to have a divorce when they break up). The third category of cases are modification cases, or cases in which a current plan is not working due to changed circumstances (such as a parental move, a new job, or simply because the children are getting older).

Family mediators deal with a number of complicated financial, emotional, and property issues. These mediators must have baseline competencies in issues such as custody arrangements, child support, spousal support, property division—including the division of retirement accounts—power and control dynamics, emotional content, and family systems, to name a few. The American Bar Association Model Standards of

---

109. Susan Nauss Exon, ADVANCED GUIDE FOR MEDIATORS 275–82 (2014).
110. *Id*. at 276.
111. *See supra* Section 5.04[A].
112. Uniform Mediation Act § 6(a)(5).

Practice for Family and Divorce Mediation devotes an entire ethical standard to mediators having the requisite educational competencies in the area of family law and family issues.[113]

Key among the competencies of family mediators is the ability to ask about and determine whether the parties are competent to engage in mediation free from the presence of domestic violence or serious power and control issues. Domestic violence is a particular concern to mediators because the victim of domestic violence may not be able to make freely informed decisions about the children, property, or financial consequences of the situation.[114] Mediators must understand that power and control issues in a family extend well beyond physical violence. Mediators should be able to recognize other types of abuse, including psychological, emotional, sexual, and economic abuse. In some cases, mediation may not be appropriate due to power and control issues. In other cases, specialized mediators may still be able to mediate the case, provided that safety protocols exist for the process.[115]

Family mediations may occur in other types of family situations other than divorce or custody. When children are removed from the home because of the parents' abuse or neglect, some jurisdictions use a process similar to mediation to aid extended families in finding alternative placements for the children.[116] Mediation is also a viable option in cases of elder law and probate law when conflict arises among adult siblings regarding the caretaking of an elderly parent or in the distribution of assets in an estate.

---

113. American Bar Association, Model Standards of Practice for Family and Divorce Mediation, Standard II (2001).

114. *Id.*, Standard X.

115. *Id.* Safety protocols may include separate sessions on different days, allowing support persons to accompany the parties to mediation, encouraging attorney representation, or referring the parties to appropriate community resources.

116. A more detailed discussion of restorative practices in family matters can be found *infra*, Section 10.08[C].

Chapter 6

Mediation Advocacy

§ 6.01 Introduction — How Mediation Advocacy Differs from Any Other Kind of Advocacy

From the lawyer's perspective, mediation is a very different process compared to negotiation, arbitration, and litigation. In some respects, the lawyer is expected to make a presentation in front of a third-party neutral, and those portions may feel similar to an adjudicatory procedure. On the other hand, the third party is powerless to make decisions, and the decision-making capability rests in the hands of the parties at all times. In that regard, mediation is similar to negotiation.

Given the similarities and differences to other types of processes, lawyers in mediation walk a tightrope trying to determine effective advocacy. Too often, lawyers treat mediation similar to a mini-trial, using all of the same advocacy tools that they might use in a courtroom. The lawyers may make inflammatory and overconfident statements regarding the facts or the law. They make insulting offers or demands during the negotiation portion of the mediation. Lawyers may act in an adversarial manner in order to try to "win" the mediator and convince the mediator of the rightness of the client's position.

Advocacy that is too aggressive often backfires during mediation. Attorneys who try to "win" the mediator in the same way that they would try to "win" a judge or jury completely miss the benefits mediation provides. In mediation, the decision-maker is not a neutral third party. Instead, the decision-maker is the actual *party* on the other side of the negotiating table. Conscientious lawyers recognize this distinction and gear their advocacy and presentations toward convincing the other side of the reasonableness of their own clients' positions. Stated another way, the audience for a mediation is primarily the opposing client, and secondarily the mediator. No matter how eloquent (or bombastic), the opposing party will not likely bow down to the opposing counsel's legal and factual recitation. However, the opposing client will likely be interested in hearing how the other side's proposal is reasonable under the circumstances and meets the needs of all parties.

This chapter considers the mediation process from the advocate's point of view and provides guidance on how advocates can effectively approach the mediation process.

§ 6.02 The Mediation Process — Advocate's Point of View

[A] Pre-Mediation

The mediation process begins well before the parties meet with the mediator. The best way to have a successful mediation is to agree with the other side on procedural issues prior to the mediation and to prepare not only as the advocate, but also to prepare the client as to what to expect. There are many steps to cross off the to-do list before getting to the mediator's office. First, examine the local jurisdiction's governing rules on mediation to protect the client.[1] After reading the governing rules, the parties will need to formulate a mediation agreement, select a mediator, and prepare for the mediation session. These steps and more are discussed below.

[1] Agreements to Mediate

A mediation agreement is essentially a contract between the parties and the mediator. A pre-dispute mediation agreement may be included in the parties' business or employment contract, and one side need only invoke the provision to initiate mediation.[2] In some cases, the parties or lawyers draft the mediation agreement after the dispute arises.[3] In other instances, the parties have a mediation agreement in place to resolve future disputes between the parties. Parties may draft their own standalone mediation agreement or use a standard form agreement supplied by the mediator.

Agreements to mediate after the mediator has been chosen can be provided by the mediator in a form document. Most mediation agreements share common elements.[4] These provisions include who may or may not attend the session, the payment of mediation fees, confidentiality and privilege, scheduling, procedure, and other various items that counsel may want included.[5] Despite these common provisions, lawyers and clients should review the provisions carefully in case they want to change or add to the agreement.

The agreement to mediate may include the identity of a specific mediator, or the parties may agree to set forth mediator qualifications within the contract. For example, the parties could agree on certain mediator credentials, such as specified training, experience, mediator orientation,[6] subject matter expertise, neutrality and personal traits.[7] The agreement could also specify a single mediator or co-mediators. The parties may also consider a procedure to choose a mediator, such as using a mediator from a provider organization's panel, such as the AAA or JAMS.[8] Additionally, the contract-drafting stage is a good time to determine if the relevant jurisdiction has any requirements for

---

1. Spencer Punnett, REPRESENTING CLIENTS IN MEDIATION 19 (2013).
2. Harold I. Abramson, MEDIATION REPRESENTATION 176 (2013).
3. Spencer Punnett, REPRESENTING CLIENTS IN MEDIATION 74 (2013).
4. *Id.* at 75.
5. *Id.* at 76–82.
6. A more detailed discussion of mediator orientations can be found supra Section 4.07.
7. Harold I. Abramson, MEDIATION REPRESENTATION 178 (2013).
8. *See* AMERICAN ARBITRATION ASSOCIATION, COMMERCIAL ARBITRATION RULES AND MEDIATION PROCEDURES (2013); JAMS, JAMS INTERNATIONAL MEDIATION RULES (2011).

mediators or mediation. Section [2] herein, dedicated to choosing your mediator, explores the pros and cons of each of these decisions.

[a] Is the Case Appropriate for Mediation?

Most cases are appropriate for mediation. Mediation is common in a variety of disputes, including contract, family, construction, employment, personal injury, health care, intellectual property, bankruptcy, elder, probate, and many other types of law. In some instances, mediation may not be appropriate. There are many factors to consider when deciding whether mediation is the appropriate forum for the case at hand. Cases dealing with abuse, issues of public, moral, legal concern, or where a confidential agreement might be inappropriate are instances where mediators, lawyers, or parties may decide that mediation is not the best way to come to a resolution. When a case deals with an important issue of public concern, the public may have an interest in the result of the mediation. The public could face harm if the result of the mediation is bound under a confidentiality agreement. While there is no set approach to determine whether a case should go to mediation, considering these factors can help settle any concerns one might have.[9]

Mediators and Law Professors Douglas Frenkel and James Stark posed questions for mediators to explore when deciding whether or not to take a case, and the same questions are helpful for advocates to use. Is a party seeking to use mediation as a means of discovery, inimidation, or delay? Are both parties able to come to an agreement that is valid? Do all the parties have authority to settle? Are the parties coming to the table in good faith?[10] These questions should be addressed when determining whether mediation is the best route.

Although the lawyer believes the case should go to mediation, the chosen mediator may decline to mediate. If a mediator is reluctant to take a specific case, consider whether a new mediator should be chosen or whether the case is appropriate for mediation at all. For example, a mediator might refuse to take a child custody case because she was recently divorced and would feel a bias toward the mother in the case. Here, it would be appropriate to search for a new mediator. A mediator might also believe a case is not appropriate for mediation because he believes that one party has too much power over the other and therefore an agreement would not be valid. If this is the case, the lawyers should reevaluate taking the case to mediation.

[b] What Rules Should Govern the Mediation?

The parties' mediation agreement is subject to applicable court and statutory rules governing mediation as well as the rules of designated provider institutions. Mediation rules vary from state to state. For example, Florida has statutory provisions for court-ordered mediation that provides its mediators immunity from liability from the performance of their mediation duties, provided they are not acting in bad faith.[11] The California Evidence Code includes a provision specifically related to mediation. Under § 1121, a mediator or anyone else involved in the process may not submit to a court or other adjudicative body, and a court or other adjudicative body may not consider, any report or finding of any kind by the mediator concerning a mediation conducted by the

---

9. Douglas N. Frenkel & James H. Stark, THE PRACTICE OF MEDIATION 95 (2008).
10. *Id.*
11. *See* Fla. Stat. § 44.107 (2015).

mediator, unless that report that was mandated by court rule or other law. This report can only state whether an agreement was reached, unless all parties to the mediation expressly agree otherwise in writing or orally.[12]

One of the most important considerations is the rule of confidentiality. In most forums, the confidentiality rule is stipulated by an alternative dispute organization or the mediator. For parties using a mediator from a large ADR provider organization, such as the AAA, JAMS, or FINRA, the organization's rules include confidentiality protections.[13] Whether or not the parties are already covered by confidentiality provisions by law, court rule, or provider organization rule, confidentiality obligations should still be addressed explicitly.[14] The agreement to mediate with the other party and the mediator is another document to govern the session "layered on top of whatever else applies, such as the procedural rules of a court-annexed mediation program or alternative dispute organization, statutes or mediators' professional-association rules regulating mediator conduct and confidentiality, state ethics-board opinions and so forth."[15]

[c] Do Lawyer Ethics Require Client Counseling on the Mediation Option?

Rule 2.1 of the Model Rules of Professional Conduct provides that "in representing a client, a lawyer shall exercise independent professional judgment and render candid advice."[16] Additionally, in rendering that advice, "a lawyer may refer not only to law but to other considerations such as moral, economic, social and political factors that may be relevant to the client's situation."[17] This professional judgment could include informing a client about the process of mediation and how mediation may or may not be a better option than going to court. Generally speaking, a lawyer is not expected to give advice until the client asks, but a lawyer might have a duty under Rule 1.4 to give advice relating to the representation if the client wants to do something that has adverse legal consequences.[18]

The mediation option can be presented at various times during representation. The first opportunity arises when the client consults the lawyer. Explaining the mediation process to the client and how the client's interests and goals can be satisfied outside of the courtroom can be risky, as some clients want to take an aggressive strategy.[19] Some lawyers might find that it is better to discuss the mediation process after a court has ordered the case to mediation, or after a significant amount of discovery is complete.[20] Again, this would include explaining the process, the advantages and disadvantages, and how the client's goals can be met.

[2] Choosing a Mediator

Choosing the mediator is one of the most important steps of pre-mediation. In fact, the biggest mistake attorneys make is not putting enough thought into selecting the

---

12. Cal. Evid. Code § 1121
13. *See* American Arbitration Association, Commercial Arbitration Rules and Mediation Procedures (2013); JAMS, JAMS International Mediation Rules (2011).
14. Spencer Punnett, Representing Clients in Mediation 80 (2013).
15. Harold I. Abramson, Mediation Representation 75 (2013).
16. Model Rules of Prof'l Conduct r. 2.1 (2016).
17. *Id.*
18. Model Rules of Prof'l Conduct r. 2.1 Comment 5 (2016).
19. Harold I. Abramson, Mediation Representation 172 (2013).
20. *Id.* at 173.

proper mediator.[21] In some cases, the parties may not have an option regarding the choice of the mediator. In some court-connected cases, a judge may assign a particular mediator to a case. On some court-connected mediation panels, an administrator may systematically assign a mediator to rotate through panel members and evenly distribute the mediation work. When parties use a community mediation center, the center may choose which mediator will mediate a given case. In many cases (including court-connected cases), the parties have the ability to choose the mediator.

A key consideration for choosing a mediator, arguably the most important, is the mediator's training and experience. Organizations have varied requirements for mediator certification. These certifications allow parties to see what training or experience the mediator has completed.[22] Also investigate a mediator's experience in the mediation process. How many mediations has he or she done? Have they completed training outside of their initial certification? Depending on the type of case, one may be interested in the mediator's familiarity with a specific area of law. A mediator who only has experience resolving intellectual property cases might not be as effective in a child custody case.

What type of approach the mediator normally takes can also be an issue to explore when deciding on a mediator. This can have an impact on what the parties can expect during the mediation process and how to effectively represent the client.[23] Four questions help guide this analysis, and the first two relate to the Riskin Grid, discussed in Chapter 4.[24] First, should the process be managed in a facilitative or evaluative manner? Facilitative mediators assist the parties working together to solve their problems. They help with the process, but the resolution is in the parties' control.[25] Evaluative mediators assess the situation and tell the parties what they believe the outcome of the case would be. They evaluate the legal case and predict the outcome.[26] In the case at hand, which approach is better and what does the client need to reach a settlement? Next, a decision should be made on whether the parties will benefit from the mediator taking a narrow or broad approach to the problem. This will primarily be determined by the needs of the client and whether they are worried specifically about the legal claim involved or if there are other issues that need to be worked out. Third, consider how the mediator interacts with the clients. Does the mediator focus on the lawyer instead of the client or work in a way that lets the client remain involved, but respects the role of the attorney?[27] Also think about the mediator's use of caucusing. There are many different opinions on this issue and the choice might not be the same every time depending on what the client needs. Is it better for the parties to negotiate directly with each other or would they benefit from talking through the mediator?

Answers to these questions ultimately depend on the needs of the client and the relevant facts in the mediation. It is important to look at what would create the best outcome for the parties and what mediator techniques would best fit those needs. However, the parties' needs do not always result in the same mediator choice. This is why it is important to agree on a selection process. There are different ways to select a mediator. The easiest is counsel for one party picking the mediator and the other side agreeing to

---

21. Spencer Punnett, REPRESENTING CLIENTS IN MEDIATION 47 (2013).
22. Harold I. Abramson, MEDIATION REPRESENTATION 178 (2013).
23. Harold I. Abramson, MEDIATION REPRESENTATION 184 (2013).
24. *See supra* Section 4.07.
25. Harold I. Abramson, MEDIATION REPRESENTATION 188–189 (2013).
26. *Id.* at 190.
27. *Id.* at 194.

that option without question.[28] One party can submit a list of candidates to the other side to have them choose the mediator. Alternatively, counsel for the parties can exchange lists of potential mediators with each other or have a conversation and decide together.[29]

[3] How to Prepare for Mediation

Preparation is key in a mediation. Although mediation tends to be less formal than the courtroom, attorneys must be prepared. There is a lot to be done before arriving at the session to avoid wasting time during the mediation. In order to make a plan that will be successful, lawyers should look at their client's interests and prepare accordingly. How the lawyer prepares will also depend on when the mediation session occurs. If the mediation is held too early, the lawyer knows less about the case, which makes preparing more difficult and time-consuming. On the other hand, if the mediation is held late, the parties could be too entrenched in the litigation process and not want to settle.

Like any legal process, research needs to be done to protect the client's interests, overcome any potential impediments, and specify what information should be shared.[30] Preparing for a mediation is similar to preparing for trial because the attorney needs to gather factual and legal research to know the case well. This includes gathering all the facts and determining what is relevant to the issue in mediation, what facts are not helpful to the client, and developing a plan for the session. Attorneys should attempt to give the case a financial value in order to come to the table with a realistic idea of settlement.[31] This should be done with the client so they can understand why settlement might be beneficial and potentially why the case is valued lower than they believe it should be. By determining a financial value, attorneys can also get an idea of where the other side is at.[32] In order to determine the value of a case, some attorneys use decision trees as a form of litigation risk analysis. This process estimates the probabilities of different litigation outcomes and the various damages awards.[33] Attorneys should be aware of this and look to relevant law in addition to this form of preparation.

Mediation submission statements are helpful to prepare both the attorneys and also the mediator. How these are prepared will depend on the mediator's overall approach and some might not ask for them at all.[34] If they do, their request will likely specify the information they want to know. These statements are discussed further in this chapter.

A major part of the preparation stage includes preparing with the client. Attorneys should focus on the clients because the result of the mediation will directly affect them. If the clients are unprepared for the mediation process, the attorney has not truly done their job. Preparing the clients should include discussing the weaknesses of the case, the risks of not settling in mediation, and a realistic view of the outcome.[35] Attorneys want to prevent the clients from being blindsided during the session and that includes preparing them for how the other side will likely react to offers. Meeting with the clients can also provide the attorney with a chance to gather more information to help them

---

28. Spencer Punnett, REPRESENTING CLIENTS IN MEDIATION 49 (2013).
29. *Id.*
30. Harold Abramson, MEDIATION REPRESENTATION 246 (2013).
31. Spencer Punnett, REPRESENTING CLIENTS IN MEDIATION 175 (2013).
32. *Id.*
33. *Id.* at 176–177.
34. Harold I. Abramson, MEDIATION REPRESENTATION 108 (2013).
35. Spencer Punnett, REPRESENTING CLIENTS IN MEDIATION 205 (2013).

prepare their case.[36] While most of the important information should be known at this stage, there is always a chance for more facts to be uncovered.

If the parties are headed to mediation, it is likely the client already knows about the process and what to expect. It is still a good idea to explain the process by discussing the nature of mediation, who will be there, everyone's roles, and the procedure.[37] Client counseling is a major part of preparing a case and should be done throughout the representation.

[4] Client Counseling Prior to Mediation

Whether preparing for trial or mediation, client counseling is critical and starts the minute the client walks into the office for their initial consultation. This book has already discussed the ethics involved in counseling, but what exactly should lawyers discuss with their clients?

Before the mediation starts, the client should be able to list and explain his overall interests and goals from the session. An attorney might think she knows the underlying interests of a case based on the facts, but it is not always as simple as it seems. Interests are what motivate people.[38] This means the client might not even realize what the real interests are. Attorneys should probe for these interests and help the client understand them in order to ultimately reach a settlement he can be satisfied with. As mentioned previously, the client also needs to know about any issues or impediments the case may face in the mediation process. By discussing these obstacles, the attorney can prepare ways to overcome them.[39] This part of client counseling can be done early in the attorney's representation.

Mediation requires counsel to take a step away from their adversarial nature and work with the other side to find a suitable result.[40] A client unaware of this shift in the lawyer's role might not think he is being represented adequately. Explaining not only how the attorney role is different, but how the client's role differs from the courtroom setting will help the mediation run smoothly. The client should be aware that the process is collaborative, not adversarial, and they should act respectfully to the other side.[41] In many cases, clients control the mediation, not the lawyer. The client should know that and the lawyer should decide with the client prior to the mediation who will handle what aspect of the case. Perhaps the most important role clients should be aware of is that of the mediator. Not all clients will have knowledge of the mediation process, so explaining that the mediator is meant to be a neutral third party who is there to facilitate the negotiation is crucial.[42]

[B] Mediation Sessions

The day of the session has arrived. Countless hours have been spent preparing the client what to expect. The attorney has prepared arguments in order to advocate strongly.

---

36. *Id.* at 207.
37. *Id.* at 208–210.
38. Harold I. Abramson, MEDIATION REPRESENTATION 147 (2013).
39. *Id.* at 157.
40. *Id.* at 372.
41. *Id.*
42. Spencer Punnett, REPRESENTING CLIENTS IN MEDIATION 211 (2013).

What happens now? This section will discuss stages of the process and strategies for effective client representation in mediation.

[1] Opening Statements

Opening statements start the mediation process by providing an opportunity for both parties to explain their side of the story. Essentially, opening statements allow counsel to present their legal case in a less formal way. The presentation of the case will depend on who goes first, but the tone of the opening statement sets up the rest of the session. An attorney who opens the session with personal attacks and a rude demeanor can damage rapport with the other side, but a lawyer who concedes too much right away is not truly advocating for her client.[43] The tone of an opening statement should be respectful and show an understanding of the other side's interests.[44] It should avoid any sensitive issues that could create major problems early on. Attorneys should also be aware of their body language and how they are speaking, in order to ensure they are sending a positive message.[45]

In the opening remarks, the lawyer should demonstrate a willingness to learn more information and work together with all parties involved. Parties should be able to ask questions about specific information they are curious about.[46]

Presenting the opening statement second may require a slightly different approach. The party presenting second should acknowledge the views of the other, but try not to react specifically to the other's opening statement and instead focus on expressing their primary concerns and issues and framing them in a neutral manner.[47] Once both parties have shared, the mediator might use this time to start asking questions in order to clarify information from both sides.

In some situations, an opening statement might not be necessary, such as the mediator has requested pre-mediation submission statements. Even if there is no pre-mediation briefing, some mediators and attorneys believe opening statements are an unnecessary step.[48] Some reasons for this belief are that they do not provide any new information, attorneys do not want to give information to the other side, and beliefs that opening statements are just a way to grandstand and insult the other side.[49] In certain circumstances opening statements are not advisable, such as when there are extremely hostile feelings involved. In this situation, having the opportunity to directly speak with each other might cause more harm than good and risk ending the mediation before it is even started.

[2] Information Exchanges

Exchanging information is a crucial part of the mediation process. A party can only gather so much information on his or her own and may have information not accessible by the other party, preparing questions prior to the session helps the parties identify information that is needed. Because both sides will have questions, attorneys should also

---

43. Harold I. Abramson, MEDIATION REPRESENTATION 282–283 (2013).
44. *Id.* at 283.
45. *Id.*
46. Harold I. Abramson, MEDIATION REPRESENTATION 275 (2013).
47. *Id.* at 276.
48. *Id.* at 280.
49. *Id.*

be prepared to share information with the other side and promote a positive relationship with open communication. This is done by presenting information in a reasonable way and being respectful to the other side.[50] If a positive rapport is built, prepared questions have a greater likelihood of receiving a detailed response.

Both parties will ask questions to gather information, so it is important for everyone to be open to sharing information without exploiting clients in any way.[51] What is the client willing to share? Is it helpful to share this information? For mediations in caucus, the mediator can help to determine information the other side may want to know and how to frame that information in a way that would be productive to the process. Private caucusing provides an opportunity for parties to disclose private information to the mediator in order to determine whether it is appropriate to share with the other side or not.[52] Parties should remember that discussions in caucus are confidential unless they allow the mediator to share information.

[3] Problem Solving and Negotiation

After parties have engaged in the information gathering phase, they can begin to shift the discussion on how to resolve the stated concerns.

When parties reach the problem-solving stage, a good way to get the ball rolling is to start brainstorming for creative options. This might seem difficult if the case is focused on monetary solutions, but brainstorming can open the door to a wide range of possibilities.[53] If parties are hesitant to be creative, they can allocate a certain, small amount of time to brainstorming. Even if this does not end with a solution, it does not hurt to try.[54]

If the mediation is caucus-based, parties should use the mediator in a proactive manner. Because parties are separated at this stage, this might be a good time to fill the mediator in on any private facts that help the client and their position.[55] Once the mediator is given all the facts, it might be beneficial to use the mediator as a reality check for the client to how settling the case may actually be in that client's best interests.[56] Deciding the next move can be tricky, so attorneys are encouraged to discuss possible moves with the mediator. In caucus-based mediation, the mediator can give insight on how the other party might feel about an offer. Mediators can use their previous experiences to provide opinions on what they would do in the situation.[57] While discussing the next move, advocates should keep in mind the minimum offer at which their client will accept a settlement. Whether or not parties disclose this bottom line to the mediator is a personal choice, but it can help the mediator provide better advice.

It might seem difficult to communicate in a caucus-based mediation, especially when it seems just numbers are passed back and forth. Advocates should try to interpret what the opposing party's numbers are saying and be aware of what their offers are

---

50. Harold I. Abramson, MEDIATION REPRESENTATION 314 (2013).
51. *Id.*
52. Spencer Punnett, REPRESENTING CLIENTS IN MEDIATION 342 (2013).
53. *Id.* at 395.
54. *Id.* at 396.
55. Spencer Punnett, REPRESENTING CLIENTS IN MEDIATION 342 (2013).
56. *Id.* at 346.
57. *Id.* at 352.

comunicating in return.[58] When the range of offers start to become closer, it is likely that the other side is reaching their bottom line. Parties need to adapt their negotiation plan to the other side during the session, and advocates should be prepared for anything. If the negotiation does not happen the way the parties expected, emotions can become involved and create bigger problems for the session. Emotions from the client are typical, especially when the first offer (or counteroffer) is much different from what they believe it should be.[59] The likelihood of an emotional reaction can be reduced if the client is properly prepared for this possibility prior to the mediation.

Attorneys should track offers and counteroffers during the negotiation stage. This helps provide a more accurate sense of where the negotiations are heading[60] and allows the attorney to make changes if they believe negotiations are heading in the wrong direction. If an offer needs to be justified, writing down the reasons and specific numbers can also help provide clarity.[61] It is important to remember that advocates can take private caucuses with their client at any time during the negotiation stage to discuss offers and counteroffers separately.

[4] Impasse Breaking

There are times when the mediation process can reach an impasse. Different factors can come into play and create an impasse which can result from the client needing something they are not getting from mediation. Section 4.05[C][3] discusses various techniques that a mediator may employ to avoid impasse in cases involving monetary damages.[62] Those techniques include bracketing, using a "black box" method, or receiving a mediator's proposal, among others. Sometimes the mediator will try to resolve an impasse by asking one party (or both) to concede a little bit more as a favor.[63] This is usually done at the end of the process and may require the mediator to tell the other side it was only done as a favor to the mediator.[64] Mediators are likely to use various impasse-breaking techniques to get parties toward a resolution, but there are ways advocates can do the same. If an advocate thinks that the case is suitable for one of these types of techniques, the lawyer can suggest that the mediator try the technique in order to keep the mediation session moving. If the mediator suggests such an option the advocate should consider whether these types of techniques would be helpful to the client. If the lawyer determines that the suggested technique would be detrimental to the client's case, then the lawyer should decline the mediator's suggestion or propose an alternative impasse-breaking technique.

Examples of issues that could arise for the client include wanting a realistic assessment of facts, likely court outcomes or damages, a realistic interpretation of the law, vindication, protections of principle, an opportunity to go for a jackpot, participation by another party, or good faith participation by the other side.[65] When this happens, it might be a good idea to suggest an alternative process where the result cannot be controlled by

---

58. *Id.* at 392.
59. *Id.* at 398.
60. *Id.* at 377.
61. *Id.* at 378.
62. A more detailed discussion of breaking impasse can be found *supra* Section 4.05[C][3].
63. *Id.* at 410.
64. *Id.*
65. Harold I. Abramson, Mediation Representation 436 (2013).

either party.[66] Attorneys should be cautious in these situations, though, and weigh the advantages and risks that come with each alternative.

If parties decide that they want to work through the impasse instead of looking to an alternative process, there are ways for the advocates to counsel their client. When the client is unwilling to budge on an offer during the session, it might be appropriate to discuss their BATNA again and analyze other potential outcomes. Reviewing the decision tree (if one was made) or looking at the probability of winning the case if it went to trial (and the realistic range of the award in comparison to what is at the table) could help a client realize they are being unrealistic. In addition, there are costs to preparing for trial that they might not be considering. Sometimes settlement becomes stuck on something as simple as an apology. Advocates should think about their client's underlying interests and brainstorm ways to cater to those needs in finding a solution.

[5] Enlisting the Help of the Mediator

In most cases, the mediator was selected by the parties to bring something to the table that counsel (and the other client) did not. They are being brought in to help and collaborate, so they should be used as much as possible. How the mediator will be used will vary depending on their style, preferences, and special techniques, but parties can influence what the mediator does, no matter their default process.[67]

Not all mediators choose to use a caucus-based process. When it is used, the mediator can act as more than a messenger.[68] The mediator can be used to help with the negotiation process, technique, as well as help with the testing of settlement offers, as described earlier. If the advocate wants to share information with the other side that the client is not comfortable with, the mediator can help assess the benefits and risks of sharing that information and assure the client that it is in their best interests.[69] They can also be another person to listen to the client's frustrations, allowing them to vent. This can be helpful to allow the client to feel better and also allow the mediator to get a deeper look into how the client is feeling. Even though it is recommended that the advocate know their client's interests before getting to the mediation session, the mediator can sometimes help clarify those interests.[70]

Outside of caucus-based negotiations, the mediator can be trusted to help parties overcome issues with each other. If one side is having trouble with problem solving and that is harming the negotiation, the mediator can employ skills such as active listening and reframing to help them figure out a solution and can use those techniques to help resolve a relationship conflict. A party who does not think that a specific technique is working, that side should feel free to ask the mediator to try another technique.[71] Mediators are not perfect, so if there is a technique that is not helping the parties come to a resolution, it is okay to move in a different direction.[72] However, this should be done respectfully because even though the process is taking place for the client's benefit, the mediator's expertise should be taken into account.

---

66. *Id.*
67. Spencer Punnett, Representing Clients in Mediation 342 (2013).
68. Harold I. Abramson, Mediation Representation 235 (2013).
69. *Id.* at 236.
70. *Id.*
71. Harold I. Abramson, Mediation Representation 387 (2013).
72. *Id.* at 388 (2013).

[C] Post-Mediation Issues

Even though the mediation session is over and the parties have settled, the advocate's job is not yet complete. The parties will need a way to wrap up the mediation process; many believe the mediation process should not end without the parties signing an agreement or document that contains the agreed-upon terms.[73] This prevents either party from arguing later that the settlement agreement was not what they agreed to.

[1] Contract Drafting

Where clients are represented, generally attorneys draft the settlement. Although issues have been resolved, the agreement needs to satisfy the client's interests and properly reflect the settlement terms.[74] No matter which attorney drafts the settlement agreement, attorneys should be careful to follow traditional contracting principles in order to avoid vulnerability to legal challenges.[75] The attorney who does not draft should carefully review the agreement to make sure it is accurate and does not cause issues for their client, legally or personally.

Whoever is drafting the settlement agreement should be mindful to use clear language that is specific, but mutual, positive, and personal.[76] The agreement should be something that the parties can realistically achieve and complete to avoid any future issues.

[2] Enforcement of Mediated Agreements

A settlement agreement is essentially a contract. Therefore, contract law governs the enforcement of the agreement. When an issue does arise between parties to a mediated agreement, possible claims include fraud/misrepresentation, duress, undue influence, mistake, unconscionability, or that there was no meeting of the minds.[77] Parties should remember that evidence from the mediation will not be allowed in to prove the contract due to confidentiality, unless there is an exception in the law.[78] Between 1999 and 2003, 64 percent of cases enforced the mediated agreement.[79]

§ 6.03 Client Involvement in Mediation

Although lawyers have an important role to play in mediation, the mediation process is still a party-centered process, and the mediator will likely involve the client in the process. Court rules, statutes, and mediators often require the parties' attendance.[80] When

---

73. *Id.* at 417.
74. *Id.*
75. *Id.* at 421.
76. Douglas N. Frenkel & James H. Stark, The Practice of Mediation 95 (2008).
77. Harold I. Abramson, Mediation Representation 421 (2013).
78. *Id.*
79. Spencer Punnett, Representing Clients in Mediation 471 (2013).
80. Courts generally find that good-faith participation in mediation requires a party's attendance at the mediation. See Megan G. *Thompson, Mandatory Mediation and Domestic Violence: Reformulating the Good-Faith Standard*, 86 Or. L. Rev. 599, 606 (2007).

the parties are in the room, they can make decisions on whether or not to settle the case after they have heard everything that the parties, the lawyers, and the mediators have had to say. In some instances, parties may be able to participate remotely through technology such as teleconference or videoconference, or the parties may be available by telephone to make a decision if a conflict prevents actual attendance. The use of technology, however, often disconnects parties from the process and prevents full engagement.[81]

If a judge or court rule requires client attendance, parties or their lawyers may be sanctioned if the client fails to appear. For example, a Florida judge sanctioned the lawyers of basketball legend Shaquille O'Neal $13,000 when O'Neal failed to attend a court-mandated mediation session in person.[82] Sanctions for failure to appear at a mediation could include the cost of the mediator, the travel and preparation time of the client, and attorney's fees for the other side's client.

This section discusses the client's role in mediation, including the issues of who should attend the mediation, what part the client should take during the mediation process, and how to use the mediator to rein in client expectations. All clients, however, are different and bring different skills and values to the mediation table. Some clients present well to the mediator and opposing side through articulate comments and understanding. Other clients may be less presentable or articulate, so the attorney may limit the involvement of those types of clients. These suggestions are flexible, and individual circumstances may inform a different strategy for client involvement in mediation.

[A] Who Should Attend the Mediation?

In most instances, clients will be required to attend the mediation. When the client is an individual, the "who" question is relatively easy. Determining which member or members of a corporate client should attend the session is a more difficult question. This section considers these issues, as well as issues dealing with third-party involvement in the process.

[1] Individual Client

When the client is an individual, that individual should attend the mediation. In a divorce action, the husband and the wife should both mediate. In a personal injury case, the injured party should be in attendance. In a workplace conflict, the parties to the conflict should be at the table. As individual, named parties, these people have the power to make the decisions on whether and what terms to settle the outstanding dispute. These individuals also likely have the greatest amount of perspective and information that can be useful in trying the resolve the dispute. Often, lawyers attend the mediation in addition to the client. Whether the lawyer attends will be discussed separately below.

---

81. The pros and cons of using technology in mediation are discussed in Chapter 10.04[C].

82. Julie Kay, *No Special Treatment for Shaq! Attorneys Fined for Allowing Him to Skip Mediation*, Daily Business Review, Feb. 23, 2016, available at http://www.dailybusinessreview.com/id=1202750395697/No-Special-Treatment-for-Shaq-Attorneys-Fined-for-Allowing-him-to-Skip-Mediation?slreturn=20160410210420.

An individual client may want to have another person attend the mediation for emotional or psychological support. For instance, in a divorce mediation, one of the parents may want a new significant other or his or her own parent to be at the session for advice or to talk through settlement options. In a personal injury case, a spouse or friend might be helpful for many of the same reasons. If a party intends to bring a non-party support person, the party or attorney should let the mediator know in advance. Mediators often like to confer with the other party and ensure that the presence of the third party is welcome and not a distraction.

In some instances, the mediator may need to create special circumstances to accommodate a third-party support person into the mediation. For example, if one spouse objects to the other spouse bringing a new significant other to the mediation, then the mediator may try to find a way for the support person to be available in caucuses or breaks, even if that person cannot be in the room with both spouses together. In cases with sensitive topics, such as trade secrets, client lists, or financial information, the presence of outsiders may also need to be limited.

Clients may have a legal right to bring a lawyer or support person to the mediation. Under the Uniform Mediation Act Section 10, "An attorney or other individual designated by a party may accompany the party to and participate in a mediation."[83] The official comments clarify that the representative need not be a lawyer, but may be a non-attorney support person.

Whether children can or should attend mediation sessions is a particularly delicate topic. Children occasionally attend mediations involving custody issues, and those mediations usually involve teenage clients. Children — particularly older children — may also attend a mediation if the child is directly involved in the lawsuit, such as a personal injury case involving a car accident. Young children and children with disabilities may not be able to contribute to the mediation and should not attend the mediation.

[2] Corporate Client

Who should attend mediation from the perspective of a corporate client is a more difficult question and the answer likely depends on the individual circumstances. Often, the mediator (or court rule or judge) requires the representative to have authority to settle the case if that is in the best interest of the client. A typical rule for a small to mid-size corporation is to ensure that someone of "vice president" status (or equivalent status at institutions such as non-profit or educational organizations) attends. Whether counsel for the corporation (i.e., in-house counsel) qualifies as an appropriate company representative may vary across the country depending on local custom. Note that many mediators and attorneys would not consider in-house counsel alone an appropriate corporate representative.

Choosing a corporate representative to attend a mediation often involves weighing the balance between bringing a person with sufficient status to demonstrate that the business takes the mediation seriously and bringing a person with sufficient knowledge of the underlying situation. Other factors may also be important, such as bringing someone who can show compassion for the other side (especially when an individual sues a corporation for an alleged consumer or employment wrong) or bringing a person who has a relationship with the other party (in cases involving long-term business

---

83. Uniform Mediation Act § 10.

relationships). Of course, the corporate client need not choose only one delegate. The corporate client may wish to bring multiple representatives, such as one with broad settlement authority and another with personal knowledge of the facts. Bringing additional representatives may also create a numerical advantage for the corporate client from a negotiation perspective.[84]

An example may illustrate some of the difficulties in determining an appropriate corporate representative. Consider a chain shoe store with locations in malls across the country. A former employee brings a lawsuit against the company for sexual harassment based on the conduct of the manager of her store. The case is set for mediation. A large number of potential client representatives *could* attend. The chief executive officer could go, but she does not have personal knowledge of the facts and is busy overseeing the operation of hundreds of stores nationwide. The chief financial officer is another possibility, but he also does not have relevant knowledge. The vice president of human resources could attend, and she is likely apprised of the situation, but does not have firsthand knowledge. The store manager could attend, but he is the alleged harasser and might make the situation more emotional than necessary. Other possibilities exist, too, such as regional managers, other personnel in human resources, and other types of executives within the company. The company representative should be apprised of the situation (whether through firsthand knowledge or through briefing) and be able to make decisions on behalf of the company.

The lawyer may need to ensure that that the company representative has been authorized by the Board of Directors (or Trustees, etc., as appropriate) to make or accept settlement offers. A party may open itself up for sanctions if it enters the mediation without any real authority to settle the case. In many cases, particularly personal injury cases, a representative from the insurance company with authority to make a decision in the case must also be in attendance. In some jurisdictions, an insurance adjuster need only be available by telephone to approve a final settlement.

[3] Witnesses, Experts, and Other Support Personnel

Additional third parties may be necessary or wise to have at a mediation session. Lawyers who plan on inviting such personnel should notify the mediator in advance and allow time for the other side to consent or refuse the presence of these additional people at the table.

A variety of people may be helpful to a mediation, including financial experts, party expert witnesses, "neutral" or jointly retained expert witnesses, or witnesses with personal knowledge. Although mediation is intended to be a forward-looking process, sometimes parties are not ready to make a decision until they have a clearer idea on past, factual issues that an eyewitness or expert witness may be able to address.

In other instances, outside parties may be necessary to ensure that the parties are able to understand the mediation and make informed decisions. Translation help should be afforded to parties whose primary language is different from the mediator and other parties. Health issues for one party may require the presence of a caretaker or nurse. These types of support personnel are not intended to influence the course of mediation,

---

84. *See, e.g.,* Edward Brunet, Alternative Dispute Resolution: The Advocate's Perspective Cases and Materials 152–53 (2012).

but instead act as reasonable accommodations to ensure that the parties have the requisite capacity to participate.[85]

[4] Lawyers

This chapter has largely assumed that lawyers should attend the mediation session; however, the presence of lawyers in the mediation room may not always be expected or productive in individual situations. Lawyers bring skill and expertise to mediation and are almost always a welcome resource in mediation. Lawyers and clients can confer in real time, they can ask and answer questions with the opposing party, and they may be able to articulate the client's wishes and ideas better than the client. On the other hand, lawyers may make the process unduly adversarial and steer the conversation away from client interests—such as apologies and non-monetary settlement options and increase mediation costs.

Local custom may also determine whether lawyers attend mediation. In some jurisdictions, the practice is for lawyers to prepare clients for mediation but not attend the sessions with the clients—particularly in family law cases. In other jurisdictions and other subject-matter areas, it is assumed that lawyers will accompany their clients. In general, lawyers often enhance the mediation process, especially when they have taken the time to prepare with their client, understand the clients' needs and interests, and have created a plan for an effective mediation.

[B] What Role Should the Client Play in Mediation?

Presuming the lawyer will be at the mediation, the next consideration is the role of the client in the room. During the client counseling preparation session, the lawyer should alert the client that the mediator will likely want the client to take a role in the process, if not an active role in the process. In most circumstances, the mediation process proceeds optimally when both the lawyer and the client remain active and engaged in the mediation process.

The division of roles between attorney and client should be somewhat intuitive. Each participant should address issues within their areas of expertise. Lawyers, naturally, should handle the legal arguments and legal issues. Lawyers, too, are often the proper persons to make, reject, or modify potential settlement options—especially in an evaluative mediation process. Clients, on the other hand, are often in the best position to discuss issues relating to the facts of the case, any effects of the conflict, and the underlying interests that would resolve the dispute. Clients are often the experts of their own case and can communicate those facts, feelings, and interests with greater credibility and sincerity than the lawyer.

Some clients have particular expertise that lawyers do not sharee. For example, in a case that involves lost business profits, asking the company's chief financial officer to explain the financial situation in mediation may be more effective than using a lawyer to summarize the same information. In cases involving technology, having the inventor to explain how the widget works, how it is different from other widgets, or how the widget was defective can be very powerful and convincing to the other side. Cases involving complicated business transactions, medical procedures, construction plans, or

---

85. ABA/AAA MODEL STANDARD FOR MEDIATION: Party Capacity.

the like may all benefit from direct client involvement, either in joint session or in private caucus with the mediator.

When a lawyer's client presents well and would make a good witness in a litigated case, allowing more robust client participation can be a strategic advantage. The lawyer can show off her client and use the client's demeanor as an additional reason to value the case favorably. On the contrary, if the client does not present well for any number of reasons—including being inarticulate, having bad manners, demonstrating a temper, or breaking down emotionally—the lawyer may decide to limit the client's direct involvement. In those situations, the lawyer may want to take the lead role in both the presentation and answering mediator questions.

As discussed above,[86] the lawyer may ask the client to give part of the opening remarks. Client involvement in the opening statement gives both the attorney and the client a voice in the process from the very beginning. During the mediation, the clients should be prepared for the mediator to ask the clients questions directly. The attorney and client should discuss in advance whether the client may answer the mediator's questions or if the attorney should answer them on behalf of the client. Some attorneys prefer to do all of the talking in joint sessions but to allow their clients considerably more freedom to speak in private caucus. Other lawyers will discuss with their clients in advance the types of questions that they should answer and the types of questions that they should allow the attorney to answer.

The correct amount of involvement of attorneys and clients will depend on the type of case, the client's goals, and the personal characteristics of the individual client. Ideally, both attorney and client will have an active role in the process and neither of them will become the proverbial "potted plant" in the room.

[C] Using the Mediator as a "Reality Check" for Clients

In some situations, lawyers can use the mediation process in order to help deliver bad news to their own client. A certain percentage of clients have unrealistic expectations of their own chances of victory in court. On the plaintiff's side, some clients are almost certain that they will receive millions or tens of millions of dollars for the alleged wrongs suffered. On the defense side, some defendants are completely unwilling to consider the possibility of a finding of any wrongdoing. In most situations, these types of expectations are unfounded and not conducive to settling cases for a realistic amount.

Clients do not always believe their own attorneys' evaluation of their cases, especially when the evaluation is not what the party wanted to hear. Mediation, then, can act as a neutral second opinion, especially when the mediator uses the evaluative style. In some cases, when the client hears the bad news not only from a lawyer but also from a neutral third party, the client may be more likely to believe the less favorable case assessment. For clients who are more risk averse, they may become more willing to settle the case in conformity with a more realistic evaluation of the available options.

---

86. *See supra* Section 6.02[B][1].

§ 6.04 Pre-Mediation Position Papers

Mediators generally request the parties submit written summaries prepared by attorneys in advance of the mediation session. The name of this summary can take many forms, but mediators may call it a "Pre-Mediation Position Paper," a "Pre-Mediation Submission," a "Pre-Mediation Brief," or other similar name. This section covers why mediators request these types of submissions, the question of whether the submission should be confidential to the other side, and a practical guide to items the mediator may request in such a paper.

[A] Overview

Pre-mediation submission statements help prepare the mediator understand the case and the parties' respective positions. For some mediators, pre-mediation submission statements replace party opening statements. Those mediators recognize that attorneys and parties will likely repeat what has already been presented in the brief for the opening statement, and eliminating the opening statement may make the mediation less contentious from the beginning.[87]

Lawyers often attach important documents, such as contracts, legal pleadings, and key pieces of evidence, to pre-mediation submission statements. Many mediators prefer to review this type of material in advance in order to have a sense of what the case is about prior to arriving at the mediation. After reviewing the information, the mediator is always free to request additional information, as needed.

Pre-mediation submission statements generally look like one of two types of documents. First, the statements can be formatted like letters addressed to the mediator. Second, the submission can take the form of a traditional legal brief, with a case caption at the top. In either case, the parties generally attach the important documents to the submission as either appendices or exhibits.

The tone of the mediation submission differs significantly from that of a traditional court filing. The primary goal of the submission is to show the mediator and other side (as permitted) how reasonable the lawyer and client are. The language should be simple and accurate, without significant embellishment or posturing. Mediators and opposing counsel will look straight through grandstanding and inflammatory remarks—that type of advocacy may be detrimental to obtaining a settlement in the case. On the other hand, the lawyer will have to share the brief with the client, so the tone must also demonstrate the lawyer's dedication to the client's case.

[B] Confidential or Open Briefing

Pre-mediation submission statements may be made confidentially to the mediator, shared with the other side, or a combination of both. Some mediators prefer one type of briefing over another, and some lawyers have their own preferences, too. Each of these forms has distinct advantages and disadvantages.

---

87. *See supra* Section 6.02[B][1].

Confidential briefing allows the parties to confide in the mediator and candidly discuss both the strengths and weaknesses of their side. Lawyers are more willing to make concessions and discuss client interests if that information will not be disclosed and later used against the client. If the memos are not exchanged, the parties can treat the discussion almost as if it were a caucus session. The biggest downside to confidential briefing is that the information is not shared with the other party, and the mediator may be required to hold a significant amount of confidential information from each side and juggle the type of information that can and cannot be shared.

Open briefing, on the other hand, is shared with all parties and increases the amount of information known to everyone. If the parties share their submissions with each other, they may be more likely to identify areas of commonality as well as pinpoint the true differences and items in dispute. Lawyers and parties, however, may not be nearly as candid in open briefing compared to confidential briefing. Further, open briefing has the potential for advocates to use more adversarial language and position the parties in a way that may be detrimental to settlement.

Another alternative is to use a combination of open and confidential briefing. The parties can exchange certain information with the mediator and each other while still submitting confidential information to the mediator. This technique combines the best of both situations, and many mediators utilize this format.

[C] Items to Include

Often, an individual mediator will alert the parties to the information that they would like to see covered in the briefing. The following is a nonexhaustive list of the types of information that a mediator may want covered:

- **Factual Summary of the Case**—The factual summary should describe to the mediator what the case is about. The ideal tone of this section is factual and non-inflammatory, yet still highlighting the best facts for the individual client. The factual summary should also acknowledge factual shortcomings and gaps, to the extent that they are relevant. Lawyers can organize this section either chronologically or topically, depending on the situation.

- **Legal Summary of the Case**—This section gives an overview of the legal case. The summary should be a snapshot, as opposed to a detailed account of every possible scenario. Again, the tone should be direct and non-inflammatory, recognizing both strengths and weaknesses in the legal argument.

- **Relief Sought or Damages Claimed**—This section will give the mediator a beginning idea of the monetary and non-monetary issues in the case.

- **Pending Motions**—Cases may be less likely to settle while dispositive motions, such as a motion to dismiss or a summary judgment motion, are pending. Mediators will want to know if pending legal motions could dismiss or limit the issues in a case.

- **Discovery Status**—As discussed above, many cases do not settle until the parties have enough information to make an informed decision regarding case value and potential options.[88] Mediating a case early in the discovery window may require

---

88. *See supra* Section 3.02.

more information-gathering techniques on the part of the mediator compared to cases that are mediated after the close of discovery.

- **Client Interests** — Some mediators may explicitly ask about the client's interests in order to have the client consider both monetary and nonmonetary settlement options.

- **Overview of Settlement Discussions** — Most mediators will want to understand how settlement discussions have proceeded up to the time of the mediation. In some cases, the parties will have engaged in substantial settlement discussions. In other cases, the lawyers may have put settlement discussions on hold pending mediation. The lawyers may have insight for the mediator on why the case has not settled as of that date.

- **Attendance** — The submission should indicate who will attend, including the identity of any corporate representatives.

- **How the Mediator Can Help** — Lawyers may want to include a section in their briefing regarding how the mediator can help in this particular case. Some lawyers may specify that the mediator use a particular mediation style (facilitative or evaluative), organize the session in a certain way (caucus or no-caucus, especially in multi-party disputes), or use certain techniques (such as brainstorming or bracketing). Most mediators will take very seriously suggestions by the lawyers and clients on how the mediation may be most successful.

Chapter 7

Collaborative Law

§ 7.01 Introduction to Collaborative Law

Collaborative law, sometimes simply called "collaborative," is a process in which two parties hire two collaborative lawyers so that the four participants can engage in problem-solving negotiations to resolve their dispute. The lawyers agree at the outset that they will engage in collaborative and cooperative techniques throughout the course of the case. One of the most distinctive features of collaborative law is the participation agreement (or "four-way agreement") that is signed by the lawyers and their clients. The participation agreement sets forth the code of conduct under which all of the participants will operate. Additionally, the participation agreement will call for the withdrawal of the lawyers for both sides in the event that the parties reach impasse. In essence, collaborative lawyers are counsel for negotiation purposes only. In this regard, they operate on a limited basis for the purposes of collaboration and negotiation. If the parties cannot reach a negotiated agreement, then the parties must both fire their lawyers and start the litigation process over with new lawyers.

The idea of collaborative law is generally attributed to Stuart G. Webb, a Minnesota trial attorney who became disenchanted with the litigation process. Around 1990, he decided to start a new type of practice—a "family law settlement" practice.[1] He was frustrated at the acrimonious way spouses and their attorneys treated each other, as well as frustrated with the way that courts were not servicing the couples and their families in a helpful way. Instead of representing clients in litigation, Mr. Webb limited his practice to helping the parties resolve their dispute out of court. He specifically agreed with his clients that he would be more than happy to help them with their divorce, but only for negotiation purposes. If a client wanted to litigate, then he would tell the client to find other litigation counsel. From these beginnings, collaborative law was born.

Mr. Webb's concept of collaborative law has grown to a viable practice in most major legal communities throughout the United States, as well as in Canada. As discussed in more detail below,[2] lawyers who want to practice collaborative law form practice groups in their locality. While some lawyers solely practice the collaborative model, other lawyers use the collaborative model in some cases and the traditional litigation model in other cases. In recent years, collaborative law has gained legitimacy with the enactment of court rules and legislation governing the process. Although collaborative law started and remains popular in the area of family law, collaborative practice is beginning to be used in the business community.

---

1. John Burwell Garvey & Charles B. Craver, ALTERNATIVE DISPUTE RESOLUTION: NEGOTIATION, MEDIATION, COLLABORATIVE LAW, AND ARBITRATION 195 (2013).
2. *See infra* Section 6.03[A].

§ 7.02 The Collaborative Process

The collaborative process draws some aspects of litigation and other aspects of dispute resolution, resulting in a hybrid process that seeks to take a case from factual development all the way through resolution by settlement. Since its inception in 1990, the collaborative process has become a practice with a relatively consistent structure based on the underlying philosophies of a client-centered practice, informed decision-making, and peaceful resolution to disputes.

[A] Collaborative Lawyers

The collaborative law process starts with collaborative lawyers. Not all lawyers are suited for the collaborative process, and the collaborative process only works with lawyers who are able to embrace the collaborative philosophy and practices. Sherrie Abney, collaborative attorney and trainer, describes collaborative lawyers as lawyers who work tremendously hard, but with the benefit of working solely toward settlement, as opposed to simultaneously working toward litigation and settlement options.[3] In this way, the collaborative lawyers have the freedom to only pursue settlement and can focus all of their attention on resolving disputes. Lawyers who live for the thrill of trial and advocacy based on taking advantage of every technicality and loophole are generally not well-suited for the collaborative practice.

Many collaborative lawyers have backgrounds in trial advocacy. These lawyers have firsthand experience in the stress and trauma the litigation process can impose on lawyers, clients, and families. Some of these lawyers may describe themselves as "burnt out" or as "recovering trial lawyers," having experienced little peace or justice in the traditional system. As collaborative law is being taught in the law schools,[4] some lawyers now enter directly into collaborative practice. Lawyers who are well-suited for collaborative practice are those who are interested in problem-solving, information sharing, collaboration, honesty, and interest-based negotiations.

Compared to traditional litigation attorneys, collaborative lawyers often view conflict as a holistic problem encompassing aspects well beyond the legal aspects of the case. Collaborative lawyers often work with and refer their clients to experts and coaches, such as mental health professionals, child specialists, financial resources, and other types of experts to solve the whole problem, and not only the legal aspect. These lawyers take seriously their role as counselor, in addition to their role as advocate.[5]

Lawyers that follow the true collaborative law method form practice groups within their localities. Unlike practice groups within a single law firm, these are groups of

---

3. Sherrie Abney, Avoiding Litigation: A Guide to Civil Collaborative Law 23 (2005).

4. For instance, Sherrie Abney teaches a three-credit-hour course on Collaborative Law at Southern Methodist University Dedman School of Law. Her syllabus reads: "Practical application of interest-based negotiation to disputes involving various areas under the law. Topics will include collaborative and cooperative law, informed consent, the Uniform Collaborative Law Act, ethics of unbundled legal services, case facilitation and management, use of experts, non-adversarial communication skills, case studies, drafting forms and agreements, and participation in role play." SMU Dedman School of Law Graduate Programs 2014–15 Catalog 97, available at http://catalogs .smu.edu/i/428201-2014-2015/32.

5. See Model Rules of Prof'l Conduct r. 2.1 (Lawyer as Counselor).

people who come from across law firms, with many of these lawyers being from solo and small practices. The International Academy of Collaborative Professionals, one of the leading collaborative law associations, defined a "practice group" as:

> an association of two or more professionals who have come together for purposes of enhancing their skills and understanding of Collaborative Practice, educating the public and promoting the use of the Collaborative process. Practice Groups are typically comprised of professionals who work the same geographic region and may be organized as formal legal entities or more loosely as professional associations. A law firm is not considered a Practice Group.[6]

As noted, most collaborative practice groups are based on a geographical region, especially for collaborative professionals in the family law area. The purpose of these groups is to support other collaborative professionals, to educate others on collaborative law, to build a referral network for clients seeking the collaborative process, and to foster a working environment when these lawyers work as counsel for opposing clients on the same case.

Most collaborative lawyers have training in the collaborative process. Training can be offered by national and international collaborative law associations, such as the International Academy of Collaborative Professionals (IACP) or the Global Collaborative Law Council.[7] These, and other, organizations offer training opportunities for new and existing collaborative law professionals. In addition, local practice groups may host training for lawyers within the community. These trainings often span more than one day, and they involve role-playing simulations. Practice groups may require that the lawyers in the group have taken training in collaborative law before other members of the group will engage in the collaborative process with them.

[B] The Participation Agreement

The Participation Agreement (sometimes called the "Four-Way Agreement") is the legal contract stating that all of the lawyers and clients agree to follow the guidelines or rules of collaborative law. It is important to note that both the lawyers and the clients sign the Participation Agreement. This agreement is a contract *in addition* to any engagement letter or agreement between the individual client with his or her attorney. A comprehensive sample Participation Agreement can be found at the end of this chapter, courtesy of the Global Collaborative Law Council.

The purpose of the Participation Agreement is to set forth clearly the terms of the collaborative process. Items covered in the agreement generally include, but are not limited to: (1) commitment to the collaborative process, (2) information exchanges, (3) the role of joint and consulting experts, (4) confidentiality, (5) meeting procedures, (6) good faith negotiations, (7) communication protocols, (8) a promise not to resort to litigation activities (except uncontested matters needed to secure a legal divorce), (9) termination provision, and (10) the withdrawal of the collaborative counsel upon termination of the process.[8] Practitioners who work in a jurisdiction that has passed the Uniform

---

6. International Academy of Collaborative Professionals, Collaborative Practice Group FAQs, at https://www.collaborativepractice.com/professional/resources/collaborative-practice-groupfaqs .aspx.

7. *See* Global Collaborative Law Council, *at* www.collaborativelaw.us.

8. *See* Abney, *supra* note 3, at 269–80.

Collaborative Law Act, discussed below, may not need to have all of these items covered if they are elsewhere covered by state law or court rule.[9]

At its heart, the Participation Agreement and the terms of engagement or retainer agreement between the attorney and his or her client constitute agreements for limited scope representation.[10] Collaborative law is a form of limited scope representation because the attorneys only agree to provide negotiation counsel, and they will not represent the parties on any litigation component that the case may present. The ethics of this arrangement, including the issue of informed consent, are discussed below.

[C] Jointly Retained Experts

One feature of collaborative law is that the parties jointly retain many of the expert witnesses. Jointly retained experts meet a number of the goals of collaborative law. First, sharing experts comports with collaborative law's principle of shared information and everyone having equal access to information. Second, shared experts should theoretically lower the cost of the process if the parties share the cost of joint experts, as opposed to shouldering the burden of separate experts. In family law cases, parties typically share financial experts and experts relating to issues dealing with children. In cases requiring a valuation (of a house, business, or other asset), jointly retained experts can make recommendations in those areas. In some cases, mental health practitioners may be jointly retained, as well. In other types of collaborative cases, jointly retained experts may include medical professionals, engineers, scientists, forensic accountants, or any other type of expert witnesses.

Unlike expert witnesses in litigation, jointly retained expert witnesses in collaborative law specifically agree to be non-testifying witnesses. In other words, the experts and their reports are used solely for the purposes of negotiation. During the process, the experts may appear and participate at the four-way sessions, and they are generally available to both of the parties and their collaborative attorneys. If the process is not successful, these experts are not available as trial witnesses.

If the collaborative process is unsuccessful, the information used to create the reports and expert opinions may still be useful.[11] As with mediation, the underlying information collected and relied upon in the collaborative process is still subject to discovery and admission into evidence at a later trial on the merits. Although the expert witness's opinion would not be admissible, the parties will still have the benefit of knowing the expert's opinion and basing future settlement offers with that piece of information in mind. In addition, the parties would be able to show that expert report to a future testifying expert for informational purposes.

---

9. Sample agreements provided by the IACP demonstrate variations depending on whether the lawyers work in a UCLA jurisdiction or not. IACP Model Participation Agreements and Guides, available at https://www.collaborativepractice.com/media/82862/IACP_Model_Participation_Agreements_and_Guides.pdf.

10. Scott R. Peppet, *The Ethics of Collaborative Law*, 2008 J. Disp. Resol. 131, 132 (2008).

11. Gary L. Voegele et al., *Collaborative Law: A Useful Tool for the Family Law Practitioner to Promote Better Outcomes*, 33 Wm. Mitchell L. Rev. 971, 1015–16 (2007).

[D] The Role of Coaches, Consulting Experts, and Mental Health Professionals

In addition to jointly retained experts, many collaborative law attorneys also highly recommend that their clients seek advice and counsel from consulting experts. Consulting experts are *not* jointly retained, and their opinions and ideas are used for the benefit of the party retaining the expert. In family law cases, consulting experts may include life coaches, conflict coaches, negotiation coaches, counselors, mental health professionals, child specialists, and other types of experts that are used to help the client assess their situation and prepare the clients for the four-way meetings. In civil cases, any number of these same types of professionals may be involved, particularly conflict coaches and mental health professionals.

Many collaborative law attorneys recognize that conflict is multidimensional, and the legal aspect of conflict is simply a part of the whole situation. Resolving the legal conflict will help the parties, but that assistance alone may not deal with the underlying problems. Many—if not most—legal problems stem from breakdowns in communication and relationships between parties, especially in the areas of family law and business (less so in negligence-based cases such as automobile accidents). The traditional legal process often exacerbates communication problems between parties, and relationships usually deteriorate over the course of litigation as parties become more entrenched in their positions.[12]

Collaborative lawyers recognize the multidimensional nature of conflict and rely on the appropriate experts from other disciplines to deal with the issues within their areas of expertise. The collaborative lawyer neither ignores the mental health and other aspects of conflict nor provides services outside of her area of expertise. Instead, the collaborative attorney involves these additional resources in the collaborative process.

Collaborative law practice groups may include not only collaborative lawyers but also other collaborative professionals. Joint and consulting experts may also participate in the practice groups, and collaborative lawyers may recruit these professionals not only for individual cases, but also to join the collaborative community within a location. David Hoffman, founder of the Boston Law Collaborative, operates a multidisciplinary practice, including dispute resolution, legal representation, training, financial advice, psychological assistance, and workplace consulting.[13] The successes of the Boston Law Collaborative are well documented, and David Hoffman has won awards for his innovations in this area of practice.[14]

[E] Document Exchanges

Under collaborative law participation agreements, the parties and their attorneys agree to exchange documentary and other information freely, in good faith, and without any formal requests from the other side. In an ideal situation, the collaborative

---

12. Jacob E. Gerson, *Markets and Corporate Conflict: A Substitution-Cost Approach to Business Litigation*, 24 L. & Soc. Inquiry 589, 591 (1999) ("Most relationships that end up in court are either already ruined or destroyed by the process of litigating.").

13. *See* www.bostonlawcollaborative.com.

14. Boston Law Collaborative, Firm Overview, available at http://www.bostonlawcollaborative.com/blc/firm-overview.html.

process commences prior to the filing of any lawsuit, and it concludes with a settlement agreement that is confidential. In many situations, however, including divorces, court intervention is necessary in order to secure the ultimate resolution, such as a divorce. In those situations, lawyers must be permitted to initiate litigation (such as a complaint and response for divorce) and file uncontested documents to close the case (such as a divorce decree and parenting plan).

Outside of the limited involvement of the court in divorce cases, the collaborative lawyers agree to not engage in any litigation activity. This agreement to refrain from litigation activities includes an agreement to not engage in traditional discovery.[15] In the collaborative process, the parties will not make document requests, sit for depositions, or request answers to interrogatories. Instead, the parties agree to disclose freely all of their relevant information to their attorneys, and the attorneys agree to provide that information to each other without any requests. In divorce cases, the parties are expected to disclose freely all of the assets and debts of the marriage, whether or not the property may be considered the separate property of either spouse. In medical malpractice cases, the parties would be expected to disclose fully all of the medical records, employment records (if relevant), financial information, and any other relevant information regarding the effects of the injury. In business cases, the parties would be expected to share all information relating to the dispute, including contracts, relevant email messages, damages information, and other information relating to the dispute. Engaging in consensual information gathering is a large cost savings for the parties in the collaborative process.[16] The clients are involved and participate in the process (thus shouldering some of the financial burden), and the parties will not need to take legal action to compel the other party's compliance with answering discovery requests.

Sharing information is essential to the collaborative process. When collaborative lawyers first meet their clients, they should thoroughly explain the information-sharing component of collaborative law. The attorney should gauge whether her own client is willing to comply with this requirement, as well as ask the client for an assessment as to whether the opposing client will also be able to follow this requirement. For example, an attorney for a wife in a divorce case should ensure that the wife is willing to disclose information freely as well as gauge whether the husband will also follow these same rules. If the lawyer's own client is unwilling to cooperate in information sharing, then the case would not be suitable for collaborative law. Similarly, if the client is wary that the opposing client would hide information (such as secret bank accounts in a divorce case), then the client may be better served using the traditional litigation process to gather important information.

[F] The Four-Way Sessions

The four-way sessions are the heart of the collaborative process. After document and information sharing, meeting with joint and consulting experts, and preparing with clients, the clients and the attorneys sit down together in a four-way session (or a four-way meeting) in order to engage in group problem solving.

---

15. Kevin Fuller, *Collaborative Law: What Is It? Why Do It?* Texas Collaborative Law Council (2004), http://www.collaborativelaw.us/articles/How_It_Works.pdf.

16. Abney, *supra* note 3, at 50–51.

[1] Creating the Environment

As in the case of mediation,[17] creating an environment for collaboration is important in collaborative law. The collaborative process relies on trust—primarily on the part of the parties, but also by the attorneys. Creativity is important, and the environment should encourage creative thinking, free flow of information, and group problem-solving.[18] Many of the same considerations for preparation of the facilities in mediation[19] should apply equally to collaborative law. The attorneys and parties should find facilities at which everyone will be at ease, which may be a neutral location instead of the offices of one of the attorneys. The facility should have sufficient resources to meet the needs of the participants, including telephone, Internet, photocopying, snacks, meal services, or other amenities needed to make everyone feel comfortable. The room will need to accommodate four (two parties and two attorneys) or more (experts, facilitator, or other support personnel) comfortably. Flip chart paper, markers, and other accommodations may be necessary for those attorneys and clients who like to use visual aids during the discussion.

[2] Use of Agendas and Minutes

Prior to arriving at the four-way meeting, the attorneys and their clients should have collaborated and agreed upon an agenda for the meeting. Crafting an agenda in a collaborative practice may take time and energy, but these agendas give structure to the in-person four-way meetings. Preparation is a key to the four-way meetings, and the work put into the planning should lead to a more productive meeting. Collaborative lawyers recognize that, despite having a plan for how the sessions should go, sometimes the four-way meetings will move along a different path and stray from the original agenda. Flexibility is another key to collaboration, and the agendas aid in preparation and planning, but all participants should remain open to the discussions moving in different directions.

At the four-way sessions, one of the participants should be assigned to take minutes of the meeting. The collaborative process often spans multiple sessions, and the time between meetings may feel significant to the parties. Minutes taken in good faith will help the parties craft future agendas and recall the events of past meetings. Working together on seemingly mundane items such as agenda crafting and minute taking help foster a collaborative environment and keep all participants on the same page going forward.

[3] Four-Way Sessions

After the preparation, the parties and their lawyers (and experts and facilitators, as necessary) get together for face-to-face four-way sessions. Although the hallmark of the four-way meeting is that both lawyers and both clients meet in person for the meeting, in some situations, the meeting may proceed without all four participants. For example, in a divorce case, a spouse that is still not ready to confront the other spouse because of the emotional issues surrounding the divorce may be excused from one or more of the sessions.

---

17. *See supra* Section 4.05[A].
18. Abney, *supra* note 3, at 76–77.
19. *See supra* Section 4.05[A].

The four-way meetings may begin with a discussion of the guidelines and the ground rules for the process. Some collaborative attorneys like to spend part of the first session discussing the benefits of the process and why collaborative is a good choice for this particular situation. Goals and interests are often identified early, and both parties and their attorneys contribute to the discussion. The goals and interests then guide the remainder of the process.

After the participants determine the goals and interests, the participants can begin to gather information during the session. The parties and their counsel may have questions of each other, or they may want to present some additional information that has not been disclosed in the documents. Documents exchanged by the parties may need additional explanation, and the parties and their attorneys can clarify confusing information. For instance, if one spouse primarily took care of household finances, that spouse may need to take time going over the debts and assets of the marriage and explain why certain deposits or withdrawals appeared in the exchanged documents. The information-gathering phase of collaborative law may take more than one session, depending on the situation. If the parties do not have the information at the time, they might be assigned to determine the answers prior to the next four-way session.

Similar to mediation, after the parties have sufficient information, they may begin prioritizing issues and working on problem solving. The parties may engage in brainstorming activities and other types of techniques to generate potential options. After the parties and their counsel identify the range of options, they will work to determine the suitability of those options, keeping in mind the overarching goals and interests of the parties. Ultimately, the parties work toward agreeing on an option and settling their case.

[4] Debriefings and Additional Meetings

The collaborative process takes time, often over many months or even a year or two. The four-way sessions may be difficult to schedule due to the logistics of finding compatible times for all of the participants. In a typical divorce, the process may take three or four sessions, setting aside separate time to cover issues such as temporary arrangements, the division of property, parenting time, and child and spousal support, among other topics. Civil cases may have some sessions devoted to liability with other sessions devoted to damages, insurance coverage, or other issues.

Because the process takes time, collaborative attorneys and their clients must meet and review after four-way sessions, as well as prepare before the next four-way session. Shortly after (or immediately after) a four-way session, individual attorneys and clients should meet and discuss how the session progressed. The attorney should check in with the client and ensure that the client is satisfied with the progress and that the client's goals are being met. Although the process is collaborative, the lawyer only represents one party, and the lawyer's duties are to her own client.[20] The attorney and client should review the accomplishments and draft or approve the meeting minutes.

Prior to the next four-way session, the attorney and client should meet again. The participants will begin working on a new agenda, which will likely be informed by the previous agendas and the work done at the last meeting. The attorney and client should also be aware of any changes in circumstances or new plans for the upcoming session.

---

20. The ethical duty of loyalty is covered in Section 6.04[D].

[G] Use of a Facilitator

The traditional model of collaborative law calls for four-way meetings with the lawyers, clients, and any jointly retained experts, if needed. Because the collaborative law training for attorneys and other professionals includes many of the tools of a mediator (active listening, information sharing, agenda setting, and problem solving, among other techniques), many collaborative lawyers do not see the need for a third-party mediator or facilitator to assist in the meetings.

In recent years, more collaborative professionals have turned to the use of facilitators to run the four-way meetings. The role of the facilitator is similar to that of a mediator, but the facilitator's role is generally limited to organizing the meeting and ensuring that the parties stay on track. The facilitator would not give any advice or opinions on the merits of the potential solutions. Instead, the role would be limited to facilitating the conversation, crafting an agenda, and otherwise keeping all of the participants moving in a productive direction.

[H] Good Faith Drafting and Closing the Process

Once the parties have agreed to a resolution in principle, one of the attorneys will draft the final document. The drafting attorney's work will be reviewed and edited by the other attorney and the clients, and the participants may work on multiple drafts before a final document is complete. The attorney who is tasked with drafting must endeavor to draft the settlement in good faith, meaning that the attorney will not slant the document toward one client or otherwise add provisions to which the other party and attorney had not agreed. Good faith drafting is essential to the collaborative process. By the time the parties have agreed in principle to a resolution, they may have been working on settlement for more than a year. If one lawyer attempted to take advantage of the ability to draft the document, trust in the process would vanish, and the parties and the other lawyer would have wasted a significant amount of time and energy. Further, this type of activity would tarnish the reputation of the attorney within the collaborative community.

Often, collaborative attorneys and their clients engage in a final four-way meeting in order to sign final documents. The purpose of this final meeting is twofold. First, the meeting aids in the logistics of final document execution. Second, and more importantly, the closing session has an air of ceremony.[21] Ceremony demonstrates the importance of what has been done and recognizes the accomplishment for all of the hard work that the attorneys and clients have put into the process.

§ 7.03 Advantages and Disadvantages of Collaborative Law

In many ways, the collaborative practice is revolutionary to the practice of law. Collaborative law shifts the paradigm from "winning" to "winning through settlement."

---

21. Garvey, *supra* note 1, at 198–99.

The paradigm shift is so radical that some scholars have questioned whether the practice is even ethical for lawyers. This section highlights the advantages and disadvantages of the collaborative process, both in theory and in practice over the last 25 years.

[A] Advantages

Perhaps the biggest advantage of the collaborative law process for both the lawyers and the participants is in the promise of collegiality, harmony, and cooperation. The litigation process can ruin relationships, cause considerable stress, drag on for years, and waste a considerable amount of time for both the lawyers and the participants. Many collaborative lawyers turn to this type of practice after becoming disenchanted with the litigation process, and they find collaborative law to be a better way not only for their clients, but also for themselves. For the clients, the collaborative process treats everyone with dignity, as the parties and their lawyers work on solving problems together. In fact, the process is built on the GETTING TO YES principle of separating the people from the problem and relying on joint problem solving.[22]

The collaborative process centers on the virtue of openness, particularly as it relates to discovery matters. When the parties engage in collaboration by sharing information and exchanging documents, they establish trust not only in the process, but also in each other. Mutual cooperation during discovery and the four-way meetings helps the parties reach negotiated agreements.

Optimally, the decisions reached during the collaborative law process are ideal negotiated results. Everyone will have the same information through openness in discussions and document exchanges. Openness in collaborative law is not simply about the factual exchange of information. The process intends to create a safe space for the participants to discuss their feelings, emotions, and interests. If everyone is operating on the same factual information and is open to understanding the underlying interests and emotions of the other parties, then the parties have maximized their opportunities to create customized outcomes that will hopefully be lasting resolutions for the parties.

Collaborative law has great potential to preserve the relationship between the disputing parties. In some instances, the relationship between the parties may be repaired or even strengthened by participating in the collaborative process and learning how to make decisions together. The benefit of repairing and maintaining relationships is a significant reason collaborative law is used in family law. When parents divorce, they will necessarily still be a part of each other's lives because they have children together. If they can learn how to co-parent and make decisions as parents through the collaborative process, they will hopefully be better parents who can reduce the amount of parental conflict in their children's lives.

The nature of the collaborative practice groups is also a benefit to the parties using collaborative law. Lawyers in a collaborative practice group are familiar with the other lawyers who practice in this area. Through regular meetings, these lawyers get to know one another and respect one another as professionals. They become part of a community. The lawyers within the group come to trust one another and become familiar with how each lawyer engages in the practice. As a practical matter, the lawyers understand how

---

22. Roger Fisher, William Ury & Bruce Patton, GETTING TO YES: NEGOTIATING AGREEMENT WITHOUT GIVING IN 17 (2d ed. 1991)

the other collaborative lawyers operate, which reduces considerable uncertainty for both the lawyers and the clients. There may even be some reputational pressure to follow the rules of the collaborative process because of the small community in which they operate.

The disqualification agreement also promotes settlement. If the collaborative process results in impasse, then the parties will both have to fire their own lawyers and hire new lawyers. In other words, the parties will essentially have to start over. If the process results in impasse, the clients are able to take their files and documents with them, but the new lawyer will have to start over from scratch and be educated on the process to date. Given the expenses associated with the process, the parties may have a significant amount of "sunk costs," and psychologically, the parties may think that they should stay with the process rather than adding new expenses to the litigation.[23] Collaborative lawyers often boast very high settlement rates,[24] and part of the success may be due to the disqualification agreement and the monetary cost, and perhaps psychological fear, of starting over with new lawyers in court.

Finally, collaborative law may potentially save parties money. When the lawyers and clients abide by the collaborative philosophy, many litigation costs disappear. With parties engaging in voluntary document exchange, the expense of the discovery process is all but eliminated. Further, the parties share expert witnesses, so those expenses are shared. If the process is successful, then no one is paying attorney fees for litigation, and litigation fees are among the highest costs that lawyers charge. Further, when cases settle well before trial, the parties save not only money, but also time.[25] In collaborative cases, an early resolution via cooperation, combined with the potential to repair relationships, might allow parties to resume their normal activities faster than if they were in a litigated case.

[B] Disadvantages

Despite these many advantages, the process has some downfalls, and collaborative practice is not the right fit for every lawyer or every client. Whether collaborative law is the right process may depend on the situation, the lawyers, and the clients' goals.

One disadvantage of the collaborative process is that it requires both parties to be represented. In other words, a lawyer cannot use the collaborative style if one party is proceeding pro se. The National Conference of Commissioners on Uniform State Laws considered this issue when it promulgated the Uniform Collaborative Law Act (UCLA). In the prefatory note, the UCLA drafters stated that collaborative law should be limited to cases in which both parties have counsel.[26] The reason for two lawyers in the process is to avoid role confusion. If one party has a collaborative lawyer and the other party is pro se, the pro se party may believe that the collaborative lawyer works for both parties. The lawyer would also run the risk of an attorney/client relationship forming with the

---

23. Hal R. Arkes and Catherine Blume, *The Psychology of Sunk Cost*, Org. Beh. & Human Decision Process 35, 1985, at 124.

24. Linda Wray, *IACP Research Regarding Collaborative Practice*, Disp. Resol. 2010, at 6.

25. *See* Ad Hoc Panel on Dispute Resolution, Nat'l Inst. For Dispute Resolution, Paths to Justice: Major Public Policy Issues of Dispute Resolution, *reprinted in* Leonard L. Riskin & James E. Westbrook, Dispute Resolution and Lawyers 695–96 (2d ed. 1997).

26. National Conference of Commissioners on Uniform State Laws, Uniform Collaborative Law Rules and Uniform Collaborative Law Act, Prefatory Note 22 (2010).

unrepresented client. For these reasons, collaborative law can only occur when the parties are both represented by lawyers. Requiring lawyers, however, adds expenses, and not all parties are able to afford lawyers. Collaborative law, then, may not be an option for low-income clients or others who do not want to hire an attorney.

Not only must the parties have lawyers, they must have *collaborative* lawyers for the collaborative law process to work. In many jurisdictions, those who practice collaborative law and want to be in a collaborative practice group must also take training in collaborative law. The training may be an extra expense and take extra time for the lawyers. Lawyers who are not properly trained may not be able to represent a client in the collaborative process. Further, the collaborative process is not for every lawyer. Lawyers who enjoy the gamesmanship of the law and thrive on the trial experience may not be good collaborative lawyers. Lawyers who believe that the other side must "work" to get every last piece of information may also not make good collaborative lawyers. If one client insists on having a lawyer who does not practice collaborative law, then the case cannot go forward as a collaborative case. If the lawyer on the other side is a collaborative lawyer, that lawyer may still take the case, but that lawyer would have to handle the case in a traditional manner.

In addition to needing two collaborative lawyers, the process requires two collaborative clients. Not all clients are willing to work together collaboratively, and those that cannot work together should use the traditional litigation process. In particular, clients who may hide information are not suited for this process. For example, if one divorcing spouse has no intention of sharing information with the other spouse regarding off-shore or other secret bank accounts or assets, then this case is not suited for collaborative law. Cases involving extreme power and control dynamics, including domestic violence issues, are also not good candidates for collaborative law. The collaborative process requires active participation by all four participants — the lawyers and the clients. If one party does not feel comfortable in a room with the other party or otherwise cannot participate, then those parties should not be using collaborative law.

In addition to the expense of lawyers, collaborative law may also be expensive because of the use of experts. Although some experts are shared, other experts are simply consulting experts, and those expenses are borne by the party retaining them. The collaborative process relies heavily on experts. In the divorce context, parties often jointly retain a financial expert and a child specialist. In addition, the lawyers may highly recommend that the parties also engage consulting experts, such as mental health professionals, life coaches, conflict coaches, and other experts as needed. The collaboration with all of these individuals will require an additional expense that may not have been needed in the traditional litigation process.

Although the disqualification provision incentivizes parties to stay with the collaborative law process, in those cases that end in impasse, the parties may suffer serious economic and psychological disadvantages. If the process ends in impasse, the parties must start over with new attorneys. The clients would have spent a considerable amount of money on the collaborative lawyers and the experts. The clients will then have to spend more money on new lawyers, including money to get those new lawyers up to speed. The parties will also need new expert witnesses. A failed collaborative process may have a psychological effect on the parties as well. If the collaborative process failed because one or both parties were hiding information, acting obstreperously, or using the process to take advantage of the other, then the party who participated in good faith may feel used or cheated.

A final disadvantage worth noting is the question of "who is the client?" Collaborative lawyers must be certain to remain loyal to their client, not to the process, not to the family, and not to the other client. The focus on collaboration theoretically may cause a lawyer to push their clients into a settlement that they do not want or does not meet their interests. This issue will be considered in more detail in the next section.

§ 7.04 Ethical Issues in Collaborative Law

Because collaborative law turns the traditional paradigm of advocacy on its head, significant questions have arisen regarding the ethics of the practice. To date, ethics opinions in the area of collaborative law have largely approved the process,[27] but collaborative practice still generates a number of ethical questions and considerations. This section considers the most significant of the ethical considerations.

[A] Zealous Representation

One of the earliest ethical questions regarding collaborative law was whether the process met a lawyer's duty to "zealously represent" his or her client. Although "zealous representation" used to be an explicit duty of lawyers in the 1969 Code of Professional Conduct,[28] in today's Model Rules of Professional Conduct, zealous representation is mentioned in the preface,[29] but the idea of "zealousness" is not a separate rule. The philosophy behind the zealousness concept is the reminder that one of the lawyer's roles is to be an advocate.[30]

Critics of collaborative law have questioned whether a lawyer can be a zealous advocate and a problem solver at the same time.[31] The traditional model of advocacy involves lawyers taking advantage of every opportunity for the benefit of the client, no matter the consequence (within ethical bounds, of course). If, in fact, "win at all costs," is the only way to be an ethical attorney, then collaborative law may not survive a challenge on the grounds that the lawyers are not adversarial enough.

This critique fails to account for the lawyer's other (sometimes competing) duty — that of counselor and advisor.[32] In their role as advisor, lawyers may counsel their clients as to both the legal and nonlegal ramifications of the conflict and representation. In other words, lawyers have a general ethical duty to be advisors, and such advice should take into account the *client's* goals regarding the representation.

---

27. Phyllis Rubenstein, Esq., *Collaborative Law: Effectively Resolving Conflict Without Going to Court*, VT. B.J., Fall 2010, at 40

28. MODEL CODE OF PROF'L CONDUCT Canon 7 ("A Lawyer Should Represent a Client Zealously Within the Bounds of the Law").

29. MODEL RULES OF PROF'L CONDUCT, Preamble (2002) ("As advocate, a lawyer zealously asserts the client's position under the rules of the adversary system.").

30. MODEL RULES OF PROF'L CONDUCT r. 3.1–3.9.

31. John Lande, *Possibilities for Collaborative Law: Ethics and Practice of Lawyer Disqualification and Process Control in a New Model of Lawyering*, 64 OHIO ST. L.J. 1315 (2003).

32. MODEL RULES OF PROF'L CONDUCT r. 2.1.

Not all clients are interested in a "win at all costs" type of representation. Some clients are interested in maintaining relationships, working together with the other side, cost savings, and seeking a peaceful resolution to the problem at hand. The collaborative lawyer can help meet those client goals by using a different process—notably a collaborative process—in order to achieve these client goals that may appear to be "nonlegal" goals. In other words, the mere fact that collaborative law seeks cooperation above zealousness does not mean that the process is unethical if the client's ultimate goals include cooperation and collaboration. For these reasons, too, collaborative law is not the right choice in every situation. Once the attorney and the client both agree to the collaborative process and confirm that collaborative law can meet the client's goals, then proceeding with the process is an ethical choice for the lawyer.

[B] Informed Consent

Collaborative law is essentially a form of limited scope representation. The collaborative lawyers agree to represent the clients in negotiations only, and not in litigation activities. The limitation of the lawyer's activities to those involving settlement is what makes the arrangement "limited scope," even if the collaborative lawyer does resolve an entire case through the collaborative process.

The Model Rules of Professional Responsibility cover limited scope engagements. Under Rule 1.2, a "lawyer may limit the scope of the representation if the limitation is reasonable under the circumstances and the client gives informed consent."[33] Collaborative law attorneys must assess with the client whether the process is reasonable under the circumstances and ensure that the client gives informed consent. In most cases, limiting the lawyer's involvement to negotiation counsel will be reasonable under the circumstances. The collaborative process may not be reasonable under the circumstances if the parties are under significant time pressure and cannot put the time and effort needed into the process. In other instances, the process may not be reasonable under the circumstances if the parties cannot negotiate together because of incapacity or power and control dynamics (particularly in high-conflict divorce cases).

In addition, the parties must give informed consent to proceed with collaborative law. Informed consent "denotes the agreement by a person to a proposed course of conduct after the lawyer has communicated adequate information and explanation about the material risks of and reasonably available alternatives to the proposed course of conduct."[34] For collaborative lawyers, this means that the collaborative lawyer must explain the collaborative process and alternatives, and the lawyer should have some indication that the client understands what the lawyer is saying.

Specifically, the collaborative lawyer should explain the collaborative process and the role of the collaborative attorney. The lawyer should also explain how this process is different from the traditional litigation process. The lawyer must determine whether his or her own client is willing to participate in a process that requires openness and full disclosure. In addition, the collaborative lawyer must be careful to explain the withdrawal provision and the consequences of not settling the process through collaborative law.

---

33. MODEL RULES OF PROF'L CONDUCT r. 1.2(c).
34. MODEL RULES OF PROF'L CONDUCT r. 1.0(e).

Although the ethics surrounding limited scope arrangements only require informed consent, the best practice for the collaborative lawyer is to have informed consent *in writing*. Attorney/client engagement letters and the participation agreements are standard protocol in collaborative practice groups, and these types of contractual arrangements help ensure that the parties consent to the process knowing what that process entails.

[C] Withdrawal Provision

The withdrawal provision has also drawn some attention as potentially unethical. Interestingly, the concern is not over the withdrawal of the client's own lawyer, but the potential for one party to have control over the lawyer of the opponent.[35] The default rule in the United States is that parties have the freedom to hire and fire lawyers of their choosing because the attorney/client relationship is an agency relationship. On the hiring side, parties certainly have every right to hire collaborative lawyers.

The issue with collaborative law is that if one party decides to end the collaborative process, then *both* parties must get new lawyers. If one party goes into the process with bad intentions, then that party could strategically wait until an opportune time and fire his or her own lawyer, thus forcing the party who participated in good faith to also lose his or her attorney, too. This arrangement is contrary to the traditional agency relationship because a third party (the opposing client) can force the termination of an attorney and a client.

Informed consent should alleviate this problem. Both parties know at the beginning how the collaborative process works and the circumstances under which the process may be terminated. Provided that the parties are fully aware, the clients have the right to contract for this type of representation. Having all of these conditions in writing is certainly a best practice for the collaborative attorney to do everything possible to ensure that the client gives informed consent.

[D] Who Is the Client?

The final ethical concern raised about collaborative law is the question of "who is the client?" Skeptics sometimes contend that the client may be: (1) both clients, (2) the process, or (3) the family in divorce cases. If that were to be true, then the lawyer would have a significant ethical dilemma in representing opposing parties.[36]

The collaborative lawyer must only serve that attorney's client. Although the parties and their attorneys agree to use collaborative techniques (including information sharing, open and honest communication, and problem-solving skills), each lawyer represents his or her own client. The lawyer will still advise that client on whether ultimate decisions are in the client's best interest given all of the goals and interests of the client. As mentioned above, those interests need not be solely legal, but the lawyer must keep the primary focus on the interests and goals of the individual client.

---

35. Christopher M. Fairman, *A Proposed Model Rule for Collaborative Law*, OHIO ST. J. DISP. RES. Vol. 21 No. 1 (2005).

36. MODEL RULES OF PROF'L CONDUCT r. 1.7 (dealing with conflicts of interest).

§ 7.05　The Uniform Collaborative Law Act

In 2010, the National Conference of Commissioners on Uniform State Laws passed the Uniform Collaborative Law Rules and Uniform Collaborative Law Act. The Commission drafted the Act in a format that could be used either as a set of court rules or as an act that could be passed into law. Most commonly, scholars and lawyers refer to the Act as the Uniform Collaborative Law Act, or UCLA for short. The Prefatory Note begins with a definition of collaborative law as a "voluntary, contractually based alternative dispute resolution process for parties who seek to negotiate a resolution of their matter rather than having a ruling imposed upon them by a court or arbitrator."[37] Unlike some ADR processes, the lawyers and the clients all participate in the negotiations.[38]

The drafters of the UCLA left open the scope of the Act. In the broader scope of the Act, the UCLA would apply to any matter "described in a collaborative law participation agreement."[39] Individual jurisdictions, however, may limit the scope to solely family law matters.[40] The UCLA places requirements on the participation agreement. Under the Act, the participation agreement must be in writing, signed, state the parties' intent to engage in the collaborative process, describe the matter to be resolved, and identify the collaborative lawyers and their intent to engage in the collaborative process.[41] The record in writing satisfies the informed consent obligations discussed above,[42] and in practice most collaborative lawyers are already using very detailed participation agreements.[43]

The UCLA gives significant detail on the intersection of the collaborative process and the courts. As a general matter, in jurisdictions following the UCLA, pending litigation is stayed once the court has notice that the collaborative process has commenced.[44] The stay remains in effect until the process concludes (either by settlement, impasse, or a party's agreement to withdraw from the process).[45] Although a judge may request status reports on collaborative cases, a tribunal may not dismiss a case for failure to prosecute without notice and a hearing or require the lawyers to divulge privileged information.[46] Tribunals may, however, issue emergency relief, as necessary.[47] Courts may approve agreements created as a result of the collaborative process,[48] such as divorce decrees, property settlements, and parenting plans. The drafters of the UCLA were mindful of the practicalities of divorce law and the fact that divorces require courts to take certain actions—such as approving divorce decrees and other documents. In a typical divorce case, the collaborative attorneys may invoke the courts to initiate the process and approve

---

37. Uniform Collaborative Rules and Collaborative Law Act [hereinafter UCLA], Prefatory Note (2010).

38. *Id.*

39. UCLA § 2(5)(Alternative B).

40. UCLA § 2(5)(Alternative A).

41. UCLA § 4(a).

42. *See supra* Section 6.04[C].

43. A sample Participation Agreement is available in Section 6.07.

44. UCLA § 5, 6(a).

45. UCLA § 5, 6(b).

46. UCLA § 6(c), (d), & (e).

47. UCLA § 7.

48. UCLA § 8.

final documents. For the rest of the case, the court issues a stay and the parties and their attorneys work on the case without court involvement.

The UCLA codifies another hallmark trait of collaborative law, i.e., the disqualification of collaborative attorneys if the process is unsuccessful in reaching a settlement.[49] The Act also provides that, as a general rule, if a collaborative lawyer is disqualified, then the entire law firm is also disqualified from representing a party who participated in that collaborative process.[50] The prohibition against representing a collaborative client in court does not extend to the permissible court representation noted above, including requesting approval of final documents or asking for emergency relief.[51] Although the general rule applies in most cases, the UCLA would not disqualify other attorneys from the same law firm from representing a collaborative client if the client meets one of two criteria: (1) the client is low income and would qualify for free legal representation,[52] or (2) the client is a government agency.[53]

The UCLA also codifies the requirement to engage in the free exchange of information. The Act states that "on the request of another party, a party shall make timely, full, candid, and informal disclosure of information related to the collaborative matter without formal discovery."[54] In addition to primary disclosures, the collaborative attorney also has the responsibility to supplement the information exchange, particularly if the information exchanged has materially changed since the time of disclosure.

Collaborative lawyers have a duty to assess that a case is appropriate for the process. The lawyer must do an independent assessment of suitability, ensure that the client understands the collaborative process, and advise the client as to the voluntary nature of collaborative law and the effects of the disqualification agreement.[55] The lawyer must also determine whether the parties have a "coercive or violent relationship."[56] If a case screens positive for these types of power and control issues, the case may still be appropriate for collaborative law if the lawyers can ensure participation safety.[57]

Like the Uniform Mediation Act ("UMA"), the UCLA allows for confidentiality of process communications as agreed by the parties,[58] and provides for privilege for these communications by law. As with the UMA, the parties to the collaborative process have the broadest privilege, covering all collaborative law communications.[59] Non-party participants, including lawyers and experts, have a privilege over the statements made by those particular participants.[60] Again, similar to the UMA, the parties have the ability to waive the privilege, and the privilege does not extend to all situations (i.e., threats of harm to self or others).[61]

---

49. UCLA § 9.
50. UCLA § 9(b).
51. UCLA § 9(c).
52. UCLA § 10(b).
53. UCLA § 11(b).
54. UCLA § 12.
55. UCLA § 14.
56. UCLA § 15(a).
57. UCLA § 15.
58. UCLA § 16.
59. UCLA § 17(b)(1).
60. UCLA § 17(b)(2).
61. UCLA §§ 18-19.

As of 2016, the UCLA has been enacted as statutory law in 14 jurisdictions, including Texas. In addition, the North Dakota courts adopted the UCLA as court rule. The bill continues to be introduced into state legislatures each year, and additional jurisdictions may adopt the UCLA over the next decade.

§ 7.06 Use of Collaborative Law Outside of Family Law

Although collaborative law is most common in the family law arena, lawyers in other areas of law are using the collaborative process. Admittedly, the use of collaborative law outside of family law has been slow. That said, collaborative attorneys have been instrumental in championing the process and its application to other areas of the law. Many collaborative law attorneys are also interested in educating other lawyers about the process. In those educational opportunities (ranging from continuing education programs to informal discussions), many collaborative attorneys discuss the process generally, as opposed to a process used in family law.

The success of collaborative law outside of family law often depends on the lawyers within a given jurisdiction. To date, the most successful collaborative law practices have arisen in geographical localities with many collaborative attorneys. In many divorce cases, both parties live in the same jurisdiction, and the lawyers and the clients are physically close to one another. The lawyers will work with one another in many cases and create reputations in the collaborative community. In the world of civil litigation, the parties and the attorneys may be geographically diverse. For instance, an automobile accident case that occurred in Iowa may involve an Iowa injured party, a Virginia driver, an insurance adjuster in New York, and attorneys from all of these (or other) jurisdictions. The likelihood that all of these clients and lawyers are trained, ready, and willing to participate in collaborative law is small. Even if the parties and lawyers are *willing*, they would not know each other or their reputations as collaborative lawyers.

Some areas of the law may be ready and ripe for increased collaborative practice. The International Academy of Collaborative Professionals suggests that collaborative law may be an ideal process in healthcare, employment, probate, construction, and religious disputes.[62] Like family law, these articulated types of conflicts generally involve parties who are geographically close. In addition, these types of conflicts involve people with continuing relationships, such as employment relationships, family relationships, service provider relationships, community relationships, educational relationships, and project relationships.

The use of collaborative law in other areas of the law is a tremendous growth area. Increased education in the collaborative processes through training, continuing legal education, law school exposure, and broader collaborative practice groups may help increase awareness and willingness to use collaborative law in any area of law.

---

62. Civil Collaborative Practice, https://www.collaborativepractice.com/professional/resources/civilcommercial-practice-information.aspx.

§ 7.07 Processes Similar to Collaborative Law

Many lawyers are intrigued by the ideas and theory surrounding collaborative law, but they have concerns about the harsh realities of the disqualification provision required in collaborative practice. To remedy this perceived problem, some lawyers created different systems and processes to meet the need of having the same counsel even if the parties reach impasse. Cooperative law and settlement counsel are the two most popular outgrowths of collaborative law. These types of processes are used primarily in business context, while family law generally uses collaborative law.

[A] Cooperative Law

Cooperative law is essentially collaborative law without the disqualification agreement. The lawyers and clients agree to work together and exchange information without formal requests or court intervention. The clients take an active role in the negotiation process. The process is focused on settlement, and the priority of the attorneys is working toward a mutually agreeable settlement. The cooperative process may also utilize jointly retained experts and mental health professionals as needed.

Cooperative law attorneys generally believe that the withdrawal agreement is too draconian a measure for a failed negotiation. Many also believe that the disqualification agreement puts too great of pressure on the clients to settle. Allowing counsel to remain on the case after impasse is reached may lessen structural pressure to settle. Further, this process would eliminate the need to educate a new attorney and save clients considerable expense in cases of impasse. Cooperative attorneys argue that the clients make better decisions when they are free from the weight of the disqualification agreement.

Critics of cooperative law argue that the attorneys are not fully engaged in settlement in the same way as collaborative law attorneys. Cooperative law attorneys must be planning for litigation contingencies, which is exactly the problem that collaborative law sought to avoid. The disqualification agreement makes clear the parties' and the clients' intent on working toward settlement, and the cooperative process has the potential of losing focus on settlement as a priority. Ultimately, attorneys and clients should discuss these nuances and choose a process based on the individual circumstances of a given case.

[B] Settlement Counsel

Another variation to collaborative law is the use of settlement counsel. Settlement counsel are lawyers who work on a case solely with the purpose of settlement, while other counsel are working on litigation aspects simultaneously. Settlement counsel are most often employed in large civil cases where the clients can afford to hire multiple sets of counsel.

The use of settlement counsel has some distinct advantages. First, unlike cooperative lawyers, settlement counsel are fully engaged in the settlement process. Settlement counsel has the flexibility and the advantage of being singularly focused on the negotiation aspects of the case. They will be working with litigation counsel in order to determine the factual and legal issues involved in the case and to determine alternatives to settlement. The primary disadvantage of using settlement counsel is that the litigation and the settlement avenues are being pursued simultaneously. Although different lawyers are engaged in different activities, the client must be considering settlement options and litigation options simultaneously. In addition, the discovery portion of the case generally involves the traditional litigation context, and no stay exists while the parties pursue settlement options.

Settlement counsel may be from the same law firm as the litigation counsel or from a different law firm. If settlement attorneys are lawyers from the same law firm, all of the lawyers likely have access to all of the same information, and the client and lawyers would not need additional engagement letters or practical arrangements in the hiring and sharing of information. On the other hand, if all of the lawyers are in the same law firm, the settlement attorneys may be subject to pressure from litigation counsel. Settlement counsel, too, must stay focused on settlement, and that focus and discipline may be difficult if litigation counsel are within the same firm. If settlement counsel is from a different law firm, they will likely have a more singular focus on settlement because of the physical and perceived separateness of the two law firms. On the other hand, counsel and the clients may need to have special contractual relationships with settlement counsel. Those additional engagement letters will need to outline the role of settlement counsel and the information sharing among counsel to ensure privilege and confidentiality.

Settlement counsel may be an effective way for clients to have at least some attorneys dedicated solely to settlement. For clients who are skeptical of the collaborative or cooperative concepts—especially if the clients are critical of the ability of the other side to be forthcoming—employing settlement counsel may be a valuable option for those clients.

§ 7.08 Collaborative Law Participation Agreement

ADOPTED BY THE BOARD OF DIRECTORS

GLOBAL COLLABORATIVE LAW COUNCIL
(formerly Texas Collaborative Law Council)
August, 2004

Revised by the Council
August, 2007

PARTICIPATION AGREEMENT

PARTICIPATION AGREEMENT

Adapted with permission of the

Collaborative Law Institute of Texas, Inc.

This document is provided as a guideline for use by licensed attorneys who are trained in the collaborative dispute resolution process. It should never be used or relied upon by anyone who is not represented by a trained collaborative lawyer. This document should not be construed as legal advice or as creating an attorney-client relationship.

THIS AGREEMENT ("Agreement") is made by and between

1_____   2_____

3_____   4_____

(each, a "Party" and collectively, the "Parties"),
and their respective Lawyers ("Lawyers")

1_____   2_____

3_____   4_____

1.0   PREMISES

1.1   A dispute ("Dispute") has arisen between the Parties concerning _____
_____
_____
_____.

1.2   The Parties wish to resolve the Dispute and any other claims or potential claims which any Party has or may have against any other Party through the collaborative process without resort to litigation, and the Parties have entered into this Agreement for that purpose.

1.3   The Parties have engaged their respective Lawyers as collaborative counsel to assist their clients in identifying issues, goals and interests, analyzing relevant information, developing options and understanding the consequences, and reaching the goal of the collaborative process which is an agreed resolution of the Dispute.

1.4   The Lawyers agree to adhere to the Protocols of Practice for Collaborative Lawyers adopted by the Global Collaborative Law Council ("GCLC") and any laws or rules of court governing the collaborative process in the jurisdiction of the dispute. The GCLC protocols should be interpreted in a manner consistent with such laws and/or rules.

2.0   ESSENTIAL ELEMENTS OF THE COLLABORATIVE PROCESS

The Parties and Lawyers understand and agree that the essential elements of the collaborative process are:

a.   Identification of the goals and interests of the Parties;

b.   Full and complete disclosure of relevant information;

c.   Efficient communications;

d.   The Parties' empowerment to make decisions on a level playing field;

e.   Confidentiality, and

f.   Good faith negotiations.

3.0   COMMUNICATIONS

3.1   The Parties understand the process will involve vigorous good faith negotiation in face-to-face settlement conferences during which the Parties will be represented solely by their respective Lawyers. The settlement conferences will be conducted with the Parties and their Lawyers present, and with any other person the Parties agree may be present. The settlement conferences will be focused on giving consideration to all Parties' interests, and to developing options for the constructive resolution of the Dispute. To maintain an objective and constructive process, the Parties agree to discuss resolution of issues with each other only in the settlement conferences, unless they agree otherwise. Any Party may request termination of a settlement conference at any time and such a request shall be immediately honored.

3.2   The Lawyers will confer to plan agendas for settlement conferences and to draft or review documents, but no agreements will be made by the Lawyers on behalf of the Parties.

3.3   The Parties agree they shall not take advantage of known mistakes, errors of fact or law, miscalculations, or other inconsistencies. Once a participant discovers a mistake, error of fact or law, miscalculations, or other inconsistencies, such participant shall identify it and provide an opportunity to correct it.

3.4   The Parties may agree to discuss the likely outcome of a litigated result; however, neither the Parties nor their Lawyers shall threaten to resort to litigation or any other adversarial proceeding.

4.0   UNDERSTANDINGS

4.1   The Parties understand that the Lawyers are independent from each other, and each Lawyer represents only their respective client in the collaborative process. The Parties further understand that each Lawyer is an advocate only for their respective client. No legal duty, by contract or otherwise, is owed to a Party by another Party's Lawyer. No lawyer-client relationship exists between one Party's Lawyer and any other Party by virtue of this Agreement or the collaborative process.

4.2   The Parties acknowledge there is no guarantee they will be successful in resolving the Dispute in the collaborative process.

4.3   The Parties are expected to express their own interests, and give consideration to the other Parties' interests. The Lawyers will assist their respective clients in doing so.

4.4   The process, even with full and honest disclosure, may involve intense good-faith negotiations. Best efforts will be used to create options that meet the interests of all Parties. The Parties recognize that compromise may be needed to reach resolution of all matters in dispute.

4.5   The Parties acknowledge this is a voluntary agreement. The Parties understand that by agreeing to the collaborative process, they are voluntarily giving up certain rights, including the right to conduct formal discovery, and the right to participate in adversarial proceedings unless otherwise agreed or the collaborative process is terminated.

4.6   A Collaborative Lawyer may not serve as a lawyer in any adversarial proceedings among any of the Parties regarding the subject matter of the Dispute, and this prohibition may not be modified. A Lawyer associated in the practice of law with the Collaborative Lawyer may not serve as a lawyer in any adversarial proceedings regarding the subject matter of the Dispute among any of the Parties, unless the Parties agree otherwise in writing.

4.7   In the event that in-house counsel serves as a collaborative lawyer for his/her employer and the process terminates prior to resolution of the Dispute, no other lawyer employed by such Party may represent the Party in any adversarial proceeding among the Parties regarding the subject matter of the Dispute. A lawyer with the employer other than the collaborative lawyer should arrange transfer of documents and information to the litigation attorney retained by the employer, and the lawyer arranging the transfer may monitor or participate in such proceeding according to the employer's normal business practices regarding matters which are referred to the litigation attorney. No lawyer employed by the collaborative lawyer's employer shall sit at the counsel table in any adversarial proceeding among the parties regarding the subject matter of the Dispute.

5.0   FULL DISCLOSURE OF INFORMATION AND DOCUMENTS

5.1   The Parties will make a full and candid exchange of all information, documents and tangible things in their control ("Information") on which they rely and which are consistent with and support their position on any matter in dispute, and all Information in their control which is inconsistent with their position and/or supports the position of any other Party.

5.2   Any material change in Information must be promptly updated.

5.3   The Parties authorize their respective Lawyers to fully disclose all Information, which in the Lawyer's judgment must be provided to other participants in order to fulfill the full disclosure commitment; provided that such authorization does not constitute a waiver of the attorney-client privilege.

5.4   The Parties agree to give complete and timely responses to all requests for documents and other Information relevant to the resolution of the Dispute. Unless otherwise agreed in writing, during the collaborative process the Parties will not engage in formal discovery as in an adversarial proceeding. Affidavits may be utilized to confirm specific matters, such as the unavailability of certain Information, or the existence or non-existence of documents or tangible things.

5.5   The Parties agree not to conduct surveillance of another Party's activities, including the use of an investigator, detective or other individual paid for or engaged by a Party or third party, or the use of electronic listening or tracking devices during the collaborative process.

6.0   CONFIDENTIALITY

6.1   The Parties agree to maintain the confidentiality of oral and/or written communications relating to the Dispute made by the Parties or their Lawyers or other participants in the collaborative process, whether the communication was made before or after the institution of formal adversarial proceedings.

6.2   All communications, whether oral or written, and the conduct of any Party, Lawyer, or retained expert in the collaborative process constitute compromise and settlement negotiations under the rules of the authority having jurisdiction over the subject matter of the Dispute and the Parties. Unless the Parties otherwise agree in writing, these communications and any written materials, tangible items, and other Information used in or made a part of the collaborative process, are only discoverable and admissible in any adversarial proceeding regarding this Dispute, or in any other proceeding among the Parties to this Agreement, if they would otherwise be admissible or discoverable independent of the collaborative process. This exclusion does not apply to the admissibility of a fully executed Collaborative Settlement Agreement.

6.3   A Party and that Party's Lawyer may disclose all Information to a lawyer engaged to render an outside legal opinion for the Party in the collaborative process, or to that Party's successor collaborative lawyer. In the event the collaborative process is terminated, a Party may disclose all Information to that Party's litigation lawyer.

7.0   LEGAL PROCESS

7.1   The Parties and the Lawyers agree that, as to the Dispute, Court intervention shall be suspended while the Parties are participating in the collaborative process pursuant to this Agreement. Unilaterally seeking Court intervention for any adversarial hearing regarding any portion of the Dispute automatically terminates the collaborative process.

7.2   The Lawyers' representation of the Parties is limited to the collaborative process. Once the process is terminated, the Lawyers cannot participate in any manner in an adversarial proceeding as to any portion of the Dispute, nor can a Lawyer subsequently represent any Party in an adversarial proceeding involving any other Party when the proceeding involves the subject matter of this Dispute.

7.3   Upon termination of the collaborative process, or upon the withdrawal of a Lawyer, the Lawyers shall not be joined as a party or called as a witness in any adversarial proceeding among any of the Parties regarding any portion of the Dispute. Any Party or Lawyer violating this provision shall pay all fees and expenses, including reasonable attorneys' fees, incurred by a Lawyer opposing such effort.

7.4   No documents will be prepared or filed which would initiate Court intervention, except if necessary to preserve causes of action, defenses, or to obtain some extraordinary relief. In such situations, service of citation or other processes, and any pleadings will be accepted by the Parties' respective Lawyers. The Parties and Lawyers will endeavor to reach agreement to eliminate the necessity for any such filings. No hearing shall be set, other than to submit agreed orders to the Court.

8.0   RETAINED EXPERTS

8.1   The Parties will jointly engage retained experts as unbiased neutrals if needed, unless the Parties agree in writing to separately engage neutral retained experts.

8.2   The Parties may engage retained experts, including lawyers, for any issue which requires expert advice and/or recommendations. The Parties will agree in advance how retained experts' fees will be paid.

8.3   Retained experts must sign and agree to abide by the terms and conditions of a Retained Expert Participation Agreement.

8.4   A retained expert who is an attorney, and any attorney associated in the practice of law with such attorney, shall not serve as the litigation attorney for any party in any adversarial proceeding arising from the subject matter of the Dispute.

8.5   Retained experts shall not serve as fact or expert witnesses, and their work product, opinions, mental impressions, and the factual basis of them are not discoverable or admissible in any adversarial proceeding regarding the Dispute, or in any other proceeding among the Parties.

8.6   Retained experts may communicate with the Parties, their Lawyers, and any other retained experts. Retained experts may participate, and their work product, opinions, mental impressions, and the factual basis of them may be utilized in any confidential ADR process which is a part of the collaborative process governed by this Agreement.

8.7   The Lawyers shall instruct retained experts to report openly to all Parties the following: (1) all communications the expert has had with any other person regarding the matter for which the expert has been engaged; (2) the expert's work product, opinions, mental impressions; and (3) the factual basis for them.

9.0   CONSULTING-ONLY EXPERT

9.1   A Party may privately retain a consulting-only expert. A consulting-only expert is an expert who: (1) has no firsthand knowledge about the Dispute; (2) has no factual knowledge about the Dispute except for knowledge that was acquired through the consultation; and (3) whose work product, opinions, or mental impressions have not been reviewed by retained experts.

9.2   A consulting-only expert's identity shall be disclosed to all Parties.

9.3   Communications between the consulting-only expert and the Party engaging that expert, and the expert's work product, opinions, mental impressions, and the factual basis for them shall remain confidential.

9.4   A consulting-only expert may review the reports of any retained expert; however, should a retained expert review the work product of a consulting-only expert, the consulting-only expert becomes a retained expert whose work product and opinions must be disclosed to all Parties. The engaging Party's Lawyer shall so advise the consulting-only expert.

9.5   By Addendum to this Agreement the Parties should agree whether or not a consulting-only expert is disqualified from testifying as a fact or expert witness in any adversarial proceeding arising from the Dispute.

9.6   A consulting-only expert who is a lawyer, and any lawyer associated in the practice of law with such lawyer, shall not serve as the litigation lawyer for the engaging party in any adversarial proceeding arising from the subject matter of the Dispute.

9.7   The Lawyers shall instruct consulting-only experts that (1) the Parties are engaged in a collaborative process; and (2) the role of the consulting-only expert is to assist the Party in identifying issues, analyzing relevant information, developing options, and assisting in reaching the goal of the collaborative process which is an agreed resolution of the Dispute.

10.0   OUTSIDE LEGAL OPINIONS

10.1   A Party may privately engage a lawyer, including a litigation lawyer, outside of the collaborative process for the limited purpose of obtaining an opinion on a specific issue or issues. Before beginning consultation with an outside lawyer, the identity of any such lawyer must be disclosed to all Parties. If a Party has engaged a lawyer other than the Party's collaborative Lawyer prior to signing this Agreement, the identity of such lawyer shall be disclosed to all Parties before signing this Agreement.

10.2   Any lawyer engaged outside of the collaborative process for the purpose of giving an opinion on any issue or issues, should be given all information necessary to give informed advice, including reports of retained experts whose services have been engaged in the collaborative process regarding the Dispute.

10.3   The Parties agree the work product, opinions, mental impressions, and the facts upon which they are based of a lawyer engaged outside of the collaborative process for the limited purpose of obtaining an opinion on a specific issue or issues, are not discoverable in any adversarial proceeding regarding the subject matter of the Dispute or in any other adversarial proceeding among the Parties, unless the Parties agree otherwise.

10.4   By Addendum to this Agreement, the Parties should agree whether or not such lawyer, and any lawyer associated in the practice of law with such lawyer, may testify as fact or expert witnesses, or may serve as litigation counsel for the consulting Party in any adversarial proceeding resulting from the Dispute, or in any other adversarial proceeding among any of the Parties regarding the subject matter of the Dispute.

10.5   Should all the Parties jointly seek an opinion from a lawyer outside of the collaborative process, including a litigation lawyer, such lawyer is a retained expert whose work product and opinions must be disclosed to all Parties.

11.0   OTHER ALTERNATIVE DISPUTE RESOLUTION PROCESSES

To avoid termination of the collaborative process or to further facilitate the process, the Parties may agree in writing to mediate in good faith with a mediator who has received training in the collaborative process, or to utilize other alternative dispute resolution procedures with third party neutrals who are trained in the collaborative process.

12.0   WITHDRAWAL FROM THE COLLABORATIVE PROCESS BY A PARTY

12.1   A Party may withdraw from the collaborative process at any time and shall notify that Party's Lawyer in writing. The withdrawing Party's Lawyer shall give prompt written notice to the other Parties through their respective Lawyers.

12.2   If the Dispute involves more than two Parties, the remaining Parties may choose to continue the collaborative process without the withdrawing Party. The withdrawing Party shall not proceed in any adversarial manner until the sooner of completion of the collaborative process or 180 days from the date the withdrawing Party gave notice.

13.0   TERMINATION OF THE COLLABORATIVE PROCESS BY A LAWYER

13.1   If a Party refuses to act in good faith, for example, by refusing to disclose relevant Information which in the Lawyer's judgment must be provided to other participants; by answering dishonestly any inquiry made by a participant in the collaborative process; or by proposing to take an action that would compromise the integrity of the collaborative process, and the Party persists after counseling by the Lawyer, then the collaborative process shall be terminated.

13.2   If the offending Party refuses to terminate the collaborative process, all Parties acknowledge that their respective Lawyers have a duty to terminate the collaborative process on behalf of their clients, and all Parties authorize their Lawyer to terminate the process by written notice to all participants and the Court. The Lawyers shall not reveal whose decision it was to terminate the collaborative process or the reason the process was terminated.

13.3   Upon termination of the process, Lawyers shall withdraw from the representation. The Lawyers may not serve as a litigation lawyer in the Dispute or in any other adversarial proceedings among any of the Parties regarding the same subject matter. If any lawyer associated in the practice of law with the Lawyers intends to serve as a litigation lawyer, the Parties must agree to such representation in writing prior to the termination of the collaborative process.

13.4   All Lawyers will cooperate in returning the clients' original documents, to facilitate transfer of the client's documents and notebooks to litigation lawyers.

14.0   WITHDRAWAL BY A LAWYER

14.1   A Lawyer may withdraw unilaterally from the collaborative process for any reason by giving three days' written notice to the Lawyer's client and the other Lawyers. The withdrawing Lawyer does not have to state a reason for the withdrawal.

14.2   The Party whose Lawyer has withdrawn may retain a new collaborative lawyer, or may continue in the collaborative process without a lawyer but only upon the written agreement of all Parties. A newly engaged collaborative lawyer must sign this Agreement.

15.0   THIRTY DAY MORATORIUM

15.1   Upon notice to all Lawyers of termination of the collaborative process, the Parties will observe a thirty day waiting period, unless there is an emergency, before requesting any court hearing, to permit all Parties to engage other lawyers and make an orderly transition from the collaborative process to litigation or any other adversarial proceeding.

15.2   All written agreements previously entered into by the Parties shall remain effective until modified by agreement or Court order. A Party may bring this provision to the attention of the court in requesting a postponement of a hearing.

16.0   LAWYERS' FEES AND EXPENSES

The Parties understand that the Lawyers and all experts engaged in the collaborative process shall be paid for their services whether or not the collaborative process results in resolution of the Dispute. The Parties agree that all such fees and expenses incurred by the Parties shall be paid in full prior to signing a final Collaborative Settlement Agreement, and/or the submission of an agreed judgment to a Court.

17.0   MISCELLANY

17.1   "Court" as used in this Agreement refers to any adjudicatory body having jurisdiction over the Parties and the Dispute. Lawyers may appear in Court only by written agreement of all Parties or as required by law. Temporary orders may be submitted to a Court upon the written agreement of all Parties.

17.2   "Good faith" as used in this Agreement means truthfulness, an honest commitment not to take advantage of a Party through technicalities of law and an intention to meet the legitimate needs of all Parties to the extent it is feasible to do so.

17.3 The participants shall require that any retained expert, consulting only expert or outside legal opinion attorney disclose any previous consultation and/or representation with any participants in the collaborative process under this Agreement.

17.4 This Agreement shall remain enforceable as a contract between the Parties and may be the basis for a claim against a Party violating its terms. If any provision of this Agreement is held to be invalid or unenforceable for any reason, all remaining provisions shall continue to be valid and enforceable.

17.5 Any written agreement, whether partial or final, which is signed by all Parties and their respective Lawyers, may be filed with the court as a Collaborative Settlement Agreement in accordance with the rules of the Court having jurisdiction over the subject matter of the Dispute and the Parties. Such an agreement is retroactive to the effective date of the written agreement and may be made the basis of a Court order.

17.6 The Lawyers shall cooperate in preparing the documents necessary to effectuate the Parties' agreements made hereunder.

17.7 The Parties and their Lawyers acknowledge that they have read this Agreement and agree to abide by its terms and conditions, to remain faithful to their duties and obligations under this Agreement and pledge to comply with the spirit and letter of this Agreement.

Signed on this _____ day of _____, 20___.

_____   _____
[Party 1]   [Party 2]

_____   _____
Street Address   Street Address

_____   _____
City, State, Zip   City, State, Zip

_____   _____
Telephone   Telephone

_____   _____
Fax Number   Fax Number

_____   _____
E-mail   E-mail

_____

[Party 3]

_____

Street Address

_____

City, State, Zip

_____

Telephone

_____

Fax Number

_____

E-mail

_____

[Lawyer for Party 1]

_____

State Bar Number

_____

Street Address

_____

City, State, Zip

_____

Telephone

_____

Fax Number

_____

E-mail

_____

[Party 4]

_____

Street Address

_____

City, State, Zip

_____

Telephone

_____

Fax Number

_____

E-mail

_____

[Lawyer for Party 2]

_____

State Bar Number

_____

Street Address

_____

City, State, Zip

_____

Telephone

_____

Fax Number

_____

E-mail

_____   _____
[Lawyer for Party 3]   [Lawyer for Party 4]

_____   _____
State Bar Number   State Bar Number

_____   _____
Street Address   Street Address

_____   _____
City, State, Zip   City, State, Zip

_____   _____
Telephone   Telephone

_____   _____
Fax Number   Fax Number

_____   _____
E-mail   E-mail

ADDENDUM TO THE PARTICIPATION AGREEMENT

The purpose of this Addendum is to assist the Parties in making choices regarding how they wish to conduct the collaborative process. The Parties may agree to postpone a decision on any item, or agree to not address any item in this Addendum. The Addendum should be modified to suit the needs of the Parties and the Dispute.

1.   The second joint meeting will be held at:

_____ on _____ __.m.

Third   _____ on _____ __.m.

Fourth _____ on _____ __.m.

If additional meetings are necessary, the Parties will agree on subsequent meeting times and places during the fourth meeting.

_____
_____

2. Meetings will be at least ____ hours, but no meeting will last longer than ____ hours.

3.   The Parties and Lawyers shall attend all face to face meetings. After signing a participation or confidentiality agreement, other persons who may attend are:

_____
_____
_____
_____

4. The Parties agree that they will __ will not __ discuss among themselves issues regarding the Dispute outside the face to face meetings.

5. The Parties shall retain all experts jointly ____ separately ____, –or– ____ the Parties will decide if the expert will be retained jointly or individually as the collaborative process progresses.

6. Each Party shall pay _____ % of any fee of any expert, –or– ____ the Parties shall pay all fees and expenses as follows:

_____
_____
_____
_____

7. The Parties agree that a retained expert may ___ may not ___ participate in a subsequent adversarial proceeding among the parties regarding subject matter **not** addressed in this Dispute.

8. The Parties have ___ have not ___ engaged a lawyer to render an outside legal opinion prior to the execution of the Participation Agreement. (List names of Party and any previously engaged lawyer.)

_____
_____
_____
_____

9. The Parties have ___ have no ___ present intention to engage an outside legal opinion attorney. (List names of Party and any proposed attorney.)

_____
_____
_____
_____

10. The Parties agree that any privately engaged outside legal opinion attorney

   a.   may _____ may not _____ represent the engaging party in any adversarial proceeding involving any other Party to the Dispute, regarding the subject matter of the Dispute.

   b.   may ___ may not ___ testify as an expert or a fact witness in any adversarial proceeding involving any other Party to the Dispute, regarding the subject matter of the Dispute.

11. There are _____ are not _____ any consulting-only experts who have been privately engaged prior to the execution of the Participation Agreement. (List names of Party and any previously engaged consulting-only expert.)

12. There are ___ are not ___ parties who presently intend to engage a consulting-only expert. (List names of Party and of such consulting-only expert.)

_____
_____
_____
_____

13. If a Party engages a consulting-only expert, the expert may__ may not __ testify as an expert or a fact witness in any adversarial proceeding regarding the subject matter of the Dispute which involves any other Party to the Dispute.

14. The Parties agree that any consulting-only expert or an outside legal opinion attorney is __ is not __ required to have the expert/attorney disclose any previous consultation and/or representation with any participants to the collaborative process.

15. The Parties agree that any consulting-only expert or an outside legal opinion attorney will __ will not __ sign an agreement explaining the collaborative process and that person's role in the process.

16. During face to face meetings, the Parties may __ may not __ discuss possible outcomes if the Dispute were to be decided in an adversarial proceeding outside of the collaborative process.

17. The Parties will ___ will not ___ participate in formal discovery in the collaborative process. (List any type discovery the Parties have agreed to.)

_____

_____

_____

_____

18. Should the Parties proceed to an adversarial proceeding outside of the collaborative process, any formal discovery, such as affidavits, depositions, or written interrogatories, developed within the collaborative process will ____ will not ____ be admissible, –or– ____ the Parties will decide as the process progresses.

19. The Parties agree that should they reach impasse they may:
        (Number in order of preference)
_____ select a mediator and mediate the issues.
_____ select a single arbitrator and participate in non-binding arbitration.
_____ select a panel of three arbitrators and participate in non-binding arbitration.
_____ select a single arbitrator and participate in binding arbitration.
_____ select a panel of three arbitrators and participate in binding arbitration.
_____ file the binding arbitration award or mediated settlement agreement with a court having jurisdiction over the subject matter of the Dispute and the Parties for the purpose of reducing the arbitration award to a judgment.
_____ terminate the collaborative process and proceed to litigation.

20. Minutes will be taken at each meeting and _____
will serve as secretary, or _____ the collaborative lawyers shall take turns serving as
secretary.

21. Other agreements: _____
_____
_____
_____
_____
_____
_____
_____
_____

By their signatures below the Parties and Lawyers acknowledge that they have read, discussed, and understand this Addendum, and that the decisions they have made as set forth in this Addendum are binding on each Party and Lawyer as of this date. It is understood that this Addendum may be amended at any time during the collaborative process, but only by the written agreement of all participants.

Signed on this ____ day of _____, 20____.

_____   _____
[Party 1]   [Party 2]

_____   _____
[Party 3]   [Party 4]

_____   _____
[Lawyer for Party 1]   [Lawyer for Party 2]

_____   _____
[Lawyer for Party 3]   [Lawyer for Party 4]

Chapter 8

The Arbitration Process

§ 8.01 Overview

The preceding chapters described the essential features of consensual, nonbinding dispute resolution processes, such as negotiation or mediation, in which the parties have ultimate control over the resolution of their transaction or dispute. A negotiated deal or mediated settlement results in a binding contract, but the process itself is not binding on the parties in that they may choose to walk away from discussions and opt to not accept a deal. Contrast such non-binding processes with processes in which parties have total control over the outcome, with arbitration.

Arbitration is a private, adjudicatory process for resolving disputes. Arbitration is a consensual process in that the parties have agreed to have their existing or future disputes heard before and decided by a neutral third party. However, unlike mediation or negotiation, the parties in arbitration cede control to the arbitrator to render a final and binding decision. Federal and state legislation provides for the judicial enforcement of written agreements to resolve disputes by arbitration, and for the judicial enforcement, and vacatur, of private arbitration awards.

Arbitration has a long history of use in specialized business, commercial, and labor-management settings, traditionally where parties have a continuing relationship and consider that their business relationship, and other interests, are best served by agreeing to a binding dispute resolution process that is generally faster and less expensive than litigation. Parties also choose arbitration because of the ability to select decision-makers who have specialized knowledge in the subject matter, as well as the ability to control the application of procedural rules governing the process.

At its heart, arbitration is a creature of contract. Most often, parties determine at the beginning of their contractual relationship (such as a business or employment relationship), that they will resolve all future disputes through arbitration. In a minority of cases, parties agree to arbitrate after the dispute arises. Resolving disputes through arbitration is customary in some industries, such as construction or insurance. In today's market, arbitration agreements are customary with some employers, and in many consumer contracts, including contracts for financial services and cellular telephone service.

As with the coverage of mediation, the discussion of arbitration spans two chapters. This chapter discusses the arbitration process from start to finish. Chapter 9 covers the legal issues in arbitration. The combination of these two chapters gives the reader an introduction to the process and the intersection of the arbitration and legal processes. These chapters should leave the reader with a greater understanding of what arbitration is, why parties choose arbitration, how the arbitration process works, and the legal framework surrounding the process. Although these chapters focus primarily on arbitration within the United States, they will highlight the international arbitration process to give a more complete view of arbitration globally.

§ 8.02 History of Arbitration

Arbitration has deep historical and even biblical roots as a method for settling disputes. In the Middle Ages, merchants often traveled from town to town, and the court systems were incredibly slow. If merchants had a dispute, they often had no remedy because of their transient nature and inability to access the court system as they traveled. For instance, if a tanner purchases hides from another merchant, but the hides were not of the expected quality, the buyer may not have sufficient time to resolve that dispute before the seller moved to the next town. The merchant class, then, created a system of arbitration that would resolve trade disputes quickly. In addition, the system they created used experts as decision-makers. In the dispute regarding the quality of the animal hides, the buyer and seller could hire another tanner as the arbitrator because that third party would already understand the commercial norms in the trade.

The history of arbitration in the United States' economy can be traced from use among these merchants, the medieval guilds, and English maritime law, to English arbitration law.[1] Religious communities in the colonial period also used arbitration to resolve disputes. Arbitration enabled the parties to resolve their dispute privately and outside of the public court system. Church elders could be selected as arbitrators to enforce the norms of the community.

Although arbitration was widely used in the United States among the merchants during the late nineteenth century, courts were reluctant to enforce executory arbitration agreements. Executory arbitration agreements are those in which the parties agree to arbitrate a future dispute that does not yet exist. If one party to an arbitration agreement asked for specific performance of the arbitration agreement (i.e., to order the parties to arbitrate), Court would reject party requests on the basis that the parties were attempting to "oust" the courts of supervision or jurisdiction over legal disputes. In the nineteenth and early twentieth centuries, courts would refuse to enforce arbitration agreements — even if the arbitration had already begun. The courts, however, would become involved to enforce an arbitration award for an arbitration that was completed.

Merchants, thus, could not predictably rely on arbitration because both parties needed to agree to arbitrate after the dispute arose in order for the arbitration agreement to be enforceable. In the 1920s, New York, at the urging of merchants and its Chamber of Commerce, enacted a statute to require courts to enforce agreements to arbitrate both current and future disputes. A few other states followed New York's lead shortly thereafter.

In 1925, the United States Congress passed the Federal Arbitration Act ("FAA"), which is based on the New York statute. The FAA reversed the common law and provided that agreements to arbitrate are specifically enforceable, even if the arbitration agreement covers future disputes. To accomplish this goal, Congress gave the federal courts two important powers. The first power is the power to stay any current litigation if the dispute should be in arbitration. The second power is the power to compel arbitration, which is essentially a remedy similar to specific enforcement, meaning that arbitration agreements will be enforced according to their terms. The FAA is discussed in considerably more detail in Chapter 9.

---

1. Kuluundis Shipping Co., S/A v. Amtorg Trading Corp., 126 F.2d 978 (2d Cir. 1942).

Congress passed the FAA in response to urging by the business community that arbitration was faster, less expensive, and less contentious than litigation and could preserve business relationships and improve commerce and standards by allowing certainty in how disputes would be adjudicated.[2] These advantages are discussed more robustly in the next section. The FAA reads as if it were a procedural statute applicable in federal courts. The statute references the federal courts, and it discusses what appear to be procedural powers. Nonetheless, the Supreme Court has since construed the FAA to apply in state courts to preempt state laws that conflict with the FAA.[3] Federal preemption and its consequences, are important legal considerations discussed in Chapter 9.

The use of arbitration has expanded dramatically since the initial merchant days of the 1920s. Today, arbitration is commonly used to resolve disputes in numerous sectors, including consumer, commercial, employment, labor-management, professional and international sports, entertainment, and international, as well as disputes under the terms of international agreements involving governments and nations. An individual may be subject to dozens of arbitration agreements whether or not that person realizes it!

U.S. Supreme Court decisions interpreting the FAA depict a transformation from the initial judicial hostility toward arbitration to a modern infatuation regarding FAA as a federal policy favoring arbitration. Yet fairness concerns regarding contemporary use of compulsory arbitration in consumer, employment, and other disparate power or bargaining situations have again raised the specter of hostility to arbitration. These issues are developed throughout this chapter and Chapter 9.

§ 8.03 What Is Arbitration?

[A] Basic Concept and Definition

Arbitration is process of dispute resolution in which a third-party neutral — the arbitrator or panel — renders a decision after a hearing at which both parties have an opportunity to be heard. Arbitration is fundamentally a matter of contract. The parties agree to submit an existing or future dispute to the final and binding decision of a third party. Parties may also agree as to the selection of the arbitrator. Prior to arbitration, the parties exchange documents and evidence, and some depositions may be taken. Ultimately, the parties will have a hearing at which each side makes arguments and presents evidence, similar to a trial. Following the hearing, the arbitrators deliberate and come to a decision regarding the merits of the dispute. The arbitrators issue an award, which is a binding resolution that can be transformed into a court judgment and enforced like any other court judgment.

This description probably sounds very similar to litigation, and arbitration and litigation share many characteristics. Both are adversarial processes that put the decision-making power into the hands of a third-party neutral. Both involve the

---

2. Margaret L. Moses, *Statutory Misconstruction: How the Supreme Court Created a Federal Arbitration Law Never Enacted by Congress,* 34 FLA. ST. L. REV. 99, 101 (2006) (FAA's historical background and intended scope).

3. Southland v. Keating, 465 U.S. 1, 12 (1984).

presentation of lawyer arguments, witness testimony, and documentary evidence. Both involve hearings with live witnesses. Both may involve the discovery process, expert witnesses, objections to evidence, and motion practice. Over time, arbitration has begun to look more and more like litigation. Most of these changes have been fueled by concerns over arbitration's fairness and potential for due process. These fairness concerns are discussed in more detail throughout this chapter and Chapter 9.

The two processes, however, have a number of key differences. Unlike litigation, arbitration is a private process that occurs outside of the public view and without public knowledge. Hearings take place in conference rooms, not courtrooms, and the public rarely knows they are occurring. The arbitration process may also be confidential, meaning that the parties have agreed that the process not only be private, but also that they will not disclose information about the arbitration to other people, including the press. The process should be expedited and less formal than litigation. Unlike litigation, which involves a generalist judge, many times arbitrators are selected for their expertise in a subject matter. The parties also have the ability to choose their arbitrator, unlike the judicial process. Unlike public judges in litigation, arbitrators are directly paid by the parties. Arbitration awards, compared to litigation judgments, have only a limited right to appeal. These characteristics sometimes contribute to arbitration's benefits, while at other times they contribute to the disadvantages of the process.

[B] Essential Characteristics

Surprisingly, the term "arbitration" is not defined in the Federal Arbitration Act or in Supreme Court jurisprudence. However, arbitration has certain defining characteristics that distinguish it from other forms of evaluation or review. Whether a process is "arbitration" is significant because of the attendant legal protections of the arbitration statutes. As discussed in more detail in Chapter 9, if a process is "arbitration," then the courts are required to enforce the agreements to arbitrate and enforce arbitration awards, with rare exceptions.

Arbitration is customarily defined as "a simple proceeding voluntarily chosen by parties who want a dispute determined by an impartial judge of their own mutual selection, whose decision based on the merits of the case, they agree in advance to accept as final and binding."[4] The signifying features of arbitration are: (1) the parties must agree or consent to have their dispute settled; (2) by a third-party decision-maker, and (3) the award is final and binding. Although the other types of ADR processes discussed thus far are also all consensual, arbitration is the only one discussed thus far that includes a third-party *decision-maker*. Mediators, by contrast, do not make decisions, but rather help the parties make their own decision. This is also the only process discussed thus far that ensures a final and binding outcome for the dispute.

The first central element of arbitration is the parties' intention or agreement to arbitrate. The agreement can determine and control much of the arbitration process, affected parties, arbitrator selection, applicable rules, and arbitral powers. Parties can agree to arbitrate before or after a dispute arises. In an overwhelming majority of the time, the agreement to arbitrate is reduced to writing. In some instances, the agreement to arbitrate says little more than "X and Y agree to arbitrate all disputes arising out of this contract."

---

4. Elkouri & Elkouri, How Arbitration Works 2 (Volz & Goggins eds., 5th ed. 1997).

On other occasions, the arbitration agreement may be an extensive document outlining all of the different procedural choices the parties have made—such as the location of the arbitration, the arbitration rules, the method of arbitrator selection, the amount of discovery, time limits for the hearing, applicable governing law, whether the resulting award must be written, and so on. Perhaps the primary reason parties have written arbitration agreements is because federal and state laws provide that courts will only enforce agreements to arbitrate "evidenced" through a written contract.[5] Whether the courts would enforce an oral agreement to arbitrate is unclear, and unlikely.

In the classic sense, arbitration occurs when "parties in dispute choose a judge to render a final binding decision on the merits of the controversy and on the basis of the proofs presented by the parties.'"[6] An "arbitral tribunal" is "a body consisting of one or more persons designated directly or indirectly by the parties to an arbitration agreement and empowered by them to adjudicate a dispute that has arisen among them."[7] The only qualification necessary for an arbitrator is that the parties agree that the person can serve as their arbitrator. Arbitrators need not have any special credentials, education, or expertise. Although many arbitrators are lawyers, not all arbitrators are lawyers. Historically, arbitrators were merchants or other laypersons with expertise in the subject matter. In many cases today, the parties choose an organization to administer the case, such as the American Arbitration Association (AAA), and the provider organization has arbitrators available to hear the case.

The third essential characteristic is that the arbitrator's award be final and binding. The arbitration process ensures a resolution to the dispute. The promise of finality is one reason parties choose arbitration. Finality is ensured through a limited right of appeal by parties under federal and state law. The availability of post-arbitration review is discussed at the end of this chapter.

§ 8.04 Advantages and Disadvantages of Arbitration

[A] Advantages of Arbitration

Arbitration offers the potential for substantial benefits to the parties. Arbitration is generally considered faster, more economical, and less formal than litigation. Many arbitration proceedings can occur from start to finish in approximately one year, which is significantly faster than litigation in most court systems. A shorter timetable means that attorneys spend fewer hours on the case, which tends to equate to cost savings for the parties. The informality surrounding discovery and the arbitration process also may lead to cost savings for the parties—especially if informality results in less motion practice, discovery objections, and other types of lawyer activities that take a considerable amount of time and money.

---

5. *See, e.g.,* 9 U.S.C. § 2.

6. Rush Prudential HMO, Inc. v. Moran, 536 U.S. 355 (2002).

7. Restatement (Third) of the U.S. Law of International Commercial Arbitration § 1-1, note to cmt. E.

Arbitration also permits the parties to agree to privacy and avoidance of precedent. Parties may be interested in a non-public type of dispute resolution for legitimate reasons. Some parties may not want their dirty laundry in the courts, and perhaps in the press. Businesses may not want sensitive information about their business, technology, or finances available for review by the public at large and business competitors. Many cases do not require the development of precedent, and some parties may not want precedent made from their individual cases.

Arbitration provides the unique opportunity for parties to ensure a neutral forum and choose their own decision-maker. The neutral forum can be particularly attractive to parties who live far apart. In those situations, the arbitration agreement may specify a neutral location that would require both parties to travel (which is an economic disincentive to bring arbitration cases). In the international context, arbitration provides a unique opportunity for the parties to choose a location that is outside of either party's "home court." Parties rarely like to utilize the court systems of foreign countries, and many would prefer to use the arbitration process with simplified rules instead of navigating a foreign court system.

Further, parties may choose arbitration to ensure enforcement of the final and binding arbitration award through application of state, federal, and international arbitration laws and conventions.[8] Because of these laws, arbitration awards are actually more enforceable than court judgments. A large number of countries have adopted conventions that allow the enforcement of arbitration awards, meaning that arbitration often results in binding decisions in either the United States or in other countries.

Arbitration also offers procedural flexibility. Parties may designate applicable procedural rules that are streamlined and less complex than most national rules of civil procedure. Court rules, such as the Federal Rules of Civil Procedure and the Federal Rules of Evidence, generally do not apply to the arbitration forum. Although arbitrators may use these rules as a guide, they are not hard-and-fast rules that must be strictly enforced. In arbitration, parties can stipulate as to the level of discovery, motions, choice of law, situs, and award forms. Parties generally desire the right to select the arbitrator(s) and designate arbitrator qualifications, experience, and industry expertise. Arbitration, in and of itself, does not require the application of any specific rule of law. The parties are free to specify the law that applies, but arbitrators have some flexibility on how rigidly they apply the law. Arbitrators may make rulings based on equity, rather than the strict application of legal rules. Similarly, arbitrators have a greater flexibility of the types of remedies they can award. Unlike courts, arbitrators have greater flexibility to award non-monetary judgments, such as reinstatement and specific performance.

Consider that a court case in litigation is randomly assigned to a judge who may have no familiarity with the subject matter, can take one to three years to adjudicate, is a matter of public record, involves formal procedures, a judgment that can set undesirable precedent, and involve rights to appeal and a broader scope of judicial review. In comparison, the arbitration process brings many features that seek to remedy the shortcomings of the litigation process.

The key to arbitration's advantages is party control. The parties have the ability to create a forum that best meets their needs. Parties can craft nearly every aspect of the

---

8. The United Nations Convention on the Recognition of Foreign Arbitral Awards, also known as the New York Convention, (1958) is a multilateral treaty for the enforcement of arbitral awards to which more than 145 states are party.

dispute resolution process, although few parties actually take advantage of these opportunities.

[B] Drawbacks of Arbitration

Depending upon your perspective, some of the touted advantages of arbitration—speed, limited discovery, privacy, and limited appeal, for example—may also be considered drawbacks of the process. Let's unpack these benefits to show their downsides. In some circumstances, the efficiencies of speed and limited discovery can be a drawback of the process. If a case proceeds too quickly or if the discovery process is too truncated, the parties may not have sufficient time to develop their case for presentation to a third-party neutral. What the parties gain in time and money, they may lose in terms of completeness and preparation. In cases involving a business entity and an individual, the business entity likely has a great deal more information than the individual, and the individual may have a difficult time getting the necessary information to put on the individual party's case.

While many parties value privacy and confidentiality, the flip side of privacy is "secrecy." Parties may choose arbitration in order to keep bad publicity from the public eye, even when the public might have a right to know. The public and press may be interested in knowing if some companies or individuals are engaging in sexual harassment, polluting the environment, or defrauding others. As discussed in Chapter 5, Legal Issues in Mediation, confidentiality is a double-edged sword that is usually beneficial, but not always.

Because of the non-public nature of arbitration, the resulting arbitration awards are rarely made available to the public. Thus, both the process and the resulting decision are both out of the public view. In some instances, arbitration awards are made available through print or online resources,[9] but the vast majority of arbitration awards are either not easily accessible or not accessible at all.

Under federal and state law, parties have a very limited right to appeal arbitration awards. The limited appeal is the other side of the finality coin. Arbitration awards may rarely be overturned based on the "rightness" or "wrongness" of the decision itself. Instead, the parties must point to some type of procedural error or ethical violation for a court to overturn—or "vacate"—the award.

One major drawback to the process is the cost of the arbitrator. Parties who avail themselves of the court system do not have to pay a judge because they are paid out of taxpayer dollars. Arbitrators, on the other hand, are private individuals who need to be paid for their time. Arbitrators often charge hefty fees (either on a per-hour or per-day basis). When the parties choose to have a panel of three or five arbitrators, the costs multiply quite quickly. Some arbitral providers have cost-savings and cost-shifting measures for consumers and employees, but not in every case. In consumer arbitrations before the AAA, the AAA requires a business entity to pay a much greater share of the fee compared to a consumer party.

Arbitrators are individuals who serve in private practice because of their expertise, neutrality, reputation, or other attributes. Arbitrators, however, work on an hourly basis

---

9. In the labor/management context, labor arbitration awards are available through BNA. In the securities area, FINRA posts all of its arbitration awards online.

and may have an economic incentive to maximize hours spent on a given case. Parties who are frequent users of arbitration services are usually called "repeat players." Repeat players have the power to hire arbitrators over the course of many different cases, while individuals likely would only ever hire one arbitrator in a lifetime. Unscrupulous arbitrators may be swayed toward ruling in favor of business entities out of the hope that they would be hired again for additional cases with the same company.

Although no qualifications exist regarding who can legally serve as an arbitrator, in practice much of the work is dominated by small group of people. These individuals are often white men, lawyers and former judges. However, organizations are attempting to bring more diversity into the arbitrator ranks.[10] Arbitrators with experience are often chosen over inexperienced arbitrators. This phenomenon weighs in favor of a small number of people who have served as arbitrators for many years.

[C] Examples

Examples of two typical cases provide a helpful illustration of the advantages and disadvantages of arbitration. The first case is one between two business entities in an arms-length transaction. The second example is an increasingly common example of an agreement to arbitrate in a "take it or leave it" consumer contract.

Arbitration agreements in the business context are included in business-to-business contracts (sometimes called B2B contracts). Consider a contract between a grain supplier ("GS") and a food manufacturer ("FM") for the sale of wheat and corn to be used to manufacture breakfast cereal. Both parties have sufficient bargaining power to form a contract that meets both of their needs. They choose to put an arbitration agreement in their contract for a number of reasons. First, both businesses want to resolve their disputes quickly and maintain their relationship, even if a conflict arises. Likely, any dispute between the parties would not require the creation of new law, and the parties would like the ability to appoint an expert as arbitrator. The arbitration forum is more expensive than litigation, but the parties hope that the money they save on attorneys' fees will more than compensate for the arbitrator and other forum fees. Sure, the parties will lose most of their right to appeal, but they are interested in finality and getting back to selling grain and making cereal.

In contrast, consider a contract between a consumer and a computer company for the sale of a $1,500 laptop computer. The consumer bought the laptop online and was required to "click through" a series of legal forms, one of which was an arbitration agreement. The consumer can only "agree" or not purchase the computer. When the computer arrives at the consumer's house, the box contains a written version of the arbitration agreement. The arbitration agreement may or may not be in fine print and written in a way that a layperson could understand. The computer company chose all of the terms of the agreement, which may or may not be friendly to the consumer. If the company has a consumer-friendly arbitration agreement, the contract would limit the consumer's fees, require arbitration at a location geographically close to the consumer, and ensure

---

10. The American Bar Association Section of Dispute Resolution has standing committees on Women in Dispute Resolution (WIDR) and Minorities in Dispute Resolution (MIDR) in an effort to increase networking and business opportunities for women and minorities who act as neutrals. In addition, some of the arbitration providers are making efforts to have a more diverse group of arbitrators on their panels for selection.

the selection of a neutral arbitrator. If the company takes advantage of the power differential between the parties, the company could require arbitration fees to be split evenly, arbitrating at a remote location, and controlling the arbitrator selection list. In a large number of today's consumer contracts, consumers are required to waive the ability to join their claims as a class action in either arbitration or litigation. Although the law restricts some of the most egregiously unfair arbitration clauses, businesses have considerable control over the arbitration process.

In the consumer context, arbitration's nonpublic nature may prohibit the world at large from learning of a problem affecting a large number of computers (or other consumer goods). The consumer may pay significantly more for the arbitration forum than he or she would have paid for court filing fees. On the other hand, if the process is faster than court, then both parties can move on with their lives sooner.

Arbitration's advantages and disadvantages are different for each case. Arbitration is widely used in a variety of industries in B2B contracts, such as insurance, construction, commercial goods, and intellectual property. Now, arbitration is also relatively common in contracts between individuals and businesses, including consumer contracts and employment contracts. In some of these situations, the parties are quite sophisticated — such as contracts for executive-level and professional employees, celebrities, and sports stars. In many other situations, the parties are unsophisticated and have no bargaining power (even sophisticated parties often have no bargaining power when buying a consumer good). When parties can bargain for the terms of the arbitration agreement, they have the power to mold the process to meet specific needs of the parties. When business entities draft contracts with individuals, the business has a significant amount of power, and the business entity should consider a wide variety of legal and ethical considerations when drafting arbitration agreements.

§ 8.05 How Cases Get into Arbitration

As with mediation, parties must agree to access the arbitration forum. That agreement takes the form of a contract, almost always written. Unlike mediation, courts cannot order parties to binding arbitration absent the parties' agreement. Such a referral to arbitration would be violative of the parties' Seventh Amendment right to a trial.[11] This section considers the types of cases that are most appropriate for arbitration, and also discusses contracts for arbitration before and after a dispute arises.

[A] Choosing Arbitration in a Specific Situation

In determining whether to choose arbitration, consider the parties involved, the type of dispute, the location or situs of where a hearing may be held, and the respective advantages/disadvantages noted above.

The CPR International Institute for Conflict Prevention and Resolution "ADR Suitability Guide" presents questions to assist in the decision whether to opt for arbitration

---

11. Kimberly J. Mann, *Constitutional Challenges to Court Ordered Arbitration*, 24 Fla. St. U. L. Rev. 1055 (1997).

or litigation.[12] Arbitration may be a good choice where the following considerations are important goals for a party:

- Is selection of the decision-maker important?
- Will the dispute require understanding of complex or technical factual issues?
- Is control over case scheduling important?
- Does a party want to prevent the specter of a massive or unpredictable jury award?
- Is less than full discovery satisfactory?
- Are less than full legal rights and procedures satisfactory?
- Is a final and binding award important?

Whereas a public court filing may be more appropriate where a party would answer "yes" to the following questions:

- Is establishment of precedent or articulation of public policy an important goal?
- Does the case involve vital corporate interests that require the full panoply of judicial procedural protections and appellate rights?
- Is the ability to conduct full discovery an important objective for either party?
- Is there a need for continuing court supervision of the case or parties?

Of course, these considerations are guideposts. Further, they do not discuss the use of other processes, such as mediation, which might also be viable alternatives.

In the case of sophisticated parties, they should consider whether arbitration is a better forum than litigation. In the case of business entities entering into take-it-or-leave-it contracts, those businesses should also consider the merits of arbitration or other options. If arbitration is the preferred option, the parties can then discuss how to craft the arbitration process, which will be discussed in subpart [D] of this section. Further, the parties could consider arbitration to be one step in a multi-step dispute resolution procedure, which begins with negotiation, mediation, or both.

[B] Post-Dispute Agreements to Arbitrate

In some instances, parties decide after a dispute arises that they would prefer to resolve the dispute by arbitration. Let's return to the hypothetical contract between the grain supplier and the food manufacturer. This time, assume that that grain supplier and the food manufacturer did not include an arbitration agreement in their contract. Instead, the contract said nothing about dispute resolution. Assume also that nine months into the contract, an unexpected pest contaminated the grain supplied. A dispute arose between the grain supplier and the food manufacturer as to whether the contaminated grain met the contractual requirements.

After the dispute arose, counsel for both parties considered their options and decided that arbitration would be the best way to resolve their dispute. The parties wanted to resolve the dispute quickly, privately, and with an expert decision-maker. They made

---

12. CPR International Institute for Conflict Prevention & Resolution, *CPR ADR Suitability Guide*, https://www.cpradr.org/Portals/0/Resources/ADR%20Tools/Tools/ADR%20Suitability%20 Screen.pdf.

this decision not only in an arms-length transaction, but also with their eyes wide open as to the nature of the dispute.

Post-dispute arbitration is not controversial, and all parties have the right to choose the arbitration option after a dispute arises. At that point, the parties have presumably understood their right to a trial and knowingly have chosen arbitration instead of a court proceeding. Employers and employees, or consumers and merchants, always have the option to agree to arbitration after the dispute arises, and such a decision should be honored.

[C] Pre-Dispute Agreements to Arbitrate

In many other situations, the parties agree to arbitrate a dispute before any dispute arises. These types of agreements are significantly more controversial, especially in employment and consumer contracts with individuals. Scholars commonly refer to pre-dispute arbitration agreements as requiring "mandatory arbitration."[13] Pre-dispute arbitration agreements are made by parties before the dispute arises.

Let's return to our grain supplier and food manufacturer. This time, the parties agreed in their initial contract to arbitrate "any dispute arising under or relating to this contract." At the time of drafting, the parties can anticipate—but do not know for certain—what types of disputes might arise during the course of their relationship. The grain supplier and food manufacturer may be able to anticipate some common types of disputes—such as the grain supplier failing to meet its quotas, the food manufacturer failing to pay for grain received, the grain supplier providing inferior quality product, and so on. Some, all, or none of these situations may arise over the course of their relationship.

Large companies and other sophisticated entities presumably can consider future events and plan for them in advance. Can the same be said for consumers and employees—especially when they have no bargaining power and are presented with a "take it or leave it" contract? Most individuals do not consider breach when they enter into contracts because they are hopeful that the relationship will be a good one and they do not want to anger their soon-to-be contractual partner. New employees rarely consider the possibility that they will be treated unfairly or illegally on the day they are hired. Consumers do not buy goods or services anticipating unfair practices. Even when individuals contemplate why they may want to sue the company, they almost never consider that the company may want to sue them—for disclosing trade secrets, or failure to pay for goods or services received.

Consumers and employees frequently sign contracts without reading or understanding them. Those contracts may contain surprise terms that have nothing to do with dispute resolution. Parties may waive or limit important warranties, agree to penalties, or even shorten the statutes of limitations. If consumers and employees can agree to these types of provisions, why are we concerned about arbitration clauses? One reason is that some people are concerned that arbitrators and businesses might act unfairly in

---

13. *See, e.g.*, Jean R. Sternlight, *Creeping Mandatory Arbitration: Is It Just?*, 57 Stan. L. Rev. 1631 (2005); Alexander J.S. Colvin, *From the Supreme Court to Shopfloor: Mandatory Arbitration and the Reconfiguration of Workplace Dispute Resolution*, 13 Cornell J.L. & Pub. Pol'y 581 (2004); Michael Z. Green, *Debunking the Myth of Employer Advantage from Using Mandatory Arbitration for Discrimination Cases*, 31 Rutgers L.J. 399 (2000).

arbitration, and parties might effectively "lose" legal rights they might otherwise have. These concerns are addressed in more detail in the Ethics section of Chapter 9. Parties generally expect that they can go to the courts if they have a problem with a contract, so an arbitration clause may come as a surprise—even if the parties had sufficient time to read the contract and have a lawyer explain it to them.

These concerns are counterbalanced with the parties' right to contract for arbitration services, often described as the parties' freedom of contract. This freedom of contract covers both post-dispute arbitration clauses and pre-dispute arbitration clauses. Further, most arbitrators are conscientious human beings who are trying to do the right thing and make the right decision based on the information given to them. As these chapters progress, consider how the advantages and disadvantages of arbitration play out in cases dealing with consumers and pre-dispute arbitration agreements.

[D] Drafting the Arbitration Agreement

Parties have the incredible opportunity to craft an arbitration agreement to meet their individual needs. In post-dispute arbitration agreements, the parties will likely know how much discovery they need, what type of arbitration they would like, and how long the arbitration hearing should last, among other factors. In pre-dispute arbitration agreements, the parties must anticipate the types of disputes that might arise under the relationship and how those disputes should be handled. In practice, lawyers do not appear to pay much attention to dispute resolution at the contract-drafting stage. The authors of this text view this as a missed opportunity.[14]

Arbitration is a creature of contract. By agreeing to arbitration, parties relinquish their rights to have their legal dispute decided in a court. This agreement to arbitration is typically contained in an arbitration clause, which is usually embedded as a provision in the primary commercial, employment, or service contract. Under the judicial doctrine of separability, the arbitration clause itself is considered a separate and distinct contract obligating the parties to arbitration even where the primary (container) contract is potentially invalid.[15] The doctrine of separability is discussed in more detail in Chapter 9.

The agreement to arbitrate is the contract that governs the parties' obligation to arbitrate, the scope of disputes subject to arbitration, the terms of the arbitration, and the powers of the arbitrator or panel. The arbitration clause may also designate the framework for arbitration, such as the rules under which arbitration will occur, as well as identify preconditions or preliminaries to arbitration, if any (mediation, etc.), and provide for judicial enforcement of the award. Arbitrators only have the power to resolve the dispute specifically given to them by contract. Parties can draft their arbitration agreements broadly or narrowly, depending on their intent and what it is they would like the arbitrator to decide.

In short, the scope of the arbitration agreement is determined by the arbitration agreement itself. Consider an arbitration agreement between an employer and the employee, which states that "the parties agree to arbitrate all employment disputes relating to this

---

14. *See,* Kristen M. Blankley, *The Ethics and Practice of Drafting Pre-Dispute Resolution Clauses,* 49 CREIGHTON L.R. 749 (2016).

15. Prima Paint Corp. v. Flood & Conklin Mfg. Co., 388 U.S. 395 (1967).

agreement." If the employee steals product from the employer, both parties would be required to arbitrate that dispute because it is an employment dispute relating to their employment agreement. On the other hand, if the employee slips and falls in the parking lot after hours, the employee may not have to arbitrate that tort action because the parking lot incident is likely not an employment dispute relating to the employment agreement.

An arbitration clause may be elaborate or simple. A contract may be as simple as: "Any disputes arising between the parties to this contract shall be arbitrated . . ." A standard pre-dispute clause suggested by the American Arbitration Association (bracketed language indicating options) states:

> Any controversy or claim arising out of or relating to this contract, or the breach thereof, shall be settled by arbitration administered by the American Arbitration Association in accordance with its Commercial [or other] Arbitration Rules, and judgment on the award rendered by the arbitrator(s) may be entered in any court having jurisdiction thereof.[16]

Similarly, JAMS offers its standard arbitration clause:

> Any dispute, claim or controversy arising out of or relating to this Agreement or the breach, termination, enforcement, interpretation or validity thereof, including the determination of the scope or applicability of this agreement to arbitrate, shall be determined by arbitration in [insert the desired place of arbitration] before [one/three] arbitrator(s). The arbitration shall be administered by JAMS pursuant to its Comprehensive Arbitration Rules and Procedures [and in accordance with the Expedited Procedures in those Rules] [or pursuant to JAMS' Streamlined Arbitration Rules and Procedures]. Judgment on the Award may be entered in any court having jurisdiction. This clause shall not preclude parties from seeking provisional remedies in aid of arbitration from a court of appropriate jurisdiction.[17]

The foregoing examples demonstrate arbitration clauses that designate a broad scope ("all") of disputes subject to arbitration. Parties may have specific reasons to define a narrower scope of questions or disputes for arbitral review, and leave other questions to be decided in a judicial context. Some contracts have a narrow scope, and whatever is not within that scope can be litigated. Other contracts have a broad scope, but then contain exceptions for types of disputes that should be litigated. A common example can be found in many consumer arbitration agreements these days. Those arbitration agreements have a broad scope, but then they take out of the scope disputes that can be resolved in small claims court. The reason for this particular exception is to keep the cost of dispute resolution low, and to resolve claims quickly. For these parties, small claims court may be even better than arbitration for low-dollar claims.

Arbitration agreements may also be quite complex and lengthy. At a minimum, all arbitration agreements should: (1) identify the parties; (2) define the scope of arbitrable disputes (e.g. all or specific); (3) commit the parties to arbitration; (4) select a set of rules (ad hoc or institutional); and (5) provide for entry of judgment. These are the

---

16. Am. Arb. Ass'n, *Drafting Dispute Resolution Clauses*, https://www.adr.org/aaa/ShowPDF?doc=ADRSTG_002540. A submission agreement to arbitrate an existing dispute would read to the effect that the identified parties agree to submit their controversy to arbitration.

17. JAMS Clause Workbook, *A Guide to Drafting Dispute Resolution Clauses for Commercial Contracts* (April 1, 2015), available at http://www.jamsadr.com/clauses/#Standard.

essential arbitration provisions that will bind parties to arbitration, either pre- or post-dispute.

The parties can agree to many other provisions to meet their needs. Common provisions include designating the number and qualifications, if any, of arbitrators; the place of arbitration; confidentiality; the timetable for proceedings and rendering award; the extent of discovery; the choice of law; the form of the award; any limitations on arbitrator powers. International arbitration provisions may include the language of the arbitration and nationality of the arbitrators. These types of provisions help shape the resolution of the dispute. Presumably, parties to an employment agreement would want different procedures compared to parties to an intellectual property dispute. Domestic parties may want different procedures from parties to an international contract. Parties in a business-to-business dispute may want different rules from parties to a consumer dispute.

As the American Arbitration Association stated:

> The agreement to arbitrate or mediate can empower the parties with a great deal of control—over the process and the arbitrator who hears the case, or the mediator who assists the parties in settlement efforts. A well-constructed AAA dispute resolution clause can provide certainty by defining the process prior to a dispute, after which agreement becomes more problematic.[18]

Thoughtful parties and their attorneys can help save time, money, and hassle by putting thought into dispute resolution before a dispute even arises. They can also capture some of the unique benefits of arbitration—such as a binding decision by a subject-matter expert—unavailable in litigation or other forums.

§ 8.06 Getting Arbitration Started and Arbitrator Selection

Once a dispute arises, the first step in the arbitration process is to draft a "demand," which is similar to a complaint in litigation. The person filing the demand is referred to as the "claimant," not the plaintiff. The party receiving the demand is the "respondent," not the defendant. The respondent generally has a few weeks to file an answering document, which is called an "answer." As in litigation, the respondent may file counterclaims against the claimant, which will then need an answer as well. The initial pleading process is usually complete in one to two months.

[A] Appointment—Number and Qualifications

After the initial pleadings are complete, the parties then choose an arbitrator. In some instances, the parties' contract specifies the arbitrator. For example, the parties could agree that your textbook author Professor Maureen Weston be appointed as the

---

18. Am. Arb. Ass'n, *Drafting Dispute Resolution Clauses*, available at https://www.adr.org/aaa/ShowPDF?doc=ADRSTG_002540.

arbitrator. Professor Weston would then have to accept the appointment, and the parties could move on to the next phase of the process. If Professor Weston declines or is otherwise unavailable to take the case, the parties would have to agree on another arbitrator.

More often, the parties agree to the number of arbitrators and the arbitrator's qualifications, as opposed to agreeing in advance to a specific person as arbitrator. Almost always, the number of arbitrators is an odd number—usually one or three. The reason for the odd number is simple. Arbitrators rule on motions and cases individually, as opposed to by consensus. An odd number of arbitrators prevents ties and ensures a final outcome. On rare occasions, parties may have five or seven arbitrators. On even rarer occasions, parties will appoint two arbitrators.

The parties may also specify the qualifications the arbitrators must possess. In some instances, the parties may specify that the arbitrators have certain educational credentials, such as a law degree or a Ph.D. In other cases, the arbitrator may need to be a member of a certain trade or professional organization, such as the premiere association for construction professionals, engineers, or any other profession. In a large number of cases, the parties agree to arbitrate with an arbitrator who is associated with an arbitration provider organization, such as AAA or JAMS. AAA, JAMS, and other providers have their own qualifications to be on their list, and those provider organizations vet the candidates before putting them on the list. For instance, AAA requires that the arbitrators on its list have the following qualifications:

a. Minimum of 10 years of senior-level business or professional experience or legal practice.

b. Educational degree(s) and/or professional license(s) appropriate to your field of expertise.

c. Honors, awards, and citations indicating leadership in your field.

d. Training or experience in arbitration and/or other forms of dispute resolution.

e. Membership in a professional association(s).

f. Other relevant experience or accomplishments (e.g. published articles).[19]

Because the parties trust the provider organization, they also trust the arbitrators associated with their organization.

In at least one industry, arbitrators may be selected precisely because they do *not* have experience in a given field. In the area of securities, the Financial Industry Regulatory Authority (FINRA) announced a new rule in 2011, which would allow consumers in securities disputes to have arbitrators who are labeled as "public arbitrators," who are people without connections to the financial services sector.[20] Historically, securities arbitrators were industry insiders, chosen for their expertise in the industry. More recently, consumers wanted to have all-public panels to reduce any potential industry bias by industry arbitrators toward institutional parties.

---

19. Am. Arb. Ass'n, *Qualification Criteria for Admittance to the AAA National Roster of Arbitrators* (2011), at https://www.adr.org/aaa/ShowPDF?doc=ADRSTG_003878.

20. FINRA, *New Optional All Public Panel Rules*, *at* https://www.finra.org/arbitration-and -mediation/new-optional-all-public-panel-rules.

[B] Selection Methods

If the parties can agree on an arbitrator, and the arbitrator agrees to serve, then the parties have successfully selected their arbitrator. In most cases, however, the selection process is more complicated. If the parties' contract specifies the characteristics of the arbitrator, then the parties may be able to generate a list of potential arbitrators meeting those characteristics. After the list is generated, the parties will seek to narrow down the list to one (or three) to serve.

When the parties use a provider organization, that provider organization will provide the parties with a list of potential arbitrators who could serve on the case. Once the parties have the list, they can select an arbitrator in a number of ways. One common way is to remove from the list anyone who is unacceptable to one of the parties and rank the remainder from best (1) to worst. Then the parties return the list to the provider organization. The provider organization will appoint the arbitrator with the lowest total score. If the parties do not have an arbitrator in common between the two lists, the provider organization will give the parties a new list, and the process starts again.

If the parties are together, they can take a list and alternatively strike names off the list until only one name remains. If there are challenges to arbitrators, then those names should be removed first. Striking names off a list one at a time would be difficult to do remotely because it would take an excessive amount of time.

When parties would like to have a panel of three arbitrators, sometimes the parties use one of these selection methods to get all three arbitrators. In other circumstances, each party chooses one arbitrator, and then those two arbitrators choose a third arbitrator. Historically, the party-appointed arbitrator was an arbitrator who could communicate with the appointing party, and the arbitrator could have a bias in favor of the appointing party.[21] Today, the party-appointed arbitrators are presumed to be neutral unless the parties agree from the beginning that the party-appointed arbitrator can be biased in favor of the appointing party and have ex parte communications with that side.[22] This type of arbitration is often called *tripartite arbitration*.

How do parties know who to pick from a list of arbitrators? Certainly, a lawyer can do Internet research on the potential arbitrators. Lawyers can also get advice from other lawyers, especially if those lawyers have used any of the arbitrators on the list in the past. In areas where arbitration awards are published — such as in the securities or labor/management context — lawyers may be able to read opinions rendered by the arbitrators in other cases. Past awards may give a lawyer an idea of how an arbitrator reasons through a case, but it is no guarantee that an arbitrator will rule in a particular way in a future case.

After the arbitrator is appointed, the arbitrator must conduct a conflicts check to determine whether the arbitrator has a conflict of interest with any of the parties or their counsel. The arbitrator must disclose any "direct or indirect" personal interest in the case, as well as any "existing or past financial, business, professional, or personal relationship which might reasonably affect impartiality in the eyes of the parties."[23] The duty to disclose is a continuing duty, meaning that if an arbitrator discovers a dispute at a later time in the case, the arbitrator must still disclose. Common examples of

---

21. ABA/AAA Code of Ethics for Arbitrators in Commercial Disputes (2003), Canon X.
22. *Id.*
23. ABA/AAA Code of Ethics for Arbitrators in Commercial Disputes, Canon II(A).

disclosures include owning (or previously owning) stock in a company that is a party to the arbitration; sitting on a board of directors with a client, witness, or lawyer involved in the arbitration; or knowing one of the participants from the PTA, religious organization, or a social club. After the lawyer discloses, the parties have the ability to object to the arbitrator's continued work on the case. If even one party objects, the arbitrator should withdraw.[24] The one major exception to this rule is that party-appointed non-neutral arbitrators do not need to withdraw on the basis of bias toward the appointing party.[25]

If the parties cannot appoint an arbitrator on their own, they can ask the courts to get involved and help with the appointment process. Under the FAA, if the parties do not provide for a selection method or, if that method fails, "upon the application of either party to the controversy the court shall designate and appoint an arbitrator or arbitrators or umpire, as the case may require."[26] The policy reason behind court involvement is to ensure that parties who agreed to arbitrate will, in fact, arbitrate.

[C] Costs and Fees

As mentioned above, arbitration involves some costs that are not associated with the litigation process. Two sets of costs are common in arbitration—administrative costs and arbitrator costs. In cases that are administered through an organization, such as the AAA or JAMS, the parties must pay an administrative fee. The administrative fee is generally charged once on a per-case basis. The purpose of the fee is to pay for administrative support, such as case managers, technological support, administrative support, arbitrator training, education, outreach, and the like. For many provider organizations, the amount of the administrative fee is contingent on the amount of the claim. For example, the AAA charges fees anywhere from $1,550 (for claims under $75,000) to $14,700 (for claims between $1,000,000 and $10,000,000).[27] Often, arbitration providers have a different fee schedule for consumers, in which the business entity pays the majority of the fee while the consumer pays a small fraction, comparable to what a consumer would pay in litigation filing fees.[28] Ad hoc arbitrations—or arbitrations taking place outside of a service provider—should not have any administrative fees.

The second—and more costly—fee is the arbitrator's fee. The arbitrator's fees are those that are paid directly to the arbitrator for the his or her services. Arbitrators are generally independent contractors who are paid on an hourly or a daily rate. Arbitrators charge different rates, depending on the market, and costs for arbitrators vary widely—from $200 to $1,000 per hour. Arbitrator daily rates can start at $1,000 and go upward. In the securities field, FINRA regulates the amount of mediator pay, which is generally $300 or $450 (for the chair of the panel) per half-day session. The FINRA rates are on

---

24. ABA/AAA Code of Ethics for Arbitrators in Commercial Disputes, Canon II(G).

25. ABA/AAA Code of Ethics for Arbitrators in Commercial Disputes, Canon X.

26. 9 U.S.C. § 5.

27. Am. Arb. Ass'n, *Commercial Arbitration Rules and Mediation Procedures, Administrative Fee Schedule*, at https://www.adr.org/aaa/ShowPDF?doc=ADRSTAGE2031504. In cases valued more than $10,000,000, the AAA charges a partial flat fee and a partial fee based on a percentage of the value of the claim, with fees capped at $77,500. *Id.*

28. *See, e.g.*, Am. Arb. Ass'n, *Consumer Arbitration Rules, Costs of Arbitration*, at https://www .adr.org/aaa/ShowPDF?doc=ADRSTAGE2026862. The AAA caps the consumer's administrative costs at $200, and the business entity pays the remainder.

the low end of the scale. In cases involving more than one arbitrator, the parties will split the costs of the additional arbitrators. The chair of the arbitration panel on a three- or five-person panel may demand a higher rate than the other arbitrators (colloquially referred to as the "wings" of the arbitration panel).

§ 8.07 The Arbitration Process

In many ways, the actual arbitration process is similar to the litigation process. The biggest difference is the degree of formality. This section gives a general overview of the arbitration process, as well as the use of provider organizations and provider rules.

[A] Overview

As mentioned above, the arbitration process starts with the presentation of a demand and an answer. Then, the parties appoint an arbitrator according to the method set forth in their contract. The arbitrator has the power to hear the cases defined in the scope of the agreement to arbitrate. What next?

After the close of the pleadings and the appointment of the arbitrator, the attorneys for the parties usually have a conference call with the mediator to set a scheduling order. The scheduling order designates a hearing date and schedules the number of days needed for the arbitration. In addition, the parties and arbitrator will agree on discovery deadlines and motion deadlines, if the parties desire. The discovery process is similar to the discovery process in litigation. Parties may exchange documents, answer interrogatories, and take depositions. Comparted to litigation, however, the discovery process is shorter and, hopefully, more cooperative. Parties usually take fewer depositions in arbitration compared to litigation. If problems arise during the discovery process, the arbitrator or arbitrators can rule on discovery motions.

After the parties complete discovery, they are ready to have their hearing. Although arbitrators may entertain motions for summary judgment, that type of relief is still uncommon in arbitration. Arbitrators likely deny these types of rulings in order to comply with their duty to hear all pertinent evidence. The lack of motion practice helps speed the process and get to a resolution quickly.

If the case goes to a hearing, the hearing proceeds similarly to litigation; however, the location will be significantly different. Most arbitration hearings take place in conference rooms, rather than courtrooms. Unlike courtrooms, everyone sits on the same "level"—usually around a conference table. The chair of the arbitration panel swears in the witnesses, and the arbitrators and the lawyers deal with any preliminary matters. After all preliminary issues are resolved, the claimant will open the session with an opening statement, followed by the respondent. The claimant side can then call witnesses. The witnesses will sit in a witness chair at the foot of the conference table. The witness will be subject to direct and cross-examination. Occasionally, the arbitrator will allow re-direct or re-cross examination. Arbitrators have the ability to ask questions of the witnesses directly, which is generally not allowed in litigation.

Compared to litigation, attorneys make fewer objections in arbitration because arbitrators rarely sustain them. Arbitrators commonly overrule rejections and allow in the evidence "for what it's worth." The rules of civil procedure and evidence do not formally apply in arbitration. As expert decision-makers, arbitrators can be trusted to correctly value hearsay testimony and otherwise unreliable evidence. The attorneys will enter documents into evidence for the arbitrators to consider. After the claimant presents its case, the claimant will rest and turn the case over to the respondent. The respondent, then, will present its case. At the conclusion of the respondent's witnesses, the respondent will give the first closing argument. The claimant—having the right to speak first and last—will give the second, and final, closing argument. Replies and rebuttals are rarely allowed. At the close of the arguments, the arbitrators close the hearing and take the case under advisement. Following the hearing, the parties may file post-hearing briefs, summarizing the arguments and legal arguments. Ultimately, the arbitrators issue their award within a few weeks to a few months following the hearing. Additional information about arbitration awards is discussed later in this chapter.

In some cases, special arrangements may be necessary to accommodate the parties. In large international disputes, translation services may be necessary. When arbitrations involve numerous parties, the arbitrators will need to take care to find a facility large enough to handle all of the parties, counsel, and arbitrators. Parties with special needs should be accommodated, as necessary.

Many cases never go to a hearing. As with litigation, often cases settle short of a hearing on the merits in arbitration. These cases may settle through traditional lawyer negotiation, or in mediation, if the parties decide to try to mediate the case while they are also engaging in arbitration discovery.

[B] Arbitration Procedural Rules versus Ad Hoc Proceedings

In an ad hoc arbitration proceeding, the parties do not necessarily follow any set of rules. The parties can specify certain procedures in their arbitration agreement—such as number of depositions, length of the hearing, etc.—or they can allow the arbitrator to determine those types of issues as they arise. Ad hoc procedures have significant flexibility, but they lack in certainty because the parties may not have clear expectations of the procedural guidelines. In some situations, parties may have an ad hoc (i.e., unadministered) arbitration, but the parties might agree that a certain arbitrator provider's rules would apply. For instance, the parties might agree that Professor Weston be the arbitrator in an unadministered case, but the parties want to follow AAA rules. What that means is that although Professor Weston is arbitrating and administering the case on her own, she will run the case under the same set of procedures as if it were a case administered by the AAA.

Many other cases are administered by a provider organization, such as the AAA or JAMS. In those cases, the rules of the provider organization will automatically apply, unless the parties stipulate to a different set of rules. In designating the application of institutional provider rules and procedures, the sample clauses incorporate the procedural and administration aspects of the arbitration, such as the arbitrator selection process, determination of the locale, and institutional rules of arbitration procedure. These clauses also provide that the arbitration will be final and binding and that the award may be entered as an "entry of judgement" in a court of law.

Stipulating the procedural rules, number of arbitrators, seat or legal place of the arbitration, and governing substantive law in the arbitration clause provides certainty in the event the contracting parties need arbitration. The arbitration clause thus can have a significant impact on whether dispute resolution by arbitration will proceed with ease and clarity, or lack thereof. If the parties do not agree or address these details in advance, debates on the management of the arbitration could hinder the process. In the absence of specific contrary agreement by the parties, the rules establish a "safety net" for the management of the arbitration.

In addition to the traditional set of arbitration rules, many provider organizations have specialty rules for different types of cases. For example, AAA and JAMS have specialized rules and procedures designed for various industry-administered arbitrations, such as commercial, construction, consumer, labor, and employment. In addition, these providers have rules specifically for consumer cases, class actions (consumer or otherwise), and international cases.[29]

The procedural rules help flesh out the basic agreement of the parties regarding some or all aspects of the arbitration process from initiation to award—and in some cases beyond. Among the matters to address in the management of an arbitration are arbitrator selection and qualifications, if any; pre-hearing procedures and rights in terms of discovery; disclosures; witness and issue identification; conducting the hearing; applicable "law"; burdens of proof; and the form, content, and impact of the arbitral award.

Institutional providers can assist in providing the administrative support for the arbitration, the roster and appointment process for arbitrator selection, fee collection, ethical codes for neutrals, and other guidelines for the arbitration process.[30] UNCITRAL or CPR have published rules for non-administered or ad hoc arbitration, which can also provide support in appointing arbitrators and considering challenges to arbitrators.

[C] The Role of Substantive Law in Arbitration

Most of the law governing arbitration governs the process, not the substance, of the underlying dispute. The parties choose the substantive law that applies to the ultimate resolution of the dispute. Parties should designate the substantive law to apply in their situation in their agreement to arbitrate. The parties can choose any substantive law to apply. Many parties choose the substantive law of the jurisdiction where at least one of the parties resides. On the other hand, some parties choose a substantive law of a different location for business or other reasons. For instance, business parties may choose Delaware law because that law is considered to be the most business-friendly in the nation. A business with operations across several states may select the substantive law of the state in which the company is headquartered.

---

29. Am. Arb. Ass'n, *AAA Court-and Time Tested Rules and Procedures,* available at https://www .adr.org/aaa/faces/rules/searchrules?_afrLoop=1905527693734854&_afrWindowMode=0&_afr-WindowId=1dvwhwthcg_1#%40%3F_afrWindowId%3D1dvwhwthcg_1%26_afrLoop%3 D1905527693734854%26_afrWindowMode%3D0%26_adf.ctrl-state%3D1dvwhwthcg_83; JAMS, *ADR Rules and Procedures,* available at http://www.jamsadr.com/rulesclauses/xpqGC.aspx?xpST =RulesClauses.

30. Thomas Stipanowich & Zachary P. Ulrich, *Arbitration in Evolution: Current Practices and Perspectives of Experienced Commercial Arbitrators,* 25 Am. Rev. Int'l Arb. 395,433–34 (2014).

In some cases involving religious institutions, the arbitration agreement may call for dispute resolution under religious principles. These types of religious organizations often involve places of worship, hospitals, and schools. Cases involving these types of organizations include employment disputes, malpractice actions, and educational disputes. Religious arbitration has been utilized in the Christian, Jewish, and Islamic faiths in the United States. As an example, consider a private Christian school that hires a new teacher. The contract between the school and the teacher may include an arbitration agreement requiring the arbitration be "informed by Christian [or biblical] principles." In these types of cases, the parties can achieve dispute resolution under theological principles, which is not offered in the traditional court systems.

Despite the application of choice of law, arbitration is ultimately a court of equity. Arbitrators must consider the law, but ultimately, they have significantly greater freedom in their rulings than courts traditionally do. Because the rules of evidence are lax, arbitrators may consider and be moved by information that a judge or jury may otherwise not be able to consider. As discussed in the next section, arbitration awards cannot be overturned simply because one party thinks that the arbitrator "got it wrong" on either the facts or the law. Arbitrators, then, have the power to rule in a way that is informed by the law, but perhaps not strictly following the law.

Students of arbitration might ask: Is there such thing as arbitral common law? The answer to that question is somewhat complicated. On the one hand, arbitration awards are commonly confidential, and arbitrators might not know or be able to find out how other arbitrators ruled in similar cases. In some situations, arbitrators may have access to other awards, particularly in areas such as labor/management or securities. Whether arbitrators are permitted to rely on the rulings and reasoning of other arbitrators may depend on the parties' contract. In 2009, the Supreme Court cast some doubt on the use of arbitral common law when it overruled a class action arbitration finding based, in part, on the prevalence of other arbitrators ruling in favor of class action arbitration.[31]

[D] Remedies Available in Arbitration

Many of the remedies available in arbitration are similar to the remedies that are available in litigation. Arbitrators, however, have a greater flexibility to award remedies not otherwise available in court. For example, in the employment realm, arbitrators are free to award reinstatement, which is not a legal remedy for courts. Arbitrators also have significantly more flexibility to award specific performance, especially if equity dictates that the parties should perform the contract, where a court might simply award damages.

Arbitrators also have the ability to award interim relief and preliminary injunctions. Historically, parties would go to a court to obtain preliminary relief, but still submit the merits of the main dispute to the arbitrator. In today's arbitration practice, arbitrators are becoming more and more comfortable issuing preliminary and injunctive relief. The AAA, JAMS, and CPR (the Institute for Conflict Prevention and Resolution) now all have specific rules allowing arbitrators to issue preliminary relief. Common examples of preliminary and injunctive relief include orders prohibiting a party from disposing of assets during the arbitration, orders preventing a former employee from disclosing

---

31. Stolt Nielsen S.A. v. Animalfeeds Int'l Corp., 559 U.S. 662 (2010).

trade secrets, or orders to dispose of perishable items in a way that reduces potential waste.

Arbitrators have the ability to issue sanctions against parties who engage in misbehavior in the arbitration process.[32] Possible sanctions include an award of attorney's fees (usually associated with the cost of bringing the ethical issue to the attention of the arbitrator), deem certain facts as admitted or drawing adverse inferences (such as when a party destroys evidence), or even throwing out some claims or the entire case if the misbehavior is particularly egregious.

For the most part, arbitrators also have the ability to award punitive damages. Parties often request punitive damages, especially when the claim involves a statutory claim where the law would otherwise permit an award of attorney's fees. In the past, some states attempted to limit an arbitrator's ability to award punitive damages; but those statutes are likely unenforceable.

As with any other aspect of arbitration, the parties can specify the types of remedies available in arbitration in their agreement. In addition to specifying the permissible remedies, the parties may also restrict available remedies. Drafting parties, however, should be careful to not unduly restrict the available remedies such that the arbitration agreement might be deemed unconscionable by a federal or state court.

§ 8.08 The Arbitration Award

The final act by the arbitrators is to render an award. After the arbitrators issue the award, their jurisdiction is over, under the doctrine known as *functus officio*. This section considers the types of awards, how awards are enforced, and also provides an overview of the potential for judicial review.

[A] Types of Awards

Arbitration awards generally take one of two forms — either simple or "reasoned." A simple award does little more than identify the parties and who wins. A simple award may look something like:

> In the matter of Claimant vs. Respondent, who appeared before us in an arbitration hearing on [DATE], we find in favor of Claimant. We hereby award Claimant $[DOLLAR]. /Signed and Dated by the Arbitrators

Some arbitral providers have pre-printed forms for arbitrators to use to simplify and standardize the award-writing process. Simple awards have two primary benefits. First, they are inexpensive — it does not take a long time for the arbitrators to draft a simple award or fill in a standardized form. Parties theoretically can receive their awards sooner because they do not take a long time to craft. Secondarily, the awards are almost impenetrable on appeal. When the arbitrators do not state any reasons for the award, courts have very little evidence on which they can overturn an award.

---

32. Kristen M. Blankley, *Lying, Stealing, and Cheating: The Role of Arbitrators as Ethics Enforcers*, 52 Louisville L. Rev. 443 (2014) (detailing the ability of arbitrators to issue sanctions and other remedies in response to unethical behavior on the part of parties, attorneys, and witnesses).

In contrast, other arbitrations end with a reasoned award. A reasoned award is an award that also includes the reasoning for the final award. Often, arbitrators will format their reasoned awards by first making findings of fact, and then setting forth their conclusions of law. The length of reasoned awards varies by case, but they can range from a handful of pages to more than 100 pages. Reasoned awards give considerably more detail to the parties as to why they won or lost the arbitration, and that reasoning may give the parties peace of mind. Parties who contract for reasoned awards may feel more comfortable employing those arbitrators again because they have a better idea of how and why they rule a specific way. One of the biggest downsides of reasoned awards is that they are costly. The parties will have to pay for the arbitrator's "study time" and time writing the award. Additionally, when the arbitrators have a reasoned award, the award may be more likely to be appealed. Although great deference is given to arbitration awards by courts, parties may worry that the more is known about the arbitrators' decision, the more likely it will be overturned on appeal.

In addition to final and binding awards, arbitrators often issue interim awards throughout the course of a case. Preliminary awards and injunctive relief have already been discussed above. In other cases, the parties may have multiple motions, and the arbitrators decide those cases by issuing interlocutory awards. For example, the arbitrator may issue an "Award Regarding Discovery Motion" or "Award Denying Summary Judgment." These types of interlocutory awards are generally unappealable prior to the conclusion of the entire case.

Class action arbitrations generally involve a complicated procedure that involves multiple stages. The AAA, the leading provider organization in the area of class action, instituted a comprehensive set of rules for class action cases, which will be discussed in more detail in Chapter 9. The class action process generally involves a number of stages, including class certification. The AAA rules generally allow for interlocutory appeals at the various stages of class action arbitrations, and the courts have exercised jurisdiction over them.

[B] Enforcement of the Award

Arbitration awards are binding and enforceable under federal and state law. Under federal law:

> If the parties in their agreement have agreed that a judgment of the court shall be entered upon the award made pursuant to the arbitration, . . . then at any time within one year after the award is made any party to the arbitration may apply to the court . . . for an order confirming the award, and thereupon the court must grant such an order unless the award is vacated, modified, or corrected as prescribed in sections 10 and 11 of this title.[33]

The courts are required to confirm the award, unless the court decides to modify or vacate the award. Under federal law, one of the parties to the arbitration award must apply for confirmation within a year of the issuance of the award. State law is very similar. Under the Uniform Arbitration Act, "upon application of a party, the Court shall confirm an award, unless within the time limits hereinafter imposed grounds are urged for vacating or modifying or correcting the award, in which case the court shall proceed"

---

33. 9 U.S.C. § 9.

under those sections.[34] States vary in the time frame allowed for confirming an award, some of which are shorter than the federal time allowance.

Once the award is confirmed, a party can enforce it the same way as a party can enforce any other court judgement. A party with a confirmed award can take that court judgment and attach it to the real property of the other side, garnish the losing party's wages, or take any other measures allowed by state law for the collection of the amount due.

[C] Judicial Review

In some circumstances, the parties seek to have the court overrule the arbitrator's award. If the court overrules the award, the award is said to be "vacated." The grounds for vacatur are quite limited. Those grounds are:

(1)   where the award was procured by corruption, fraud, or undue means;

(2)   where there was evident partiality or corruption in the arbitrators, or either of them;

(3)   where the arbitrators were guilty of misconduct in refusing to postpone the hearing, upon sufficient cause shown, or in refusing to hear evidence pertinent and material to the controversy; or of any other misbehavior by which the rights of any party have been prejudiced; or

(4)   where the arbitrators exceeded their powers, or so imperfectly executed them that a mutual, final, and definite award upon the subject matter submitted was not made.[35]

In addition, the courts have created two additional grounds for review — "manifest disregard of the law" and an award "in violation of public policy." All of these grounds are narrow, and only one in about four arbitration awards are ever overturned. The grounds for vacatur are nearly identical in the state courts.

The timing for vacatur is different than the timing for confirming the award. In the federal courts, the law gives any party the right to confirm an award within a year. The timeline to vacate an award, however, is only three months.[36] What that means is that if the losing party fails to move to vacate an award within three months, and the winning party thereafter moves to confirm, that motion will be automatically granted. Because the federal courts do not have jurisdiction in all arbitration cases, lawyers should consult the statutory timelines for confirmation and vacatur in all relevant jurisdictions.

As for the grounds for vacatur, none of the statutory grounds have anything to do with the merits of the arbitration award. This fact might be surprising, because appellate review in the court system centers around the correctness of the award. In arbitration, judicial review is purposely limited to promote finality, and the statutory grounds all center on whether or not the hearing was *fair*. Under § 10(a)(1), an award can be vacated for fraud or other misconduct committed by the arbitrator, opposing party, lawyer, or witness. A procedure rife with misconduct would not be fair, and the resulting award could be vacated. Section 10(a)(2) allows an award to be vacated if the arbitrators were biased. Vacatur under § 10(a)(2) is most common when a party finds out after the award

---

34. Uniform Arbitration Act § 11 (1956).
35. 9 U.S.C. § 10(a).
36. 9 U.S.C. § 12.

is issued that an arbitrator had an undisclosed conflict of interest. Procedural misconduct is grounds for vacatur under § 10(a)(3), which provides that an award may be set aside if the arbitrator did not allow in material evidence, or if the arbitrator did not grant reasonable requests for delay. Section 10(a)(4) allows vacatur if the arbitrators "exceeded their powers" because the arbitrators' powers are determined by contract. Although this ground is somewhat less defined than the others, it is still quite narrow.

Over time, the courts have also added two grounds of review. Whether these grounds are valid has never been explicitly addressed by the Supreme Court. The Supreme Court has been asked to consider this question, but every case involving one of these common law grounds for vacatur has been decided on other grounds. The "public policy" grounds are cited most often in the labor/management context, especially when arbitrators order reinstatement. For instance, an arbitrator who orders reinstatement for a pilot or a truck driver who has a history of alcoholism or drug abuse has been considered an award against public policy. An arbitrator may have acted in "manifest disregard of the law" if a party can prove that the arbitrator knew the law and then purposefully acted in disregard of it. Vacating an award under these two grounds are also still limited, but these are the only two grounds that involve vacatur based on the contents of the award, as opposed to a deficiency in the process.

Because arbitration is a creature of contract, parties at one time attempted to draft clauses broadening or limiting the scope of the review. This type of clause appeared to make sense because party autonomy and party control over the process are central policy benefits of arbitration. In this area, however, the Supreme Court ruled that the grounds for vacatur are limited to those stated in the statute, and they cannot be altered by party agreement.[37] In that decision, the Court avoided answering the question of whether judicially created grounds, such as manifest disregard, were also valid.

Given the limited availability of judicial review, parties should think very carefully about even attempting to vacate an arbitration award. In client counseling sessions, lawyers for losing arbitration parties should be frank about the low likelihood of success and the costs of pursing the appeal. Lawyers in that position should also consider local trends in arbitration and compare the likelihood of success in the relevant federal and state courts.

---

37. Hall St. Assoc., L.L.C. v. Mattel, Inc., 552 U.S. 576 (2008).

Chapter 9

Legal Issues in Arbitration

§ 9.01 Introduction

Although arbitration is intended to be a private, consensual process, numerous legal issues arise in the context of this process. Rather ironically, disputes over various applications and interpretations of arbitration questions have spawned extensive litigation, sometimes making the arbitration process more expensive than if the parties had simply litigated the merits of the case. The Supreme Court decided more than 30 arbitration-related cases between 2000 and 2016. Congress, state legislatures, and federal and state courts have similarly been concerned with arbitration policy and legal issues.

The following material sets forth the legal framework governing arbitration and discusses the legal questions that can arise in arbitration. The intersection between arbitration and the court system is surprisingly long, and it governs nearly every aspect of "Do I have to arbitrate?" This section considers the laws governing arbitration, who decides (arbitrators or courts) issues relating to arbitration, defenses to arbitration agreements, and ethical issues. The courts have been very active in these areas, and the law is changing. This chapter will give the reader some context as well as describe emerging trends.

§ 9.02 The Laws Governing Arbitration

[A] The Federal Arbitration Act

Recall that Congress enacted the Federal Arbitration Act (FAA) in 1925 to provide for the enforceability of agreements to arbitrate and to overcome the historical judicial hostility to arbitration. The FAA remains the primary federal legislation governing commercial arbitration. Its basic provisions are largely unchanged since the statute's inception. In early arbitration law, some questions existed as to whether Congress passed the FAA under its power to regulate the courts (i.e., as procedural court rules) or under its powers to regulate interstate commerce.[1] In 1984, however, the Supreme Court definitively ruled that Congress passed the FAA pursuant to its Commerce Powers, meaning that it applies in cases involving interstate commerce and is substantive law for the purposes of preemption.[2] Given that the scope of "interstate commerce"

---

1. Kristen M. Blankley, *Impact Preemption: A New Theory of Federal Arbitration Act Preemption*, 67 Fla. L. Rev. 711, 713 (2015).
2. Southland v. Keating, 465 U.S. 1 (1984).

is broadly interpreted, the FAA's reach is expansive and can apply to most contractual transactions.[3]

The FAA regulates the interface between private arbitration and the courts and is a fairly short procedural statute comprised of 16 sections.[4] The FAA generally deals with how cases get into the arbitration forum and how to enforce arbitration awards. Several interrelated policies are accomplished through this Act. The first policy is to ensure that parties who agree to go to arbitration will, in fact, go to arbitration. Second, the Act encourages minimal court involvement so that the parties can get to the merits of the dispute with the arbitrator. Third, the Act respects arbitration awards by enforcing them as court judgments and limiting the grounds for post-arbitration court review.

On the other hand, the arbitration process is largely unregulated. The Act does not cover *how* arbitrators conduct a hearing or deal with the parties during discovery. The Act does not address issues such as evidentiary standards or rules of procedure. Presumably, those types of issues are left to parties' contracts or to arbitrator discretion. The remainder of this section briefly explains the 16 provisions of the FAA. The provisions will be discussed in order, although the flow of one provision to another does not always make intuitive sense.

Section 1 sets forth certain definitions. Oddly, "arbitration" is not defined in the statute. Section 1 defines the categories of "maritime transactions" and "commerce" covered under the Act, and also expressly states that "[n]othing herein contained shall apply to contracts of employment of seamen, railroad employees, or any other class of workers engaged in foreign or interstate commerce."[5] This exemption for "[c]ontracts of employment of . . ." was interpreted in *Circuit City v Adams*,[6] a 5-4 U.S. Supreme Court decision, as exempting only workers in the specified transportation industries, requiring the arbitration of Adams' state employment discrimination law claim. Thus, the FAA applies to general employment contracts providing for arbitration, as well as to domestic arbitration contracts generally.[7]

FAA Section 2 is the heart of the statute. Under this Section, agreements to arbitrate can be specifically enforced by the courts. The statute provides for the validity and enforcement of written agreements to arbitration, "save upon such grounds as exist at law or in equity for the revocation of any contract."[8] Section 2, interpreted as requiring that written agreements to arbitrate are "enforceable according to their terms," has been the

---

3. Allied Bruce Terminix Co. v. Dobson, 513 U.S. 265 (1995).

4. Complete text of the Federal Arbitration Act is reproduced at Appendix A.

5. 9 U.S.C. § 1. *See also* See Maureen A. Weston, *Preserving the Federal Arbitration Act by Reining in Judicial Expansion and Mandatory Use*, 8 Nev. L.J. 382, 396 (2007).

6. 531 U.S.105 (2001).

7. 9 U.S.C. § 1 (applying to contracts involving interstate commerce). *See also* AlliedBruce Terminix Co. v. Dobson, 513 U.S. 265, 269 (1995).

8. 9 U.S.C. § 2 (Validity, irrevocability, and enforcement of agreements to arbitrate. "A written provision in any maritime transaction or a contract evidencing a transaction involving commerce to settle by arbitration a controversy thereafter arising out of such contract or transaction, or the refusal to perform the whole or any part thereof, or an agreement in writing to submit to arbitration an existing controversy arising out of such a contract, transaction, or refusal, shall be valid, irrevocable, and enforceable, save upon such grounds as exist at law or in equity for the revocation of any contract.").

source for FAA preemption of conflicting state laws or policies that are hostile to arbitration.[9]

The FAA's enforcement mandate, however, is subject to two exceptions in the last clause of Section 2, which is referred to as the "savings clause."[10] First, arbitration contracts are subject to the same defenses applicable to contracts generally, such as fraud, duress, unconscionability, and violation of public policy. Second, the FAA must yield where Congress commands. Courts typically require that such a mandate be either explicit in the text or implicit through direct conflict with another federal statute.[11]

FAA Sections 3 and 4 provide a procedural mechanism to ensure that parties who agree to arbitrate will actually arbitrate. In some cases, parties to arbitration agreements file lawsuits in court, rather than submit claims in arbitration. In those instances, FAA Section 3 provides for a court to stay court proceedings brought "in any of the courts of the United States" upon finding a valid arbitration. Section 4 permits a U.S. district court, otherwise having jurisdiction, to compel a party to arbitrate. Thus, Sections 3 and 4 work together to stay any pending litigation and to compel the parties to arbitrate their claim when they have a valid agreement to arbitrate.

FAA Sections 5 through 8 contain a hodgepodge of specialty provisions. As discussed in Chapter 8, in some instances, the parties' method for selecting an arbitrator fails. Pursuant to Section 5, a court may appoint an arbitrator if parties fail to agree. This section, then, ensures that the parties will arbitrate, even if the court must intervene to ensure the selection of the arbitrator. Section 6 states that applications and motions pertaining to arbitration are heard in the same manner as court motions. The purpose of Section 6 is to ensure that arbitration matters are treated in a summary manner so the parties can arbitrate, rather than spending a considerable amount of time litigating. Section 7 confers on arbitrators the power to issue "summons (subpoenas) for witnesses to appear before them . . ." Section 8 addresses maritime litigation.

Sections 9 through 12 concern court intervention following the issuance of an arbitration award. Under Section 9, a party, within one year of entering the arbitral award, may seek judicial confirmation of the award as a judgement. Section 9 advances the policies of enforcement of arbitration awards and simplicity of proceedings.

Section 10 specifies four grounds upon which a federal court may vacate an arbitral award upon a party's application. These include "(1) [w]here the award was procured by corruption, fraud, or undue means; (2) [w]here there was evident partiality or corruption in the arbitrators, or either of them; (3) [w]here the arbitrators were guilty of misconduct in refusing to postpone the hearing, upon sufficient cause shown, or in refusing

---

9. *See e.g.,* AT&T Mobility v. Concepcion, 563 U.S. 333 (2011) (FAA § 2 preempts California's rule classifying most collective-arbitration waivers in consumer contracts as unconscionable"); CompuCredit Corp. v. Greenwood, 132 S. Ct. 665, 669 (2012) (holding that the FAA requires courts to enforce agreements to arbitrate unless Congress has directed otherwise); Preston v. Ferrer, 552 U.S. 346, 359 (2008) (FAA preemption of California Talent Agency Act); Mitsubishi Motors Corp. v. Soler Chrysler-Plymouth, Inc., 473 U.S. 614, 628 (1985) ("Having made a bargain to arbitrate, the party should be held to it unless Congress itself has evinced an intention to preclude a waiver of judicial remedies for the statutory right at issue."); Southland Corporation v. Keating, 465 U.S. 1 (1984) (holding the FAA preempted California's Franchise Investment law which required a judicial forum for franchisee disputes).

10. 9 U.S.C. § 2.

11. Additional analysis of FAA Section 2 can be found *infra* at Section 9.02[B].

to hear evidence pertinent and material to the controversy; or of any other misbehavior by which the rights of any party have been prejudiced; [and] (4) [w]here the arbitrators exceeded their powers . . ."[12] These grounds are purposefully narrow to promote the policy of finality in arbitration.

The standard for vacatur is extremely high and relates to significant deficiencies in the arbitral process rather than to substantive errors on the merits. *Hall Street v. Mattel* held that the statutory grounds for vacatur are exclusive and that courts would not enforce a private contract for judicial review of an arbitral award beyond the grounds set forth in the FAA. Lower courts are divided on the continued viability of judicially created exceptions to allow vacatur of awards determined in "manifest disregard of the law" or "contrary to public policy" or under state statutes that provide additional grounds for vacatur.

Section 11 permits courts to correct or modify awards containing evident formalistic or technical errors. These types of errors are items such as typographical or mathematical errors. Under § 12, notice of motions to vacate or modify awards must be made within three months after the award is filed. Again, the short timeframe to vacate awards helps preserve the policy of finality of arbitration awards.

Section 13 sets forth administrative requirements for filing papers with motions seeking relief under the Act. Section 14 clarifies that the Act was not retroactive to 1926. Section 15 speaks to the "[i]napplicability of the Act of State doctrine." Finally, Section 16 provides for a right of interlocutory appeals that may be taken from orders essentially denying arbitration.[13] Section 16, by allowing an immediate appeal of orders denying arbitration, but not for orders compelling arbitration, further reinforces the policies in favor of arbitration and resolving issues in arbitration if the parties so agreed.

Although the FAA's 16 provisions seem fairly straightforward and designed to ensure enforcement of written agreements to arbitrate, voluminous litigation has ensued regarding the FAA's meaning, scope, application, and preemptive effect. Discussion of judicial decisions involving the FAA is set forth *infra in* Sections 9.03 through 9.05.

[B] State Arbitration Laws and Preemption

Although the FAA prescribes procedural courses for judicial enforcement of arbitration agreements (e.g., stays of judicial proceedings pending arbitration, judicial confirmation of arbitral awards, and limited grounds for review or vacatur of arbitral awards), the statutory text directs its application in "[c]ourts of the United States," thus, in federal courts. Moreover, the FAA does not provide an independent basis for federal jurisdiction.[14] The lack of independent federal court jurisdiction means that the parties must have either diversity or federal question jurisdiction, and invoking the FAA is not enough to bestow the federal courts with jurisdiction. The fact that the FAA is substantive law that does not bestow jurisdiction on federal courts is something of an anomaly in federal law.

---

12. 9 U.S.C. § 10(1) (1–4).

13. *See* Weston, *supra* note 5 8 Nev. L. J. at 391.

14. Vaden v. Discover Bank, 556 U.S. 49 (2009) (holding that the FAA does not confer federal court subject matter jurisdiction and requiring federal courts to apply the "well-pleaded" complaint rule and look through to merits of claim to determine whether a claim arises under federal law).

Concerned that the FAA applied only in federal courts, each state adopted arbitration legislation to ensure similar enforcement in state courts. In 1955, the National Conference of Commissioners on Uniform State Laws (NCCUSL) promulgated the Uniform Arbitration Act (UAA), which states adopted and whose provisions were virtually identical to the FAA, intended to ensure enforcement of arbitration agreements and confirmation of arbitration awards in state courts. It is important to note that both federal and state courts have jurisdiction to hear arbitration matters. As a matter of practice, parties who need the court's assistance in an arbitration case may have the discretion to choose between federal or state court.

In 1956 in *Southland v. Keating,* the Supreme Court announced that the FAA applies in both state and federal courts and that the FAA preempts state laws in conflict with the FAA.[15] Since *Southland*, the U.S. Supreme Court has consistently cited the FAA as establishing a "national policy favoring arbitration."[16] Despite the confusion about whether portions of the FAA that address "[c]ourts of the United States" apply to state courts, the FAA's central enforcement provisions are held to apply and are given substantial preemptive effect over state laws that conflict with the FAA or its pro-arbitration policy.[17] The practical effect of the preemption ruling is that states cannot enforce anti-arbitration law (legislation, administrative rules, or common law), such as requiring arbitration agreements to appear in a special font,[18] creating special legal tests for class action arbitrations,[19] or permitting litigation in a certain context, even when the parties have an otherwise enforceable arbitration agreement.[20]

Against this backdrop, in 2000, the NCCUSL proposed a Revised Uniform Arbitration Act (RUAA) seeking to address many issues that neither the 1955 Act nor the FAA addresses.[21] For example, the RUAA contains provisions regarding a range of issues, such as arbitrability, provisional remedies, initiation of an arbitration proceeding, consolidation, arbitrator disclosures, arbitrator immunity, arbitrator testimony, prehearing management, arbitral remedies, waiver, subpoena power, vacatur, and notice standards.[22] Many of these issues are also addressed in institutional procedural rules. The drafters, however, noted that the preemption doctrine may invalidate state law.

State and federal arbitration laws can both govern an arbitration, with the FAA's substantive provisions prevailing in the event of a conflict. Although the FAA can apply in state courts, parties can expressly designate to have their arbitration governed by state arbitration law. Most state arbitration legislation largely mirrors the FAA; however, certain state arbitration laws may vary. For example, California's Arbitration Act governs

---

15. Southland v. Keating, 465 U.S. 1 (1984). Under the Supremacy Clause of the U.S. Constitution, federal law preempts, and thus invalidates, conflicting state law. Although the FAA does not contain an express preemption clause, the U.S. Supreme Court has on several occasions ruled the FAA preempts state laws that attempted to regulate agreements to arbitrate or the arbitration process.

16. Southland v. Keating, 465 U.S. at 10.

17. Laura Kaster, *The Revised Uniform Arbitration Act at 15*, (noting the "ongoing "confusion in state courts as to the role of federal arbitration law), available at http://www.americanbar.org/content/dam/aba/publications/dispute_resolution_magazine/winter2016/9_Kaster_Winter_2016.authcheckdam.pdf

18. Doctor's Associates, Inc. v. Casarotto, 517 U.S. 681 (1996).

19. ATT Mobility, Inc. v. Concepcion, 563 U.S. 333 (2011).

20. Perry v. Thomas, 482 U.S. 483 (1987).

21. Rev'd Uniform Arb. Act, http://www.uniformlaws.org/c.aspx?title=Arbitration%20Act%20(2000).

22. Weston, 8 NEV. L. J. at 389. RUAA Commentary, (2000)

arbitrations seated in California.[23] Unlike FAA § 3, which provides for a judicial stay of litigation where any issues are referable to arbitration, the California Act permits a court to stay arbitration pending resolution of related litigation.[24] In *Volt v. Board of Trustees of the Leland Stanford Jr. Univ.*, the Supreme Court held that the FAA did not preempt application of the California statute because the parties agreed that their arbitration agreement would be governed by the California arbitration law.[25]

State arbitration law may address procedural matters not covered by the FAA and applies where the FAA or designated procedural rules do not address the question or where the parties have specified application of the state arbitration law. Of course, those state laws must not be hostile to arbitration, or they will be preempted. If parties wish to incorporate a specific state's arbitration law into their contract, they should specifically state this; a general state choice-of-law provision may not be sufficient. For instance, if the parties desired their arbitration agreement to be governed by Wisconsin law, the parties should include a clause such as: "This agreement to arbitrate shall be governed by Wisconsin law." A general choice-of-law clause designating Wisconsin law may not be enough.

Because of the preemptive effect of the FAA, states are limited in enacting legislation intended to address particular concerns regarding the compulsory imposition of arbitration provisions in adhesion contracts in contexts such as employment, consumer, and franchisee disputes. Although states normally have the power to issue laws regarding employment or consumer protection, arbitration preemption bars them from making laws that are hostile to arbitration even in those areas that traditionally fall under the state's police power.

[C] International Arbitration Treaties and Conventions

Arbitration is the leading alternative method of dispute resolution for international commercial transactions and is the preferred method for dealing with disputes involving parties from different countries. Consider that fear of litigation in a distant forum fuels interest in domestic arbitration in general, and this concern is even more pronounced in the international context. Parties may fear uncertainty in dealing with an unfamiliar legal system, foreign law, language, and concern about cultural differences and possible bias in the courts of an opponent's country. As a party will often prefer not to submit to the jurisdiction of another party's national courts, international arbitration can provide a neutral forum for dispute resolution. Arbitration rules are streamlined, flexible, and far less complex than most national rules of civil procedure, making them better suited to parties from different jurisdictions. Arbitrators can be selected for their familiarity with relevant commercial practices, trade usages and legal structures, and their ability to apply different national laws and deal with comparative law issues.

International arbitration law applies to arbitration agreements reached to settle disputes arising from international trade between parties or entities of different countries. International law has made arbitration very conducive to resolving disputes mainly by

---

23. Cal. Code Civ. Pro. §§ 1280-1294.2.
24. *Id.* at § 1281.2.
25. *See* Volt v. Board of Trustees of the Leland Stanford Jr. Univ., 489 U.S. 468 (1989).

providing uniformity for the enforcement of arbitration in a large number of countries. International arbitration agreements and awards are governed under international conventions. The Convention on the Recognition and Enforcement of Foreign Arbitral Awards (1958), popularly known as the New York Convention, is a multilateral treaty ratified by more than 145 countries.[26] The New York Convention requires that national courts of signatory countries recognize and enforce arbitral awards entered in member foreign states. Under Article V of both treaties, enforcement may be refused in limited situations, such as where the subject matter is nonarbitrable—that is, not capable of settlement by arbitration, or where enforcement violates the public policy of the country where recognition is sought.[27] Other grounds for non-enforcement include party incapacity, invalid arbitral agreement; inadequate notice of the arbitrator's appointment or the arbitration proceedings or inability to present his case; the award decides matters not within the scope of the arbitration agreement; the composition of the arbitral tribunal or the procedure used did not accord with the parties' agreement or applicable law; or the award has not yet become binding or has been set aside or suspended by a competent authority of the country where the award was rendered.[28]

The 1975 Inter-American Convention on International Commercial Arbitration, called the "Panama Convention," similarly provides for the enforceability of arbitration agreements and arbitral awards in Latin American countries.[29] These international arbitration treaties provide certainty to the international trade industry by ensuring the enforceability of valid arbitration agreements and awards. The United Nations Commission on International Trade Law (UNCITRAL) Model Law on International Commercial Arbitration (1985), as amended (2006), provides a model law for countries to adopt to harmonize laws on international arbitration procedures. The international arbitration conventions are implemented in the United States through Chapters 2 and 3 of the FAA (not discussed above), thus requiring U.S. courts to recognize arbitration awards rendered in a foreign country, or involving parties who are citizens of different nations or U.S. citizens if the "relationship involves property located abroad, envisages performance of enforcement abroad, or has some other reasonable relation with one or more foreign states."[30]

[D] Private Institutional Rules

A number of domestic and international private organizations have developed procedural rules that provide a framework for conducting the administration and also offer services to administer arbitrations. An arbitration agreement may designate application of a particular provider's rules or services. These organizations may provide general or industry-specific services and include the American Arbitration Association (AAA) and its International Centre for Dispute Resolution, JAMS, the International Chamber of Commerce International Court of Arbitration (ICC) located in Paris, the London Court

---

26. United Nations Convention on the Recognition and Enforcement of Foreign Arbitral Awards, 1958, ("New York Convention"), available at http://www.uncitral.org/pdf/english/texts /arbitration/NY-conv/XXII_1_e.pdf.

27. New York Convention, Art. IV(2).

28. *Id.* at Art. V(1).

29. O.A.S. Ser. A20 (S.E.P.E.F.), 14 I.L.M. (1975), available at http://www.oas.org/juridico /english/treaties/b-35.html

30. 9 U.S.C. § 202.

of International Arbitration (LCIA), as well as the Court of Arbitration for Sport (CAS). As discussed in Chapter 7, an arbitration conducted under the supervision of one of these organizations is referred to as an "institutional arbitration." An "ad hoc" arbitration is not administered by an institution. Parties to an "ad hoc" arbitration may still incorporate a provider organization's rules. In those cases, the arbitration is not administered by the organization's staff and no fees are paid to the organization, but the chosen arbitrator will be required to abide by the procedural rules chosen by the parties.

§ 9.03 Allocation of Authority between Court and Arbitrator

Over the years, substantial questions have arisen regarding "who decides" if the parties agreed to arbitration. These questions include: Should a court decide if the parties agreed to arbitrate? Should the arbitrator decide? What if the parties agreed to arbitrate, but that agreement is arguably unenforceable? Will either courts or arbitrators act in self-interest in making the decision about who should handle the case? Can the parties' contract designate whether the courts or the arbitrators answer these questions? This section will discuss these questions, keeping in mind the policies in favor of arbitration and speedy dispute resolution.

[A] Substantive Arbitrability and Court Authority

As arbitration is fundamentally based upon consent, arbitration may be compelled only where the party is subject to the agreement and the dispute is within the scope of the arbitration clause. A valid arbitration clause is the "gateway" prerequisite to obligate parties to arbitration. Intuitively, this rule makes sense. Parties should be required to arbitrate disputes they agree to arbitrate; parties should not be forced to arbitrate disputes that they did not agree to arbitrate.

Parties may contest arbitration on a number of grounds, some of which are more likely to be successful than others. For example, a party may contend that the arbitration clause is invalid and subject to a defense, that the party is not required to arbitrate for having never been a party to an arbitration agreement, or that the particular dispute, claim, or issue is not within the scope of an otherwise admitted arbitration agreement. A party may also raise a number of other objections to arbitration, such as alleged failures of procedural conditions, including time limitations or waiver.

Arbitrability is the term given to the array of "gateway" determinations that must be resolved before arbitration on the merits may be compelled,[31] or litigation stayed due

---

31. A party seeking to enforce arbitration may file a motion in court to compel arbitration. 9 U.S.C. § 3 ("A party aggrieved by the alleged failure . . . to arbitrate under a written agreement for arbitration may petition any United States district court . . . for an order directing that such arbitration proceed . . . .").

to arbitration.[32] A critical preliminary question, however, involves identifying who decides—the court or arbitrator—these threshold questions of "arbitrability."

The U.S. Supreme Court in *First Options of Chicago, Inc. v. Kaplan*[33] set forth a general allocation of authority between the court and arbitrators in accord with parties' presumed expectations. Although parties can explicitly agree otherwise,[34] courts are primarily directed to deciding three questions: (1) is there a valid arbitration agreement? (2) did the parties agree to arbitrate? and (3) is this claim or dispute within the scope of such agreement? The *First Options* test is predicated on FAA Section 4. Under §4, the Court has an obligation to "hear the parties, *and upon being satisfied that the making of the agreement for arbitration or the failure to comply therewith is not in issue*, the court shall make an order directing the parties to proceed to arbitration in accordance with the terms of the agreement."[35] Because courts must be satisfied as to the making of the agreement, issues of contract validity and scope are questions initially for the court, not an arbitrator (unless the parties give that power to the arbitrator).

Having a court determine the gateway agreements serves two important policy issues. First, the courts can ensure that parties have actually agreed to arbitrate so that parties are not subject to a process to which they did not agree. Second, a question of arbitrator self-interest lurks in the background. Arbitrators are only paid for cases that they spend time on and actually hear—compared to judges, who are paid a salary no matter the number of cases in their courts. Critics state that arbitrators are influenced by self-interest (to be paid) and are more likely to find that parties agreed to arbitrate so that they can keep the work, rather than rule that the parties never agreed to arbitrate and send those cases back to the courts. Whether or not this self-interest exists, having courts determine this gateway issue will help curb this type of offense.

[1] Arbitration Clause Validity

A court may hear only challenges to the validity of the arbitration agreement itself and not to the overall contract. Under the *separability* doctrine, announced in *Prima Paint v. Conklin*, the arbitration provision is considered a separate contract, severable from the primary (container) contract, and a court decides only challenges to the arbitration provision itself. Again, this rule is based on the text of FAA Section 4, stating that once the court is satisfied that an agreement to arbitrate has been made, the court will refer the case to arbitration. Because of Section 4, the court will *separate* the arbitration agreement from the remainder of the contract to determine first whether the parties agreed to arbitrate. If the parties agreed to arbitrate, the remaining questions go to the arbitrator. If the parties did not agree to arbitrate, then the courts will retain jurisdiction over the matter. This rule ensures that agreements to arbitrate are honored and enforced, and courts give deference to arbitration.

---

32. 9 U.S.C. §4 ("If any suit or proceeding be brought in any of the courts of the United States upon any issue referable to arbitration . . . the court in which such suit is pending . . . shall on application of one of the parties stay the trial of the action until such arbitration has been had . . . .").

33. 514 U.S. 938 (1995) (holding that a court should decide whether the arbitration contract bound parties who did not sign the agreement).

34. *See infra* Section D.

35. 9 U.S.C. §4 (emphasis added).

Thus, for example, even where a party alleges that an entire contract is fraudulent or illegal, the arbitrator is to decide the question regarding the overall contract's validity.[36] The court hears only challenges that are directed to the validity of the arbitration provision itself, such as that the arbitration clause itself was induced by fraud or duress, or was defective under other contract law defenses, such as unconscionability, incapacity, or mistake.[37] Consider this rule for a moment. Which might be easier — challenging a whole contract for fraud, or challenging the arbitration clause within the contract for fraud (or mistake, or duress, etc.)? Making a pointed challenge at the arbitration clause is a difficult task, and the courts cannot consider an argument that a defense to the whole contract indicates a problem with the arbitration agreement. Later in this chapter we outline how parties can make the specific challenge to the arbitration agreement. Note, however, that such challenges are difficult and good lawyers will counsel their clients on the low chance of success before engaging in this endeavor.

[2] Only "Parties" Are Bound to Arbitrate

As consent is the foundation of arbitration, only parties to the arbitration agreement can seek to compel arbitration or to be required to arbitrate.[38] Thus, one may object to arbitration on the grounds that he was not a party to the arbitration agreement. For example, if one party asks for a court to compel arbitration, but the other party never signed the arbitration agreement, a court would have to determine whether those parties ever agreed to arbitrate. In the case of one party not signing the agreement, a court would likely find that the parties never did come to an agreement to arbitrate.

What about other interested parties, who are not necessarily signatories? In *EEOC v. Waffle House*, although the employee was bound to arbitrate individual claims, the EEOC was not a party to the arbitration contract and thus was free to pursue relief in federal court against the employer for victim-specific discrimination.[39] Under the *Waffle House* case, the agreement of an individual to arbitrate employment claims does not affect the government's ability to litigate claims based on the same facts. Keep in mind, however, that the individual employee will still have to arbitrate. The *Waffle House* case only stands for the principle that the government — who did not sign an arbitration agreement with the employer — does not have to arbitrate by virtue of the employee's arbitration agreement.

In other cases, third parties may be required to arbitrate even if they are not signatories to the arbitration agreement. Although arbitration contracts must be "in writing" and can only be enforced by or against a "party" to the contract, it is not always essential that each party physically sign the agreement. Certain nonsignatory third parties with a relationship to the primary contracting party can be bound by an arbitration agreement under relevant state agency and contract law.[40] Nonsignatories can thus be bound to arbitrate, for example, when theories of third-party beneficiary, agency, incorporation by reference, corporate veil-piercing or alter ego, assumption, or estoppel are used as

---

36. Buckeye Check Cashing, Inc. v. Cardgena, 546 U.S. 440 (2006).

37. *See* discussion on FAA "Savings Clause" defenses *infra* Section § 8.05.

38. Howsam v. Dean Witter Reynolds, Inc., 514 U.S. 79 (2002) (stating that "[c]ourts should not assume that the parties have agreed to arbitrate unless there is clear and unmistakable evidence that they did so.").

39. 534 U.S. 279, 296–98 (2002). The U.S. Equal Employment Opportunity Commission (EEOC) is a federal agency responsible for enforcing federal anti-discrimination laws.

40. *See* Thompson-CSF, SA v. Am. Arb. Ass'n, 63 F.3d 773 (2d Cir. 1995).

the basis to compel.[41] These are the same theories that would bind a nonsignatory to a contract under general contract law. Because arbitration applies general contract law to agreements to arbitrate, these well-established contract principles also apply to arbitration agreements.

Consider an example. A woman owns a lawn care business, and she is the sole shareholder and employee. She secures a loan in the company's name with an organization that lends money to local small businesses. As part of the loan process, she gives the company information that is later discovered to be untruthful. The signed contract includes an arbitration agreement, and the parties to the contract are the bank and the lawn care company. Ultimately, the company defaults on the loan and the bank initiates arbitration against *both* the lawn care business and the owner. The owner does not want to arbitrate personally and petitions the court to issue an order that she does not have to arbitrate. In this instance, the court will be required to consider the local state's law of corporate veil-piercing or alter ego to determine whether the lawn care owner must also arbitrate — despite not signing the arbitration agreement — because the owner may also be personally liable.

This arbitrability question of whether a person is bound to arbitrate is to be decided by the court unless the parties "clearly and unmistakably" delegate that function to the arbitrator.[42] What does "clear and unmistakable" look like? Perhaps unsurprisingly, "clear and unmistakable" may not be as clear or unmistakable as laypersons might expect. The following examples of contract language would all pass the "clear and unmistakable" test:

- The Parties agree to arbitrate all disputes arising out of or relating to this contact, including all issues of arbitrability.

- The Parties agree to arbitrate all disputes arising out of or relating to this contract, including issues relating to the jurisdiction of the arbitrator, the enforceability of this arbitration agreement, and the scope of the agreement.

- The Parties agree to arbitrate all disputes arising out of or relating to this contract, and the Parties agree to follow the Commercial Rules of the AAA.

Why would incorporating the rules of the AAA create a clear and unmistakable waiver? In those AAA rules, Rule 4 gives the arbitrators the ability to determine their own jurisdiction. Courts have generally said that when a party incorporates AAA rules, the rule governing jurisdiction is "clear and unmistakable" that the parties intended to submit the issue of arbitrability to the arbitrators instead of the courts. This rule is based on the presumption that incorporating the AAA rules makes them part of the arbitration agreement — whether or not the parties have actually read them prior to signing the arbitration agreement. These "clear and unmistakable" waivers are called "delegation clauses," which are discussed below.

---

41. *See* Jaime Dodge Byrnes & Elizabeth Pollman, Comment: *Arbitration, Consent and Contractual Theory: The Implications of EEC v. Waffle House,* 8 Harv. Neg. L. Rev. 289 (2003).

42. Prima Paint Corp. v. Flood & Conklin Manufacturing Co., 388 U.S. 395 (1967) (ruling that courts, not arbitrators, are to decide whether the parties have agreed to arbitration unless the parties "clearly and unmistakably" assign that function to the arbitrator."); First Options of Chicago, Inc. v. Kaplan, 514 U.S. 938 (1995) (holding that a court should decide whether the arbitration contract bound parties who did not sign the agreement).

[3] Whether Claim or Dispute Is within the Scope of the Arbitration Agreement

Parties circumscribe the scope of disputes to be submitted to arbitration through the exact wording of their arbitration agreement. Therefore, knowing whether a particular claim or dispute is subject to arbitration requires interpreting the relevant arbitration agreement. The scope of disputes covered under an arbitration cause may be broad, such as "All disputes arising out of or related to this agreement . . . ," or more narrow. For example, the clause providing for arbitration of "[A]ny controversy or claim arising out of this Agreement . . . ," "covered only those disputes 'relating to the interpretation and performance of the contract itself.'"[43] Whether or not a particular claim is within the scope of an arbitration provision is a matter of "substantive arbitrability," typically decided by a court.

An example may help illustrate the issues of the scope of an arbitration agreement. Consider that a non-unionized factory employee and the factory have an arbitration agreement stating: "Employer and Employee agree to arbitrate all employment disputes." A dispute about the working conditions, pay, or employee misconduct would easily fall within the scope of the agreement. But other types of disputes may or may not fit within the definition of "employment disputes." What if the employee slips and falls on ice in the parking lot? What if a burglar breaks into the employee's car in a dimly lit parking lot? What if two employees get into a fistfight during the working hours or on a break, and the employee wants to hold the employer responsible? These types of questions are much more difficult, and a court would be in the position to determine in the first instance if these types of disputes fall within the agreement.

[B] Procedural Arbitrability

The general allocation of authority is for courts to decide the "substantive" arbitrability issues regarding the arbitration clause's validity and coverage. However, a party may also raise a number of challenges regarding procedural defects and claims that the merits and entire contract—which includes the arbitration provision—is unenforceable. For example, a party may raise objections to the duty to arbitrate, such as expired time limitations, inadequate notice, estoppel, and the alleged failure of other conditions precedent to the obligation to arbitrate.[44] Although these procedural conditions must be satisfied to trigger arbitration on the merits, these questions of procedural arbitrability are decided by the arbitrator, on the theory that they are matters expected to be decided by an arbitrator, given an otherwise valid arbitration contract.[45]

The criticism regarding arbitrator self-interest can also be found in the area of procedural arbitrability. Is an arbitrator *really* going to find that an entire claim is barred by the statute of limitations if that ruling will close the case before the arbitrator has had a chance to work on the merits of the case? Generally, the system trusts that the arbitrator

---

43. *See* Tracer Research Corp. v. National Environmental Services Co., 42 F.3d 1292 (9th Cir. 1994).

44. *Howsam v. Dean Witter Reynolds, Inc.*, 537 U.S. 79 (2002) (ruling that interpretation of six-year time limit rule to file arbitration was a "procedural" question presumptively for an arbitrator to decide).

45. *See* Richard Reuben, *First Options, Consent to Arbitration, and the Demise of Separability: Restoring Access to Justice for Contracts with Arbitration Provisions*, 56 S.M.U. L. Rev. 820 (2003).

will act ethically and not in his or her self-interest, but it is interesting to consider the arbitrator's financial interests when analyzing the courts' rules regarding arbitrability.

[C] Delegation Clauses

The general presumption that courts decide substantive arbitrability issues can be overcome by an agreement delegating these issues to the arbitrator. For example, an arbitration clause may contain a provision that gives the arbitrator "exclusive authority to resolve any dispute relating to the . . . enforceability . . . of this Agreement." Such a provision was contained in the arbitration contract in *Rent-a-Center, West., Inc. v, Jackson.*[46] The consumer challenged arbitration in court, contending that the arbitration procedures called for by the contract—fee-splitting and limitations on discovery and the delegation provision itself, were unconscionable. The Supreme Court ruled, however, that these objections that the arbitration agreement was unconscionable, ordinarily reserved for court determinations, should be decided in arbitration because the agreement explicitly delegated that decision to the arbitrator. Many institutional arbitration procedural rules now contain "delegation" clauses conferring authority to arbitrators to decide all arbitrability issues.[47]

Above, we asked whether it would be more difficult to levy a contract defense against an arbitration clause or against the entire container contract. As a general matter, challenging the arbitration agreement would be more difficult. Now, consider the effect of the delegation clause. The delegation clause puts the ability to handle gateway matters squarely in the hands of the arbitrator. To challenge a contract involving an arbitration delegation clause in court, the party opposing arbitration must challenge *only* the delegation clause. Understanding that a party faces an uphill battle when challenging an arbitration agreement, consider the even greater challenge of only being able to challenge the delegation clause. How can a party prove that a delegation clause is unconscionable or the product of duress? Parties who are keenly interested in arbitrating future disputes would be wise to include a delegation clause to further insulate the contract from judicial challenge.

§ 9.04 Arbitrating Statutory and Regulatory Claims

An arbitration clause may state that a broad range of disputes, "any and all disputes between the parties . . . ," will be heard in arbitration. Traditionally, arbitration involved claims relating to the parties' contract. But can a private arbitrator also determine claims between the parties that involve statutory, regulatory, or public rights?

---

46. Under the *delegation doctrine* announced in *Rent-A-Center, W., Inc. v. Jackson*, 561 U.S. 63 (2010), an arbitration clause may assign authority to the arbitrator to decide challenges to the arbitration agreement, which otherwise are arbitrability questions for the court under the FAA. *Id.* ([a] district court may *not* decide a claim that an arbitration agreement is unconscionable, where the agreement explicitly assigns that decision to the arbitrator).

47. Applicable rules may also provide arbitrator authority to rule on own jurisdiction. *See e.g.*, AAA. R-7.

Initially, courts were hostile to the notion that arbitrators, who did not necessarily have legal training or procedural review, would decide claims involving statutory rights enacted for public protection.[48] Citing the FAA as a federal policy favoring arbitration,[49] the Supreme Court has since made clear that, absent a clear congressional mandate to require a judicial forum, statutory claims may be heard in arbitration.[50]

The Court has reasoned that "[b]y agreeing to arbitrate a statutory claim, a party does not forego the substantive rights afforded by the statute; it only submits to their resolution in an arbitral, rather than a judicial forum."[51] Provided the arbitration clause is broadly worded, few statutory claims are considered inarbitrable.[52] Even a federal consumer protection statute that provides for a "right to sue" was held not to preclude arbitration.[53] Thus the range of federal statutory claims involving securities fraud, employment, civil rights discrimination, or antitrust violations on a domestic and even international scale, may be heard in arbitration. The FAA's command to enforce arbitration agreements also supplants recourse to a state administrative agency, such as with the employee who sought to file a claim with the Labor Commission under California's Talent Act in *Presten v. Ferrer*.[54]

A potential limit on the doctrine making statutory claims arbitrable is where another federal statute provides a comprehensive regulatory scheme or a state statute "deputizes" a party to assert a representative action on behalf of the state under a Private Attorney General Act.[55] The federal circuit courts presently divide on whether an arbitration agreement containing a ban on class actions violates a party's rights to collective

---

48. Wilko v. Swan, 346 U.S. 427 (1953) (involving federal securities law and investor-protection issues).

49. Moses Cohn v. Mercury Const. Corp., 460 U.S. 1, 24 (1983) (instructing courts to presume a dispute is arbitrability).

50. Scherk v. Albert-Culver Co, 417 U.S. 506 (1974) (upholding international arbitration agreement involving U.S. securities claims); Shearson/American Express, Inc. v. McMahan, 482 U.S. 220 (1987); Gilmer v. Interstate Johnson, 500 U.S. 20 (1991) (holding Age Discrimination in Employment Act claims arbitrable).

51. Mitsubishi Motors Corp. v. Soler Chrysler-Plymouth, Inc. 473 U.S. 614 (1985) (holding that federal antitrust claims arising from international contract were arbitrable and could be heard by arbitral tribunal in Japan).

52. *Cf.* Dodd-Frank Wall Street Reform and Consumer Protection Act of 2010, 12 U.S.C. § 5301 (2012); Sarbanes-Oxley Act of 2002, 18 U.S.C. § 1514A(e)(2) ("No predispute arbitration agreement shall be valid or enforceable, if the agreement requires arbitration of a dispute arising under this section."); Motor Vehicle Franchise Contract Arbitration Act, 15 U.S.C. §§ 1226(a)(2) (permitting only post-dispute arbitration in dealer-franchisee disputes).

53. CompuCredit Corp. v. Greenwood, 132 S. Ct. 665, 669 (2012) (ruling that claims arising under the Credit Repair Organizations Act are arbitrable, despite Act's requirement that credit organizations notify consumers that they "have a right to sue a credit repair organization that violates the Credit Repair Organization Act" does not reflect Congressional intent to preclude arbitration of claims arising under the Act). *See also* Gilmer v. Interstate/Johnson Lane Corp., 500 U.S. 20, 28 (1991) (enforcing arbitration agreement despite claim under the Age Discrimination in Employment Act of 1967, 29 U.S.C. § 626(c)(1)).

54. Preston v. Ferrer, 552 U.S. 346, 359 (2008) ("[w]hen parties agree to arbitrate all questions arising under a contract, the FAA supersedes state laws lodging primary jurisdiction in another forum, whether judicial or administrative."). *See also* Sonic-Calabasas A, Inc. v. Moreno (Sonic I), 247 P.3d 130, 134 (Cal. 2011), vacated, 131 S. Ct. 496 (2011); Sonic II, 311 P.3d 184, 188 (Cal. 2013) (FAA preempted state wage and hour administrative claim process), *cert. denied*, 134 S. Ct. 2724 (2014).

55. Iskanian v. CLS Transp. L.A. LLC, 327 P.3d 129, 133 (Cal. 2014), *cert. denied*, 135 S. Ct. 1155 (2015).

action under the National Labor Relations Act.[56] In some instances, Congress may explicitly state that disputes may not be subject to a pre-dispute arbitration agreement. As part of the Dodd-Frank Act, for instance, Congress prohibited mortgage companies from including pre-dispute arbitration agreements in mortgage contracts with residential home buyers.

[A] Unaffordability and the Effective Vindication of Rights

What if a consumer, employer, or other party cannot afford the expenses of arbitration? As discussed in Chapter 7, arbitration involves costs that parties do not normally bear in litigation, such as arbitrator fees and administrative costs charged by arbitration provider organizations. The inability to pay for the forum is particularly concerning when a party must arbitrate cases falling under state or federal statutes. In the Supreme Court's case of *Green Tree Financial Corp. v. Randolph*,[57] the Court indicated that if a party could prove that it could not afford to access the arbitral forum, then the party could litigate the claim. Parties who would like to take advantage of the *Randolph* ruling would need to demonstrate with admissible evidence that the party cannot afford the costs of arbitration due to arbitration fees that would not be otherwise required in litigation.

The *Randolph* decision has been limited in some respects over the years. The argument that prohibitive costs of individual arbitration would effectively deny a party the right to vindicate statutory antitrust claims was rejected in *American Express Co. v. Italian Colors Restaurant*.[58] A class of merchants filed an antitrust lawsuit against American Express, contending that the amount of expenses necessary to prove each case individually would dwarf any potential individual recovery.

- FAA does not permit courts to invalidate a contractual waiver of class arbitration on the ground that the plaintiff's cost of individually arbitrating a federal statutory claim exceeds the potential recovery

American Express Co. v. Italian Colors Restaurant upheld enforcement of an arbitration class waiver provision under the FAA, despite the merchant plaintiffs' claim that doing so prevented them from "effectively vindicating" their federal statutory rights because the cost of individually arbitrating an antitrust claim would exceed the potential recovery.

Italian Colors and *Randolph* can be distinguished based on the types of costs associated with the case. In *Randolph*, the party claimed that the arbitrator and forum fees were prohibitive for the plaintiff. In *Italian Colors*, the merchant class could afford the arbitrator's fees and the fees due to the arbitration provider organization. What the merchants could not afford, however, were the costs of expert witnesses. If the merchants could proceed as a class, they could share the cost of the expert witnesses. If the merchants were required to arbitrate individually, then the cost of expert witnesses would

---

56. Lewis v. Epic-Systems Corp. 833 F.3d 1145 (7th Cir. 2016).
57. 351 U.S. 79 (2000).
58. 133 S. Ct. 2304 (2013) (J. Scalia) (5-3-1 Sotomayor recused) (rejecting the argument that FAA enforcement of an arbitration class waiver denies a party's "effective vindication" of their federal statutory rights by removing their economic incentive to bring the antitrust claims).

significantly dwarf any recovery they might receive. Of course, if the merchants were in litigation (class action or individually), they would still have to bear the costs of expert witnesses. In ruling against the merchants in *Italian Colors*, the Supreme Court limited *Randolf* to the incremental costs of the arbitral forum over the costs of the litigation process.

§ 9.05 Contract Defenses

The FAA's mandate to enforce arbitration agreements is subject to '[s]uch grounds as exist at law or in equity for the revocation of *any* contract."[59] The statute enforces contracts to arbitrate and recognizes that enforcement is subject to contract law defenses. Defenses that may be raised in opposition to a request to compel arbitration include unconscionability, fraud, duress/undue influence, material breach, waiver, contrary to public policy, illusory contract, statutes of limitations, or failure to comply with conditions precedent (e.g., mediation or notice requirements), and lack of capacity, consideration, contract formation, due process, or mutuality of obligation. Note that the range of defenses can encompass what are considered substantive and procedural arbitrability claims, and objections should be directed to the court or to the arbitrator accordingly.

[A] Unconscionability

Unconscionability arguments are typically made in objection to arbitration clauses contained in adhesion form contracts involving employees, consumers, or franchisees. Arbitration may be imposed as a condition of employment or consumer transaction. An employee or consumer may be surprised that their right to a judge or jury trial is waived by virtue of a pre-dispute arbitration provision in the contract. But the fact that an arbitration provision is presented on a "take-it-or-leave-it" basis and non-negotiable is not alone unconscionable. Courts will require a showing that the arbitration agreement is both substantively and procedurally unconscionable in order to deny enforcement. Procedural unconscionability concerns the formation of the contract and whether the arbitration contract was presented as "take it or leave it" or in a rushed manner so as to deny adequate notice. The court will consider factors such as disparity in bargaining power, knowledge or sophistication, the use of complex legalistic language, or inconspicuous print. Substantive unconscionability measures whether the arbitration terms are overly harsh, or so one-sided as to oppress, unfairly surprise, or "shock the conscience." An arbitration provision may be unconscionable it presents "an overall imbalance in the obligations and rights imposed by the bargain."[60]

For example, in *Zaborowski v. MHN Gov't Servs.*, the arbitration provision in the employment contract contained multiple oppressive provisions, including a shorted limitations period, a $2,600 filing fee, punitive damages waiver, costs, and fee-shifting (even where plaintiffs prevailed on some but not all claims), and granting MHN near-unfettered discretion to select three preferred arbitrators. The clause was struck in its entirety as

---

59. 9 U.S.C. § 2 (emphasis added). *See also* Allied-Bruce Terminix Cos. v. Dobson, 513 U.S. 265, 281 (1995).

60. RESTATEMENT (THIRD) OF CONTRACTS.

"unjustifiably one-sided" and effectively a "practical abrogation of the right of action."[61] The more one-sided the arbitration agreement in an adhesion contract, the more likely that the court will find the contract unconscionable.

The following is a nonexhaustive list of the types of clauses that will weigh in favor of the court finding the contract unconscionable:

- Requiring an individual to pay a large portion of arbitrator and forum fees (even if the party could pay them under *Randolph*)
- Instituting a "loser pays" rule for the arbitrator and forum fees
- Shortening the applicable statute of limitations
- Limiting the remedies that would otherwise be available in court
- Requiring the individual to travel a great distance for an arbitration hearing
- Arbitrator selection processes in which the company controls the list of potential arbitrators
- Rules requiring the individual to comply with rules that the company need not follow (such as one-sided discovery limitations or witness disclosures)—these types of rules lack "mutuality of obligation" between the parties

Courts will consider each contract individually. The more offensive provisions a contract contains, the more likely it will be considered unconscionable. The presence of a class action waiver, which is discussed in more detail below, may also weigh in favor of a finding of unconscionability.

[B] Other Contract Defenses

Because FAA Section 2 incorporates state contract law, any contract defense available for contracts generally is also available as a defense to an agreement to arbitrate. The following is a nonexhaustive list of potential contract defenses that might apply to arbitration agreements:

- The arbitration agreement (not the entire contract) was secured by fraud, perhaps to ensure secrecy in resolving a pattern of misconduct
- The arbitration agreement was procured by duress or undue influence
- A party did not comply with a condition precedent to arbitration, such as "good faith" negotiation, mediation, or notice requirements
- The party seeking arbitration committed a material breach of the arbitration agreement
- The arbitration agreement is illusory

---

61. *Zaborowski v. MHN Gov't Servs.*, 2014 U.S. App. LEXIS 23738 (9th Cir. Cal. Dec. 17, 2014) ("Although the Federal Arbitration Act expresses a strong preference for the enforcement of arbitration agreements, the Act does the terms of an arbitration agreement."); Hooters of America, Inc. v. Phillips, 173 F.3d. 933 (4th Cir. 1999) ("By promulgating this system of warped rules, Hooters so skewed the process in its favor that Phillips has been denied arbitration in any meaningful sense of the word."); Jackson v. Payday Financial, 764 F.3d 765 (7th Cir. 2014) (provision one-sided, potentially biased process, illusory rules and sham process).

- The party seeking to avoid arbitration did not have the requisite capacity (due to minority or mental incapacity)
- Consideration was not given for the arbitration agreement (especially in cases in which an arbitration agreement is inserted into a contract during the course of an employment or business relationship between the parties)

Certainly other defenses exist and are also available. These are simply illustrative of the types of defenses available. All of these defenses are difficult to make to a court, and clients should be advised of their likelihood of success before undertaking these types of legal issues.

§ 9.06 Policy and Fairness Issues

As can be imagined, a system of arbitration that is outside of the public view and utilized on a wide scale between large companies and individuals can lead to a number of questions dealing with policy and fairness. The legal test for unconscionability is essentially a test based on fairness, but this section considers some additional policy considerations, including the presence of "repeat players" and issues regarding class actions.

[A] Repeat Players and One-Shot Players

The "repeat player" notion posits that employers or parties who more frequently use arbitration and select arbitrators are not only more experienced with the process, but also obtain more favorable outcomes.[62] The plaintiff in *Gilmer v. Interstate Johnson*, cited several concerns with the arbitration process, arguing that arbitration would inadequately address the statutory discrimination claims. But the Court determined that these concerns were not well founded. Despite the repeat player concern, the court said there was no reason to presume arbitrators will be biased; moreover, rules applicable to the arbitration require impartiality.

Repeat players have a series of advantages over individual arbitration participants. First, repeat players likely have more information about the arbitration process and individual arbitrators than "one shot" players. Repeat players can collect information about the process and individual arbitrators over time as they experience multiple arbitrations. Because this information is otherwise confidential, one-shot players cannot get the information, leaving a significant informational asymmetry. A critical view of arbitration is that arbitrators will prefer and rule in favor of repeat players because the repeat players can bestow new business on the arbitrators — something that a one-shot player cannot do.

[B] Class Action Issues

In the early 2000s, parties started considering the possibility of class action arbitrations, particularly in the areas of consumer and employment arbitration. The 2003

---

62. Lisa B. Bingham, *Employment Arbitration: The Repeat Player Effect*, 1 EMP. RTS. & EMP. POL'Y J. 189, 191 (1997).

Supreme Court case of *Green Tree Financial Corp. v. Bazzle*[63] appeared to bless the idea of class action arbitrations as a way to resolve disputes. The AAA responded to the *Bazzle* decision and created a new set of rules for arbitrators to follow in class action arbitration cases. Companies, however, did not want to use arbitration for class actions. Instead, they began revising their arbitration agreements to ban class action procedures — in *both* arbitration and litigation. Instead of class action procedures, the companies preferred to require each case to be arbitrated individually. Companies then started utilizing "class action waiver" clauses to accomplish this controversial goal.

The increase in the use of consumer arbitration also led to more companies inserting class action waivers or bans in form pre-dispute arbitration contracts. According to a report by the Consumer Financial Protection Bureau (CFPB), arbitration clauses are included in "hundreds of millions of consumer contracts" for consumer financial products and services, from bank accounts to private student loans to payday loans. These clauses often require consumers to submit any dispute to individual arbitration, rather than raise their claims as part of a class action.[64] States have also sought to address public policy concerns about arbitration through judicial and legislative actions.

Prior to 2011, federal and state courts were divided on the legality of class action waivers in arbitration contracts. On the one hand, the FAA requires that an arbitration contract be enforced "according to its terms." Yet other courts, such as the California Supreme Court, considered such waivers substantively unconscionable if the waiver meets a three-part test: (1) the waiver is in a contract of adhesion; (2) the dispute involves a predictably small amount of damages, and (3) the plaintiff alleges that the party with superior bargaining power has carried out a scheme to cheat large numbers of people out of small amounts of money.[65]

In 2011, the U.S. Supreme Court in *AT&T v. Concepcion* ruled that the FAA preempted a California Supreme Court decision, which deemed, as a matter of California law, that class waivers in consumer arbitration contracts had the practical effect of exempting a party "from responsibility for [its] own fraud" and thus were unconscionable.[66] The court reasoned that the state application of the unconscionability rule "stands as an obstacle" to FAA objectives and was not just a "ground that 'exist[s] at law or in equity for the revocation of any contract' under FAA § 2."[67]

Since *AT&T*, the debate on the propriety of class action waivers has escalated, as well as the use of class action waivers in consumer contracts.[68] Proposals to ban class action waivers in consumer and employment contracts have been introduced legislatively in the Arbitration Fairness Act, but that bill has gained little traction. On the other hand,

---

63. 539 U.S. 444 (2003).

64. Consumer Fin. Prot. Bureau, Arbitration Study: Report to Congress, Pursuant to Dodd-Frank Wall Street Reform and Consumer Protection Act § 1028(a), §§ 1.1–1.4.1 (2015).

65. Vaden v. Discover Bank, 556 U.S. 49 (2009).

66. AT&T Mobility LLC v. Concepion, 563 U.S. 333 (2011).

67. *Id.* (The overarching purpose of the FAA, evident in the text of §§ 2, 3, and 4, is to ensure the enforcement of arbitration agreements according to their terms so as to facilitate streamlined proceedings. Requiring the availability of classwide arbitration interferes with fundamental attributes of arbitration and thus creates a scheme inconsistent with the FAA.")

68. http://www.nytimes.com/2015/11/01/business/dealbook/arbitration-everywhere-stacking -the-deck-of-justice.html 2) http://www.nytimes.com/2015/11/02/business/dealbook/in-arbitration -a-privatization-of-the-justice-system.html?action=click&contentCollection=DealBook&module =RelatedCoverage&region=Marginalia&pgtype=article.

the CFPB has proposed a rule banning the use of predispute arbitration class waivers in financial contracts.[69] The California Supreme Court has not retreated, either. Although conceding that the FAA preempts state laws deeming class waivers unconscionable, the court insists that the FAA does not preclude unconscionability challenges to the arbitration clause itself.[70]

§ 9.07 Arbitration Ethical Standards

Arbitration can only be a successful process if the forum is fair. Fairness, of course, requires that the arbitrators be fair and that the parties respect the process. Regulating the fairness and ethics of arbitration is similar to regulating the mediation process. Most of the regulation takes place in the private sector, as opposed to positive law. The leading code of ethics for arbitrators was promulgated by the American Arbitration Association and the American Bar Association, and this Code of Ethics for Arbitrators in Commercial Disputes (the Code) will be discussed throughout this section. As discussed in Chapter 7, ethical violations are the primary reason arbitration awards are vacated by a court on appeal. Protecting the forum, then, is of utmost important for all of the participants.

This section covers the major ethical obligations found in the arbitral forum. It begins with the ethical duties of arbitrators, followed by the liability and immunity afforded to arbitrators, the costs of the forum, and concludes with the ethical obligations on arbitration participants.

[A] Independence and Impartiality

The primary ethical obligation on the part of the arbitrator is to be free from bias and conflicts of interest. This issue is so important that Canons I and II of the Code deal with the issues of independence, impartiality, and ultimately, fairness. Under Canon I, the arbitrator must be able to "serve impartially" and "independently from the parties, potential witnesses, and the other arbitrators."[71] The arbitrator should not only avoid actual partiality, but also the "appearance of partiality."[72] Freedom from partiality includes refraining from engaging in business or other activities with any of the arbitration participants after appointment.

---

69. *See, e.g., CFPB Proposes Prohibiting Mandatory Arbitration Clauses that Deny Groups of Consumers their Day in Court*, at https://www.consumerfinance.gov/about-us/newsroom/consumer-financial-protection-bureau-proposes-prohibiting-mandatory-arbitration-clauses-deny-groups-consumers-their-day-court/.

70. Sanchez v. Valencia Holdings, LLC., 353 P.3d 741 (Cal. 2015) (holding the FAA preempted provision anti-waiver of judicial forum provision in state Consumer Legal Remedies law; but noting that the FAA does not preempt contract law defenses, applied even-handedly). *See also* Sonic-Calabasas A, Inc. v. Moreno (*Sonic I*), 247 P.3d 130, 134 (Cal. 2011), *vacated*, 131 S. Ct. 496 (2011); *Sonic II*, 311 P.3d 184, 188 (Cal. 2013) (remanding preempted law for wage and hour administrative review for unconscionability determination), *cert. denied*, 134 S. Ct. 2724 (2014).

71. AAA & ABA, Code of Ethics for Arbitrators in Commercial Disputes, Canon I(B) (2004).

72. *Id.*, Canon I(C).

Prior to taking the appointment, each arbitrator must make a series of disclosures of any types of conflicts or potential conflicts of interest with any of the participants. Canon II of the Code states: "An arbitrator should disclose any interest or relationship likely to affect impartiality or which might create an appearance of partiality."[73] The duty to disclose is continuing,[74] meaning that if the conflict arises later in the course of the proceeding (such as when the parties exchange witness lists or after the arbitrator recognizes one of the participants in person) the arbitrator must make a timely disclosure at the point he or she learns of the conflict. The arbitrator should disclose any known existing or past financial, business, professional, or personal relationships that might reasonably affect impartiality or lack of independence in the eyes of the parties."[75] Under this rule, an arbitrator should disclose facts such as: stock ownership in one of the parties, previous employment with one of the parties or law firms associated with the case, service on a board of directors with an arbitration participant, or a friendship with an arbitration participant. If an arbitrator does not disclose a conflict of interest, the award may be subject to attack on appeal.[76]

For arbitrators who arbitrate under a provider organization, such as AAA, JAMS, CPR, or FINRA, the duty of disclosure will be required under the organization's rules. Many providers require that arbitrators maintain a series of "usual" disclosures, such as previous employment, which should be updated periodically. The provider, then, provides the disclosures to the parties and requests that the arbitrators make additional disclosures, as necessary. In some states, notably California, state law requires more stringent disclosures.[77] California arbitrators must make disclosures not only on their own behalf but also on behalf of anyone living in their household.

In some instances, the parties choose the arbitrators precisely because they are *not* neutral. As discussed in Chapter 7, some of these non-neutral neutrals are party-appointed arbitrators in a tripartite arbitration.[78] In other instances, the parties agree at the beginning that the arbitrator be associated with one of the parties, usually for expediency's sake or because the person has expertise. Examples of such "structural bias" occur with some frequency in the realm of public construction projects.[79] In its collective bargaining agreement, the National Football League (NFL) reserves the right to have the Commissioner be the arbitrator,[80] which is another example of structural bias.

[B] Other Obligations

In addition to the obligation to neutrality and independence, arbitrators have a series of other ethical obligations to ensure a quality and ethical process. As with judges, arbitrators have a duty to refrain from ex parte communications with the parties.[81] Because arbitrators make binding decisions, it would be unfair for one side or the other to have

---

73. *Id.*, Canon II.
74. *Id.*, Canon II(C).
75. *Id.* at Canon II(A)(1).
76. *See supra* Ch. 7.08[C]; *see also* 9 U.C.C. § 10(a)(3).
77. Cal. Code Civ. Proc. § 1281.9 (2015).
78. *See supra* Ch. 7.06.
79. *See, e.g.*, MCI Constructors, LLC v. City of Greensboro, 610 F.3d 849 (4th Cir. 2010)
80. *See, e.g.*, Nat'l Football League Mgmt. Council v. Nat'l Football League Players Ass'n, 820 F.3d 527 (2nd Cir. 2016) ("Deflategate" decision).
81. Code of Ethics for Arbitrators in Commercial Disputes, Canon III.

a private audience with the arbitrator to try to sway the ruling. Arbitrators must also ensure that the proceedings are fair by treating the parties evenhandedly, allowing the parties to be represented, and giving adequate notice of the hearing to the parties.[82] Arbitrators also have a general duty to rule in a deliberate and independent way, as well as to maintain the confidentiality of information learned in the arbitration.[83]

These types of ethical rules inspire confidence that the process will be fair and that all parties have an equal right to put on their case. These duties apply from the beginning of the case, through the discovery period, through the hearing, and then finally as the arbitrators deliberate and determine their award. These ethical rules hopefully instill confidence in the process and ensure that the procedure is fair.

[C] Costs, Fees, and Advertising

The ethical obligations of arbitrators also extends to costs, fees, and advertising, just as ethical obligations surround lawyers' billing and advertising practices. In terms of fees and costs, arbitrators have an ethical duty to abide by "integrity and fairness."[84] Part of that obligation is for arbitrators to be up-front with fees, preferably in writing. When arbitrators work through a provider organization, the parties should pay the fees to the provider organization, who will then pass the fees along to the arbitrators. The provider organization provides a great buffer between the parties and the payment of fees. If a party is slow to pay, the provider organization can deal with the collection issues, allowing the arbitrators to remain neutral and unaware of these problems. In ad hoc arbitrations, the parties will pay the arbitrator directly. Arbitrators, absent extraordinary circumstances, should not increase their fees during the pendency of the arbitration.[85]

Arbitrators are permitted to advertise, provided such advertisements are "truthful and accurate."[86] The Code of Ethics provides:

> This Canon does not preclude an arbitrator from printing, publishing, or disseminating advertisements conforming to these standards in any electronic or print medium, from making personal representations to prospective users of arbitral services conforming to such standards or from responding to inquiries concerning the arbitrator's availability, qualifications, experience, or fee arrangements.[87]

These rules are flexible in allowing arbitrators to advertise, but still protect consumers from untruthful claims or practices.

[D] Arbitrator Malpractice and Immunity

What happens to bad arbitrators? The short answer is that market corrections should keep bad arbitrators from being appointed to additional cases. Arbitration's confidentiality, however, may prevent the market from making these corrections due to incomplete

---

82. CODE OF ETHICS FOR ARBITRATORS IN COMMERCIAL DISPUTES, Canon IV.
83. *Id.* at Canons V & VI.
84. CODE OF ETHICS FOR ARBITRATORS IN COMMERCIAL DISPUTES, Canon VII.
85. *Id.* at Canon VII(B)(3).
86. CODE OF ETHICS FOR ARBITRATORS IN COMMERCIAL DISPUTES, Canon VIII.
87. *Id.*, Comment.

information on the part of the decision-makers. Sometimes word of mouth will keep an arbitrator from re-appointment. For repeat players in arbitration, they can choose to not re-appoint sub-par arbitrators. If provider organizations know about unethical conduct on the part of an arbitrator, the organization may be able to take remedial measures with the arbitrator or take that arbitrator off the roster.

What about suing an arbitrator for malpractice? Although the law is not particularly well developed, many jurisdictions apply the doctrine of immunity to arbitrators. Judges have long had immunity from malpractice actions based on official duties as judge. The purpose of immunity is to give judges freedom to act independently and to take cases without fear of lawsuits by disappointed parties. For these reasons, courts have applied immunity to arbitrators as well, particularly because arbitrators have a similar function to that of judges. Controversially, immunity effectively insulates arbitrators who have engaged in wrongdoing in the arbitral forum.[88]

[E] Participant Obligations for Fairness

What about parties, lawyers, and witnesses who abuse the arbitration forum? Parties, lawyers, and witnesses may lie, alter or destroy documents, bribe or hide witnesses, or engage in other types of bad behavior. Like arbitrators, arbitration participants are also afforded immunity from actions that take place in the arbitration forum. The policy, however, is slightly different. For parties, witnesses, and lawyers, immunity gives them the freedom to speak up and redress wrongs, as well as a freedom from being sued by the losing party. In traditional litigation, the criminal law acts as a deterrent so people do not engage in this type of behavior. Whether the criminal law applies to arbitration, however, is not very clear, and it is possible that the criminal law does not extend that far. One of your textbook authors has written extensively on this issue,[89] and she urges state legislatures to close the gap and allow for criminal redress of these wrongs, even if they occur in arbitration. For lawyers, the rules of professional conduct explicitly apply to arbitration,[90] but the criminal law could apply more clearly to parties and witnesses.

---

88. *See* Jenny Brown, *Expansion of Arbitral Immunity: Is Absolute Immunity a Foregone Conclusion?*, 10 J. DISP. RESOL. 225 (2009).

89. Kristen M. Blankley, *Lying, Stealing, and Cheating: The Role of Arbitrators as Ethics Enforcers*, 52 U. LOUISVILLE L. REV. 443 (2014); Kristen M. Blankley, *Advancements in Arbitral Immunity and Judicial Review of Arbitral Awards Create Ethical Loopholes in Arbitration*, in JUSTICE CONFLICT & WELL-BEING (2014); Kristen M. Blankley, *Taming the Wild West of Arbitration Ethics*, 60 KANSAS L. REV. 925 (2012).

90. MODEL RULES OF PROF'L CONDUCT r. 1.0(m) (defining "tribunal").

Chapter 10

Other ADR Processes

§ 10.01 Introduction

Negotiation, mediation, collaborative law, and arbitration are the primary methods of dispute resolution outside of the court system. Despite the popularity of these particular processes, a myriad of possibilities exist for dispute resolution for parties who are willing to experiment with processes to meet their needs. For example, when a large disaster strikes, a settlement fund with a specialized process could be established for the victims to receive compensation. These types of complicated settlement processes have been used for victims following the terrorist attacks of September 11, 2001,[1] and following certain natural disasters, such as Hurricane Katrina.[2]

This chapter provides an overview of some of the most commonly used dispute resolution procedures not covered in the previous chapters. Many of these processes are hybrids or variations on negotiation, mediation, and arbitration, while some are distinct processes used in certain circumstances. These processes are used in a wide variety of situations, such as private dispute resolution, governmental dispute resolution, large-scale dispute resolution, and dispute resolution in criminal law. Each of the processes described below will include a description of the process, a discussion of the pros and cons of using the process, typical scenarios involving the process, and any ethical concerns that might arise.

§ 10.02 Med-Arb

Mediation-Arbitration ("Med-Arb")[3] is a hybrid process combining mediation and arbitration. The Med-Arb process is a controversial process among dispute resolution professionals, and a limited number of neutrals offer this service to clients. This section describes the process and some of its variations, and then covers ethical issues relating to Med-Arb.

---

1. September 11th Victim Compensation Fund, *About the Victim Compensation Fund*, at http://www.vcf.gov/genProgramInfo.html
2. Katrina Levee Breach Settlement, *Vodanovich v. Boh Brothers Construction Co., LLC*, at https://www.leveebreachclass.com/
3. The "e" in "Med-Arb" may be pronounced as a long "e" sound (similar to the sound used to pronounce "mediation") or a short "e" sound (similar to the sound used to pronounce "medical"). Both pronunciations are common in the dispute resolution practice.

[A] The Med-Arb Process

Med-Arb is a process that begins with mediation and then shifts to arbitration if the mediation portion does not generate a settlement.[4] Med-Arb generally occurs in one of two circumstances. In the first circumstance, the parties agree at the beginning of the process that they will engage in this hybrid method of dispute resolution.[5] In other circumstances, parties who have become exhausted by the mediation process ask the mediator to make the final decision and give the mediator the authority to make a binding decision.[6]

The Med-Arb process eliminates one of the most fundamental downsides of the mediation process — the ability to not arrive at a decision. Mediation's lack of finality makes the process less predictable and a mediation that ends in impasse is often considered a waste of both time and money. To rectify this drawback, parties began combining mediation and arbitration to ensure that a final and binding decision was reached when the process was over. The parties would either leave the process with a mediated settlement agreement (a contract) or a binding arbitration award.[7]

In the classic form of med-arb, the neutral first works with the parties in the capacity of mediator. As mediator, the neutral engages in a process similar to that discussed in greater detail above.[8] In many circumstances, the mediator will engage in shuttle diplomacy and meet privately with each party for at least some portion of the time. During the course of the mediation, the mediator will be required to make assessments of the case, settlement value, legal arguments, party veracity, and other factors that may have an effect on how the mediator would decide the case, if need be. If the neutral settles the case as a mediator, then the case is resolved and the parties have an agreement that closes the neutral's involvement in the case.[9] If the neutral cannot settle the case, then the case switches from mediation to arbitration, and the mediator must change from the "mediator hat" to the "arbitrator hat."

The arbitration portion of the process should theoretically be relatively short. One of the benefits of med-arb is that the mediator is already familiar with the case, so the parties need not bring a new neutral up to speed. In some instances, the arbitrator does not hold a separate hearing for the arbitration portion; instead, the arbitrator will simply decide the case based on the information learned in mediation.[10] In some jurisdictions, such as Ohio, case law suggests that the arbitrator must hold a hearing on the merits because mediation communications are generally protected as confidential or privileged.[11] The Uniform Mediation Act specifically states that mediation communications are privileged and cannot be used in arbitrations.[12] In those jurisdictions, the parties must necessarily put into evidence anything on which they would like the arbitrator to rely.

---

4. Kristen M. Blankley, *Keeping a Secret from Yourself*, 63 Baylor L. Rev. 317, 323 (2011).

5. *Id*. at 330.

6. *Id*.

7. *See supra* Section 5.05 (discussing mediated settlement agreements) and Section 8.08 (discussing arbitration awards).

8. *See supra* Chapter 4.

9. Brian Pappas, *Med-Arb: The Best of Both Worlds May Be Too Good to Be True: A Response to Wiseman*, 19 No. 3 Disp. Resol. 42 (Spring 2013).

10. *Id*. at 330.

11. Bowden v. Weickert, No. S-02-017 (Ohio Ct. App. June 20, 2003).

12. Uniform Mediation Act § 2(7)(a) & § 4.

The benefits of med-arb then include the ability to combine mediation's flexibility with arbitration's finality.[13] The process is intended to be efficient by using the same neutral for both parts of the process.[14] The process, however, has some significant flaws that have drawn considerable criticism. Because the arbitration option is always looming in the background, parties in the mediation portion of the process do not have an incentive to be open, flexible, or candid about their situations or positions.[15] Instead, the parties will try to put the best case forward to support their position if the parties must resort to arbitration. In addition, the mediator may experience some confusion with the role of neutral, especially in determining whether information can and should be used from the mediation portion in the arbitration portion of the process. In particular, the mediator may not be able to separate out information learned in a caucus session with one party when the neutral issues an award.[16] Acareful in process design.

As a practical matter, few neutrals are comfortable with the med-arb process. Even parties who are interested in taking advantage of med-arb's efficiencies may have difficulty finding a neutral to conduct the process. Sophisticated parties may be better suited for the med-arb process because they can assess these strengths and weaknesses and may be better equipped for preparing for the nuances unique to med-arb.

[B] Ethical Issues in Med-Arb

Three primary issues of ethical concern surround med-arb. The first deals with the question of voluntariness and informed consent. The second concerns confidentiality. The third issue is whether the mediator can remain neutral during the process, especially after having learned confidential information. These ethical considerations are the primary reason few neutrals offer this process.

As discussed in the ethics portion of the Mediation Chapter,[17] mediation is a voluntary process founded on the principle of party autonomy and self-determination. Questions exist whether parties can give informed consent to a process such as med-arb when the neutral shifts hats during the middle of the process.[18] Whether consent is truly informed may depend on the sophistical level of the parties, the type of dispute at issue, and when in the process the parties give consent. Parties who agree to use med-arb prior to starting the mediation process arguably have more time to consider the process and its benefits and drawbacks prior to engaging in dispute resolution. Parties who switch from a planned mediation to med-arb upon reaching impasse may not fully appreciate how their choices in the mediation portion (i.e., choosing what to disclose and not to disclose) affect the arbitration portion.

---

13. Blankley, *supra* note 4, at 326.

14. Brian Pappas, *Med-Arb and the Legalization of Alternative Dispute Resolution*, 20 Harv. Negot. L. Rev. 157, 166–67 (2015).

15. *Id*. at 172.

16. Town of Clinton v. Geological Services Corp., 21 Mass. L. Rptr. 609 (Sup. Ct. Mass. 2006) (prohibiting discovery of mediation communications in the arbitration portion of the med-arb process).

17. *See supra* Chapter 5.10.

18. Jacqueline Nolan-Haley, *Mediation: The Best and Worst of Times*, 16 Cardozo J. Conflict Resol. 731, 735 (2015).

Parties who want to use the med-arb process should give their informed consent to the process in writing.[19] If the parties agree at the outset to the med-arb procedure, the written, informed consent signed by the parties should detail how the processes will work, which information will remain confidential, and how the neutral will know to switch from one process to the other, among other provisions. For a planned mediation that changes into med-arb, the neutral should endeavor to obtain informed consent in writing before the mediator begins the arbitration portion of the process. This document should detail, among other things, the parties' willingness to proceed and whether the mediation communications will be confidential in the arbitration portion.

Confidentiality is a significant ethical concern in the arbitration portion of the med-arb process. Confidentiality concerns are especially great if the mediator engaged in private caucus sessions and learned information that was otherwise confidential from the other parties involved.[20] In many situations, mediators will be privy to information learned in a private caucus session. Without informed consent, confidential information learned in mediation cannot be used in the arbitration portion of the process.[21] Participants in med-arb must have trust that the neutral will not, in fact, use confidential information to make an ultimate ruling in arbitration. Asking a decision-maker to disregard something heard during a process is not an altogether foreign concept. Judges and juries are often asked to disregard information offered into evidence.[22] If the parties do not trust the mediator to segregate the use of information between the processes, then med-arb is not the right form of dispute resolution for those parties.

The final ethical concern to address is neutrality. The mediator-arbitrator will be bound by neutrality requirements both from the codes of ethics of mediation[23] and the codes of ethics of arbitration.[24] During the mediation portion, the mediator must be keenly aware that the parties will be attempting to "spin" the mediator in the event that the parties cannot settle and the third party is required to issue a binding decision in the case.[25] During the mediation phase, the mediator may develop biases for or against a particular party, and those biases may impact the third party's decision in the arbitration portion of the process.[26]

[C] Med-Arb with Two Neutrals

In order to avoid the ethical issues that arise from single-neutral med-arb, parties could engage in the process using two neutrals—one as the mediator and a different neutral as the arbitrator. How these two neutrals work in the process can vary depending on how the parties would like to structure their process.

One option would be to simply switch from a mediator to an arbitrator in the case of impasse, and the parties would present their arbitration case to a different neutral. This procedure does not have the ethical issues regarding confidentiality and bias noted above,

---

19. Blankley, *supra* note 4, at
20. Pappas, *supra* note 14, at 172.
21. Blankley, *supra* note 4, at 361
22. *Id.* at 365–66.
23. *See supra* Section 5.10.
24. *See supra* Section 9.07.
25. Pappas, *supra* note 14, at 179.
26. *Id.* at 180.

but it does have some inefficiencies. The process would cost more than single-neutral med-arb because the parties would have to bring the new neutral up to speed on the dispute during the arbitration portion, and the whole of the process might be repetitive. On the other hand, the economic impact of putting on a full arbitration case following a complete, but unsuccessful, mediation, may be a financial incentive for the parties to settle their case during the mediation portion.

To cut down on some of those redundancies, other types of med-arb could be used instead. The second neutral (i.e., the arbitrator) could "shadow" the mediator during the mediation portion.[27] The arbitrator could "shadow" the mediator during the whole of the mediation or only during the parts that are in joint session.[28] If both neutrals are available for the whole of the session, then the arbitrator will be familiar with the case from the mediation portion, thus alleviating the amount of information that may need to be presented during the arbitration portion. For parties concerned about confidentiality, they could choose to have the arbitrator present only during joint sessions, when the information is openly discussed with all parties to the dispute. The primary drawback with using different-neutral med-arb is the cost of employing two neutrals, especially if both of those neutrals will be involved in all or part of the mediation session.

[D] Arbitration-Mediation

Another variant on med-arb is arbitration-mediation, or "arb-med" for short. As one might expect, the arbitration component occurs first, followed by a mediation.[29] At the conclusion of the arbitration, the neutral determines the award and puts the decision in a sealed envelope. The neutral then changes "hats" and becomes the mediator. The mediation process begins and if the parties settle in mediation, the parties' settlement controls. If the parties cannot agree on a settlement, then the neutral unseals the arbitration award, and that award governs the resolution of the dispute.

Arb-med has many of the advantages of med-arb. The process is relatively efficient and results in finality. The parties have an opportunity to resolve their dispute in a conciliatory manner, but that phase of the process occurs after the parties have already put on their arbitration cases. The process involves one neutral, which has certain cost-savings benefits, and when the parties arbitrate first, there is little risk that confidential information or other types of outside information would influence the arbitrator's decision. In other words, the ethical concerns of med-arb are largely alleviated in the arb-med process.

Some significant downsides still exist with this process. First, the process *always* includes arbitration and mediation, whereas med-arb may only involve the mediation component if the mediation settles the case. The guaranteed use of two processes is potentially inefficient if the case could have been settled simply with mediation. The process potentially takes longer, which may result in increased fees for attorneys and neutrals. Further, the "sealed envelope" lingers over the mediation process, and this dynamic may affect both the parties and the neutral. The parties may be more likely to settle in mediation, especially if the arbitration left lingering doubts in the minds of one or

---

27. Richard Fullerton, *Med-Arb and Its Variants: Ethical Issues for Parties and Neutrals*, 65-OCT Disp. Resol. J. 52 (2010).

28. *Id.*

29. *Id.*

more of the parties. The neutral must be careful not to give any impressions of the arbitration ruling when acting as a mediator. For evaluative mediators, this practice may be particularly difficult because the mediator may be expressing thoughts or giving recommendations based on the arbitration portion.

§ 10.03 Arbitration Variations

In addition to med-arb and arb-med, other variations of arbitration exist, and some of them have gained popularity in specific industries. This section considers four variations on arbitration, including baseball arbitration, high/low arbitration, document-only arbitration, and non-binding arbitration. These sections will highlight the processes, benefits and drawbacks of the processes, and any common ethical concerns arising in the area.

[A] Final Offer Arbitration, or "Baseball Arbitration"

Final offer arbitration, often called "baseball arbitration," is a type of arbitration popularized by Major League Baseball ("MLB"), and it is used by MLB as a final and binding method to resolve player salary disputes. A common criticism of arbitrators is that they "split the difference" and issue a compromise award, leaving both parties gaining something, losing something, and generally unhappy. In addition to widespread anecdotal evidence, some empirical evidence supports this finding.[30] In final-offer arbitration, each party submits a proposed award at the beginning of the arbitration, and then the arbitration proceeds as normal. At the conclusion of the arbitration, the arbitrators may *only* select one of the two proposed awards.[31] Consider a case involving money damages. The claimant side may request an award of $50,000 while the respondent requests an award of $10,000. After the presentation of the evidence, the arbitrator must make one decision: Do I award $50,000 or $10,000?

Because the arbitrators' award is limited to the two options presented by the parties, the parties have an economic incentive to be as reasonable as possible when presenting a potential award. The arbitrators will choose whichever award they consider the most reasonable, and this process forces each party to thoughtfully consider the settlement value of the claim. In practice, this process of determining a realistic award leads the parties to voluntarily settle because their proposed awards are numerically close and the parties can bridge the gap on their own. Only a small number of final-offer arbitrations proceed to a hearing. Most settle.

Major League Baseball has been using final-offer arbitration since 1974 to resolve conflicts regarding players' salaries.[32] In MLB, the arbitrator is asked to determine one issue: how much the player should make. The player and the team each have an hour to present their evidence of salaries made by comparable players, and both sides submit

---

30. Sara R. Cole & Kristen M. Blankley, Empirical Research on Consumer Arbitration: What the Data Reveals, College of Law, Faculty Publications, Paper 127 (2009).

31. Edward Brunet et al., Alternative Dispute Resolution: The Advocate's Perspective Cases and Materials 679 (4th ed. 2011).

32. *Id*. at 680.

documentary evidence, largely consisting of statistics of the player and similar players in the league.[33] Ultimately, the arbitrator must choose one of the two proposals if the case gets that far.

Outside of MLB salary arbitration, final-offer arbitration is used in a handful of other industries. In the area of collective bargaining, final-offer arbitration is sometimes employed during an interest arbitration (i.e., contract creation arbitration) in order to set the terms of a collective bargaining agreement.[34] Final-offer arbitration may also be ideal in cases involving a valuation, such as determining the value of real estate or even a business. Outside of valuation cases, many participants are afraid to take on the risk of losing entirely, and they opt for traditional arbitration instead. Final-offer arbitration is best suited for the resolution of a single issue. If the arbitration involves multiple issues, the arbitrators may have difficulty finding for one side on all of the issues. This process works best when the parties have a single issue, and it generally produces settlement because of the incentive to introduce reasonable results.

[B] High/Low Arbitration

High/Low arbitration is similar to final-offer arbitration, except that the arbitrators are not bound to select any particular submission, but the arbitrators may choose an award within a range capped by the parties. The parties put on a full arbitration case, but the arbitrator is limited to making a monetary award within the range that the parties have decided. In the example above, if the claimant chooses $50,000 and the respondent chooses $10,000, the arbitrator can make an award between and including $50,000 and $10,000.

In some instances of high/low arbitration, the arbitrator knows the range and then can make an award that falls within the range specified by the parties. In other instances, the parties determine the range in confidence and do not tell the arbitrator. Then the parties put on their cases, and the arbitrator makes an award. If the award falls outside of the range agreed to by the parties, then the award becomes the top or bottom amount of the range. If the range is $50,000 to $10,000, and the arbitrator awards $16,000, then the award of $16,000 would stand. If the arbitrator awarded $66,000, then the award would be reduced to $50,000 on the agreement of the parties.

High/low arbitration gives the parties some assurances as to the maximum each party could gain or lose. High/low arbitration minimizes the risk that each party will take in the arbitration. On the contrary, parties may feel remorseful after an arbitration if the arbitrator did or would have awarded more than the maximum on either side of the scale. Because high/low arbitration deals with monetary amounts, it is best suited for disputes involving damages or other payments of money.

[C] Document-Only Arbitration

Some arbitrations do not involve a live hearing. If no live hearing is required, the arbitrator will read the written submissions and make a determination based on the document submissions only. Document-only cases are generally more cost- and time-efficient

---

33. *Id.*
34. *Id.* at 681.

because the parties do not have to pay for the time of attorneys and arbitrators for the hearing. Cases most suitable for document-only arbitration are those that are simple and involve few disputed items.

Arbitrators often decide cases on the papers in consumer cases, notably consumer credit cases. In many consumer credit cases, little dispute exists regarding whether the consumer actually received the goods or services at issue. In addition, many of these cases involve no dispute regarding the costs of the goods or services. These cases involve a single issue—i.e., what amount the consumer should pay—and the arbitrator can determine the issue without the need for an oral presentation. Some of these cases involve a respondent who defaults in the arbitration, but the claimant must still put on evidence. In most of these cases, the claimant creditor wins in whole or in part.[35]

Some arbitration providers have special rules for document-only arbitration. The American Arbitration Association, for example, has a rule permitting the procedure,[36] as well as a set of guidelines for the procedure. The document-only process is significantly shorter than the traditional process, and the parties generally only meet once or twice by telephone.[37] The procedure is intended for claims and counterclaims of less than $25,000, but the process is available for all parties who would prefer a document submission in lieu of a live hearing.[38] Arbitration providers that have special rules for document-only arbitrations are only one way of instituting this procedure. The parties may decide on a case-by-case basis that a hearing is unnecessary and have the parties rule on the case based on the submissions.

[D] Non-Binding Arbitration

Non-binding arbitration is an arbitration in which the arbitrator's ruling is not binding on the parties. The award is advisory only, and it does not carry any weight. In essence, the purpose of the arbitration award is to help the parties determine what a case is worth and its settlement value. The award only becomes binding if both parties agree to be bound by it. Otherwise, either party (or both parties) may reject the award and the parties may seek a trial de novo.

Courts do not have the ability to send parties to binding arbitration. If a court orders parties to arbitrate their case in a traditional, binding arbitration, then the court is viewed as having abrogated its powers and deprived the parties of their right to a trial under the Seventh Amendment.[39] On the other hand, courts may order parties to attempt non-binding arbitration because either party may request a trial de novo following the procedure, and the ability to request a trial preserves the parties' Seventh

---

35. Sarah R. Cole & Kristen M. Blankley, *supra* note 30.

36. American Arbitration Association, Consumer Rules, R-29 (Documents-Only Procedure. "Disputes may be resolved by submission of documents and without in-person or telephonic hearings. For cases being decided by the submission of documents only, the *Procedures for the Resolution of Disputes through Document Submission* (found at the end of these Rules) shall supplement these Rules.").

37. American Arbitration Association, Consumer Rules, Procedures for the Resolution of Disputes Through Document Submission.

38. *Id.*

39. Kimberly J. Mann, *Constitutional Challenges to Court Ordered Arbitration*, 24 Fla. St. U. L. Rev. 1055 (1997).

Amendment rights.[40] Local court rules that provide for non-binding arbitration also explain how parties can receive a trial if one or both parties reject the arbitrator's decision.[41]

Non-binding arbitration is not widely utilized, and some courts are taking the power to refer cases to non-binding arbitration out of their local rules.[42] Non-binding arbitration is a potentially expensive option because the parties take on the obligation to put on a full arbitration hearing with the risk that one or more parties will disagree with the arbitrator's decision and require a trial before a judge. The advisory function served by the arbitrator is now largely filled by evaluative mediators and early neutral evaluators. These types of neutrals also give an evaluation of the value of a case, but they do not require the same level of presentation (particularly witness testimony) as an arbitration hearing.

§ 10.04 Online Dispute Resolution

Online dispute resolution ("ODR") uses technology to help parties resolve their dispute. Parties have been using ODR since the 1990s to aid in the dispute resolution process.[43] ODR is essentially the synergy of ADR and computer technology. The field of ODR includes the use of any computer assistance in dispute resolution. In some instances, ODR processes are entirely online, from claim submission to resolution. In most other instances, the dispute resolution is partly online and partly in person. In the broadest sense, ODR includes the use of email messaging, video conferencing, online forums, text messaging, cloud storage, group editing of documents, and other electronic means of communication.

ODR can be used for nearly any kind of dispute. Many disputes that arise from an online purchase or other type of online activity may be best resolved online. That said, many disputes that occur in real life may also benefit from ODR, depending on the circumstances. This section considers the advantages and disadvantages of ODR and then discusses how ODR may be used in negotiation, mediation, and arbitration.

[A] Advantages and Disadvantages of Online Dispute Resolution

The use of technology for dispute resolution purposes has any number of advantages and disadvantages, depending on the circumstances, the parties, and the dispute. The

---

40. Riggs v. Scrivner, Inc., 927 F.2d 1146, 1148 (10th Cir. 1991) (finding no Seventh Amendment violation because of ability to request trial de novo by either party).

41. *See, e.g.*, Florida Rules of Civil Procedure, R. 1.820(h) (2015) (Hearing Procedures for Non-Binding Arbitration); Order Adopting Rules Governing Alternative Dispute Resolution and Nevada Mediation Rules and Amending the Nevada Arbitration Rules and Nevada Short Trial Rules, Nevada Arbitration Rules, Rule 18 (2013).

42. In September 2015, the Northern District of California abrogated its rules on non-binding arbitration. *See* Northern District of California, Alternative Dispute Resolution and Local Rules, available at http://www.cand.uscourts.gov/localrules.

43. Ethan Katsh & Janet Rifkin, Online Dispute Resolution: Resolving Conflicts in Cyberspace (2001).

decision to use ODR, in whole or in part, should be determined on a case-by-case basis and with the consent of the parties.

Efficiency is perhaps the biggest advantage of ODR. The parties only need to have access to a computer or other electronic device to connect them for the dispute resolution process. Travel time is essentially eliminated when the parties use ODR. For parties who live a great distance apart, reducing or eliminating travel time may be the difference between attempting to resolve the dispute and simply treating losses as sunk costs.[44] If an American consumer buys a $35.00 dress from a Chinese retailer online and the dress does not meet the standards set forth in the description, the buyer likely has two choices — pursue a form of dispute resolution online or drop the issue. The consumer is not likely to travel to China to sue the company over the low-value item, and the Chinese company may not be subject to the courts in the United States. Commercial disputes are not the only ones that involve parties at great distances. Family cases, including divorce actions, probate matters, and elder care situations, may involve parties from across the country, and electronic means may help all parties participate in a meaningful manner.

Most people have the equipment needed to engage in online dispute resolution, and the forum is generally inexpensive to use. Personal computers and mobile devices are common, and many people already have access to the Internet, email addresses, and other basic computer software. Features such as webcams are often built into computers and laptops, and if not, they are relatively inexpensive to purchase and easy to install.

Communications in ODR may be done either in real time ("synchronously") or separated in time ("asynchronously"). Asynchronous communications have some distinct advantages compared to real-time communications. Parties have time to read and react to the communications, and they can respond in a way that is not fueled by emotions. Asynchronous communications also result in a record, which can be helpful in determining issues that had or had not been discussed or resolved.[45]

ODR can be even less formal than traditional ADR processes. Because people can participate in ODR from home and sight unseen (if using text-based communication messages), parties need not dress up for the process (and they may even participate in their pajamas). Participating from one's own home may make the process more comfortable, which may encourage more people to resolve their disputes.

ODR also has disadvantages. If the atmosphere is too informal, the parties may not take the process seriously. While resolving a dispute in one's pajamas may sound comfortable and convenient, too much informality may hamper the gravitas inherent in some dispute resolution processes. The processes may also be unfamiliar, and the parties may not understand what is expected of them or how the protocol works.

Although most people have access to the technology needed for a successful ODR process, not all people have computers or mobile phones.[46] Friends and families may be able to assist, and sometimes people may be able to access computers, webcams, and other conference technology at local libraries or schools. Before trying the ODR

---

44. Charles T. Autry et al., *Mediation: Effective Resolution of Contract Disputes*, Management Q. Vol. 46 (2005).

45. Randy Winn, *Issue-Spotting in Technology and Law Practice 2000–2005*, 53 Wash. St. B. News 41, 43 (1999).

46. Monica Anderson, *Technology Device Ownership: 2015*, Pew Research Center (Oct. 29, 2015).

process, the parties or neutral should determine whether everyone has the correct technology for the chosen process.

Security, especially online security, may be problematic in ODR. Security concerns may occur in one of two ways. First, because ODR does not put the parties face-to-face, other people may be helping one or more of the parties "behind the scenes" or "off camera," when the other party expects only the parties to be participating. For example, if the parties to an online divorce mediation expect that the husband and wife will be participating by themselves via webcam, security expectations may be compromised if a spouse's new significant other is sitting just out of view of the camera and providing feedback to the party regarding negotiating stances. Online security is another concern.[47] Video conferences, cloud networking, email systems, and other programs and platforms may be subject to hacking attacks. Information that needs to be stored may be compromised or lost. The converse may also be true—information that needs to be destroyed may be saved for all eternity. In addition to outside threats, electronic communications may lead to increased incidents of inadvertent disclosure of confidential, privileged, or otherwise inappropriate information. Emails may be sent to the wrong recipients, attachments may contain metadata, or incorrect documents may be electronically sent. Although ethical rules may govern these situations,[48] parties, lawyers, third parties, and others need to be vigilant in how they structure electronic communications.

Although listed as an advantage, asynchronous communications may also have disadvantages. Human communication is primarily derived from non-verbal communication. As much as 55 percent of a person's meaning can be detected from the body language of the speaker.[49] The tone, tenor, and tempo of a person's voice makes up roughly the next 38 percent of the speaker's meaning.[50] People can detect confidence, weakness, humor, sarcasm, and other characteristics from the way a person speaks. The words of the message, then, constitute only roughly seven percent of the meaning.[51] Online dispute resolution often uses text-based, telephone, and web conferencing-based methods of communication. Text-based messages lose a significant amount of information because the recipient can only guess as to the tenor, tone, and tempo intended by the speaker, and nonverbal communication is nonexistent. The recipient of the message may incorrectly guess as to the meaning, and human psychology often guides people into making incorrect assumptions.[52] Telephone and web conferencing add back some of these communication elements, but they are imperfect given limitations in technology. Text-based communications may also be cumbersome and inefficient given the time needed to draft and revise.[53]

Finally, the parties must have an appropriate level of sophistication with technology. Although more and more people are becoming competent with computer and Internet technology, gaps may still exist in knowledge of general computing or specific software.

---

47. Noam Ebner and John Zeleznikow, *Fairness, Trust, and Security in Online Dispute Resolution*, 36 Hamline J. Pub. L. & Pol'y 143 (2015).

48. *See, e.g.*, Model Rules of Prof'l Conduct r. 1.6(c), 4.4(b).

49. Albert Mehrabian, Silent Messages: Implicit Communication of Emotions and Attitudes (2d ed. 1981).

50. *Id.*

51. *Id.*

52. Charles R. Craver, Effective Legal Negotiation 233 (7th ed. 2012).

53. *Id.*

Parties and neutrals may need to have training sessions or other educational opportunities prior to beginning the ODR process in order to participate in a meaningful way.

Given the advantages and disadvantages, parties should carefully consider using ODR in whole or in part. Many disputes are well-suited for ODR, and some disputes with parties spanning a great distance may only be served by ODR. For parties where in-person dispute resolution is available, ODR may still be an option for any number of reasons, including cost efficiency, safety, and personal comfort. The remainder of this section details how ODR is commonly used in negotiation, mediation, and arbitration.

[B] Online Negotiation

Online negotiation may happen informally or with the help of computer technology. Online negotiation may be as simple as a transaction that takes place solely through email. Websites such as Craigslist work by placing an online ad and then inviting respondents to reply by email, text, or telephone.[54] The prices for items for sale on Craigslist and similar websites[55] are often negotiable, and the buyers and sellers may make a series of offers and counteroffers before arriving at a negotiated deal. Once the parties agree on terms, the contract may be completed by meeting in person for the exchange or the parties can negotiate a way to exchange goods for payment electronically or through the mail.

Some parties may wish to negotiate online even when the parties have a face-to-face relationship. Lawyers on opposite sides of a lawsuit may want to negotiate the terms of a discovery schedule through email communications, or exchanged documents online in order to preserve a record or to carefully craft the terms of the arrangement. Divorced parents may only communicate through text messaging or email communications because they have difficulty communicating over the telephone or in person. An employee may not have the courage to ask for a raise in person, but using email communication might be a way to get the conversation started.

Most of these examples are examples of "deal-making" negotiations. Deal-making negotiations look toward the future and forge new relationships. Deal-making negotiations can be contrasted with dispute-settling negotiations, which are backward-looking and seek to redress a wrong that already occurred.[56] Online negotiation may also be used in dispute-settling negotiations. Parties may try to negotiate the terms of a settlement by email, telephone, video conference, or text message. Emails may include attached documents that go through a series of edits by multiple people.

Some software exists to resolve online disputes through negotiation. Software packages can ask parties for their maximum "bids" and then mathematically determine the economically "best" settlement if the maximums on both sides overlap.[57] Software can also suggest a settlement—usually a midpoint—if the parties' maximums do not

---

54. www.craigslist.com

55. Social media sites such as Facebook host community pages that operate as fora for community buying and selling. Message boards and other online sites also facilitate buying and selling items locally.

56. FRANK E.A. SANDER & JEFFREY Z. RUBIN, THE JANUS QUALITY OF NEGOTIATION: DEAL-MAKING AND DISPUTE SETTLEMENT, 4 Negotiation J. 109 (1988).

57. Joseph W. Goodman, *The Pros and Cons of Online Dispute Resolution*, 2 DUKE L. & TECH. 2 (2003)

overlap. These types of programs can automate the process of bidding and speed up the negotiations. Programs such as these were used by eBay for a while to resolve disputes on its website, but they ultimately abandoned this program in favor of mediation.[58] The most successful fully automated system for online dispute resolution using a bidding process is Cybersettle, and studies of the program demonstrated that parties who used the process saved significant amounts of time, money, and legal expenses.[59]

[C] Online Mediation

Mediation can take place partially or wholly online. In many cases, traditional mediation is assisted through the use of technology. When parties are a great distance apart or if safety reasons dictate that they cannot be brought together, the parties may be able to meet with a mediator wholly or partially online. A mediator may be physically present with one or more of the parties, while other parties may join by telephone or online video conferencing. This type of arrangement may be ideal when one party lives close geographically to the mediator while other parties live farther away. Some risks accompany a partially online mediation. The mediator may bond more readily and communicate better with the party in the room, thus raising concerns about bias.[60] Mediators must also be sure that their security systems are sufficient to avoid breaches of confidentiality.[61] If the parties give informed consent after understanding the risks, then a partially online mediation may meet the needs of the parties.

A mediation may also be fully online using standard technology, such as Skype, Adobe Connect, Fuze, Zoom, or other commercially available software. If all parties are online, including the mediator, then the bias associated with physical proximity with fewer than all the parties would be eliminated. On the other hand, miscommunications and technical difficulties may increase as more and more people rely on their own technology. Mediators should be sure that they are competent with the technology and that the parties are competent as well. Mediators may be required to educate the parties as to the intricacies of the technology—such as how to gain access to the software or how to disconnect during private sessions. If one party requires much more assistance than another, the mediator should be careful to not demonstrate bias toward or against the party that requires additional assistance.[62]

Some companies have mediation-specific software that can be used for dispute resolution. The American Arbitration Association will provide access to software for a virtual mediation for cases involving less than $10,000.[63] AAA's process is cost-effective, and they resolve the cases in a relatively short time frame.[64] The software that AAA provides allows for parties to take advantage of web conferencing and text messaging, and the program will support both joint sessions and private meetings with fewer than all of

---

58. Ethan Katsh et al., *E-Commerce, E-Disputes, and E-Dispute Resolution: In the Shadow of "Ebay Law,"* 15 Ohio St. J. Disp. Resol. 705 (2000).

59. Susan Nauss Exon, Advanced Guide for Mediators 367 (2014).

60. Model Standards of Conduct for Mediators, Standard II.

61. Model Standards of Conduct for Mediators, Standard V.

62. Model Standards of Conduct for Mediators, Standards II and IV.

63. American Arbitration Association, Welcome to the Online Experience, *at* http://services.adr.org/eroom/faces/welcome_and_steps.jspx.

64. *Id.* In 2016, the AAA will provide this service for a flat fee if $200.00 and seek to have the dispute mediated within 30 days.

the parties.[65] Modria is a company that offers an online dispute resolution platform aimed at disputes involving ecommerce.[66] The Modria system first offers the buyer and seller an automated attempt at resolving the dispute, but online mediation is available if the automated process is unsuccessful.[67]

At least one researcher is trying to determine if mediation should be conducted using smartphone technology, as opposed to computer technology. Giuseppe Leone, the Director and Founder of Virtual Mediation Lab, suggests that mediation using mobile telephone technology has two advantages over traditional online mediation.[68] First, mobile technology is even more convenient and portable than computers and laptops. Second, mobile phones can act as a video projector or camera used to show physical evidence that might be at issue in a mediation.[69] In a situation involving home repairs gone awry, a party could use the camera on the phone to show, in real time, the condition of the claimed botched work.[70]

These examples show how online mediation can take place in a wide variety of ways. As technology continues to evolve, opportunities for online mediation will also continue to evolve. As parties and mediators can take advantage of these new opportunities, mediators must ensure that the parties have given informed consent to the process.

[D] Online Arbitration

Online arbitration, like online mediation, can take place wholly or partially online. While few arbitrations take place wholly online, many arbitrations use complex software for online case management. The Financial Industry Regulatory Authority ("FINRA") oversees the administration of the arbitration of nearly every dispute in the securities arena. FINRA operates the "DR Portal," which is its online case management system.[71] For the neutrals, the DR Portal allows the arbitrators to view case documents, case information, hearing information, and the ability to change the arbitrator's disclosure statement.[72] Parties can use the portal to view and submit documents, schedule hearing dates, and rank arbitrators for the purpose of arbitrator selection.[73] Pre-hearing conferences (including resolution of discovery disputes) often take place by telephone. In other words, nearly the whole of the FINRA process takes place online or telephonically, other than the hearing on the merits.

Other organizations are expanding into online arbitration, offering entirely online methods of arbitration. For instance, the World Intellectual Property Organization ("WIPO") is seeking to use online arbitration to deal with intellectual property concerns across the globe.[74] The type of technology needed for an all-online arbitration would

---

65. Id.

66. Modria, *The Modria Platform*, at http://modria.com/product/.

67. Modria, *How It Works*, at http://modria.com/how-it-works/.

68. Virtual Mediation Lab, *at* http://www.virtualmediationlab.com/.

69. Jenna Blakely, *Honolulu's Giuseppe Leone Launching Mobile Mediation*, Pacific Bus. News (May 20, 2013), available at http://www.bizjournals.com/pacific/blog/2013/05/honolulus-giuseppe -leone-launching.html.

70. *Id.*

71. *See* FINRA, DR Portal, *at* https://www.finra.org/arbitration-and-mediation/dr-portal.

72. *Id.*

73. *Id.*

74. WIPO, On-Line Arbitration, at http://www.wipo.int/amc/en/arbitration/online

likely need to include a combination of live video conferencing, document display, and a way to submit documents and other evidence. In international disputes, translating services would also need to be available. But because arbitrators are finders of fact, they may not be comfortable taking testimony via video or telephone conferencing. As technology continues to advance, more and more dispute resolution may take place online. Whether ODR suits a particular situation may depend on the case and the provider organization.

§ 10.05 Ombuds Procedures

The term "ombuds" is a modern version of the term "ombudsman" (or, less commonly, "ombudswoman"). The ombuds process originates from Scandinavia, and the United States' version draws from its Scandinavian roots.[75] The ombuds duties include both investigative and conciliatory aspects. Ombuds are embedded neutrals, working within the organization they serve.

Ombuds work in both the governmental and private sectors. Many states and governmental organizations have an ombuds office or an ombuds who works within the specific agency. For example, the State of Nebraska Legislature established an ombuds office, which it calls the Office of Public Counsel.[76] The Office of Public counsel investigates and resolves citizen complaints. Many public universities have an ombuds office to handle student and other complaints. Ombuds offices are also found in a number of large businesses. Hospitals, nursing homes, and large employers may have an ombudsperson on staff to resolve issues involving employees, customers, or other complaints.

Although an ombuds is generally an embedded neutral paid as a staff member of the governmental agency or large business, the role of the ombuds is to be independent. When a complaint is lodged, the ombuds will read the complaint, take it seriously, conduct factual investigations (such as talk to witnesses or examine documents), and help the parties resolve the dispute in a mutually beneficial way. Many ombuds consider themselves advocates for a fair process, as opposed to advocates for the employer. An ombuds office will only be successful if the atmosphere created by the ombuds is safe. In other words, the office gains legitimacy when people trust the process, trust the office, and trust that the ombuds is neutral. Many ombuds handle employment disputes within the organization. For the office to be effective, employees must trust the ombuds to be neutral. Ombuds services are generally confidential. The confidential nature of the office also helps instill trust in the process and allows the ombuds to remain impartial.[77]

---

75. Eric S. Adcock, *Federal Privilege in the Ombudsman's Process*, 8 Charleston L. Rev. 1, 13 (2013).

76. Office of Public Counsel, *at* http://nebraskalegislature.gov/divisions/ombud.php.

77. Adock, *supra* note 75, at 13.

§ 10.06 Summary Jury Trials and Mini Trials

The summary jury trial and mini trial are two distinct types of dispute resolution that may be confused with one another. Both involve abbreviated trial-like presentations with the purpose of helping parties settle cases before a binding trial procedure. The attorneys and clients can use these processes when settlement negotiations have stalled and the parties have significantly different ideas regarding the value of the case, or when both parties have significantly overvalued each side of the case. These types of procedures are well-suited for cases involving money damages, such as personal injury cases, product liability cases, and contract cases.

The summary jury trial is a procedure that will render a non-binding verdict that can be used as an advisory settlement. Former Judge Thomas D. Lambros of the Northern District of Ohio is credited with the creation of the summary jury trial, a process he envisioned to help resolve personal injury cases.[78] The summary jury trial is a court-annexed process, and courts have the inherent power to order parties to comply with the process.[79] In the summary jury trial, the lawyers for each case empanel a limited number of jurors (usually six) and make an abbreviated trial presentation, such as a half a day or so.[80] The procedure is usually run by a judge or magistrate, and the jurors used are actual jurors called for jury duty.[81] The attorneys may have a small number of peremptory challenges to the potential jurors. The lawyers make opening and closing remarks, and they present most of the evidence to the jurors (as opposed to calling witnesses).[82] The process varies from one jurisdiction to another, and some jurisdictions allow the lawyers to call witnesses, in addition to the lawyers' presentations.[83] Following the presentation of evidence and the lawyers' arguments, the presiding judge gives the jurors limited jury instructions, and the jury has time to deliberate and render a non-binding "verdict."[84] The lawyers in the case also have the opportunity to discuss with the jurors their rationale for their verdict and their understanding of the evidence.[85]

Summary jury trials are available as a form of alternative dispute resolution in approximately 39 federal judicial districts.[86] In the vast majority of cases—more than 90 percent of the time—cases settle within one week of learning the jury's verdict.[87] These procedures, while less expensive than a trial, may still be quite costly. A summary jury trial works best after the close of discovery, when the parties are ready to make trial presentations and test their legal theories. Compared to a trial, this summary procedure is less expensive. The presentations often last less than a day, and expert witnesses are

---

78. Judge Thomas D. Lambros, *The Summary Jury Trial and Other Forms of Alternative Dispute Resolution*, 103 F.R.D. 461 (1984).

79. *Id.* at 469.

80. *Id.* at 468–69.

81. *Id.* at 470.

82. *Id.*

83. National Center for State Courts, *The Evolution of the Summary Jury Trial: A Flexible Tool to Meet a Variety of Needs*, available at http://www.ncsc.org/sitecore/content/microsites/future -trends-2012/home/Better-Courts/1-3-Evolution-of-the-Summary-Jury-Trial.aspx#_ftnref1.

84. Donna Shetowsky, *Improving Summary Jury Trials: Insights from Psychology*, 18 Ohio St. J. Disp. Resol. 469, 472 (2003).

85. *See id.* at 472–73.

86. *Id.* at 471.

87. *Id.* at 474.

not present. Summary jury trials are particularly useful when both sides suffer from an overconfidence bias and cannot make headway in settling the case on their own.

The mini-trial also involves a trial-like presentation. This method of dispute resolution has traditionally been utilized in complex business cases between companies.[88] The lawyers make a presentation of the case, usually after discovery has closed. Unlike the summary jury trial, the audience for the mini-trial is a group of corporate representatives who have the authority to settle the case.[89] The purpose of the mini-trial is to expose the principals of the organizations to the strengths and weaknesses of the case — as well as the strengths and weaknesses of the other side. Following the lawyer's presentations, the corporate representatives may ask questions of the lawyers. After all questions are answered, the principals have the ability to try to settle the case on their own with their new perspectives on the case.

Unlike the summary jury trial, the mini-trial is a private procedure. This process does not involve the use of a judge or magistrate, and no jurors are present to give their opinions. Both sides must agree to take part in the process, and requesting a mini-trial may make the requesting party appear weak.[90] The mini-trial has many of the same advantages and disadvantages of the summary jury trial, particularly as they relate to the timing of the process and the costs. The mini-trial, too, is helpful when the parties have vastly differing views of the value of the case, and these contrasting viewpoints have led to a settlement stalemate.

§ 10.07 Early Neutral Evaluation

Early Neutral Evaluation ("ENE") is a process during which parties make abbreviated presentations of the case to a neutral, third-party evaluator. One of the first courts to adopt ENE procedures was the Northern District of California in the mid-1980s.[91] Unlike summary jury trial, the ENE process occurs much earlier in the life of a disputed case. The process can be ordered by a court in a court-connected process, or ENE can occur based on private agreement of the parties. ENE might benefit a wide variety of cases, but it is most commonly used in business disputes. Some jurisdictions also utilize ENE in domestic matters, such as divorce and child custody cases.[92] In Florida, the insurance industry regularly uses ENE in order to resolve cases involving sinkholes.[93]

The South Carolina courts define ENE as a process in which "the parties and their counsel, in a confidential session, make compact presentations of their claims and defenses, including applicable evidence as developed at the time of the evaluation, and receive a non-binding evaluation of the matters in controversy by an evaluator."[94] The

---

88. Elizabeth Sherowski, *Hot Coffee, Cold Cash: Making the Most of Alternative Dispute Resolution in High[-Stakes Personal Injury Lawsuits*, 11 Ohio St. J. Disp. Resol. 521, 529 (1996)

89. *Id*. at 530.

90. *Id*. at 531.

91. David I. Levine, *Northern District of California Adopts Early Neutral Evaluation to Expedite Dispute Resolution*, 72 Judicature 235 (1989).

92. Jordan Leigh Santeramo, *Early Neutral Evaluation in Divorce Cases*, 42 Fam. Ct. Rev. 321 (2004).

93. *See* Citizens Prop. Ins. Co. v. Trapeo, 136 So. 670 (D. Ct. App. Fl. 2014); Morejon v. Am. Sec. Ins. Co., 829 F. Supp. 2d 1258 (M.D. Fl. 2011).

94. South Carolina ADR Rules, R. 14.

evaluator may also assist "in identifying areas of agreement, offer[ing] case planning suggestions and assist[ing] the parties in settlement discussions."[95] Colorado similarly defined ENE as "an early intervention in a lawsuit by a court-appointed evaluator, to narrow, eliminate, and simplify issues and assist in case planning and management. Settlement of the case may occur under early neutral evaluation."[96]

During the ENE process, the lawyers give a truncated presentation of the case. The presentation consists of a factual and legal summary, summarizing potential witness statements and documentary evidence.[97] The neutral considers the presentations and has great freedom to give an evaluation on a wide variety of matters, including the strengths and weaknesses of the parties' claims and arguments, the likelihood of liability, damages assessments, likely litigation costs, and potential settlement options.[98] The process is confidential. Courts have the power to order parties to try the ENE process, either from court rule or by relying on inherent powers.[99]

The ENE process has the benefit of having an outside evaluator weigh in and give thoughts on the case early. Even if ENE does not settle the case, the process may result in the narrowing of claims or limiting the scope of damages. Because ENE happens so early in the life of the case, the parties have the ability to save considerable time and money. On the other hand, the timing of the presentation may be too early in the process before the parties understand the legal landscape and all of the available evidence. Before engaging in this type of process, the parties should understand the risks associated with the timing of ENE.

§ 10.08 Restorative Justice Processes

Restorative justice processes apply the use of ADR to criminal law and other situations involving wrongdoing. Unlike the traditional criminal model, restorative justice is a victim-centered approach to crime.[100] In the criminal justice system, the victims of crime have little autonomy in the process. Victims do not get to decide trial strategy; they do not have a chance to ask questions of the offenders; and they only participate in the process if they are called as a witness to testify at trial. Dr. Mark Umbreit has likened victims in the criminal justice system to little more than pieces of evidence controlled by the prosecutors.[101] "Marsy's Law," in the California Victim's Bill of Rights Act of 2008, advocated by the family of Marsy Nicolas who was murdered by an ex-boyfriend, guarantees victims the right to be notified and heard at every stage of legal criminal proceedings.

Restorative justice processes view crime as a wrong to individuals as well as a wrong to the community or the fabric of society. Restorative processes, then, seek to remedy the harm done by the offender to make the victim and the community whole. In contrast, the traditional criminal justice system typically considers "the state" to be the wronged

---

95. *Id.*
96. Colorado Stat. § 13-22-302(2) (Colorado Dispute Resolution Act).
97. *See generally* WAYNE D. BRAZIL, EARLY NEUTRAL EVALUATION 4–9 (2012).
98. South Carolina ADR Rules, R. 15.
99. *See, e.g.*, Wis. Stat. 802.12(2).
100. MARK UMBREIT, THE HANDBOOK OF VICTIM OFFENDER MEDIATION xxvii (2001).
101. *Id.* at 87.

party, and the prosecutor has the ability to act on behalf of the state. Restorative practices actively use collaboration and problem-solving techniques in order to repair the loss suffered to specific persons and specific communities, as opposed to the "state" at large. Restorative justice can be defined as "a process to involve, to the extent possible, those who have a stake in a specific offense and to collectively identify and address harms, needs, and obligations, in order to heal and put things as right as possible."[102]

Restorative practices could theoretically be used to resolve any type of crime. A system of restorative justice generally meets the following nine criteria:

1. focus on the harms of wrongdoing more than the rules that have been broken;

2. show equal concern and commitment to victims and offenders, involving both in the process of justice;

3. work toward the restoration of victims, empowering them and responding to their needs as they see them;

4. support offenders while encouraging them to understand, accept, and carry out their obligations;

5. recognize that while obligations may be difficult for offenders, they should not be intended as harms, and they must be achievable;

6. provide opportunities for dialogue, direct or indirect, between victims and offenders as appropriate;

7. involve and empower the affected community through the justice process, and increase its capacity to recognize and respond to community bases of crime;

8. encourage collaboration and reintegration rather than coercion and isolation;

9. give attention to the unintended consequences of our actions and programs; and

10. show respect to all parties including victims, offenders, and justice colleagues.[103]

Given these guiding criteria, any wrongdoing may be suited for restorative justice. In practice, restorative justice has been used in a wide variety of situations, including crimes involving both juvenile and adult offenders. In recent years, restorative justice programs have found particular success with juvenile offenders. For juvenile offenders, this type of intervention may reduce recidivism and serve as an early intervention so that these young people may turn away from future criminal activity.

Although any type of offender and any type of offense may be suitable for restorative justice practices, many programs focus on property crimes, as opposed to personal crimes. With property crimes, the victim is readily identified (property owner), and the emotional content may not be overwhelming. Crimes such as theft, vandalism, and burglary are well-suited to these processes, even if the victim is a corporate entity (such as a store) and not an individual person (such as a homeowner). Violent crimes may also be appropriate for restorative justice practices, whether they involve strangers or loved ones.[104] Some jurisdictions are also employing these types of practices in cases of violence between people of different ethnic groups, such as cases involving hate crimes.[105]

---

102. Howard Zehr, Changing Lenses 130 (1990).

103. Mark Umbreit et al., *Restorative Justice in the Twenty-First Century: A Social Movement Full of Opportunities and Pitfalls*, 89 Marq. L. Rev. 251, 258–59 (2005).

104. *Id.* at 265.

105. *Id.*

"Victimless" crimes, such as drug possession or traffic violations are generally not good candidates for restorative practices.

For restorative practices to be successful, the program needs the support of many stakeholders. Because these practices are at the intersection of ADR and criminal law, it is imperative to have the support of the prosecuting authorities, such as the district, county, city, or state attorneys. Without the support of the prosecuting authority, a restorative justice program will not succeed on a system-wide level. With juvenile offenders, cases may also initiate from individual schools or school districts, even when the child is not facing criminal charges. On individual cases, the process also requires buy-in from the offender. Because restorative justice processes are based on making individual victims and communities whole, many programs require that the offender be willing to admit fault and work to repair the harm done to the victim or society.

Interestingly, victim participation may not be necessary to have a successful restorative practice process. Restorative processes are victim-sensitive processes, recognizing that not all victims want to participate. If a victim does not want to participate, most of these processes can still proceed with a "victim surrogate." That victim surrogate may be a person who was the victim of a similar crime or simply an interested community member. Victim surrogates who have been victims of similar crimes may have a perspective that they can share with the offender in order to share the perspective of what it is like to be a victim of crime. Interested community members can also fill this role by relaying to the offender how crimes can have a detrimental effect on the community.

Different programs may have different requirements for when the restorative justice process happens. An offender may have the opportunity to participate in the process as part of a diversion program that would prevent the offense from showing up on the offender's record. Other programs may use this program as part of probation, which would occur after a person pleads guilty to the crime. In schools, restorative practices may be alternatives to suspensions, so that children do not miss too much school or drop out.

The two most common types of restorative practices in the criminal arena are victim-offender mediation and circle processes, which are discussed in turn. This section also explains the process of family group conferencing, which is a program that can help place children whose parents have engaged in abuse or neglect of their children. Although these processes involve remedying different types of wrongs, they all have a basis in restoring the victim, the community and, in some cases, the family.

[A] Victim-Offender Conferences or Mediation

Victim-offender mediation, which is often called victim-offender conferencing, is one of the most widely used restorative justice practices. This practice has been used in the United States for more than four decades, and empirical research repeatedly validates its use in the criminal justice system.[106] Victim-offender mediation programs have involved both juveniles and adults, and are used in both property and violent crimes.

Victim-offender mediations are facilitated by trained mediators or facilitators. The purpose of the conference, however, is not the same as traditional mediation.

---

106. *Id.* at 282; *see also* ADR HANDBOOK FOR JUDGES 197 (Donna Stienstra & Susan M. Yates eds., 2004)

Traditional mediation, as discussed in Chapter 4,[107] largely focuses on coming to a resolution and solving the conflict between the parties. Traditional mediators also generally shy away from determining fault. In contrast, victim-offender mediation is focused on repairing harm between parties to the community. The offender will generally admit responsibility for the wrongdoing and try to make reparations.[108] In some programs, the case is not appropriate for mediation unless the offender has admitted fault and is willing to make reparations.[109]

Pre-session preparations with both the victim and the offender are critical to the success of a conference. Many mediators routinely meet privately with the parties or their attorneys prior to a mediation session.[110] This step takes on new importance in victim-offender situations. During the meeting with the victim, the mediator should ascertain the comfort level of the participant, whether the victim wants to participate, what the victim would like to achieve from the session, what the victim would be interested in receiving in reparations, and what measures might be necessary to ensure safety.[111] The mediator should meet in advance with the offender. The mediator may need to ascertain whether the offender is willing to make reparations, the potential reparations that may be offered, whether the offender can be sympathetic to the victim, and how the victim and offender can be in the same room together in a safe and respectful manner.[112] During the pre-mediation sessions, the mediator should be able to determine if the case is appropriate for mediation, and whether the victim or a victim surrogate would be best for the situation. Pre-mediation sessions are also invaluable for setting expectations for the full mediation.

The mediation session generally revolves around three conversations, told from both the victim's and the offender's perspectives: (1) What happened? (2) What is the effect of the crime or harm? and (3) What reparations may be made to the victim or the community?[113] The first discussion regarding "what happened" fills in important gaps in the victim's and the offender's understandings of the situation. In most cases, the timelines of the event will be different—and perhaps drastically different, especially if the victim was not present when the crime happened (such may be the case in property crimes). After each side has had a chance to talk about what happened, the parties may have the opportunity to ask questions of each other. For example, the victim may inquire as to why he or she was the victim (i.e., was the crime targeted or simply random?).

The second conversation covers the effect of the crime on both the victim and the offender. The effect of crime is multidimensional. The crime may have left physical damage to persons or property. Property may have been stolen, real estate may have been vandalized, cars may have broken windows, or people may have injuries and hospital bills. All of these tangible effects can be discussed. The process, however, should also discuss the emotional, psychological, and non-physical effects of the incident. Victims may want to discuss how the crime has affected their sense of safety, changed their daily routine, or affected their relationships with other people. Offenders also experience an

---

107. *See supra* Chapter 4.
108. Ilyssa Wellikoff, *Victim-Offender Mediation and Violent Crimes: On the Way to Justice*, 5 Cardozo Online J. Conflict Resol. 2 (2004).
109. *Id.*
110. *See supra* Section 4.05[A].
111. Mark Umbreit, The Handbook of Victim Offender Mediation 29–33 (2001).
112. *Id.* at 27–29.
113. *Id.* at 51.

effect from the experience. Offenders may have suffered negative school or job consequences; they may have emotional reactions, such as regret; or they may be trying to improve their lives in positive ways following the incident. The mediator can help the parties work through these issues and help with the exchange of information if the victim or the offender has questions regarding these effects.

The third portion of the conference involves reparations. This third conversation concerns how the offender may repay the harm caused and ameliorate the harmful effects discussed in the second conversation. The victim (or surrogate) and the offender are asked to negotiate and agree on the method by which the offender pays back the debt owed to the individual or society. Compared to traditional criminal law, the victim has a significant amount of power in determining the outcome, because the prosecutor is not the decision-maker. Typical reparation agreements include the return of property, the payment of money (in full or over time), and community service hours. Community service hours may be tied to a particular organization that is meaningful to the victim, depending on the situation. For example, if the offender engaged in an act of cruelty to the victim's dog, the victim may be interested in having the offender donate time to a local animal shelter or clinic. In appropriate cases, the parties could agree to reparations that include personal services to the victim. For instance, in a case involving a juvenile offender, the juvenile may make reparations by offering lawn care or snow removal services to the victim free of charge. Following the mediation, the mediator may have to follow up as needed to ensure that the agreement between the parties is being honored.

Compared to traditional mediation, the mediator/facilitator in victim-offender mediations typically takes a less forceful role. The mediator's job is to create an atmosphere that facilitates a conversation and to keep the conversation moving in a productive manner. If the parties are engaging in a dialogue between themselves, the mediator has done a successful job, and the parties can and should talk freely, without too much interruption by the mediator. Successful pre-mediation conferencing with the parties individually should pave the way for a smooth session that is only guided by the mediator while the parties take the lead on the discussion.

[B] Circle Processes

Another common restorative justice practice is known as the "circle process." Circle processes involve more people than victim-offender mediation; notably, these processes may also involve community members, support personnel, and officers from the penal system. A circle process generally involves the following elements: (1) the circle itself, which is to symbolize equality, connection, and inclusion, (2) items placed in the middle of the circle, which represent common ground, (3) elements of ceremony to formalize the process, (4) a talking piece, (5) circle keepers, (6) guidelines and ground rules, and (7) consensus decision-making.[114] Circles may be used in a wide variety of contexts, such as sentencing circles to determine sentences in criminal cases, pre-sentencing healing circles, reintegration circles when a person is about to be released from a correctional facility or aging out of the child welfare system, workplace circles, or community circles.[115]

---

114. Nicole Concordia, *Preserving Liberty in the American Justice System Through Circle Processes*, 5 U. St. Thomas J. L. & Pub. Pol'y 67, 81 (2011).

115. *Id.*

Trained mediators or facilitators guide the circle process. The attendees are often those who have committed the wrong, victims who would like to participate, interested community members, support persons for the victim or the offender (such as family members, friends, or clergy), lawyers, and representatives of the criminal justice system. As with victim-offender mediation, a significant amount of preparation takes place before the circle is convened.[116] The facilitator may have individual meetings with every participant before the group meets as a whole. The preparation is to gauge everyone's interest in participating and ready them for the process. The facilitator must also arrange appropriate facilities, such as a room and chairs to accommodate everyone who will participate.

At the circle meeting, the participants will actually sit in a circle (usually without a table, which could be viewed as a barrier between the participants). The parties and facilitator will establish guidelines and ground rules for participation. Perhaps the most important ground rule is that a participant may only talk when he or she has the talking piece.[117] The talking piece could be one used by the mediator before, or it could be customized for the occasion. In a case involving vandalism to a vehicle, the talking piece could be a toy car. If the victim or offender has a particular love of cooking, the talking piece could be a kitchen utensil. The talking piece moves around the circle, and when a participant has the talking piece, that participant may share thoughts or feelings on the topic being discussed. As the talking piece moves around the circle, any participant may share or "pass" and give the talking piece to the next person without sharing.

The topics of conversation will be similar to those discussed in victim-offender mediation. The participants will likely talk about the crime and what happened. They may all discuss how the crime has impacted them individually or the community, and ultimately, the group will talk about how the harm will be repaid. Because circle processes work on a model of group consensus, a larger number of stakeholders will have to agree to a particular sentence or other reparations.

[C] Family Group Conferencing

"Family Group Conferencing" (FGC) is a restorative process used primarily in the area of child welfare. The FGC concept originates from New Zealand, and it is a process that is often used when children may be removed from the home because of abuse or neglect on the part of the parents. Although these processes may be resource-intensive, the hope is that the process can smooth the path to permanent placement for the children at issue, either reunited with the parents or placed with another member of the family.

FGCs utilize trained facilitators to locate the children's relatives and to facilitate a meeting with the nuclear family, the extended family, attorneys, case workers, and other interested people. Once a case is referred to the FGC process, the facilitator must do preparation work in locating and inviting interested family members to participate.[118] In some programs, the facilitators try to locate adult siblings, aunts, uncles, grandparents, great aunts and uncles, and other relatives. Although none of the family members are required to participate, they are all invited to attend.

---

116. *Id.* at 83–84.
117. *Id.* at 84–85.
118. Jesse Lubin, *Are We Really Looking Out for the Best Interests of the Child? Applying the New Zealand Model of Family Group Conferences to Cases of Child Neglect in the United States*, 47 Fam. Ct. Rev. 129, 136 (2009).

At the conference, everyone is invited to discuss the family, the children, the children's needs, and also the parents' needs. One critical element of FGCs that differs from other types of restorative justice processes is that it includes a private time for the family to meet without any interference by the facilitators, case workers, attorneys, or other support personnel.[119] During this private time, the family can work together on their own to determine the best course of action for the children. Often, the family agrees on a placement for the children within the family, as opposed to having the children removed and put with a foster family or in a group home.

The private family time lasts until the family reaches a consensus or an impasse. At that point, the rest of the group reconvenes. If the family reaches an agreement, the facilitator will work with the group to record the agreement and ensure that the children will be safe under the agreement. If the family cannot decide, the case may revert back to the court system. As with many of the other restorative practices, the facilitator may need to reconvene the group periodically and monitor the situation going forward.

§ 10.09 Negotiated Rulemaking

Negotiated Rulemaking (often called "neg-reg") involves the use of a consensual process whereby government agencies and interested stakeholders collectively negotiate the terms of an agency's regulations. The process dates back to the 1970s and 1980s, but Congress officially endorsed it in 1990 when it passed the Negotiated Rulemaking Act of 1990.[120] Negotiated rulemaking came about because critics thought that the agency rulemaking processes were becoming too controversial.[121]

Negotiated rulemaking does not replace the traditional notice and comment rulemaking. Instead, the negotiated process takes place at the beginning of the process, and the negotiated rule is then put up for notice and comment.[122] Theoretically, the negotiated rulemaking process is more efficient and leads to better agency rulemaking. Although reaching consensus may take time, a rule that is drafted through a negotiated process with all of the relevant stakeholders and the agency should fly through the notice and comment process with little or no objection.[123] The time to the ultimate rule is potentially shorter because of the work completed during the negotiations. In addition, if the stakeholders all agree to the rule at the outset, then the amount of post-rulemaking litigation should diminish significantly.[124] Presumably, the negotiated rule will be a better rule because of the amount of work that goes into a negotiation with multiple stakeholders. The parties to the negotiation will have incentive to determine their true interests and seek a rule that prioritizes those interests, rather than taking extreme positions in the traditional notice-and-comment process.[125]

---

119. Ann Reyes Robbins, *Troubled Children and Children in Trouble: Redefining the Role of the Juvenile Court in the Lives of Children*, 41 U. Mich. J.L. Reform 243, 252 (2007).

120. Cary Coglianese, *Assessing Consensus: The Promise and Performance of Negotiated Rulemaking*, 46 Duke L.J. 1255, 1256–57 (1997).

121. Danielle Holley-Walker, *The Importance of Negotiated Rulemaking to the No Child Left Behind Act*, 85 Neb. L. Rev. 1015, 1035–36 (2007).

122. Coglianese, *supra* note 120, at 1256.

123. *Id.* at 1262.

124. *Id.*

125. Holley-Walker, *supra* note 121, at 1040.

The process, however, is not without criticism. Unlike traditional rulemaking, negotiated rulemaking potentially takes a lot of power out of the hands of the agency by inviting interested stakeholders to negotiate. If the agency is one of many equal bargaining parties, the role of the agency may be viewed as being reduced to a mere "participant."[126] Agencies are the bodies assigned to implement legislation, and negotiated rulemaking potentially distorts the intent of Congress by asking stakeholders—who may wield significant private power—to help create the rules.[127] Depending on the agency and the statute, the role of the agency may turn into that of a mediator, trying to help broker a compromise among many interested private parties. Whether negotiated rulemaking theoretically leads to better rules is also questionable. Government agencies are tasked with creating and implementing rules that are in the best interests of the public. The neg-reg process, however, only indirectly considers the public interest. The primary interests served may be those of the private stakeholders, and those stakeholders may or may not care about the public.[128]

Many important pieces of legislation have included a statutory grant to use negotiated rulemaking. The No Child Left Behind Act of 2001 included a requirement that the Department of Education use the negotiated rulemaking process to implement the Act.[129] The Environmental Protection Agency, Occupational Safety and Health Administration, and some portions of the Department of Health and Human Services have all used negotiated rulemaking with considerable success over the years.[130] Since its inception in the 1970s, negotiated rulemaking has enjoyed some successes,[131] and it will likely continue to be employed by federal agencies in the future. Certainly, the time and effort needed to create negotiated rules preclude its use in many—particularly emergency—situations. The process, however, has been demonstrated to work well when the interested parties are all involved and they are willing to work together to prioritize interests and meet as many interests as possible to create stronger and better-lasting legislation.

§ 10.10 Limited Scope Representation and ADR

Although not a form of process per se, it is worth noting that lawyers may provide limited scope representation services in ADR processes to help achieve client goals and increase access to justice. Limited scope representation refers to the ability of a lawyer and client to limit the services that the lawyer will provide for the client, provided that the limitation on services is reasonable and the client gives informed consent to the arrangement.[132] Low-income clients who may not be able to afford "full service" legal representation may still be able to afford legal counsel for a smaller portion of the overall goal.

---

126. *Id.* at 1042.

127. *Id.*

128. William Funk, *Bargaining Toward the New Millennium: Regulatory Negotiation and the Subversion of the Public Interest*, 46 Duke L.J. 1351, 1373 (1997)

129. Holley-Walker, *supra* note 121, at 1016–17.

130. Julia Korbick, *Negotiated Rulemaking: The Next Step in Regulatory Administration at the Food and Drug Administration?*, 65 Food & Drug L.J. 425, 526 (2010).

131. Phillip J. Harter, *Assessing the Assessor: The Actual Performance of Negotiated Rulemaking*, 9 N.Y.U. Envtl. L.J. 32, 33 (2000).

132. Model Rules of Prof'l Conduct r. 1.2(c).

Limited scope representation has grown in popularity for providing access to attorneys to perform discrete tasks, such as drafting complaints or taking depositions.[133] These types of litigation activities, while important, generally prolong legal problems — as opposed to resolving them.[134] Lawyers can use the concept of limited scope representation and offer services relating to settlement, such as negotiation, mediation, or arbitration counsel.

Negotiation-only representation or "settlement counsel" could help a client determine a settlement position and actually represent a client in settlement negotiations. Lawyers can help with factual determination, negotiation strategy, setting realistic goals, and negotiation preparation. Engagement of settlement counsel may be advantageous in a wide variety of situations. A party to a divorce may need help determining what type of asset division is fair before that party can even begin to determine whether an offer received from the spouse is equitable. A limited-scope lawyer could counsel or represent a tenant in a case involving ignored repairs or a homeowner in a case to restructure the terms of a loan to avoid foreclosure. During the representation, the attorney and client can strategically decide whether to disclose counsel's limited representation. A lawyer only need disclose the fact of limited scope representation where required by ethical or court rules.[135]

Similarly, a lawyer could represent a party for the purposes of mediation only. Those services might include mediation preparation, mediation attendance, preparation of mediation documents (such as pre-mediation submission statements), or review of mediated agreements. Mediation is still not a household term, and even when parties understand the general concept, they might not be familiar with the process they will encounter. Lawyers could be employed on a limited basis in order to educate clients on the mediation process, prepare the case for mediation, attend the mediation, and help in any post-mediation matters, such as contract drafting. If the case does not settle in mediation, then the lawyer would no longer represent the client, unless the parties created another agreement that would continue the lawyer's services.

Just as parties may need legal counsel for litigation matters, parties may also be surprised to learn that their case is actually one requiring resolution through arbitration. Arbitration agreements are now standard portions of consumer contracts, including agreements for cellular phone services, securities transactions, and use of financial services.[136] Many large employers also use arbitration agreements to resolve workplace disputes. Given the similarities between the litigation and arbitration contexts, lawyers may be particularly well-suited to represent a client for the purposes of an arbitration process.

Lawyers may also consider providing limited scope representation services pro bono or for a reduced fee. Legal ethics rules highly encourage every lawyer to provide 50

---

133. Kristen M. Blankley, *Adding by Subtracting: How Limited Scope Agreements for Dispute Resolution Representation Can Increase Access to Attorney Services*, 28 Ohio St. J. Disp. Resol. 659, 662 (2013).

134. *Id.* at 674.

135. *See* Neb. Ct. R. Prof. Cond. § 3-501.2.

136. Jodi Wilson, *How the Supreme Court Thwarted the Purpose of the Federal Arbitration Act*, 63 Case W. Res. L. Rev. 91, 92 (2012) ("Arbitration is omnipresent. If you have a bank account, a credit card, or a cell phone, you have an arbitration agreement."). Note, too, that some major companies, such as Bank of America, are moving away from using arbitration agreements in their consumer contracts.

hours of pro bono service per year to help ensure access to justice for those who are un-able to pay.[137] Taking on clients in limited scope arrangements allows lawyers to engage in a more predictable number of pro bono hours. Lawyers who regularly take on pro bono litigation clients may experience that the overall amount of time needed for a given case may vary greatly, and the length of the case may turn into a multi-year commitment.

Of course, lawyers may also bill for the limited scope arrangement, provided that the fee is reasonable under the circumstances.[138] The billing method must be agreed upon by the attorney and client, but the method of billing could be hourly, a flat fee, a contin-gency fee, or some mixture of these methods. For example, a lawyer and client could agree that the lawyer will represent a plaintiff in mediation, and if the case settles, the lawyer will get a contingency fee, but if the case does not settle, then the client will pay a fixed or hourly fee.

---

137. MODEL RULES OF PROF'L CONDUCT r. 6.1(a).
138. MODEL RULES OF PROF'L CONDUCT r. 1.5.

Table of Cases

[References are to pages]

Index

[References are to pages]

257